From Cedar Mountain to Antietam

FROM CEDAR MOUNTAIN TO ANTIETAM

2nd Edition

Edward J. Stackpole

Commentary by D. Scott Hartwig
Foreword by William C. Davis

STACKPOLE
BOOKS

Published by
STACKPOLE BOOKS
Cameron and Kelker Streets
P.O. Box 1831
Harrisburg, PA 17105

Cover painting "Until Sundown" by Don Troiani. Photograph courtesy Historical Art Prints, Ltd., Southbury, Connecticut

Cover design by Caroline Miller

Maps by Colonel Wilbur S. Nye, USA (Ret.)

Printed in the United States of America
Second Edition

10 9 8 7 6 5 4 3 2

Library of Congress Cataloging-in-Publication Data

Stackpole, Edward J. (Edward James), 1894–
    From Cedar Mountain to Antietam / Edward J. Stackpole. — 2nd ed.
      p.   cm.
    Includes bibliographical references (p.   ) and index.
    ISBN 0-8117-2438-7
    1. Cedar Mountain (Culpeper County, Va.), Battle of, 1862.
2. Bull Run, 2nd Battle of, Va., 1862. 3. Chantilly (Va.), Battle of, 1862. 4. Maryland Campaign, 1862. I. Title.
E473.7.S77   1993
973.7'32 — dc20   92-31707
                                                 CIP

DEDICATION

To my three beloved gals
Frankie, Frances, and Esme

ACKNOWLEDGMENTS

Grateful appreciation for their invaluable assistance in the completion of this book is extended to:

Mr. Francis B. Wilshin, Park Superintendent, Mr. L. VanL. Naisawald, Park Historian, and Mr. Tom Crowson, of The Manassas Battlefield National Park. To insure accuracy in the battle maps, Mr. Wilshin took the editor to the key areas on the battlefield and explained the actions at each; he provided invaluable assistance in permitting research on the situation maps on which the developments during the battle had been plotted by himself, Mr. Naisawald, and Dr. Warren Hassler, Jr. Mr. Naisawald, in addition to furnishing basic information concerning the maps and terrain, gave a helpful and critical reading of the manuscript, and accompanied the editor in a visit to the obscure Chantilly battlefield.

Mr. Richard W. Stephenson, of the Library of Congress, for friendly and valuable assistance in locating old maps pertinent to the campaigns described.

Mrs. Prentiss Bassett, Bluff Head, Huletts Landing, Washington County, New York, whose father and uncle served in the Army of the Potomac and whose interest in the Civil War is exceeded only by her gracious generosity in sharing with the author much interesting material taken from the letters written by her uncle, Captain James Gillette.

Mrs. Rose Weiss, U.S. Army Map Depot, Dalecarlia, Washington, D.C.

Dr. Elizabeth G. McPherson, Manuscript Division, Library of Congress.

Mr. and Mrs. B. Carlin Inskip, RD, Rapidan, Va., for information concerning the Cedar Mountain Battlefield.

Colonel John E. Ray, Waterloo Ridge, Va., for assistance in checking the Rappahannock-Rapidan terrain.

Cora Martin Weeber, amanuensis extraordinary, whose patient typing and retyping served times without end to bring legible order out of chirographic chaos.

CONTENTS

Chapter 1

McClellan Fails to Take Richmond. A New General-in-Chief. John Pope Rides in from the West. Union Teamwork Sadly Lacking. McClellan Wastes Valuable Time.

Chapter 2

A New General Gets Tough. The Theater of Operations. Pope Puts Out Ineffectual Feelers. Pope Takes the Field. Tightening Union Discipline. Combat Imminent.

Chapter 3

Confusion at Orange Court House. Destination—Culpeper. Jackson and his Generals. Jackson's Favorite Division Commander.

Chapter 4

Banks Blocks Jackson's Advance. The Cedar Mountain Battlefield. 20,000 Against 8,000. General Charles S. Winder. Banks Guesses Wrong. The Meeting Engagement. Jackson's Left Driven Back. A. P. Hill Saves the Day. Jackson Attempts a Pursuit.

Chapter 5

Lee Takes Command. Stuart Loses his Hat. Pope Effects a Limited Withdrawal. Stuart's Raid on Pope's Headquarters.

Chapter 6

Jubal Early has a Rough Time. Lee "Shoots the Works." Pope's Predicament. Pope's Rear Again Exposed.

Chapter 7

The Confederates are Coming! Halleck's Frantic Order to Haupt. Taylor Makes a Noble Effort. Pope Operates in a Fog. Heavy Union Reinforcements Arrive. Pope Plans to Crush Jackson. McClellan Muddies the Waters.

LIST OF ILLUSTRATIONS

The capital letters in parentheses refer to the sources of the following pictures, as follows:

(B) *Battles and Leaders of the Civil War.* New York: Century Co., 1884.

(H) *Harpers Pictorial History of the Great Rebellion.* New York: Harper & Bro., 1868.

(L) Library of Congress.

(N) National Archives.

(P) *Photographic History of the Civil War.* New York: Review of Reviews, 1912. Brady photographs.

(S) *The Soldier in Our Civil War, A Pictorial History.* New York: Stanley Bradley Co., 1885. Sketches by Forbes, Waud, and others.

LIST OF MAPS

A discussion of map sources, and of the symbols used in plotting troop positions, is given in the Appendix.

FOREWORD TO THE SECOND EDITION

In the summer of 1862 the still-new commander of the newly designated Army of Northern Virginia faced a daunting task. He had grasped triumph from near catastrophe in late June with the Seven Days Battles, turning back Union Gen. George B. McClellan's hesitant but still powerful campaign against the Confederate capital at Richmond. But now, with a victor's laurels, Gen. Robert E. Lee could not rest upon them. Even though McClellan was beaten, he remained a nagging threat on the Peninsula south of Richmond. And the enemy had constituted another new force, the Army of Virginia, to sweep down from Washington to the north. Between the two Yankee forces, Lee, his army, the capital, even the Confederacy itself, could still be pinched to death.

Lee's response only confirmed that President Jefferson Davis had made one of the greatest decisions ever taken by a commander-in-chief when he set this general at the head of an army. In the subsequent battles of Cedar Mountain and Second Manassas, or Bull Run, Lee virtually eliminated Gen. John Pope's Army of Virginia from the equation, while McClellan idly remained an onlooker. Not content with his victories, Lee continued the initiative by invading Maryland and heading for Pennsylvania in order to put a mammoth scare into the North. His own daring almost put him in McClellan's grasp at Antietam, once the timid Yankee brought his army north to meet the threat. But even then, Lee faced him down and, while losing a tactical contest, arguably won the strategic match simply by getting his army back to Virginia safely.

While Antietam received almost constant attention from writers and historians, then and thereafter, Cedar Mountain and Second Manassas were largely ignored. One of the first, and still excellent, books to look at those battles, indeed the entire summer campaign of Lee's army, was Edward J. Stackpole's *From Cedar Mountain to Antietam*. More than three decades have passed since it first appeared in 1959, and it is still in demand by students and scholars. Crisp, well written, based on a solid foundation in the secondary and primary literature, Stackpole's work is still the only one to treat these three great battles as a continuum. His text is further enhanced by thirty-eight outstanding tactical battle maps by the late Col. Wilbur S. Nye, for many years editor of the magazine *Civil War Times Illustrated*.

But history does not stand still. New sources come to light, new interpretations emerge, and old errors are discovered. So it is with *From Cedar Mountain to Antietam*. It is time for a new edition, updated and corrected, to bring it in line with the latest scholarship. It is also time that it is once more available after being out of print for years. Civil War scholar D. Scott Hartwig has combed the book line by line, correcting errors where found and adding new material where necessary, some of it of considerable importance to understanding the turbulent summer of 1862.

The result is hardly a new book. Rather, it is a fine old book made better and made available for new generations who have awaited its coming. In General Stackpole's crisp prose readers can hear again the crunch of Rebel feet on the dusty roads of Virginia and Maryland and see their wide, swinging gait as they bravely march north to take the war to the enemy from Cedar Mountain to Antietam.

William C. Davis

PENNSYLVANIA AVENUE, WASHINGTON, IN 1862

CHAPTER 1

EARLY UNION FRUSTRATIONS

"IF General McClellan does not want to use the army for some days, I should like to borrow it and see if it cannot be made to do something."

President Abraham Lincoln, Commander-in-Chief of the Armed Forces of the United States, may have made the remark humorously in the latter days of 1861, but the grim implication of his words reflected the growing impatience of the country with the reluctance of the Army's General-in-Chief to make the slighest threatening gesture in the direction of the enemy.

Long on patience and conscious of his own lack of knowledge or experience in the military art, but sensitive to the political realities of the situation, Lincoln studied tactics and strategy diligently during the early winter of 1861-62 in a determined effort to educate himself, insofar as practicable, in the science of war. He pored over all the available books

1

on strategy, conscientiously studied sheafs of reports from the military departments, and conferred for long hours with a variety of generals and admirals. Partly as a result of his rigorous course of self indoctrination over a period of several months, the President came to the conclusion that McClellan would have to be catapulted into offensive measures by peremptory orders if the North was to get on with the war.

Having reached that decision, on January 27, 1862 Lincoln issued his first General War Order, which directed that all the land and naval forces of the United States engage in "a general movement against the insurgent forces" on February 22 (Washington's birthday). Specifically mentioned as participants in the planned general offensive were the Army of the Potomac, the Army at Fortress Monroe, the Army of Western Virginia, the Army in Kentucky, the Army and flotilla at Cairo, and the naval force in the Gulf of Mexico.

As if that were not sufficient to galvanize supreme Army commander McClellan and the War and Navy Departments into action, Lincoln followed up his initial blast, four days later, with Special War Order No. 1, this one directed specifically to the Army of the Potomac. The order instructed the Commanding General to launch the Army of the Potomac on an expedition "for the immediate object of seizing and occupying Manassas Junction," the movement to commence on or before the 22nd of February.

The President's refreshing initiative aroused new hope in the public mind and appeared to please everybody but Major General George B. McClellan, who took issue with the plan of moving overland through Virginia toward Richmond. He proposed instead a water movement to Urbanna on the Rappahannock by way of Chesapeake Bay and thence overland to the York River, to approach the Confederate Capital from the east. Declining to accept Lincoln's strategic judgment and insisting on his own conception in spite of the unequivocal order already issued, McClellan was finally given his way, doubtless because the President had concluded the general would exert more effort in a project of his own devising.

General Joseph A. Johnston, commanding the Confederate forces in Virginia, had kept the bulk of his troops massed in the vicinity of Manassas, twenty odd miles southwest of.Washington, ever since the Union defeat at the first Battle of Bull Run in July 1861. The only other organized Confederate body in the State was Stonewall Jackson's small command in the Shenandoah Valley. McClellan's propensity for vastly overestimating the strength of his enemy was so habitual, however, that he would not accept the fact that he outnumbered the Confederates three to one in the Washington-Manassas area. Lincoln's order to move on Richmond by land through Virginia was militarily sound. Had McClellan obeyed the order it is almost a certainty that Johnston would have had no recourse but to withdraw in the face of the Union army's great preponderance of armed might.

Despite the pressure from Washington, McClellan continued to postpone the movement, while the discontent of the people in the North grew to such an extent as to endanger willing public support of the war effort. Lincoln was acutely aware of the danger, but felt himself to be on the horns of a dilemma which made him hesitate to formally remove McClellan from command lest such action make a bad situation worse. For it was a fact that his little general had performed something of a miracle in welding the raw Union levees into an effectively organized and well-disciplined army, most of whose officers and men believed in and gave to him their undivided loyalty and affection.

In his own good time, then, but not until Lincoln had found it necessary to promulgate two more general orders that put additional burrs under the McClellan saddle, the general condescended to leave the comfortable camps around Washington. The President, his patience exhausted, had found it advisable on March 8, 1862 to issue an order which reduced McClellan from General-in-Chief of the U. S. Army to Commanding General of the Department of the Potomac, a rebuff that reflected in no uncertain terms the waning confidence of the Administration in "Little Mac." A victory of sorts for the radical anti-McClellan element, the action was understandable from the viewpoint of the President. But the effect was militarily a step backward in that the several Union armies in the field would for the next four months be under the direct control of two civilians, the President and the Secretary of War, a condition that left much to be desired.

Finally, however, on March 17 McClellan embarked his army of over 100,000 men for the water trip to the Peninsula. Even then his egomania would not permit him to obey Lincoln's order to leave a more adequate force to protect Washington. As a result, the President took matters into his own hands and pulled one corps (McDowell's) out from under McClellan, holding it for the defense of Washington.

McClellan's preparations to move had taken so long and his counter-intelligence measures were so inadequate that Johnston's Confederate army at Centerville had ample warning of the impending Federal move. While Stonewall Jackson's small force in the Shenandoah Valley made threatening gestures toward Washington, Johnston's army side-slipped to the south to counter McClellan's advance. After a two-day march it took positions at Fredericksburg and Culpeper, putting the Confederates as close to Richmond as was Urbanna. This neat maneuver caused McClellan to revise his plan by changing his concentration point to Fort Monroe, 70 miles from Richmond.

McClellan Fails to Take Richmond

Disembarking his army at Fort Monroe, McClellan moved slowly and ponderously up the Peninsula toward Richmond. The Confederate forces under Johnston opposed him in a series of delaying actions, then withdrew into the outer defenses of Richmond, a series of earthworks. McClellan, adhering to his obsession that the Federals were greatly outnumbered, continued to importune Lincoln for reinforcements.

However, the Confederate General Thomas J. (Stonewall) Jackson, with some 10,000 men in the Shenandoah Valley kept the three Union corps in that area at bay and even threatened Washington. Jackson's famous Valley campaign at this time established for all time his reputation as a Great Captain, secured the granary of the Confederacy, as the Shenandoah area was called, and prevented Washington from sending more troops to McClellan.

Meantime, in one of the engagements on the Peninsula, Joe Johnston was wounded and was superseded by General Robert E. Lee. Lee spent the month of May in reorganizing and refitting his army, which he now named the Army of Northern Virginia, and in preparing a counteroffensive against McClellan. This was planned as a battle of annihilation, and to make the blow more effective, Lee brought Jackson secretly from the Valley to strengthen the enveloping force on McClellan's right flank.

At last Lee's preparations were complete. He would attack Major General Fitz John Porter's isolated corps on the north bank of the Chickahominy to cut McClellan's supply line. But Jackson was late in coming up and the Confederates were repulsed at Mechanicsville on June 26, the first of the Seven Days Battles. On June 27, with reinforcements that gave them a two to one advantage over Porter, they tried again and this time were successful at Gaines' Mill, but night came before they could prevent the Federals from escaping across the river.

During the remainder of the campaign, Lee pressed the attack while McClellan was engaged in changing his supply base from White House to Harrison's Landing on the James River. A succession of rear-guard actions by the Union forces, as the Union general retired in a southerly direction toward his new base, managed to hold off the Confederates up to the final battle at Malvern Hill. There Lee unwisely attacked a strongly held Union position and was severely repulsed, chiefly through the performance of Brigadier General Henry Hunt's superbly employed Union artillery.

The Peninsular Campaign, launched by the self-assured McClellan to save the Union, as he confided in a letter to his wife, but which failed either to take Richmond or inflict a serious defeat on Robert E. Lee, was the first major campaign of the war in the East. Covering a period of three and one-half months, the campaign ended on July 1 with the Confederate repulse at Malvern Hill; that same night McClellan, with cumulative losses of 16,000 of his 105,000 troops, fell back to Harrison's Landing, where he entrenched. Lee, having lost 20,000 of his 80,000 men, withdrew behind the defense works of Richmond. It was clear that both armies needed rest and time to pull themselves together for further effort.

The year 1862 was now more than half gone. A Union victory seemed far away. With at least twice as many troops as the Confederates could muster in Virginia, the military forces of the North had made a miserable showing in the Shenandoah Valley and accomplished nothing in the vicinity of Richmond. In both areas the outnumbered Confederates had cleverly conducted active defensive campaigns in which the Federal commanders were consistently out-generaled by Jackson and Lee.

A New General-in-Chief

It had become apparent that the combination of Lincoln and Stanton as military commanders by remote control from Washington was a poor substitute for a General-in-Chief, the position held by McClellan until Lincoln relieved him. Perhaps the President had kept the post vacant from March through early July in the hope that McClellan would restore his confidence by taking Richmond, a feat that would undoubtedly have brought about his restoration to supreme command. Unfortunately the Peninsular Campaign proved to be a failure, so Lincoln turned to the Western theater in his search for a key to unlock the secret of how to win battles. The choice fell on the saturnine Halleck.

Major General Henry W. Halleck, whose intellectual qualities exceeded his command ability by a considerable margin, had on March 11, 1862 been elevated to command of all the forces in the West, in which theater the North had made notable progress. It was logical that Lincoln should cast his eyes in that direction as he mulled over the problem of finding a general to improve the Union fortunes in the East. The belief was current that Halleck, highly respected by Lincoln's colleagues in Washington, had been responsible for the western successes. The fact that Grant and other generals were really the ones who deserved the battle credit had not as yet filtered down to the man in the street.

Born January 16, 1815 in New York State, Halleck attended Union College and graduated from West Point in 1839, third in his class. A serious student of the military art, his lectures on the science of war, published in 1846 as *Elements of Military Art and Science,* became during the Civil War a manual for officers of the Army and was universally in demand by students of the military profession. After the war with Mexico, in which he served, Halleck played a leading part in drafting a constitution for the new State of California, following which he resigned from the Army, took up the practice of law, and wrote a number of books on mining and international law.

It is easy to see why he gained the sobriquet, "Old Brains," for in addition to his intellectual accomplishments he had acquired large interests and much valuable property as the head of San Francisco's most prominent law firm, served as president of a small railroad, and was in every respect one of the leading citizens of California when civil war broke out in 1861.

Halleck immediately offered his services to the Union, was appointed a major general in the Regular Army at the behest of General Winfield Scott, and was assigned to command of the Department of the Missouri, with headquarters at St. Louis. There was great need for a man of administrative ability to bring efficiency and order to the chaotic situation which existed in that department, and Halleck succeeded admirably. So effective was his work that in March 1862, the Departments of Kansas and Ohio were merged with that of the Missouri, with Halleck promoted to command the entire territory from the Alleghenies to the Rocky Mountains, the whole constituting the Department of the Mississippi.

When Halleck on July 23 was called to Washington his star was in the ascendancy. Under his overall departmental command the Confederates had been driven from Missouri, the northern half of Arkansas, Kentucky, and most of Tennessee, and the Union forces had gained a foothold in Mississippi and Alabama. But when Halleck had doffed his administrative headgear and taken command of troops in the field, the results were less than spectacular, for his abilities as a field general fell considerably short of his accomplishments as a disciplinarian and administrator.

Nevertheless, he had built a solid foundation for getting results, hence his selection to command all the Union armies was a perfectly natural one for the President to make. Interestingly enough the idea didn't appeal to Halleck, who at first declined the honor, and it was only after Lincoln had made it an order that he packed his bags for a reluctant departure from his western post.

Immediately upon assuming command of the armies in July, Halleck's first official action was to visit McClellan at Harrison's Landing. He told the latter that not more than 20,000 reinforcements could be spared for him if he would attack Richmond. McClellan agreed, but after Halleck had returned to Washington McClellan reneged, sending a wire that on reconsideration he felt it could only be done with almost twice that number of additional troops, or 35,000. This old refrain was no surprise to the President, who would have relieved McClellan then and there if Major General Ambrose E. Burnside, to whom the post was offered, had been willing to accept the responsibility. Burnside, however, a good friend and loyal to McClellan, recommended that the latter be retained.

It had become quite clear that the Federal troops in the East, other than the Army of the Potomac, needed two things and needed them desperately: unified command and a commander who could make unification work. Even as Lee was pushing McClellan back from Richmond, the latter had taken time from the operations to write Secretary of War Edwin M. Stanton urging him to combine the troops in the Valley with those in front of Washington, under a single commander. As Commanding General of the Army of the Potomac, the defense of Washington was not McClellan's concern, but that made little difference to the self-sufficient general. As it happened, Lincoln had independently reached the same conclusion and had already selected the man for the job of heading the new army about to be created.

The solution was to organize a second army by putting together the separate corps of Banks, McDowell, and Fremont, under a new commander. This army would have the same mission as the separate commands of the three corps commanders, viz, to protect Washington, control the Shenandoah Valley, and draw Confederate troops from Richmond. This time, however, a single general would head the heretofore uncoordinated fighting teams, which was a step in the right direction. The wistfully hopeful desk-chair strategists in Washington would thus have to deal only with two generals, McClellan and the new commander of the Army of Virginia, as it was to be called. Two hundred thousand men would be available to overwhelm less than half that number of Confederates.

But there was still a serious defect in the Administration's reasoning. Unity of command had not been achieved. Two armies would take the place of one army and three separate corps, and Halleck may have felt that as Commander-in-Chief the desired integration would be effected in his person. If so, firm action to produce the desired result was not forthcoming.

There was one ray of hope. The war in the east would be pursued with vigor. The summer and fall months were ideal for fighting. Lincoln saw clearly the need for offensive action, even if his field generals did not. He would keep trying to find a leader who would give the North a victory, no matter how great his frustrations. Fortunately the heavily burdened President still maintained his incomparable, dry sense of humor—an asset whose worth to the Union could not be measured in terms of dollars or manpower.

The problem that confronted Halleck, now that he had two armies in Virginia with Lee and Richmond between them, was how best to employ them in combination. Should he revive Lincoln's pincers plan, when both armies could be readied for an offensive campaign, or would it be better to unite them under a single commander? And if so, what then? The difficulty was that Halleck, who had an aversion to politicians, hated the Washington scene and had tried his best to avoid the important assignment of General-in-Chief. He liked to counsel and advise but seemed constitutionally incapable of making decisions in his new role. Really a theorist at heart, still he tried to function as General-in-Chief in fact, until after the failure of the first great eastern campaign under his direction, which culminated in the Battle of Second Manassas. Thereafter he sidestepped command responsibilities, confining himself to acting merely as the President's military adviser.

Halleck's inability to reach a firm decision on how to employ the two separate armies under his command was a keen disappointment to the President, who had plenty of problems of his own without having to solve those of the military as well. It finally became apparent that, if there was to be a solution, Lincoln himself would have to dictate it. Despairing of offensive action by McClellan, and knowing of no other general to whom he could safely entrust the job after Burnside declined to take it, Lincoln reluctantly discarded his nutcracker project, that is, to attack Lee at Richmond from two directions, and directed Halleck to call the Army of the Potomac back north with a view to operations in conjunction with the newly formed second army on the line of the Rappahannock River.

Despite McClellan's strenuous objections, the order stuck. Further operations against Richmond were suspended for the time being. McClellan was directed to withdraw his forces from the Peninsula forthwith. The lessons taught by Jackson's

Shenandoah Valley campaign, notably the disastrous results that can stem from divided command when opposed by a resolute enemy, had not been lost on Lincoln. Furthermore, McClellan's reluctance to take any risks, regardless of his preponderance in combat strength, had been proven so repeatedly that it would not do, in Lincoln's judgment, to place supreme reliance on him.

John Pope Rides in from the West

Major General John Pope of Illinois was the Administration's choice to command the newly designated Army of Vir-

MAJOR GENERAL JOHN POPE
From a photo made early in the war, when he wore a full beard.

ginia. But it was soon to become apparent that the President's military education had not proceeded far enough to master the art of successfully appraising the capabilities of generals with the potential to lead armies to victory. Lincoln had known both the general and his father before the war. Pope had achieved some little success under Halleck in capturing New Madrid and Island No. 10 in the Mississippi earlier in the year. Although conceited and a braggart, he was quick-tempered and liked to fight, a trait so lacking in many of the generals upon whom Lincoln had to rely that it undoubtedly influenced the President's decision. The fact that the corps commanders who would now be subordinate to Pope were all senior to him in rank seemed to upset only one of them, General Fremont, whose prompt resignation could scarcely be construed as a major disaster to Union armies.

Pope was gifted with a vivid imagination, was impatient of contradiction, and almost violently unorthodox in his conception of the military art. This latter trait manifested itself in the views that he freely expressed before committees of Congress and was quick to announce in orders to his new army, to the effect that "the time had come for the adoption of a truly American system of warfare. Such traditions of the past as lines of retreat, bases of supplies, positions, etc., which had bothered all commanders from Agamemnon to Banks, were to be at once discarded." This was but one of the ill-advised, and foolishly conceived pronouncements that the freshman army commander would live to regret, and soon.

Like Joe Hooker, John Pope was a striking figure who made quite an impression in uniform. His large frame and piercing eyes were balanced by a goatee,* so that the first reaction of those whom he met was extremely favorable. He also talked a great deal, but when those with whom he conferred in Washington had escaped from his conversational charm, and thought about the matter, they recalled that much of his talk had centered about John Pope.

Pope's assigned mission, somewhat similar to but with more ·offensive implications than that of the three corps which were now being combined to make up his army, was to cover Washington, exercise control over the Shenandoah Valley, threaten Gordonsville and Charlottesville, and make every effort to draw Confederate troops from Richmond. The ultimate objective,

_____

*An early photo of Pope shows him with a fairly full beard. A postwar portrait has him with only a mustache.

clearly stated in the order, would be to move against Richmond from the west as McClellan attacked from the east.

The Army of Virginia, officially brought into being on June 26, could be a powerful force for the Union when pulled together from its scattered positions and welded into a well-organized fighting team. With all present or accounted for, Pope would be in command of an army about half as large, although not so well blooded, as the Army of the Potomac. As constituted, his army included Fremont's First Corps of 11,500 men now commanded by Major-General Franz Sigel; the Second Corps, Major General Nathaniel P. Banks, 8,800 strong; and the Third Corps under Major General Irvin McDowell, strongest of the lot with 18,500 men.* These three corps represented Pope's striking force, which together with some 5,000 poorly mounted and imperfectly organized cavalry totalled 43,800. Also assigned to Pope, but not yet organized and consequently unavailable, was a small Reserve Corps under Brigadier General Samuel D. Sturgis, then being formed in the vicinity of Alexandria, in the Washington area.

Sigel reported his corps, newly acquired from Fremont, as being badly disorganized. He and Banks were in the Shenandoah Valley between Winchester and Middletown. McDowell had one division at Manassas Junction and the other at Falmouth, across the Rappahannock from Fredericksburg, the latter designated by the War Department to cover Aquia Creek Landing against a possible enemy incursion from the direction of Richmond.

Unfortunately Pope got off to a bad start in his first General Order to his new troops, when he undiplomatically informed them, with an oratorical flourish, that he was from the west "where we have always seen the backs of our enemies" and where the policy had been to seek out, attack, and defeat the enemy. This was bad psychological medicine to administer to

––––––
*For this entire campaign, the strengths adopted by any writer will depend to a certain extent on the researcher's interpretation of the available official statistics. The tables in the Appendix give the data used in this book, together with a short discussion of their derivation.

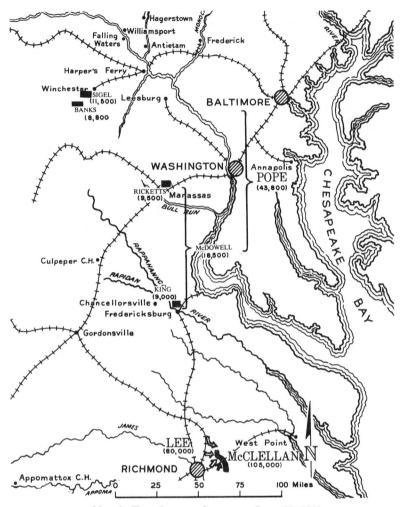

MAP 1. THE GENERAL SITUATION, JUNE 26, 1862

This sketch shows the situation, more or less schematically, on the day General Pope assumed command of the newly constituted Army of Virginia. His three corps, those of Sigel, Banks, and McDowell, are disposed as shown; Pope's total also includes some 5,000 cavalry which, except for Bayard's small brigade (at Manassas), was farmed out by regiment to the several corps and was ineffective for reconnaissance on an extended scale. Pope has the capability, but not the ability, to concentrate swiftly and sweep down the Shenandoah Valley, where he is unopposed; or to seize the important railway net center at Gordonsville; or to move directly against Lee's rear. Lee on this date launched his attack on McClellan in the Battle of Mechanicsville, the first of the Seven Days' campaign. He has the capability, and the ability, to neutralize McClellan quickly, then turn on Pope.

proud troops of whom the worst that could be said was that they had been ineffectively led. Nor did it raise Pope in their estimation when he stated that his headquarters would be in the saddle; an unfortunate remark which naturally invited the enlisted rejoinder that that was where most people placed their hindquarters.

Union Teamwork Sadly Lacking

McClellan's chronic reluctance to fight and his ridiculous habit of always vastly overestimating the strength of his opponents finally caught up with him. Had he been an effective combat leader, the decision to withdraw his large army from its position only a few miles from the enemy's capital, with a secure line of supply and communications, and with another strong Union army on the opposite side of Richmond, would have been an historic blunder of great magnitude. But the blame cannot fairly be placed on Lincoln, who had at long last reached the conclusion that McClellan simply did not have a fighting heart. Still, one cannot understand why the President failed to replace McClellan outright and give the army a decent chance to gain its objective. One reason was of course that good generals were hard to find and even then they seemed unwilling to accept responsibility for high command. It was also a fact that Halleck, going by the book as usual, advised Lincoln to unite the two armies before resuming the offensive, on the premise that otherwise they might be defeated in detail. In so recommending, Halleck ignored the fact that the position of Lee's army between McClellan and Pope placed the Confederates in a vulnerable situation which could have proven fatal had the Union's preponderant strength been utilized to advantage. In any event, the President ordered McClellan's army back to the Washington area and the groundwork was laid for a succession of battles that, coupled with McClellan's failure on the Peninsula, would make 1862 a year of great frustrations for the Union.

When Pope assumed command of the Army of Virginia on June 26, his first task was to improve the organization and supply of the separated corps and effect a concentration. Jackson's Confederates having left the Valley to join Lee for the showdown battles with McClellan, there were no hostile forces of any size in Pope's area. Keeping in mind his threefold mission, Pope ordered Sigel and Banks to move via Luray Gap to the vicinity of Sperryville and ten miles east thereof, respectively, and McDowell was directed to transfer his division at Manassas to Waterloo Bridge on the Rappahannock, leaving his other division at Falmouth.

Pope was concerned when McClellan, following Malvern Hill, withdrew south of Richmond to his new position on the James River. He felt that this was strategically unsound in that this movement away from Washington would make it difficult for McClellan to effect a junction with his own army and would likewise expose both to the danger that Lee could attack each separately from his central position between them. Pope wrote Halleck urging him to direct McClellan to halt in place, and at the same time sent a letter to McClellan offering to cooperate with him by adapting his own tactical moves to McClellan's plan, whatever it might be. McClellan's reply, full of generalities, avoided suggesting specific ways and means as Pope had requested. This was a short-sighted but typical reaction from the "little Napoleon," who evidently considered Pope an upstart competitor who was not to be given the opportunity to gain distinction if McClellan could help it. Pope at least felt keenly the need for a unified command and showed his willingness to cooperate with McClellan in achieving that result. The latter's indifference, however, convinced Pope that a superior to both was not only militarily desirable but an absolute necessity if the operations of the two armies were to be effectively coordinated.

Halleck's new plan, in July, was for the Army of the Potomac to move down the James to the Chesapeake and up the Potomac to Aquia Landing, from which new base it would be available to cooperate with Pope's army. As usual, McClellan acted with exasperating slowness, so that August was almost half gone before the movement got underway, despite repeated telegrams from Halleck to speed it up.

There was good reason for Halleck's urgency. In order to strengthen the lone division of McDowell's corps at Falmouth and more fully secure the approaches to Washington from

GENERAL ROBERT E. LEE, C.S.A.

Richmond, Halleck had ordered Burnside to embark his corps at Newport News. Burnside responded with gratifying speed and on August 3 his troops debarked at Aquia Creek for the short overland march to a position opposite Fredericksburg. Pope's army, operating from Culpeper, was by that time south of the Rappahannock River threatening Gordonsville.

With strategic foresight, Lee suspected that Washington might recall McClellan from the Peninsula, a development which would be very much to his liking. On July 13 he sent

Jackson from Hanover Court House towards Gordonsville to engage Pope with part of the Army of Northern Virginia, but held his main body at Richmond until he could be certain of McClellan's intentions. When McClellan finally started from the Peninsula, Lee on August 13 left Richmond with the rest of his army for Gordonsville, with the avowed purpose of destroying Pope before the two Union armies could be joined. By that time a preliminary engagement, the Battle of Cedar Mountain, had been fought and Jackson had retired to Gordonsville.

McClellan Wastes Valuable Time

McClellan seemed strangely indifferent to the fate of anyone but McClellan. Willing compliance with orders from Halleck, Stanton, or even Lincoln himself was rarely evidenced in his egotistical code of conduct. Directives from higher authority invariably brought long dissertations of disagreement from the general, whose letters to his wife best reveal his self-centered attitude. Since it was McClellan's opinion that he was destined as the chosen one to save the country, it seemed perfectly clear to him that all else should be subordinated to his own plans and wishes. Much has been written about Longstreet's propensity on occasion for dragging his feet in his uncooperative attitude towards orders from General Lee, but Longstreet ran a poor second to McClellan in that respect.

In spite of positive orders from Halleck, who early in August had received reliable information of Lee's probable intention to destroy Pope's army before moving on Washington; and virtually ignoring the follow-up letters and telegrams with which Halleck sought to galvanize him into action, it was August 14, eleven days after receipt of the initial order, before McClellan commenced to evacuate Harrison's Landing.

George B. McClellan was a great organizer who with even a small amount of humility in his make-up might have proven to be the man of the hour to lead the armies of the North to victory. The great flaw in his character, his egocentricity, dominated his every thought and action, however. There was no room left for those traits which might have made him a great battle leader and subsequently President of the United States— self-discipline, the ability to work in harness with others of equal or greater authority, a willingness to take the calculated risks inherent in warfare, and a readiness to do the best he could with the means available.

McClellan's personality and military deficiencies may fairly be said to have been largely responsible for the series of depressing events which plagued the Lincoln Administration in its conduct of the war in the East during 1862. McClellan had the men, weapons, and equipment with which to wage successful offensives; his strength was twice that of the Confederates; and his officers and soldiers from the division level down were just as good as their opposite numbers in the Confederate Army. But McClellan was pitted against Robert E. Lee and it was that, coupled with his own lesser character and lack of aggressiveness, together with the trial and error floundering of the Washington administration and the lack of unified field command, which came perilously close to losing the war for the Union during the summer of 1862.

There was one other prominent Union general whose fleeting appearance in the eastern theater of operations had much to do with the depressing results for the North during that summer. His name was John Pope. Zooming in from the west, he came, he saw, and almost in the twinkling of an eye was conquered.

This is the story of four battles between Union and Confederate armies that were fought in the short space of five weeks between August 9 and September 17, 1862: Cedar Mountain, Second Bull Run (Manassas), South Mountain, and Antietam (Sharpsburg). In a sense all four were constitutent, successive elements of a single campaign, during which General Robert E. Lee went over from the defensive in the Richmond area, outmaneuvered and decisively defeated Pope's Army of Virginia, invaded Maryland, and was turned back to Virginia by the Army of the Potomac under McClellan at Sharpsburg in what is reputed to have been the bloodiest single day's battle of the Civil War. In that short period, the opposing armies would suffer aggregate casualties to the number of some 50,000 and in the end nothing much would be proven beyond the fact that American boys would bravely fight and die for a cause in which they believed, that Lee was a hard man to beat, and that Lincoln would have to keep trying in his search for a competent general with ability to employ the superior strength available to the Union in order to win victories on the battle-field.

CULPEPER DURING POPE'S OCCUPATION

CHAPTER 2

POPE PLANS A CAMPAIGN

THE letters and telegrams that passed between Halleck, McClellan, and Pope during the first few weeks of the summer of 1862 are so revealing that one may pause to wonder how the North was able to maintain any sort of a military posture in the face of the crosscurrents that characterized the strategic planning in Washington and at the headquarters of the two armies.

President Lincoln's attempt to achieve unity of command in the military forces was a proper move but made with the wrong men. McClellan was the strongest of the three, Pope the weakest. Halleck had the right idea but lacked the strength of character to make his orders stick, with the inevitable result that military operations suffered from a debilitating climate of disunity, lack of harmony and cooperation, and the resulting low morale among officers and men in the field.

Lincoln and Stanton had passed the ball to Halleck, who for

21

the present at least felt constrained to call the signals, while McClellan, from his self-constructed "Olympian Heights" in the unhealthy Peninsula country, remained steadfast in the obsession that only he could save the country. In his annoyance that Halleck had succeeded him as General-in-Chief, and consistent with the savior role in which in his mind's eye he pictured himself, McClellan objected to every plan that emanated from Washington, no matter from what high source. Arguing endlessly with his superiors in favor of his own strategy, stalling interminably when peremptory and unequivocal orders reached him from an exasperated Halleck, and discouraging Pope's effort toward teamwork between the two armies, it is difficult to conclude otherwise than that McClellan wanted both Halleck and Pope to fail so that he himself could emerge as the sole leader capable of leading the North to victory. In no other way can the following excerpt from a letter to his wife be interpreted, in light of the fact that he was clearly doing everything in his own power to make it certain that Halleck's revised strategy should *not* succeed. Coincident with the final overruling of McClellan's stalling tactics by Halleck, who bluntly informed him by telegraph that "It (the order for withdrawal from the James) will not be rescinded and you will be expected to execute it with all possible promptness," McClellan wrote his wife: "They are committing a fatal error in withdrawing me from here, and the future will show it. I think the result of their machinations will be that Pope will be badly thrashed within ten days, and that they will be very glad to turn over the redemption of their affairs to me." Apparently the thought never crossed the general's little mind that he was pursuing the wrong path that leads to greatness, even though his two-point forecast would in the end prove correct.

Halleck was fully aware of the danger that Lee might attack one or the other of the widely separated Federal armies either before or during McClellan's northward movement. The latter's recalcitrance could prove fatal, so Halleck cautioned

Pope not to be precipitous, "but to avoid an advance from the line of the Rappahannock so as to expose yourself to any disaster, unless you can better your line of defense, until we can get more troops upon the Rappahannock."

The application of such a restrictive check-rein to the newly appointed, ambitious army commander was disappointing, particularly after Pope's flamboyant early orders to his troops, all breathing the spirit of the offensive and decrying such ordinary precautions as security for the rear areas. Furthermore, Pope believed that Halleck should force McClellan to cooperate by more energetic action rather than to hamstring his own army by requiring him to mark time. There is also some evidence that Pope may have pictured himself at the head of his army, sweeping across country toward Richmond and, brushing aside all opposition, pounding at Lee's back door while the latter kept an eye on McClellan in front.

However, Pope was not completely reckless, only prone to reach hasty decisions without considering all the implications; in the present circumstances he reluctantly allowed himself to be guided by Halleck's injunction to go slow.

A New General Gets Tough

The appointment of General John Pope to command the new Army of Virginia was dated June 26, 1862. For some weeks thereafter his headquarters remained in Washington while he took account of stock, conferred with War Department officials, devised plans, and issued orders to effect the concentration of his several corps and to define organizational procedures and operational policies.

As already noted, his first ill-advised general order to the troops had just the opposite effect from what he had intended. With his foot still in his mouth, during his extended sojourn in the Capital, he caused to be published General Orders Nos. 5, 6, and 7, dated July 18, setting forth the methods by which he had determined to keep the citizens of occupied Virginia territory under strict control. The series of orders prescribed that the Army of Virginia should live off the country to the maximum extent practicable. Supplies requisitioned for the army would, on presentation of vouchers to be rendered by the requisitioning officer, "be paid for at the conclusion of the war, upon sufficient testimony being furnished that such owners have been loyal citizens of the United States since the dates of the vouchers."

Furthermore, the people of the South would be notified that persons living in the vicinity of Federal camps or bivouacs were to be held responsible for damage done to all railroad tracks, telegraph lines, and roads, and for any attacks upon army trains or stragglers, whether perpetrated by private citizens or guerrillas. Payment for such damage would be exacted by turning out the local populace within five miles of the spot, not only to repair the damage but in addition to pay to the United States in money or property the full amount of the pay and subsistence of the Federal troops required to enforce performance by the citizens of the corrective measures.

Still harsher punishment was promised to any Southerner from whose house a soldier should be fired on. All such houses were to be immediately destroyed and the occupants sent to army headquarters as prisoners. If any person should be caught in the act he was to be shot forthwith, "without awaiting civil process."

There was no doubt that Pope believed strongly in the strictest kind of martial law in occupied territory. Doubtless his intent was to intimidate the Southerners as a preventive measure and to effect economy in his own operations, on the premise that his troops would thus be more secure and would not be diverted from essential military operations by excessive police duties. While his purpose may have been militarily justified, the psychology was defective, for his harsh measures only served to harden the resistance and strengthen the will of Confederate citizens to outsmart the invaders at every opportunity.

The broad latitude granted to a large army on the loose in enemy country, particularly one whose morale and discipline (in many of the units) would rate less than satisfactory on an efficiency report, inevitably resulted in depredations and pillage against innocent Southerners which shamed the more intelligent and sensitive officers and men of Pope's army.

The effect of Pope's blanket "live off the country" order was to strip handsome plantations and small farms alike of all means of livelihood, reducing the inhabitants to penury and almost complete dependence on the good will of the invading army. The heavy weight of Federal license descended indiscriminately on the just and unjust alike.

Lieutenant James Gillette, a brigade commissary officer in Sigel's corps, wrote his mother from Warrenton on July 31:

> Straggling soldiers have been known to rob the farm houses and even small cottages, the homes of the poor, of every ounce of food or forage found in them. Families have been left without the means of preparing a meal of victuals.
>
> The amenities, privations, and discomforts of those removed from the scene of war's conflicts, away from the path of armies, know nothing of suffering or inconvenience compared with the horrors undergone by the people of Virginia.
>
> The magnificent farm of the late Hon. Robert E. Scott of Virginia has lost all its crops and means of cultivation within the past few months. Mrs. Scott told me that the negroes had absconded. That she had twenty horses, but not a kernel of corn to feed them. With her cows shot, sheep and chickens ditto, she hardly knew where she was to obtain subsistence for her large family. Mr. Scott stood with John Minor Bott in opposing secession and was at last shot by a deserter to the Union Army. His farm is now being shorn of all its worth by the renegade and straggling soldiery of the army he would have upheld if he were alive. The lawless acts of many of our soldiery are worthy of worse than death. The villains urge as authority, "General Pope's order."

General Orders No. 11, issued July 23, were equally punitive in directing commanders down to brigades and detached commands "to arrest all disloyal male citizens within their lines or within their reach in rear of their respective stations." Those Southerners who were willing to take the oath of allegiance to the United States would be permitted to remain at home during good behavior; all others would be routed from their homes, conducted south beyond Federal picket lines, and turned loose under penalty of being treated as spies should they later be found within or in rear of the Union lines.

Pope subsequently defended these policies affecting the Southern people by asserting that they were in accord with accepted practice in time of war, adding that they had been publicly and wilfully misconstrued as authorizing indiscriminate robbery and plunder. He claimed that they were completely justified by the embarrassment and long delay imposed on Lee's army in its subsequent invasion of Maryland in September 1862, because of the resulting shortages of food and supplies from the country which Pope's army had wrung dry during the campaign.

Concentration of the infantry and artillery of the Army of Virginia in late July and early August was partially screened by cavalry, which at that stage of the war was little more than an aggregation of uniformed men and horses that had not been allowed either to acquire the necessary branch training or to function as organized combat units, trained or untrained. To be a good trooper called for equal efficiency either mounted or dismounted, but the steps necessary to attain the needed state of training were precluded by the wasteful use of the green Union horsemen on inconsequential duties such as orderlies and messengers for infantry corps and division commanders, outposts and patrols, and guards for slow-moving wagon trains. The resulting waste of horseflesh was disgraceful because of the lack of training and foolish dissipation of resources on inappropriate missions, so that reliability could not be placed on the Federal cavalry arm until the facts of cavalry life were finally recognized and applied by General Joe Hooker during the first half of 1863.

In spite of these deficiencies, part of Pope's cavalry, operating under two capable commanders, Brigadier Generals John Buford and George D. Bayard, displayed a bold aggressiveness that surprised the Confederates, unaccustomed as the latter were to any display of ambition or dash by the Union horsemen. Moving many miles in advance of their infantry, the two Federal detachments reconnoitered actively and tirelessly with surprising effectiveness, keeping Pope well informed of the general movements of Jackson's advance elements as they moved west toward Gordonsville.

The Theater of Operations

By way of orientation, it should be noted that the Rappahannock River, together with its branch, the Rapidan, played a significant role throughout the war in the strategic thinking and planning of the War Departments and military com-

POPE'S ENGINEERS AT WORK ON A BRIDGE OVER THE RAPPAHANNOCK NEAR SULPHUR SPRINGS

manders of both sides. Although fordable at many points in the dry season, the east-west river line afforded a sufficiently strong military obstacle to cause difficulty for armies on the offensive and, conversely, to serve as a formidable aid for defending forces.

Rail junctions at Manassas, Gordonsville, and Charlottesville were vital strategic points coveted by the contending armies. Manassas Junction was particularly important to the North, in that the Manassas Gap and Orange and Alexandria Railways, joining at that point, supplied the Union armies in northern and western Virginia. Gordonsville and Charlottesville were of equal importance to the South, in that the Virginia Central Railway, crossing the State from east to west, connected with the Orange and Alexandria at Gordonsville and with the East Tennessee and Virginia at Charlottesville, thus serving as the major supply line between Richmond, western Virginia, and the Southwestern States.

The theater of operations in which Pope and Lee were destined to cross swords in the summer of 1862 was quite heavily forested, thick in some areas, less so in others, such as the plains of Manassas. North and west of Gordonsville the Blue Ridge and Bull Run Mountains could be crossed at the various "gaps." There were numerous roads, mostly dirt, which were useful in dry weather but difficult to negotiate after severe rains. The macadam turnpikes were few and far between, being limited in this theater to the Warrenton-Alexandria Pike, the Little River Turnpike through Aldie Gap, the Orange Turnpike to Fredericksburg and one or two others.

Pope Puts Out Ineffectual Feelers

Pursuant to that portion of his instructions which called for the protection of Washington while the Army of the Potomac was returning north from the Peninsula, Pope ordered McDowell's division commander at Fredericksburg, Brigadier General Rufus King, early in July to dispatch part of his cavalry to impair and, to the extent practicable, destroy communications along the line of the Virginia Central Railroad between

Richmond and the Shenandoah Valley. At the same time General Banks was directed to send an infantry brigade, together with all the cavalry attached to his corps, to march on Culpeper Court House, seize it, and push the cavalry on towards the Rapidan and Gordonsville. Threatening Gordonsville and Charlottesville would in Pope's opinion be the best way to isolate the Shenandoah Valley and draw troops away from Richmond.

After that mission should be accomplished, Banks was to send forward his entire cavalry force from Culpeper, under Brigadier General John P. Hatch, to seize Gordonsville, destroy the railroad for a dozen miles east of that town, and then move on towards Charlottesville to destroy railroad bridges and disrupt communications as much as possible. Moving out on July 15, Hatch encumbered himself with artillery and trains, found the roads bad, and made so little forward progress that the expedition was abandoned in the face of the arrival of Confederate Major General Richard S. Ewell with the advance guard of Stonewall Jackson's troops at Gordonsville on July 16.

Still hopeful of preliminary success in the unfolding of his remote control strategy, Pope tried again. He instructed Banks to send several thousand cavalrymen, again under Hatch, to move down on the west side of the Blue Ridge, destroy the railroad west of Gordonsville and continue south to destroy the railroad between Charlottesville and Lynchburg. Hatch made a feeble start on this assignment, but for undisclosed reasons (probably Ewell's presence at Gordonsville) quickly abandoned the movement, whereupon Pope relieved him from command and sent in his stead the able Brig. Gen. John Buford to serve as Chief of Cavalry of Banks' corps.

Buford had been buried in the Inspector General's Department as a major, without influential friends to rescue him from oblivion, when he reported to Pope in the capacity of an Inspector shortly after the latter was given command of the Army of Virginia. Pope offered him a field command which

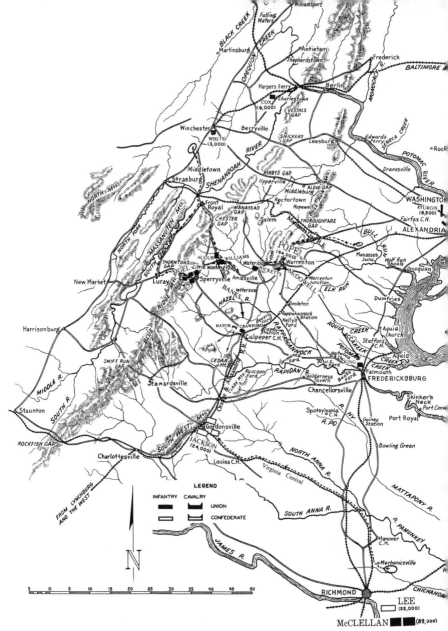

MAP 2. POSITIONS OF THE TROOPS ON AUGUST 1, 1862

Three days after General Pope left Washington to join his troops in the field, the various corps and divisions were still scattered, as shown on this map. Sigel's corps plus Milroy's brigade was at Sperryville. Banks' corps, less Crawford's brigade at Culpeper, was at Little Washington. One of McDowell's divisions is at Waterloo Bridge, the other at Falmouth. This map also shows the routes of Sigel and Banks from their positions in the Shenandoah Valley to their present locations east of the mountains.

Jackson, at Gordonsville, has been joined by A. P. Hill's division.

Buford gratefully accepted. His commission as Brigadier General of Volunteers came through promptly and Pope immediately gave him a cavalry brigade in one of his corps.

John P. Buford was a contemporary of Robert E. Lee at West Point where the two were cadets, in the latter half of the 1820's. Other fellow students were Jefferson Davis, the two Johnstons, and Leonidas Polk, all destined for military fame almost four decades later. If for nothing else the North owed a debt to John Pope for uncovering Buford, for the cavalryman injected new ideas into the mounted branch, trained his troopers to fight dismounted as well as on horseback, and reached the zenith of his career at Gettysburg, where his cavalry division, fighting on foot astride the Chambersburg pike, successfully blocked the advance of A. P. Hill's corps on the first day until Reynolds could come up.

Pope Takes the Field

At this stage Pope concluded that the time had come for him to take personal command in the field. It was high time! Jackson's advance elements had reached Gordonsville and his main body was on the way. The rest of Lee's army was still in Richmond, while McClellan's Army of the Potomac remained at Harrison's Landing. Halleck had arrived in Washington in mid-July to take over and it may be presumed that one of his first official acts was to tell Pope to take himself out of Washington and join his troops, where he belonged. There was of course no objection from Lincoln, who had temporarily used Pope as his military adviser pending Halleck's arrival.

On July 29 Pope left the Capital, reviewed Ricketts' division of McDowell's corps at Waterloo Bridge, and joined Banks at his headquarters a short distance southeast of Little Washington. Pope's strength return for July 31 shows a grand total of nearly 72,000 officers and men, but does not give a true picture of his strength. Banks, for example, had 8,800, not the 15,000 he reported. Actually Pope's three corps including his cavalry and King's division, still at Fredericksburg, totalled about 43,800. In theoretical support but too distant or otherwise engaged to be immediately available were the commands of Sturgis, Cox, and White, which brought Pope's total to 64,000. In the critical Sperryville-Culpeper-Warrenton triangle he had only 34,800.

March orders for the army now directed Banks' corps to advance to the point where the Sperryville-Culpeper Turnpike crosses the Hazel River, McDowell to move with Ricketts' division from Waterloo Bridge to Culpeper, and Sigel's corps at Sperryville to remain in place. By August 8 all of Pope's infantry and artillery except King's division at Fredericksburg were disposed along the turnpike from Sperryville to Culpeper. The cavalry covered the front from Madison Court House to Rapidan Station, with pickets posted along the Rapidan River from the Blue Ridge on the west to the forks of the Rappahannock above Falmouth on the east. Halfway between the cavalry forces under Buford and Bayard, a signal station was established on the top of Thoroughfare Mountain, ten miles southwest of Culpeper, commanding a view of the entire country as far down as Orange Court House.

Pope had misgivings about the First Corps under Franz Sigel, the German-born general who had recently succeeded the politically-minded John Fremont, whose military accomplishments had failed to measure up to his reputation as an explorer. Sigel was popular with his men but somewhat controversial in character, and far from compatible with his fellow officers of the Regular Army. "A very insignificant looking man, but a thorough soldier and gentleman," was the way one of his staff described him in a letter to his family. Banks and McDowell on the other hand enjoyed the confidence of the army commander, so it was on these two corps that Pope came to rely more fully than on Sigel's.

Tightening Union Discipline

Whether he was influenced by what he had observed of the troops after his arrival, or simply as a matter of sound administration, Pope issued a general order on August 6 whose purpose was to tighten discipline and improve the marching and combat capabilities of his army. Straggling was strictly forbidden, and to make certain that the order would be obeyed, regimental commanders were instructed to habitually march in rear of their regiments, company commanders in rear of their companies. Men could not fall out except by written permission of a medical officer and then only if sick enough to be forced to ride in an ambulance. None but ambulance and ammunition wagons would be permitted in the column of march of the respective regiments, all other wheeled vehicles to follow in rear of the troops. Shelter tents and knapsacks were to be carried in the wagons, and each officer and man would at all times on the march be required to carry two days' cooked rations on his person. Enlisted men would habitually carry 100 rounds of ammunition, and any company commander whose men were found deficient in this respect was to be arrested forthwith and reported to the War Department for dismissal from the service.

The terms of this order implied either a lack of confidence in the efficiency of his subordinate commanders or a blunt recognition of the lack of training and discipline of the troops under their former separate status. Probably some of both. Whatever the reason, Pope must be credited with a determination to put his army in a condition to make the most of its opportunities. It would appear, however, that the language of certain parts of the order was hardly calculated to raise morale, in view of the implication that the General could not trust his officers to perform their sworn duty except under the compulsion of harsh and punitive terms.

It was clear that the Army of Virginia needed a commanding general, on the field in person, capable of whipping it into shape. But that was going to be an uphill struggle, if the current reflections of a dubious lieutenant in Sigel's corps* reflected the universal view of the staff and line:

-----

*Lieut. James Gillette, Commissary of Subsistence in Cooper's brigade.

We are still in the bustle of preparation. We are going through a sort of picking over and sifting process. A General checked out here and a Colonel there; a brigade put here and another countermarched to where it was a week ago. Then shifted back again, and the whole thing knocked into Pi, sifted out, picked over, and sorted again. What they are going to do and when they are going to do it I don't know.

An immense army is in the neighborhood and some great work is being laid out for it in Washington by the Politicians. The soldiers are much disgusted with the interference of Politicians. They rule everything and the changes that daily occur evidence it. No sooner is a soldier attached to his Commander than that Commander is removed to supply a place for some favorite.

The topographical and engineering corps of our army is sadly deficient. Generals are almost without exception totally ignorant on this hand, so much so that they can't understand the maps they carry. It is not unusual for a brigade to lose its way and take wrong roads. No one knows the enemy's whereabouts. The scouting system, which is the chief pride of the rebel army, is ignored by us. We content ourselves with pickets asleep on their posts a mile from camp or obtain information from the "intelligent" negroes with which the country abounds.

The ignorance of our officers has become proverbial and patent to the men and hence the present low standard of discipline in the army. A Lieutenant of Cavalry remarked to me that he hoped he might never be a Major General, for a brigadier was a big enough fool without wanting to go higher. Unless something is done to rescue the army from the politicians, patriots will hang up their swords in disgust and despair.

On August 7 Pope rode to Sperryville to inspect Sigel's corps. While there he received several reports from the cavalry that enemy troops were crossing the Rapidan at several points between the railroad and the bridge at Liberty Mills. The reports continued to come in on the morning of August 8. Buford and Bayard messaged that the enemy was advancing on Culpeper and Madison Court House respectively, but Pope was unable to determine which of the two towns represented the principal objective of Jackson's force. In the course of the day, however, he decided to concentrate his full strength in the direction of Culpeper in order to keep his own army between the enemy main body and the lower fords of the Rappahannock. To that end Crawford's brigade of Banks'

MAJOR GENERAL NATHANIEL P. BANKS

corps was sent forward in the direction of Cedar (Slaughter) Mountain, to support Bayard's cavalry as it retired before the enemy in the direction of the mountain, and to assist Bayard in determining the strength and dispositions of the hostile forces. Buford was near Madison Courthouse. At the same time Banks and Sigel were directed to move their troops immediately to Culpeper from Hazel River and Sperryville, respectively.

Banks marched promptly, reaching Culpeper the same day, the 8th of August, but Sigel was slow and, judging from Pope's subsequent official report, stupid as well, for he sent army headquarters a note from Sperryville inquiring which road to take, although there was only the single broad turnpike between the two points. Consequently, Sigel's corps reached the assembly area almost a day later than Pope intended and was not ready to be sent in company with Banks to meet the enemy advance on August 9.

Some days earlier Banks had reported an effective strength of some 15,000 men. It turned out, however, according to Pope, that his actual effectives did not exceed 8,800. The reason for the discrepancy was never explained. At the time of the concentration Pope believed Banks' strength to be almost twice as great as it actually was, and the army commander's battle plans were predicated upon that assumption. That at least was Pope's story after the stunning defeat of his army at Second Manassas, and his statement must be judged with subsequent events in mind.

Sigel's unsatisfactory performance up to this time had thrown Pope's logistics off schedule to the extent that Banks' corps on August 8 was the only immediate complete tactical weapon of consequence available for offensive action. McDowell had but one of his two divisions, Ricketts' at Culpeper, the other being at Fredericksburg, covering the Union supply base at Aquia Creek Landing. Pope thereupon took it upon himself to order King's division up from Fredericksburg, a thirty-five mile march, and so advised Halleck by telegram at 10 o'clock on the evening of August 8. Since Burnside's corps had now arrived at Aquia Creek, it was perfectly proper for Pope to recall King.

In the same telegram Pope summed up his estimate of the situation by advising Halleck that the enemy division (Elzey's)*, which had crossed the Rapidan during the day, was probably a reconnaissance in force, which might however represent an advance upon Culpeper. He indicated his intention, as soon as Sigel's corps should join the rest of the army the following morning, of pushing the enemy across the Rapidan and then taking up a strong position in accordance with Halleck's suggestion in an earlier message.

---

*Actually a brigade of Ewell's division, commanded by Jubal Early, who had supplanted the invalided Elzey.

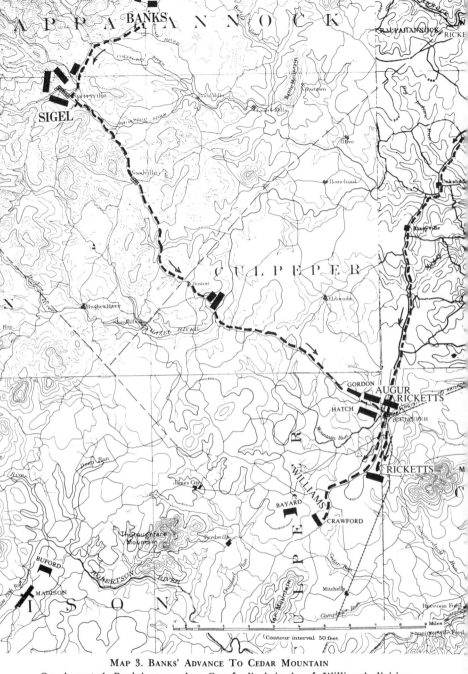

MAP 3. BANKS' ADVANCE TO CEDAR MOUNTAIN

On August 1 Banks' corps, less Crawford's brigade of Williams' division at Culpeper, was at Little Washington. On the 6th, Augur's division moved to Hazel River, followed on the next day by Gordon's brigade of Williams' division. On the 8th the corps moved to Culpeper, on the 9th it joined Crawford at Cedar Run. Meantime, Ricketts' division of McDowell's corps was moved by Pope from Waterloo Bridge on August 7 to just north of Culpeper. On the 8th Ricketts was moved to a position near Colvin's tavern (Map 5).

Combat Imminent

On the morning of August 9, Banks with his entire corps was ordered toward Cedar Mountain to join the brigade of A. S. Williams' division under General Crawford, already well forward. Banks was directed to occupy a strong position at the point reached by Crawford and to halt the advance of the enemy. Ricketts' division of McDowell's corps was posted nearby at Colvin's Tavern, where the Madison Court House-Culpeper Road intersects the Culpeper-Cedar Mountain Road, to hold that tactically important point against a possible advance by a Confederate force reported by Buford to be in strength near Madison Court House. Ricketts' division would thus be in position, three miles behind Banks' corps, either to support the latter or to serve as a strongpoint for a buildup of additional strength to counter the hostile threat from the direction of Madison Court House.

Occasional enemy horse-artillery fire was directed on Banks' position during the day, but there was no evidence in his opinion to justify a belief that the Confederates planned to attack. Enemy cavalry had been making demonstrations, but Banks reported to Pope that in his judgment the supporting Confederate infantry was not strong enough to launch an attack. Later in the afternoon, however, the tempo of artillery fire increased to such an extent that Pope became alarmed and sent Ricketts' division barging toward the front, in support of Banks as a measure of insurance.

It was late afternoon of August 9, before Sigel's corps reached Culpeper, and just about the time Pope was preparing to start for the front to see for himself what was happening. It was bad enough that Sigel was late in arriving at Culpeper, but on top of that he had compounded his earlier mistake by neglecting to enforce Pope's standing order to keep two days' cooked rations on the men's persons on all marches. This failure meant further delay until he could borrow rations from McDowell's trains at Culpeper and have a hot meal cooked for his troops.

Army Commander Pope was having his troubles. It was an inauspicious start for the Army of Virginia, which seemed to be getting off on the wrong foot in its first campaign. Pope was trying hard—that much was evident—but his tools lacked sharpness and his own attitude had not contributed materially to the development of a smooth-working, enthusiastic organization.

History is prone to overlook errors of judgment on the part of generals who win battles, and to condemn unmercifully those who fail to do so, particularly when the defeats occur in the grand manner. In the last analysis, results are what really count. Pope was one of many Northern generals who flashed briefly across the Civil War skies only to sink back into military anonymity. He was to have his big chance and fail. Whether his Army of Virginia would have written history in a more illustrious manner under another commander, or whether Pope himself might have made good under different circumstances, can only be conjectured.

JACKSON'S COMMAND MARCHING NORTH TO MEET POPE

CHAPTER 3

JACKSON MOVES TO MEET POPE

JACKSON'S successes in the Shenandoah Valley and Lee's effective neutralization of the Army of the Potomac on the James had afforded an opportunity for the commander of the Army of Northern Virginia to take the initiative, which he was quick to grasp. He was now in a position to call the turn if he played his cards carefully but boldly.

Operating in widely separated areas, but in accordance with a definite strategic concept, Lee and Jackson between them had successfully frustrated Federal designs on Richmond and the Valley. Lee's immediate task, as the summer weeks passed, was to maintain a close watch on the slow-acting McClellan and at the same time keep Pope's new army preoccupied while he sought an opening to crush the latter before the two Federal armies should succeed in effecting a junction.

Lee was fast becoming an expert in taking calculated risks by splitting his forces and reassembling them in time for the payoff battle. If he could attack Pope, keep Washington on tenterhooks, and hinder or prevent a junction between the armies of Pope and McClellan, it would immeasurably improve the fortunes of the Confederacy. It might even pave the way for an invasion of the North, a project that was dear to Lee's heart and constantly in his thoughts.

It was no secret that Pope's army was being concentrated east of the Blue Ridge in the Warrenton-Culpeper area. Lee learned of it through his efficient spy system almost as soon as Pope arrived in Washington and began to sound off. But even before the Federal Army of Virginia came into being, the "armies" under Banks, Fremont, and McDowell must not be allowed to maneuver at will along the Rappahannock.

It was natural, then, that Stonewall Jackson be ordered to retrace his steps and take up where he had left off when summoned to Lee's aid at Richmond. Lee had learned to respect Jackson's capabilities and, keen judge of character that he was, no doubt recognized—particularly after Mechanicsville—that his spirited lieutenant was at his best when working alone, and without a curb bit.

In mid-July, with the divisions of "Baldy" Ewell and Charles S. Winder, Jackson set out for Gordonsville, which was reached on July 19 after a leisurely march of three days. Ten days later Lee wrote that he was sending A. P. ("Powell") Hill's Light Division to strengthen Jackson's force, adding in diplomatic language that Hill could be trusted with Jackson's plans and implying that so large a force as Jackson would now command was too unwieldly to be handled as a one-man show. The advice was however wasted on the uncompromising Jackson, who persisted to the end of his career in treating his generals as though they were children who could not be trusted to think for themselves.

On August 1 Jackson's force at Gordonsville numbered more than 24,000 men, almost half of Lee's army, and the largest body of troops that he had commanded up to this time. The three infantry divisions, with their artillery components, were led by Hill, Ewell, and Winder. By far the largest, the Light Division, had at least 12,000 men present. Ewell's strength was 7,200, while Winder counted only 4,000 in the relatively weak outfit, which formerly had been Jackson's own division. Brigadier General Beverly H. Robertson's 1,200 cavalrymen completed the roster.

Robertson had succeeded Ashby, Jackson's dashing cavalry leader who had been killed in the Valley campaign, and whose troopers had now been reorganized into four regiments under the West Pointer whom Jackson disliked, preferring "Grumble" Jones to the man selected by President Davis. Robertson's Laurel Brigade, as the consolidated regiments were called, joined Jackson after his arrival at Gordonsville.

Jackson's men were happy to get away from the Peninsula and the swamps of the Chickahominy to the more familiar country with its clear, swift-running streams, modern (by Civil War standards) roads, and wooded country fringed by the towering ridges of the Blue Ridge Mountains. The troops were in good physical shape, the weak sisters having been weeded out in the rapid marches of the earlier campaign. The regiments were below their normal strength, few replacements having been received, but their morale was good and discipline had been restored by a strenuous regime of continuous drilling after the Seven Days Battles. They had yet to face defeat and were ready for the best that Pope could offer.

Acutely aware of Lee's hope that Pope's army might be attacked and destroyed before effecting a junction with McClellan's, Jackson was alert for any information that would enable him to apply his successful Valley technique to a portion of Pope's army if it could be caught before Pope could complete his own concentration. Jackson had his eye on the network of roads at Culpeper, which he correctly believed to be Pope's assembly point. When reports from spies disclosed that only a part of the Army of Virginia had reached Culpeper, Jackson determined to act promptly. In the late afternoon of August 7, on which date Pope's divisions were strung along the turnpike from Sperryville to Culpeper, Jackson's troops took off, bivouacked that night at Orange Court House, 20 miles from Culpeper, and resumed the march at dawn the following morning, initial objective the crossing at Barnett's Ford.

Confusion at Orange Court House

On August 8 Ewell's division led off, with Powell Hill and Winder to follow in that order. Jackson had issued sketchy written orders for the march the evening before, but neither he nor any of his staff had apparently given any thought to routine logistical factors, such as the relative strength and road distance of the several divisions and the position of organizational trains. To further confuse the issue, Jackson changed his mind about the route of the leading division under Ewell, but neglected to inform either Hill or Winder of the change in orders. Instead of following the Orange Court House–Culpeper Road, Ewell was directed to take the road to the left till he reached the Rapidan at Liberty Mills; there he would split his division and march on parallel roads to north and south of the river till he reached Barnett's Ford.

At Orange Court House, Hill, in position early in the morning, waited for the tail of Ewell's supposed column to clear. The troops he watched however turned out to be Jackson's division, under Winder's command, followed by its division trains. Ewell by this time was miles ahead. When Jackson put in an appearance he promptly inquired the reason for Hill's delay, but even then did not tell him of the change in orders; nor did he make any effort to straighten out the tangle.

The net result of the mix-up, which would never have occurred had Jackson been a bit more communicative, was threefold. Jackson's vaunted "foot-cavalry" made one of its sorriest showings, with Hill's division ordered back to Orange Court House for the night after advancing little more than two miles for their day's work. Jackson's corps, instead of reaching Culpeper on the 8th as planned, covered only about 8 miles of the 20-mile distance with less than half of the troops. Finally, a spark of mutual distrust was struck between Jackson and Hill that, fanned by subsequent winds of misunderstanding, would lead to the arrest of the latter and the filing of court-martial charges by his uncompromising superior within a matter of months. All of which could have been avoided if the close-

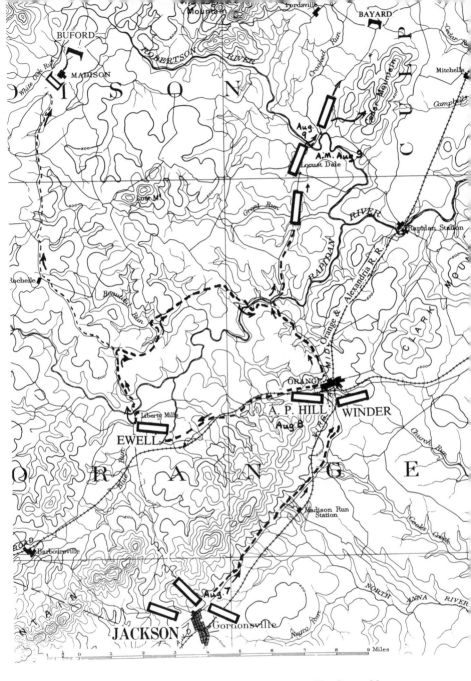

MAP 4. JACKSON'S ADVANCE FROM GORDONSVILLE TO CEDAR MOUNTAIN

The basic map used here was surveyed about 1886, hence some of the features shown, such as the railroad running through Barboursville, did not exist in 1862. The roads, towns, streams, and hills, however, were little changed if at all. After the Civil War several railroads such as the Orange & Alexandria, received new names, but otherwise were little altered. The contour interval on some sheets is 100 feet, on others fifty feet; on this sheet it is 100 feet.

mouthed Jackson had been more considerate of his subordinates and played his lone wolf role with greater acumen.

The disgruntled Jackson informed Lee of the delay, expressing a fear that because of the slow progress on August 8 the expedition would accomplish little. Federal cavalry had obstinately opposed his forward movement and the enemy now knew pretty well what he was up to. Pope was not the only commanding general having troubles. The honors were consequently about even on the morning of August 9.

The Federal cavalry under Buford and Bayard was doing a fine job of screening the movements of Pope's army, and the chances were now good that Jackson's delayed march had given Pope the additional needed time to concentrate at Culpeper. Nevertheless Jackson optimistically believed the odds were in his favor. These were the same troops opposing him that he had made monkeys of in the Valley. His own strength was much greater now; if he moved fast and took advantage of any opening that might offer, it was still possible that Pope's army could be defeated in detail.

Destination—Culpeper

A. P. Hill, determined to erase the apparent recent blot on his record, started his march that third morning long before daylight, soon caught up to Ewell and Winder. The entire force quickly put the Rapidan behind them. With part of the cavalry covering the advance and the rest marching on the left flank and toward Madison Court House, the tired Federal cavalry was pushed steadily back as Jackson, with Ewell's division still in the lead, crossed Robertson River at Locust Dale and headed down the home stretch toward Culpepper.

Off to the northeast the troops were able to observe, several miles distant, a long tree-covered ridge known locally as Slaughter Mountain, so called after a minister by that name who lived on its northern slope. The bitter fighting that was soon to take place in its vicinity would serve to confirm the name, but history would call it the Battle of Cedar Mountain or Cedar Run as a more euphonious title and in deference to the twin-forked creek whose branches, originating on either side of the Gordonsville-Culpeper Road, meandered east and south to join at Hudson's Mill, about a mile from the Slaughter home, and thence flowed on to the Rapidan.

Jackson and His Generals

The operations of General Thomas Jonathan (Stonewall) Jackson were always more effective when he held independent command and could march and maneuver on his own without restrictions beyond those required to integrate his movements and actions with the overall strategy of the Commanding General, Robert E. Lee. Jackson's great reputation was initially earned in the course of his independently conducted Shenandoah Valley campaign in the spring of 1862, while his military genius failed to shine with equal brilliance when he joined Lee before Richmond to participate in the Seven Days' Battles.

The austere pre-war professor of military science at Virginia Military Institute could never have been called loquacious or gregarious. God-fearing, methodical, reserved, earnest, determined, straightforward, courageous, and inflexible—all of those and many more adjectives fitted him perfectly. The depths of his extraordinary character were rarely plumbed by his associates, most of whom regarded him as decidedly eccentric. The irrepressible students of VMI called him "Tom Fool" Jackson, a nickname that rather failed to imply admiration or affection, but there was no lack of respect for either his knowledge or military competence.

No other general in any of the armies, North or South, could even approach him in the matter of keeping his own counsel. His reticence was proverbial; so much so, indeed, that his own division commanders were forced to function almost blindly because of his consistent policy of divulging his plans to no one, not even the members of his immediate staff, until the moment for action had arrived.

It would appear that he could not or would not trust his own people to keep their mouths shut. When a march impended, none but Jackson himself knew the precise destination until the column was headed down the road, and frequently not then. As a rule, the officers learned where they were to camp only when ordered to halt and fall out. There were occasions when, no doubt to confuse the enemy, the general would change division orders after the troops were on their way, but the word was not always passed to the other division commanders, causing inevitable and, to them at least, unnecessary confusion.

One may question the propriety or wisdom of one man playing his cards so close to his chest, when so complex an organization as an army or even a corps is involved. It can be argued that the best results from loyal, intelligent officers can scarcely be expected when they are given no information in advance as to what is expected of them. Jackson must have believed that the resulting frustrations of his chief lieutenants were more than offset by the guaranty that if his own people were not taken into his confidence there would be no danger that his plans would become known to the enemy. There was of course nothing they could do to penetrate his irritating secretiveness, although the fiery-tempered red head, Powell Hill, was goaded almost to insubordination on more than one occasion by what seemed to him to be Jackson's wilfully strange and annoying attitude.

Many writers have speculated, ad infinitum, on the reasons for Jackson's almost invariable success when operating independently with a small force, and conversely on the less energetic attitude which characterized his movements and actions on the several occasions when, with a larger independent force, or when approaching a junction with Lee's main body, as at Mechanicsville, his performance failed to measure up to the high standard Lee had come to expect from him. Certainly it was not that he was temperamentally incapable of serving under Lee, for whom he had the greatest admiration and respect. What is more likely is that he lacked a well-rounded, capable staff, as did practically all the higher ranking Confederate generals; had never developed a workable formula for exerting his will other than by issuing personal, oral orders; and, most importantly, placed too little emphasis on the science of logistics. For the principles of logistics, or to put it simply, the accurate calculation of time-and-space factors followed by the closely coordinated headwork necessary to make the logistic tables effective, were the same in 1862 as in 1918 or 1945. The only difference is that modern gadgets are now available to keep pace with the increased complexities of warfare. The more primitive tools for logistic planning during the Civil War neither lessened its vital importance in the prosecution of campaigns nor does it excuse those generals who were unskilled in the science or neglected to apply what knowledge they may have had.

There exists some evidence that Jackson's failures, few as they were, stemmed either from careless planning on that score or from an inadequate appreciation of the importance of logistics, where large bodies of troops are involved. Planning without effective execution is an idle gesture, and since Jackson's taciturnity was such that he habitually kept his own counsel, it is not surprising that execution was occasionally faulty, even though he may have had adequate but undisclosed plans. This would not have been so noticeable when he commanded only the equivalent of a reinforced division in the Valley, but would show up plainly when his force was enlarged to three divisions of widely different strengths, as occurred just prior to the Battle of Cedar Mountain; and again at Chancellorsville in the spring of 1863. On the latter occasion, when Lee turned Jackson loose with over 30,000 men for his famous eleven-mile march across Hooker's front, that culminated in the successful rolling up of the latter's right flank, Jackson was more than three hours late in starting, took almost nine hours to cover eleven miles, with little if any interference from Union forces, and attacked too late in the afternoon to exploit his success before darkness, and his own fatal wounding by his own men, halted the fighting.

Jackson's Favorite Division Commander

Richard Stoddert Ewell, one of the most colorful of the Confederate generals who rose to distinction in the Civil War, is historically linked with the name and fortunes of Stonewall Jackson in much the same way as the combinations of Longstreet and Lee, Jackson and Lee, Fitz Lee and Stuart. All were significantly close military relationships which successfully weathered fair winds and foul throughout the course of the war, until battlefield wounds caused the subsequent death of two of the most famous leaders, Jackson and Stuart.

It was the Shenandoah Valley Campaign of early 1862 from which stemmed the durable association of Jackson and Ewell, mentor and protege. Two more varied personalities it would be difficult to throw together. Jackson has already been portrayed. In striking contrast to his superior, "Old Baldy," a confirmed bachelor until he was close to fifty and the war was half over, was very much the extrovert, fond of people and always ready for a good laugh. Biographer Hamlin* pictures Ewell as "no hero, but a man who, while living on a most realistic plane, exhibited to those with whom he came in contact a noble generosity, a fairness of mind and an undeviating honesty of purpose, qualities often lacking in some of our most celebrated heroes."

Described by author Glenn Tucker† as a "hard-swearing, hard-riding, quick-tempered old trooper" with Jackson in the Valley, his later marriage to widow Lizinka Brown, his only love, would, on the surface at least, involve a surprising change in his habits. Attendance at church services would be increasingly noted by his colleagues. He would try his best to stop swearing, and in other ways Lizinka's influence was to have a marked effect on the middle-aged veteran who was destined to succeed to command of Stonewall Jackson's corps and in so doing to substantiate the validity of the old military adage

---

Old Bald Head (General R. S. Ewell), by Percy G. Hamlin, Strasburg, Va. 1940.

†*High Tide at Gettysburg*, Bobbs-Merrill, 1958.

that many a topnotch first sergeant is spoiled by converting him to a second lieutenant.

Born in Georgetown, next door to the city of Washington, on February 8, 1817, Dick was but a few years old when his family moved to "Stony Lonesome," five miles southwest of Manassas, Virginia. Father Ewell, a doctor, had decided to retire from the active practice of medicine to devote more time to the affairs of his wife's late father, who had been a soldier of the Revolution, a confidential agent of General Washington and the first Secretary of the Navy.

Unaware of the future strategic and historical importance of the countryside southwest of Washington, where he would pass his early youth, close by the plains of Manassas and the then peaceful little winding stream known as Bull Run, Dick learned in the shadow of Manassas to ride and shoot. His father's death when he was nine years of age meant that the remainder of his youth would be spent under the major influence of his mother, a woman of strong character and courage, both of which traits Dick inherited to a marked degree. He was an indifferent student, however, and it was only because of the determined tutelage of his older sister, Rebecca, that the young man managed to master the rudiments of an education in preparation for the day when he would follow Brother Ben's footsteps to the United States Military Academy at West Point.

During his four years at the Point, from which he graduated in 1840, fellow cadets included "Cump" Sherman, George Thomas, Henry Hunt, and "Sam" Grant, all four of whom became his close friends. George Meade had graduated a year before Ewell entered, but Joseph Hooker, Jubal Early, Pierre Beauregard, and Braxton Bragg were upperclassmen and hence, in the tradition of West Point, far removed from intimate or even friendly contact with the lowly plebes.

Ewell's first assignment after graduation was to Carlisle Barracks, Pennsylvania, where he found a strict disciplinarian and drillmaster in the commandant, Captain Edwin V. Sumner, who kept Ewell and the rest of the First Dragoons busy from morning to night. Service on the western plains followed, during which Ewell was engaged in convoying long wagon trains of traders along the dangerous Santa Fe trail, dodging buffalo stampedes and prairie fires, serving on recruiting duty in Missouri, Kentucky, and Indiana. After that came participation in the War with Mexico in which he experienced a little combat, but unfortunately missed the decisive battles.

Ten more long years on the western frontier involving long marches, chasing Apache Indians, and patrolling the country's expanding frontiers, brought Ewell face to face with the decision which confronted all Southerners of the Regular Army as the war clouds gathered. On April 24, 1861, immediately after Virginia seceded, Captain Ewell resigned from the U.S. Army, having completed twenty-one consecutive years of service with the same regiment, the famous First Dragoons. In May he was appointed Lieutenant Colonel of Virginia Cavalry, and within a month was made a brigadier general and given command of a brigade of Beauregard's Confederate Army of the Potomac, posted near Fairfax Station.

Although Ewell was present with his brigade during the First Battle of Manassas, the outfit was operating on the fringe and failed to encounter a single enemy soldier during the entire engagement. An order from Beauregard failed to reach Ewell and as a result his brigade spent its time fruitlessly marching and countermarching on the outskirts of the battle, waiting impatiently for orders that never came.

When Longstreet was promoted to major general, Ewell was given his brigade, whose headquarters he transferred to Centerville, the village of youthful memories, where his troops spent the miserable winter of 1861-62, ravaged by pneumonia and typhoid fever. Ewell's promotion to major general came in January 1862, at which time he was given command of 8,000 men of the Third Division, whose brigadiers were West Pointers Isaac Trimble and Arnold Elzey, and a graduate of Yale, Dick Taylor, son of ex-President Zachary Taylor.

Ewell's division was sent in April to join Jackson's forces in the Valley, where the as yet undistinguished Stonewall was conducting with his small force Lee's ordered strategic diversion while the latter was engaged in securing Richmond against McClellan's Army of the Potomac. This reinforcement greatly strengthened Jackson's hand, and although Jackson's fame overshadowed the activities of his division commanders in the Valley Campaign, Ewell's division played a leading part in the amazing exploits which on three successive occasions so alarmed Lincoln and Stanton for the safety of Washington that their plan to send McDowell's 35,000 men to McClellan's aid on the Peninsula was repeatedly shelved, with the interesting possibility that but for the Valley Campaign Richmond, and with it the Confederacy, might very well have been lost.

Unlike A. P. Hill, whose temperament was such that he was never able to adapt himself to Jackson's eccentricities, Ewell's first impression soon evaporated, as he learned to appraise Jackson's mastery of the art of war at first hand. When he joined Jackson in April, he later told friends, he thought "Old Jack" was "crazy as a March hare," because he was so secretive that he would never let Ewell know anything about his plans, not even where he could be reached or when Ewell would see him again. Ewell's first mission, as stated by the laconic Jackson, was simply to "remain at Swift Run Gap and watch Banks."

It wasn't long before Ewell figuratively mounted Jackson on a pedestal. Jackson was admired and emulated to the limit of the faithful and devoted Ewell's abilities, which were far from small. Ewell's apprenticeship under the tutelage of the hard-driving Jackson taught him many valuable lessons, from most of which he profited greatly so long as he remained a division commander. Stonewall allowed his division generals no discretion but rather conditioned them virtually as automatons to adhere strictly, and without deviation therefrom, to the terse orders which he would issue from time to time, mostly on the spur of the moment.

It was only after Jackson's death at Chancellorsville in May 1863, when Ewell was promoted to lieutenant general and given command of Lee's Second Corps, that Dick would forget some of Jackson's teachings, his old professor no longer being at hand to guide and lead him. Ewell's temperament was such, and his opinion of Jackson so high, that he followed the latter's instructions almost blindly. Part of the fault belongs to Jackson, who failed utterly to train his generals to think for themselves, with the natural result that they were likely to flounder in confused uncertainty when suddenly confronted with a situation calling for the exercise of discretionary judgment. It was exactly that kind of a situation that Ewell would be called upon to face in his first critical moment as a corps commander during the first day's battle at Gettysburg. As Ewell temporized, Union General Hancock preempted the prize, Cemetery Ridge, which for several hours would have been Ewell's merely for the asking.

Stonewall Jackson, reputedly a close student of Napoleon's campaigns, had managed to develop a few maxims of his own, many of which, it cannot be doubted, had rubbed off in the course of time on the more alert of his lieutenants, among whom "Baldy" Ewell was one of the best. Such maxims as these:

> Always mystify, mislead, and surprise the enemy if possible.

> I had rather lose one man in marching than five in battle.

> To move swiftly, strike vigorously, and secure all the fruits of victory is the secret of successful war.

> A defensive campaign can only be made successful by taking the aggressive at the proper time. Napoleon never waited for his adversary to become fully prepared, but struck him the first blow.

> Never fight against heavy odds if by any possible maneuvering you can hurl your whole force on only a part, and that the weakest part of your enemy, and crush it.

> When you strike him and overcome him never give up
> the pursuit as long as your men have strength to follow;
> for an enemy routed, if hotly pursued, becomes panic-
> stricken and can be destroyed by half their number.

The history of Jackson's campaigns and battles show either
that he practiced what he preached or that his military philosophy evolved from successful practice. The important fact is
that adherence to his rules of generalship made him a great
leader in war. The Valley Campaign and the battles around
Richmond were now history. It will be of interest to the reader
to keep the foregoing maxims in mind during the battles that
followed during the sumer and fall of 1862.

BATTLE OF CEDAR MOUNTAIN AS VIEWED FROM THE FEDERAL SIDE

CHAPTER 4

THE BATTLE OF CEDAR MOUNTAIN

AUGUST 9 turned hot and sultry as the day advanced. Some of the fast-marching Confederate soldiers, oppressed by the choking dust and enervating heat of midday, were felled by sunstroke. Others, unable to maintain the pace demanded by the driving corps commander, staggered off the road and sank down in the shade to recover. Jackson's preference for losing one man in marching rather than five in battle was being demonstrated in this forced march on Culpeper, and the ratio seemed to be working out according to formula.

Bayard's Federal cavalry, screening Banks' dispositions south of Culpeper and watchfully reconnoitering the Rapidan crossings, had discovered the enemy in force as they crossed at Barnett's Ford on August 8. The Federal pickets had then retired along the Orange Court House Road and rejoined the main body of the cavalry on wooded high ground between the branches of Cedar Run, a mile west of the highway. Here Bayard covered the right flank of Crawford's infantry brigade,

55

which was awaiting the enemy in a concealed position along the valley of Cedar Run, north of Cedar Mountain and protected from direct fire by high ground to its front and rear.

Banks Blocks Jackson's Advance

Acting upon the August 8 report of his cavalry, Pope sent forward Banks' corps of two divisions, under Brigadier Generals C. C. Augur and A. S. Williams, with orders to strengthen Crawford's defensive position and to block Jackson's advance until other reinforcements could be brought up. By noon of August 9 Banks was in position on a line running in a northwesterly direction on the high ground east of Cedar Run. The line, including the cavalry on the flanks, extended from Hudson's mill on the south, across the Orange Court House-Culpeper Road to a point somewhat more than a mile north of the pike, Augur's division on the left, Williams' on the right. Jackson's direct route to Culpeper was sealed off. He would now have to fight his way through or around his enemy if he still wished to take Culpeper as planned.

Shortly after noon the forward guns of Banks' artillery opened on the leading elements of Ewell's division as the Confederate advance guard came into view of the Federal batteries posted in front of their infantry on high ground south of Cedar Run, overlooking the highway. The word went back to Ewell and thence to Jackson. Both galloped ahead for a personal look at the terrain where the Union commander had apparently decided to contest Jackson's advance. It was partly wooded, rolling country with occasional fields of grain, but it was not possible at a glance to tell whether the Federals were there in strength. Their position would have to be developed and there was only one way to do that.

Jackson's strength, including Lawton's and Gregg's brigades guarding wagon trains, totalled some 24,000 combat effectives*.

If the Union troops in his front were only a part, or even the

---

*See Table I, Appendix.

full strength of Banks' corps, Jackson's initial target, he felt confident of his superiority. Just to make certain, however, and because it was still early in the afternoon, he decided to wait for A. P. Hill's division to come up before launching an attack.

The obvious key to the battlefield, Cedar Mountain, loomed to the right less than a mile from the highway. Ewell was directed to place his batteries on the mountain and his infantry initially on its northern shoulder supporting the guns. Winder was assigned a position directly to the front, along the Culpeper road and on Ewell's left. When Hill's division came up it would form a second line in rear of Winder.

As the troop deployment proceeded, the Federal guns reopened, firing intermittently whenever the enemy exposed themselves as they moved from column into successive lines or crossed open country within the vision of the alert Union gunners. Development for action of over 20,000 men, marching on one road in a single column seven miles or more long, would take several hours of intense effort. In the process, the Confederate artillery, moving rapidly into firing position, was given the task of neutralizing the Union guns and discouraging any tendency on the part of the Blue infantry to launch an attack that might disrupt Jackson's buildup.

As the opposing forces completed their development for action, the two Federal divisions of Banks' corps, five brigades in all, were aligned along Cedar Run for a distance of two miles, with Bayard's cavalry (less one regiment near Hudson's mill) covering Gordon's right flank brigade. Jackson's three divisions contained twelve infantry brigades, two additional brigades having been left at Robertson's River, 2 miles in the rear, to guard the trains. They were deployed from the northern tip of Cedar Mountain, on the right, to the Culpeper Road, inclusive, on the left. The divisions of Winder and A. P. Hill, on the left, one behind the other, would be prepared to attack in depth, while two of Ewell's brigades would deny to the enemy the important bastion of Cedar Mountain on the right.

The Cedar Mountain Battlefield

The field on which the battle was about to be joined was in the form of a rectangle, the Federals occupying the eastern side and northern end, the Confederates the western side and southern end. At almost the exact center of the rectangle, where a north-south dirt road crossed the Culpeper pike, which at that point ran east and west, was a broad, cultivated field, almost made to order for the inevitable clash. The terrain was ideal for troop maneuvering, with gently rolling fields broken by groves of trees, many ridge lines and plenty of defilade space. Fields of fire were greatly restricted by the woods, which meant that attacking units would have to come to close quarters with their opponents to gain a decision. Observation would be difficult, again because of the intermittent but dense woods, although the troops that occupied the high ground of Cedar Mountain would have a decided advantage in that respect.

Cedar Mountain, a partially wooded ridge running slightly east of north for some two miles, stands out prominently 200 feet above the green, gently rolling farmlands south of Culpeper. Five miles to the southeast of this hill, and somewhat larger, is Clark's Mountain, while Thoroughfare Mountain, an equal distance to the west, shows through the blue summer haze. But the Battle of Cedar Mountain was confined to the valley of Cedar Run, which, with the slopes of Cedar Mountain to the southeast, and the gradually rising ground north and west of the creek, formed a shallow bowl or amphitheater about two miles in diameter. In this the battle occurred.

A little over a half mile west of Cedar Mountain, and parallel to it, ran the Orange-Culpeper turnpike, then a somewhat meandering clay road but which today, with its kinks straightened out, is the hard-surfaced US 15. Around the northern and western base of Cedar Mountain ran the southern branch of Cedar Run, emptying into the main stream a short distance above Robert Hudson's mill and mill pond, the foundations of the mill still being visible. Viewing the area from the vicinity of Dr. Slaughter's old home, long vacant and in partial

SLAUGHTER HOUSE ON CEDAR MOUNTAIN
Home of Rev. Slaughter, near where Trimble's and Forno's brigades were in position on the north shoulder of the mountain.

ruin today, one sees an almost level farm of pastureland and wheatfields, in the approximate center of which are the white farm buildings of Mr. B. Carlin Inskip, present owner of the land. This house, the core of which is of logs now covered with weatherboarding, stands near the site of the "Clump of Cedars" —one of the focal points of the battle, where some Confederate artillery was in action and near where Early's brigade stood. This ground is a few feet higher than the creek bottoms of the two branches, being referred to in some of the reports as a "ridge." It is scarcely to be dignified by that description, but, with the standing corn in August of 1862, did offer some cover to the opposing troop units lined up on either side of the rise. Looking north toward the site of Colvin's Tavern, in the direction of Culpeper, one notes that the ground rises gradually. Here slight undulations in the terrain, together with some clumps of woods, offered cover to the Federal brigades in their initial positions.

There were more extensive woods just northwest of the Culpeper Road, approximately opposite the clump of cedars. In 1862 the road ran along the edge of the woods, but today is perhaps two hundred yards farther southeast. It was in these woods, and along their eastern and northern borders, near where one may see the monument of the 10th Maine Regiment, that the severest part of the fighting occurred. Between these woods and Cedar Run was a wheatfield in which were growing some scrub oak bushes, extending to the Run, while to the southeast of the road, and considerably more extensive, was a cornfield.

The Inskip family have found scores of Minie balls in their fields, and artillery projectiles of various types along the higher ground on both sides and imbedded in old trees. Doubtless gray- and blue-clad ghosts slip across the fields by night, though none have been positively identified.

20,000 Against 8,000

With A. P. Hill on hand, Jackson would have 20,000 muskets, Banks only 8,000, the odds greatly favoring the Confederates, unless Union reinforcements should be quickly supplied to achieve a balance. Ricketts' division of McDowell's corps, three miles away, had not yet been ordered forward, and was not under Banks' command. King's division of the same corps was not even in the picture. Sigel's corps, arriving belatedly at Culpeper without rations, could not be counted on till August 10.

Banks was an old opponent of Jackson's, who had suffered more than one humiliation at Stonewall's hands during the Shenandoah Valley fighting. It is not inconceivable that he envisaged at Cedar Mountain an opportunity to turn the tables on the wily fox by attacking quickly before Jackson could get all his troops to the field. Thus he could restore a reputation which had been somewhat tarnished by the Valley defeats. But his close-in infantry scouting from the Cedar Run position was ineffective. While Bayard's cavalry had reported the crossing in force of Confederate troops at the Rapidan, his pickets had been driven back, while Jackson's horsemen evidently did a thorough job of counterreconnaissance as the Gray infantry column advanced. As a result, Banks was simply guessing at the strength of his opponent and he guessed wrong.

Pope's instructions had been perfectly clear and unequivocal; Banks was ordered only to put his two divisions in a posture of defense to block the enemy advance. The last thing Pope wanted was to bring on a general engagement with inferior forces, the outcome of which could easily be that his separated corps would be defeated in detail.

Jackson's advance from the Rapidan, lacking the element of surprise, caused no consternation in the Union ranks. Banks, an aggressive general, welcomed another opportunity to try his luck against his heretofore victorious opponent. He would briefly follow orders and allow the enemy to commit the first overt act, but he had no intention of staying permanently on the defensive if an opportunity should present itself to make an active defense, which to the military means simply to go over to the offensive as soon as it appears profitable to do so.

Early's brigade of Ewell's division, leading the long column as advance guard, and Taliaferro's of Winder's undersized division, edged forward under cover towards the enemy position as soon as the two divisions had completed their deployment about 3 o'clock. They advanced cautiously, putting out skirmishers and taking plenty of time to allow Powell Hill's 12,000-man division to close up in reserve and assure ample support for a decisive attack.

General Charles S. Winder

As Winder's leading regiments felt their way forward, their commander, one of the most promising among the many young generals of the Confederate Army, watched the action through his field glasses from a nearby artillery position. He had gotten up from a sick bed to be with his troops for this adventure and still suffered from a high fever. Although he rode in an ambulance during the march, as soon as the column came in contact with the enemy, and in spite of strenuous objections from his surgeon, Winder mounted his horse and took active command of his division on the field.

Charles S. Winder of Maryland, age 33, was a West Pointer

who had gained a reputation in the Valley as commander of the seasoned Stonewall Bridge. He was also a strict disciplinarian whose determined attitude and, as it seemed to the men in the ranks, harsh measures in enforcing discipline had the effect of arousing the open hatred of many of them. It was

BRIGADIER GENERAL CHARLES S. WINDER, C.S.A,
KILLED AT CEDAR MOUNTAIN

common knowledge that more than one had sworn that "the next battle would be his last," an idle threat that has been hurled from time immemorial at many a general who placed his sense of duty ahead of easily-won popularity.

Jackson who thought highly of Winder, had advanced him to acting command of his own division when he himself was given a larger command. This post of honor was clear recognition of Winder's worth and the young general looked forward eagerly to winning formal appointment to command of Jackson's division as the troops moved against Pope. Nevertheless, his fame would prove to be fleeting, for the Battle of Cedar Mountain was indeed to be his last.

When the march orders had arrived, on August 7, Winder had sent a staff officer to Jackson to learn whether a battle impended. If so, he wanted to be in it. For once the taciturn Jackson had relented, softened no doubt by the courageous spirit of his promising subordinate. The word went back to Winder that there would certainly be a fight. That was all he needed to order up an ambulance to carry him into the thick of it.

Banks Guesses Wrong

Now, at 2:25 p.m. on the 9th, Banks sent Pope a message that revealed a faulty evaluation of Jackson's intentions:

> General Williams' division has taken position on the right of the pike, the right on a heavy body of woods. General Augur on the left, his left resting on a mountain occupied by his skirmishers. He will soon be in position. The enemy shows his cavalry (which is strong) ostentatiously. No infantry seen and not much artillery. Woods on left said to be full of troops. A visit to the front does not impress that the enemy intends immediate attack; he seems, however, to be taking positions.

Following the dispatch of the foregoing, an hour and a half passed while nothing much happened that would be likely to cause Banks to revise his estimate. The main bodies of both forces were concealed from the other by dense woods and folds in the ground, as the opposing troops disposed themselves under cover.

The afternoon was pretty well advanced when the opening shots of the infantry skirmishers were pressed off. Banks, having made up his mind that the Confederates were not strong enough to take the initiative, now persuaded himself that his orders were sufficiently discretionary to permit him to take the offensive. He informed Pope of the developments:

> 4:50 p.m.
> About 4 o'clock shots were exchanged by the skirmishers. Artillery opened fire on both sides in a few minutes. One regiment of rebel infantry advancing now deployed in front as skirmishers. I have ordered a regiment on the right, Williams' division, to meet them, and

one from the left, Augur to advance on the left and in front.

5 p.m.—They are now approaching each other.

The Federal line overlapped the left of the Confederate, with dense woods extending westwardly and affording an opportunity for the Blue to mass troops without the knowledge of the Confederates. That flank was vulnerable; therefore Jackson, with his quick eye for tactical details, ordered the left flank brigade of Lieutenant Colonel Garnett to be on the alert and to ask for reinforcements at that point.

By 5 o'clock the artillery duel was in full swing. Jackson had stretched out for a rest on the porch of a convenient farmhouse, awaiting the arrival of A. P. Hill before launching a coordinated attack. The booming of the guns, heard in Culpeper, became so loud and continuous that General Pope, despite the optimistic earlier messages of corps commander Banks from up front, drew his own conclusions and sent word to Ricketts' division of McDowell's corps to move at once to Banks' support. Although Ricketts had also heard the firing, and was less than three miles distant, he did not reach the field until 7 p.m., by which time the fighting was over. It would seem that this unit wasn't overly anxious to participate in Banks' affray.

The Meeting Engagement

Early initially had been to the left of the Culpeper Road, but by 5 o'clock he had moved east of it into the cornfield. Winder's three brigades were in the woods to the left of the pike, two of them being in line parallel to it and facing east. Apparently there were some incipient plans for attacking across the front of Early to capture some Federal artillery which was exposed to a swift advance. About this time the two Federal divisions, less Greene's brigade of Augur's division, which remained in place, were launched in an advance which converged slightly on Early and Winder. Garnett, commanding Winder's leading brigade, saw some of the Federal line in motion, and

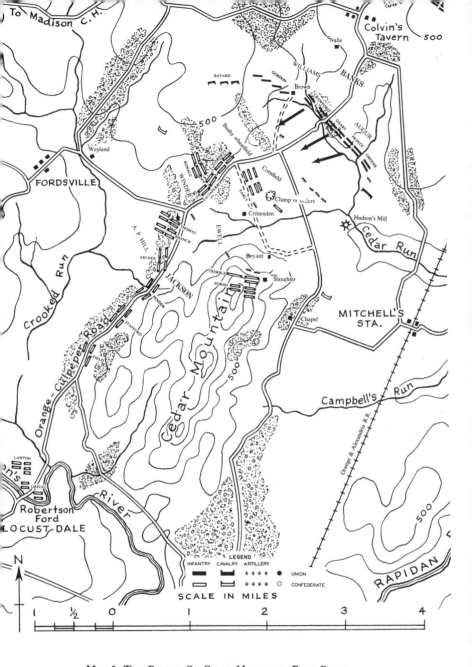

MAP 5. THE BATTLE OF CEDAR MOUNTAIN—FIRST PHASE

The situation at about 5 p.m., following the artillery duel and showing the beginning of the Federal advance.

For a more complete explanation of the symbols used to represent troop units on the battle maps, see the Appendix, section entitled *Maps*. In a book of this kind, with greatly reduced maps, it is generally impracticable to show artillery positions or sectors of fire. This map and a few others do, however, show some batteries.

CRAWFORD'S BRIGADE ATTACKING GARNETT AND TALIAFERRO
A graphic picture of the close fighting at the height of the Federal attack.

sent word to the division commander. A courier galloped up to Jackson to report trouble on the left. Winder had been mortally wounded by a direct hit from a Federal gun before he could act on Jackson's warning to Garnett to strengthen his left. In the resultant confusion, with the division commander out of action, an aggressive Union brigade, Crawford's, attacking Garnett from front and flank in a converging drive, had broken through and was exultantly driving before them two of Garnett's regiments.

Jackson's Left Driven Back

These serious reverses on Jackson's left occurred at about the time Taliaferro was taking over command of Winder's division, the sequence of events being as follows: The Stonewall Brigade, under Colonel Charles Ronald, had been formed at right angles to the other two, but was a hundred yards or more deep in the woods and not in close contact on its right flank with neighboring units. When the Federal advance was first observed, Taliaferro quickly sent word to Ronald to advance straight forward toward the wheatfield to meet the enemy. Ronald did so, but his lines reached this clearing just in time to receive a volley in the face from Crawford's oncoming regiments. The Stonewall Brigade broke, and (according to Gen. Branch) streamed rearward uttering loud cries of panic. Crawford's regiments, in hot pursuit, arrived at the east edge of the woods, about where the Tenth Maine monument now stands, which put them on the rear and flank of Taliaferro's other two brigades. The latter were still parallel to the road and at that moment were being assailed by Augur's right brigade, which was turning Early's left. Crawford delivered heavy fire into the backs of Garnett's and A. G. Taliaferro's men. The Confederate officers tried to face their rear ranks about, but the commands could not be heard. In a few moments these two brigades also broke and began to stream to the rear. A fine disaster was in the making. It began to appear that Banks' judgment was about to be vindicated.

The news of Winder's serious wound (he died a few hours later) and the accelerated tempo of artillery fire was, however, bringing Jackson himself at an extended gallop to the scene of action.

The turning point of the battle had now arrived. Banks' drive had lost its initial momentum. His units had expended most of their ammunition, and no provision had been made for a corps reserve, with which to deliver the final, knockout punch. So for a few minutes there was this general wild melee of Union and Confederate soldiers, locked in close combat, in the edge of the woods, in the cornfield, and between the road and the clump of cedars. The fight could break either way.

This was the sight that met Jackson's eye as he arrived at the front. It was a part of Stonewalls' genius that he perceived instantly that the time had come, and this was the place, to strike a counterblow. He sent hasty orders to Ewell and Hill, then without waiting for his orders to filter down through command echelons, he galloped to where he knew his reserves were waiting.

The leading brigade, Branch's, of A. P. Hill's division, was resting in the woods and listening to a pep talk by the commander, who in civil life had been a congressman and was an accomplished orator. A few words from Jackson sent Branch and his men dashing to the front. As they hurried through the

MAP 6. THE BATTLE OF CEDAR MOUNTAIN—SECOND PHASE

The situation about 6 p.m., when the Federal attack has spent its force and Jackson is beginning to throw in his reserves. The confused melee which met Jackson's eye as he galloped to the front is portrayed here, with Garnett's and Taliaferro's brigades crumpling under the Federal assault, and Ronald's and part of Early's' brigades pulling back under the blows they sustained. Thomas has been sent out to extend Early's line; and Branch, Archer, and Pender are moving up on the Confederate left.

woods they encountered Ronald's fleeing men but did not falter, merely opening ranks to allow these remnants to continue rearward.

Branch's attack struck in the flank and rear those Federal troops who had nearly surrounded the brigades of Garnett and A. G. Taliaferro. His big regiments drove the bluecoats back toward the north, as Branch slanted off somewhat toward the right so that his advance crossed to the opposite side of the Culpeper road.

By six o'clock the battle was raging fiercely all over the field. Hill's Light Division had come up to give Jackson a combat edge of $2\frac{1}{2}$ to 1. The able combination of Jackson, Ewell, and Hill, despite Banks' early success in flanking the Confederate left, could scarcely lose this battle.

Taliaferro, an excellent general who had assumed command of Winder's division, persuaded Jackson to return to a more appropriate and less dangerous position, as he and Ewell reorganized their confused brigades and made ready for the coordinated attack that Jackson now ordered.

Banks' infantry had by this time all been committed, his only reserve being Bayard's cavalry, which was not strong enough to do much except harassment or pursuit. Gordon's brigade had followed Crawford's into action on the Federal right, while Greene's brigade held the left of the line in support of McGilvery's battery in standing off a possible attack by Trimble and Forno, seen descending Cedar Mountain. The Federal losses were heavy. Crawford had lost every one of his regimental commanders and most of his field officers in the swirling fight with Winder's division. Generals Augur, Geary, and Carroll were badly wounded and Brigade Commander Prince captured.

Jackson's overwhelming strength was now thrown into the battle with the inevitable result. Ewell was directed to attack the Federal left, while A. P. Hill and the remnants of Winder's division went after the Union right. Four of Hill's six large

brigades*, averaging over 2,000 men each, were sent charging
forward in two directions. Branch, Archer, and Pender, with
the first-named in the van, were given the mission of turning
the enemy right flank, Thomas was sent to help Early's brigade
of Ewell's division; Hill's remaining brigade, under Field,
was told to form a supporting line in company with Sheffield's
brigade of Taliaferro's reorganized remnants, in order to give
depth to the attack.

A. P. Hill Saves the Day

The Confederates moved forward all along the line, as the
Federals commenced to withdraw toward Cedar Run.

It was now A. P. Hill's turn to show the stuff of which he
was made. Stripping off his jacket to reveal the flaming red
shirt that was his badge of valor, and drawing his sword as
Jackson had done before him, Hill jumped into the middle
of the action and led his cheering brigades into the. attack.

It was here at Cedar Mountain that Hill and his Light Division set the combat pattern that contributed so greatly to
its reputation as a magnificent fighting division. The im-
petuosity and fearlessness of their leader was reflected in the
attitude of the men in the ranks, who admired "little" Powell
and would go anywhere that he told them. The Virginia cavalier, a handsome man and finished horseman, had in the few
months since he received his second star forged a powerful
shining weapon in the form of the Light Division, which even
now was on its scrappy way to becoming the best in the entire
Confederate service.

Jackson's march order for August 9 originally scheduled
A. P. Hill's division to follow Ewell's division, but because of
the mix-up at Orange Court House that morning, the Light
Division followed Winder, which meant that it would be the
last to get into the fight. What effect that may have had on
the ardent spirits of the men can only be conjectured, but
there was no doubt whatever that they were rarin' to go when
they reached the battlefield, deployed rapidly, and hurled their

---

*Field was in "support," Gregg was guarding trains.

weight of numbers and driving force into Jackson's well-timed, effective counterattack.

There was no stopping the fierce charge of Hill's brigades. The Federals wavered, recoiled, and retreated, unable to stem the avalanche of greatly superior numbers which the Light Division brought to bear against them. Hill's men delivered the knockout punch in short order and completed the pattern which was destined to be repeated again and again as the war progressed.

Jackson's superior strength was quickly felt all along the line. The Federal brigades were being steadily pressed from the front and turned on the flanks. Banks' artillery was hastily withdrawn as the victorious Southerners drove the Federals in every direction. In a vain but brave effort to cover the withdrawal of the guns and stay the Confederate advance,

"BUSHY WHEATFIELD" ACROSS WHICH CRAWFORD CHARGED AND A. P. HILL COUNTERATTACKED

The edge of the distant woods marked the advance of Ronald's "Stonewall" brigade before they broke and fled to the rear.

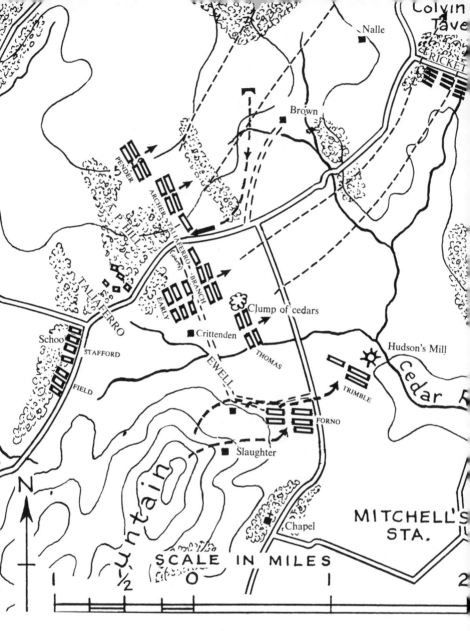

MAP 7. THE BATTLE OF CEDAR MOUNTAIN—THIRD PHASE

The situation shortly before dark. Branch has advanced to the assault, moving obliquely to the right of the road. Archer and Pender have come up, and reconstituted portions of Taliaferro's division are astride the pike. On the far right, Trimble, followed by Forno, has advanced but is held up by artillery fire and Hudson's mill pond. The Federal units, their cohesion broken by their attack, and their ammunition nearly exhausted, are withdrawing. In the center, the abortive cavalry charge is attempting to cover the withdrawal of the Federal artillery. Ricketts' division is moving up, but too late to join in the battle. Except for Ricketts and the cavalry, the Federal units are not shown on this map, only their general routes of withdrawal.

Bayard sent in a 164-man battalion of the 1st Pennsylvania Cavalry. They charged in a column of fours, parallel to the pike and into the spearhead of the Confederate counterattack. Crossfire from Branch's brigade and the remnants of Talia-ferro's division emptied many saddles, but the impetus of the charge carried the unit inside the Confederate line. Only 71 men returned, but more must have been rounded up later, since Bayard reported only 61 casualties for his entire brigade.

Jackson Attempts a Pursuit

By 6:30 p.m. the battle was over, but Jackson as usual was determined to reap the fruits of his tactical victory. Having escaped a near disaster in the early stages, by personal inter-vention at the point of greatest danger his unerring instinct enabled him to turn the enemy's initial progress to his own advantage. He had wisely delayed his attack until his opponent had revealed his strength and position, and A. P. Hill's Light Division, larger than all the other Confederate troops com-bined, had reached the battlefield. Then it was that he threw everything he had at his weaker opponent. In an hour and a half nearly 4,000 men and officers on both sides were killed, wounded, captured, or missing, and Jackson's successful troops were crossing Cedar Run in pursuit of the retreating Federals.

Although Jackson, who rarely bestowed words of praise on any of his living officers either orally or in his brief reports, gave Powell Hill no credit for the Confederate success, the Light Division and Hill himself had the satisfaction of know-ing that it was they who had tipped the scales at the psycho-logical moment, a feat they would duplicate some weeks later at the Battle of Antietam, there again preventing a disaster to Confederate arms.

Jackson and Hill would both prove by their deeds, before meeting a soldier's death on the field of battle, that they were great leaders, courageous fighters, able tacticians, and dedicated patriots to the Southern cause. They would likewise demon-strate that no matter how bitter their official relationship, neither would permit personal animosity to influence his attitude toward the other during combat.

The opportunity was present after Cedar Mountain for Jackson to heal the breach first created between the two generals by the senior's unjustified criticism of Hill at Orange Court House, but it was not in the Jackson character to admit that he may have been a bit hasty in passing judgment on what only appeared to be a disregard of his orders on the part of Hill. Hill's determined and energetic efforts to wipe out the slur by proving himself and his division to an ungenerous superior was met by complete silence on Jackson's part. The latter's message to Lee said simply: "God blessed our arms with another victory," thus allowing the Commanding General to infer that with the help of Providence Stonewall Jackson had added another wreath to the laurels gained in the Valley. It was not until May 1863 that Jackson wrote his official report of the battle, in which the name A. P. Hill appears but once, in the following cryptic sentence: "As General Hill had arrived with his division, one of his brigades (General Thomas') was sent to Early and joined him in time to render efficient service." The heroically significant part played by Branch's brigade of Hill's division, together with the supporting efforts of Archer's and Pender's brigades, also of Hill's division, was factually recorded in the report, but the division commander himself might have been a mere spectator on the scene so far as any recognition by the corps commander was concerned.

Fuel was thus added to the flame of Powell Hill's resentment, and as time passed the clashing of the two irreconcilable temperaments reached and passed the point of no return. The surprising thing about this famous Jackson-Hill feud is that both generals fought their personal cold war as though it had no relation to their official conduct toward each other. On the surface neither permitted the unfortunate bickering to color his military actions, but there can be little doubt that the repercussions were harmful to Confederate operations, difficult as it might be to quote chapter and verse.

On the other hand, Pope's report on the Virginia Campaign, verbose as it was, at least handed out a few bouquets to those who served under him in the capacity of general officers. "General Banks' conduct at the battle of Cedar Mountain," wrote Pope, "was marked by great coolness, intrepidity and zeal." To which he added that "Generals Williams, Augur, Crawford, Greene, Geary, Carroll, and Prince, of Banks' Corps, have been already noticed for their gallant and distinguished conduct at Cedar Mountain."

Union Lieutenant Gillette, a few days after the battle, wrote his parents a succinct report:

> I am sorry I can't twist the facts into a glorious victory. It was a glorious defeat if such an adjective can be used with the noun. A hotter fire than that endured by our men, I do not believe ever was poured in on soldiers, certainly not in this war. . . . My friends are stricken down on all sides. The General (Prince, the brigade commander), a good friend of mine, is a prisoner captured ahead of his brigade where he had been all day.
>
> . . . A rush to the rear about supper time caused the soldiers to forget rations and everything else and so scared the boss butcher that he abandoned his drove and the teamster his wagon load of salt beef, while they were out of reach of all possible harms way. . . . The men seemed to fall twice as fast as at Bull Run where the battle was more extended and involved greater numbers.
>
> . . . The report is that the Confederates have retreated across the Rapidan. We have been expecting a severe battle every hour since the last fight, until today.

The official reports after the battle showed total casualties of approximately 3,800 out of 28,000 engaged. Of these 2,377 were Federal, 1,355 Confederate, although there is reason to doubt the numbers reported by the Southerners, who recorded only four men missing despite the panicked rout of Winder's two brigades in the early stages. The fighting along the pike had been the most vicious, and it was there that over half of all the casualties were incurred. Crawford's Federal brigade (Williams' division) alone lost 867 men of 1,767 engaged, while Williams' other brigade under Gordon brought that division's total to 1,212. Augur's three brigades suffered 986 casualties.

Winder's Confederate division was the hardest hit on the other side, losing 707 men or close to 25% of those engaged, which exceeded by a good margin the combined losses of Hill and Ewell. The cavalry losses were negligible, 61 for Bayard and 19 for Robertson, most of the Federals falling in the final charge which Bayard launched late in the day, without effect on the outcome.

General Pope arrived with Ricketts' division of McDowell's corps as Banks' defeated troops were on their way back to their original position east of Cedar Run. The Federal withdrawal was made in good order as Pope took charge and disposed Ricketts' fresh troops on a strong position to dispute the Confederate followup, while Banks' depleted brigades were massed a short distance to Ricketts' rear in support.

As the Confederates cautiously pursued, with the heretofore unused brigades of Field and Stafford as the spearpoint, Ricketts' artillery opened, bringing Jackson's men to an abrupt halt. Darkness had fallen, Culpeper was still seven miles distant, and a cavalry patrol reported to Jackson that it had taken prisoners from Sigel's Federal corps. It was apparently not going to be easy sailing for the Jacksonians, but the general allowed the artillery duel to continue until almost midnight before deciding that the imponderables of the situation made it impracticable to advance further during the night. Orders were issued to bivouac in place. The Battle of Cedar Mountain had passed into history.

As a matter of fact, Sigel's corps *was* beginning to come up from Culpeper, having put away a good meal in the interim. Banks' corps had been rather badly used up, so Pope fed Sigel's men into the position occupied by Banks, sending the latter several miles to the rear to reorganize.

By daylight of August 10, Pope's Army of Virginia was pretty well concentrated except for King's division of Mc-

Dowell's corps, still 20 miles away, and Buford's cavalry, which was at Madison Court House. Pope reported results to Halleck, claiming a victory, which must have surprised Banks and his defeated divisions when they heard about it. Nevertheless, and in spite of his tactical victory, Jackson had suffered a strategic set-back in failing to seize Culpeper as the first step toward defeating Pope before the latter could complete his concentration.

In retrospect, Banks' corps, 8,800 against 20,000, had done very well to stop Jackson, which was their primary mission. His troops had fought with bravery and determination. They had broken and routed Stonewall Jackson's own vaunted division (under Winder) and had battled unceasingly until overwhelmed by vastly superior numbers. Yes, they could look back with pride on that engagement at Cedar Mountain, for in the Valley Jackson had repeatedly whipped them with much smaller forces, while here it took a preponderance of better than two to one in Jackson's favor to effect their defeat.

For two days the opposing armies rested within artillery distance of each other. Jackson had given up any intention of renewing the attack in the face of Pope's evident strength, but he was willing to accept battle again on his Cedar Mountain position if Pope should be interested. The intervening period was used to bury the dead* and remove the wounded, after which, when it became apparent that Pope entertained no serious offensive measures, Jackson put his troops in motion to the south and returned to his former camps at Gordonsville.

----

*They did a poor job. Averell, passing that way a year later, noted the unburied dead at Cedar Mountain.

POPE'S WITHDRAWAL ACROSS THE RAPPAHANNOCK AT RAPPAHANNOCK STATION

CHAPTER 5

UNEASY PAUSE BETWEEN BATTLES

THE alarmed reaction of the North to the defeat of Pope's advance corps at Cedar Mountain confirmed the unhappy suspicion that the unpredictable Stonewall Jackson had done it again. His most recent battle had shown most of the earmarks of his "here he comes—there he goes" maneuvers in the Valley, which a few months earlier had made him a national figure and certainly the most feared of all the Confederate generals. With a somewhat larger force than he had in the Valley, but still greatly outnumbered by Pope's slowly concentrating army, Jackson had repeated his earlier successful tactics, moved to defeat his opponent in detail, and although balked in his hope of taking Culpeper, had managed to again whip Banks' two-division corps before fading back to his base at Gordonsville.

Nevertheless, Jackson's margin of victory this time had been slimmer than in his earlier battles, and he had failed to secure his strategic objective. Banks' Federals had waged a spirited fight, with dogged courage, and in the early stages had come very close to a victory. When Banks, attacking before A. P. Hill's division had completed its deployment, disregarded Pope's order to wage a strictly defensive engagement, he had 8,800 men against Jackson's at that time only slightly greater strength, represented by the divisions of Ewell and Winder. Had Banks' drive to outflank Jackson's left been strongly supported in depth, the Confederate confusion incident to the breakup of Winder's small division might easily have resulted in the rolling up of Ewell's line as well. It might then have been too late for Jackson and Hill in concert to repair the damage and launch their victorious counterattack.

The initial setback at Cedar Mountain failed to discourage Pope, who was still in an aggressive mood and anxious to proceed with his planned offensive, now that his army was concentrated at Culpeper. The fact that two-thirds of Banks' corps had been rendered hors de combat for a period of weeks did not seem to be sufficient reason for postponement. Neither did a personal incident, with respect to which he chose conveniently to overlook the fact that he himself, contrary to his earlier bombastic pronouncement, had indeed "turned his back on the enemy" on the evening of the Battle of Cedar Mountain. That had occurred during the retreat of Banks' corps when Pope, arrived on the scene, personally ran into a hot spot east of Cedar Run at the very moment when Jackson's pursuing divisions were breathing down the necks of the retiring Federals. It was no place for an army commander to be if he wished to continue in that capacity, and Pope wisely chose discretion by participating in the retrograde movement.

It was Halleck who held Pope in check after Cedar Mountain, and it would appear that Halleck's judgment was sound. To the General-in-Chief it was more important that the armies of McClellan and Pope be closed to supporting distance of one another than that Pope should engage in a unilateral adventure by lashing out at Jackson immediately. Quite possibly, in directing Pope not to advance beyond the Rapidan at this stage, Halleck saved him from falling into a trap of Jackson's devising, for Jackson wrote Lee that he was falling back to Gordonsville in the belief that Pope would follow, and that he hoped to meet him on a position of his own choosing, with reinforcements at hand. Since Longstreet's corps was now on the way to Gordonsville from Richmond, an incautious advance by Pope could have brought about his defeat somewhat further south than the area where it actually did occur a few weeks later.

On August 15, six days after the Battle of Cedar Mountain, Pope's army was increased to almost 52,000 men by the arrival of Major General Jesse L. Reno at the head of 8,000 men comprising two divisions of Burnside's force which had just come up from Fredericksburg. Reconnaissance by Confederate cavalry located the Federal divisions resting in positions northeast of Cedar Mountain, their Rapidan River outpost line extending from Rapidan Station on the right to Somerville Ford on the left, a distance of eight to ten miles.

Lee Takes Command

On that same day General Lee in person arrived at Gordonsville and summoned his chief lieutenants, Longstreet, Jackson, and Stuart, to a conference at headquarters. Longstreet's corps of over 25,000 men had just completed a two-day rail trip from Richmond. Stuart traveled by train to make it on time, while Fitz Lee's cavalry brigade took to the road to join the main army assembled at Gordonsville. All that remained of Lee's army in the Richmond area were the divisions of D. H. Hill and Lafayette McLaws and Wade Hampton's brigade of cavalry, left behind to keep a watchful eye on the Army of the Potomac, then on its way northward by way of Fortress Monroe.

With Lee's arrival on the scene and the junction of his two wings, the Army of Northern Virginia was slightly superior to Pope numerically. The preliminaries were over and the stage set for the main event, but Lee would have to act quickly, if he was to crush the opposing force before additional rein-

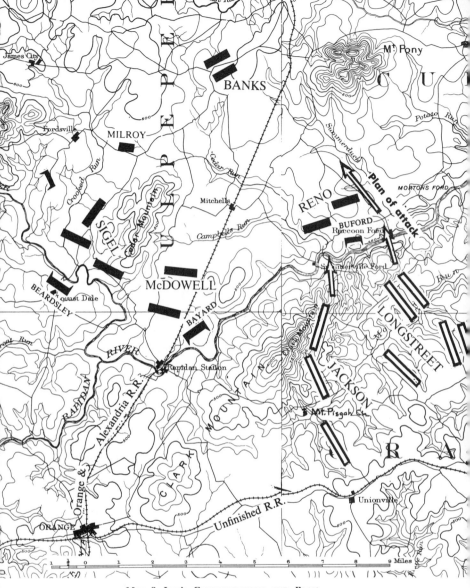

MAP 8. LEE'S CONCENTRATION AND PLAN

The situation at dark, August 17. Lee, having assembled his entire force, less Fitzhugh Lee's cavalry brigade, in the Gordonsville area about August 13, has concentrated secretly southeast of Clark's Mountain. He plans to attack around Pope's left (east) flank on or about August 18, to cut Pope off from Washington and destroy him. This plan is to be frustrated because Fitz Lee was slow in arriving from Beaver Dam, some 40 miles to the southeast, and because Jeb Stuart, at Verdiersville with a small party, was surprised by Federal cavalry who captured Stuart's copy of Lee's plan. Stuart showed moral courage in promptly apprising Lee of this. Lee also knew that Pope might have become aware of the concentration on his left flank owing to a Federal cavalry raid on Jackson's signal station on Clark's Mountain, from which point they could probably see his bivouacs.

forcements should reach Pope. He outlined his plan of action for the benefit of his lieutenants. From the concealed position of his army behind Clark's Mountain, on the south side of the Rapidan opposite Pope's left flank, he would cross at Somerville Ford, swing around the enemy left and sever Pope's lifeline to Washington. Meanwhile Stuart's cavalry would cross farther to the east, move rapidly to Rappahannock Station, and cut the railroad line northeast of Culpeper by destroying the bridge on Pope's retreat route.

However, it did not work out that way. As so often happens in war, a too-wordy order, sent by Stuart to Fitzhugh Lee, initiated a chain of events that, with overtones of comedy, served again to postpone the day of evil destiny for the braggart who was so sure of himself that he advised his army to forget about their rear. Pope in his delusion was acting much like the overconfident big-league pitcher who in the ninth inning waves his outfielders to the bench as he prepares to strike out the last batter of the opposing team.

The plan was for Stuart's cavalry to precede the forward movement of the infantry-artillery team, Robertson's brigade cooperating with Jackson, Fitz Lee's with Longstreet. The cavalry was directed to move out August 18. Fitz Lee was to meet Stuart at Raccoon Ford, but Stuart's orders neglected to impress on him the urgency of the time factor and it was because of that oversight that the first Confederate plan failed to materialize.

Fitz Lee's brigade had ahead of it almost a thirty-mile march if made directly from the North Anna River at Davenport's Ford to Raccoon Ford on the Rapidan. His wagons had already been sent ahead to Louisa Court House, en route to the original assembly point at Gordonsville, and it was imperative that he replenish his rations before going after Pope. Instead of marching directly to Raccoon Ford, he took the long way around to fill his men's empty haversacks, adding 30 more miles to the trip. Consequently he was out of touch with his commander, Jeb Stuart, for twenty-four hours.

Stuart Loses His Hat

As Stuart with his staff rode east along the Orange Plank Road on the way to Raccoon Ford on the 17th, he became increasingly puzzled at not crossing Fitz Lee's path. When at dark he reached Verdiersville, ten miles from Raccoon Ford, and was unable to find any trace of the missing brigade, he sent his adjutant to locate it and hasten its march, while he himself, with Von Borcke, Mosby, and several other officers halted for the night at the village of Verdiersville, in an old house just off the main highway.

Accustomed as he was to bivouacking wherever it suited his purpose, in friendly or enemy territory or even behind hostile lines, Stuart was unconcerned for his own safety. Surely Pope's army, well north of the Rapidan, posed no threat, and it never occurred to Jeb that any of the Federal cavalry, which at this time the Confederate horsemen held in considerable contempt, could possibly be as far south as the Orange Plank Road. Furthermore, the civilians with whom he talked had assured him that they had seen no signs of enemy cavalry in the neighborhood.

As a precaution, however, the horses of the staff were kept saddled but turned loose for the night in the yard next to the house, while Stuart curled up on the front porch for a comfortable night's sleep, blissfully unaware that within a few miles of him was a Federal cavalry detachment of Buford's brigade which had been reconnoitering the area about Louisa Court House and was on its way back to rejoin Pope's army. As luck would have it, Stuart's adjutant, Major Fitzhugh, travelling alone under Stuart's orders to locate Fitz Lee's brigade, ran smack into the arms of the Federals and was promptly taken prisoner.

That was bad enough, from the Confederate standpoint, but the really tough break was that among Fitzhugh's papers the interested Federals found R. E. Lee's letter to Stuart, in which the army commander's complete plan for the flanking maneuver against Pope's left rear was spelled out in gratifying detail.

Dawn was approaching when the Blue cavalry reached the few houses that represented Verdiersville. The sound of many horses' feet clip-clopping on the road brought Stuart out of a sound sleep. Cavalry was coming up from the direction that Fitz Lee would take, so it must be the missing brigade. Two members of the staff were told to ride out and meet the column, while Stuart himself stood by the gate to observe the troops.

Suddenly the silence of the early morning was shattered by pistol shots, as Stuart's surprised staff officers galloped back with shouts of "Yankee cavalry!" Stuart and the remaining members of his staff leaped into their saddles and scattered in all directions, heading for the nearby woods. One of them halted under cover and, finding that the Federals were not pursuing, watched as the enemy troopers searched the premises and emerged from the house waving Jeb Stuart's fancy cloak and carrying his dispatch case. One Federal liked the looks of a plumed hat he had found among the loot and placed it jauntily upon his head.

It was a close shave for the famous leader of the Southern cavalry, but Stuart probably felt the loss of the prized finery more strongly than his narrow escape from being captured. Had the commander of the Federal cavalry been less preoccupied with the thought that he had run into a Confederate hornet's nest of unknown size, he might have taken time to round up the handful of enemy horsemen who had just barely escaped him. But at the moment, unaware of the important character of his quarry, he was more concerned with the problem of getting his regiment back across the Rapidan to a safer spot.

"I intend to make the Yankees pay dearly for that hat," Stuart wrote his wife, little realizing how soon the opportunity for revenge was to come.

The fickle fates now chose to compound the unfortunate effect of Stuart's indefinite order to Fitz Lee. Added to the chain of events from which Stuart narrowly escaped capture, the combination would result in forcing General R. E. Lee to revise his tactical plan.

When Longstreet reached Raccoon Ford and discovered that the cavalry under Fitz Lee, scheduled to lead off on that flank, had not yet arrived, he made a temporary substitution of a portion of Toombs' Georgia infantry brigade to cover the crossing. When the order arrived, Toombs was out visiting a fellow Congressman who lived nearby. His second-in-command was placed in charge of the detail. When Toombs returned and spotted several of his regiments astride the road without having been ordered there by himself, he chose to assert his command prerogative and sent them back to camp. The result was that the Federal cavalry, returning by that road with Stuart's adjutant, the famous plumed hat, and Lee's captured order, found the way clear and passed unhindered to the other side of the Rapidan. Toombs, a politician turned general, was forthwith placed under arrest, but the damage had been done. After a profuse apology from the humbled general, Longstreet relented and restored him to command in time to share in the final stage of the Second Battle of Manassas.

Pope Effects a Limited Withdrawal

Pisgah Church, the intermediate rendezvous to which Lee moved his army from Gordonsville as the first stage of his offensive, lies in the shadow of a high hill known as Clark's Mountain, from which eminence it is possible to observe the countryside for many miles to the north. From the Confederate lookout on top of the mountain the Federal camps lay in full view, and, since all the topographical features of the impending battlefield could be studied, the signal station was a priceless adjunct to the mapping genius of Jackson's chief topographical engineer, Captain Jed Hotchkiss. The terrain over which the fighting in late August would shortly take place is described by Colonel G. F. R. Henderson in his classic *Stonewall Jackson and the American Civil War*:*

> On Clark's Mountain, a high hill near Pisgah Church, Jackson had established a signal station. The view from

---

*Volume II, P. 111, Longmans, Green and Co., New York, 1927.

the summit embraced an extensive landscape. The ravages of war had not yet effaced its tranquil beauty, nor had the names of its bright rivers and thriving villages become household words. It was still unknown to history, a peaceful and pastoral district, remote from the beaten tracks of trade and travel, and inhabited by a quiet and industrious people. Today there are few regions which boast sterner or more heroic memories. To the right, rolling away in light and shadow for a score of miles, is the great forest of Spotsylvania, within whose gloomy depths lie the fields of Chancellorsville, where the breastworks of the Wilderness can still be traced; and on the eastern verge of which stand the grass-grown batteries of Fredericksburg. Northward, beyond the woods which hide the Rapidan, the eye ranges over the wide and fertile plains of Culpeper, with the green crest of Slaughter Mountain overlooking Cedar Run, and the dim levels of Brandy Station, the scene of the great cavalry battle,* just visible beyond. Far away to the northeast the faint outline of a range of hills marks the source of Bull Run and the Manassas plateau, and to the west, the long rampart of the Blue Ridge, softened by distance, stands high above the Virginia plains.

In Washington General Halleck, seriously perturbed by McClellan's uncooperativeness and snail-like pace in executing the order to transfer his army to Aquia Creek for the planned junction with Pope's army, was prophetically fearful that Lee would attack and overwhelm Pope before McClellan should arrive. On August 16 he telegraphed Pope not to cross the Rapidan but instead to take position north of the Rappahannock, where he could be more easily reinforced.

Although Halleck didn't know it at the time, the captured letter from Lee to Stuart had given Pope an even more compelling reason to fall back to the north bank of the Rappahannock. He now knew for a fact that the bulk of Lee's army confronted him, and, it was reasonable to assume, with a superior force. In pleasant contrast to McClellan, however, Pope did not offer an advance alibi by magnifying the enemy strength beyond all reason.

*June 9, 1863.

Nevertheless it was time to pull back, even though a retrograde movement would violate Pope's earlier assurance to his men that there would be no turning of the backs of *his* army to the enemy. The trouble was that the position of the army was strategically as well as tactically unsound, between two rivers, the Rapidan and the Rappahannock, both of which were in the habit of rising rapidly after heavy rains and becoming unfordable in a matter of hours. Nor could there be any further doubt that Lee's purpose was to move to eliminate Pope before the Army of the Potomac could (or would) arrive.

Discretion was clearly indicated for the moment, so Pope shifted his army to the rear the few miles that were necessary, moving by corps echelon on the 18th and 19th of August. By midnight on August 20 there were no Federal troops between the two rivers except a few cavalry regiments and one small infantry support. Pope's new line extended along the north bank of the Rappahannock, with his right near Sulphur Springs and his left, except for part of Buford's cavalry, near Kellys Ford.

The Confederates followed closely on the heels of the retiring Federals, Lee's entire force moving up to the Rappahannock and feeling out Pope's new position. Finding it strongly posted at all the nearby crossings, Lee discarded his first plan and proceeded to develop a new one, as the 21st, then the 22nd of August passed with continuous artillery fire being exchanged along a length of 7 or 8 miles between the opposing armies on either side of the river.

Lee and Pope were acutely conscious of the passage of time, although for different reasons, for the minds of both were centered on the image of McClellan's Army of the Potomac. On the 21st, Pope had word from Halleck that if he could hold Lee south of the Rappahannock for two more days he would receive sufficient reinforcements to enable him to resume the offensive. By the night of August 22 General Reno's division, followed by the Pennsylvania Reserves under Brigadier General John F. Reynolds, arrived on Pope's left, in the

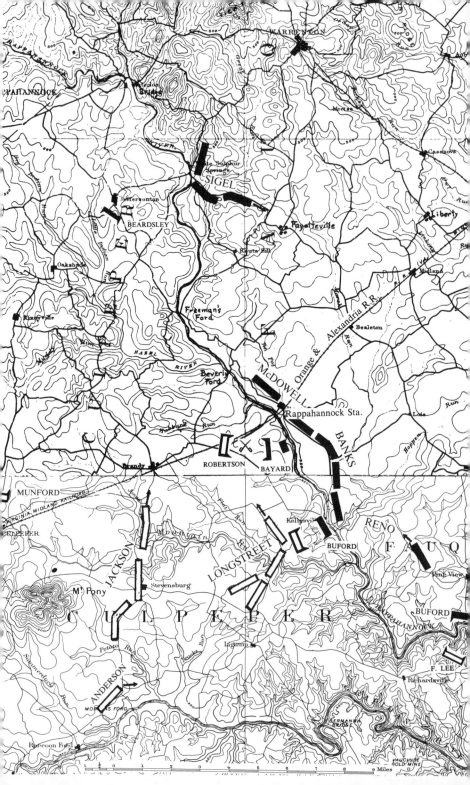

Kellys Ford area. On the 25th all of Reno's corps was present; and most of Heintzelman's corps (Hooker's and Kearny's divisions) had detrained near Warrenton Junction. Porter's corps had marched up the Rappahannock to Deep Creek, 13 miles south of Bealeton. Other divisions of McClellan's army were also on the way, although not very rapidly, as Pope waited for Lee's blow to fall.

On the south side of the Rappahannock, with its many fords, Robert E. Lee was concocting a new scheme to get at Pope. He had already used five days in probing for a soft spot in Pope's defensive armor, but which he had failed to find in that area where he had originally planned to operate around the Union left flank. Because of some heavy rains upriver the stream was now fordable only with difficulty; something had to be done quickly before it was too late. Stuart's cavalry, presently engaged in one of their circuitous rides around the Union army, was looked to for the latest intelligence.

On August 19, after Fitz Lee had arrived, twenty-four hours later than expected and with men and horses jaded by their sixty-mile march, Stuart had moved part of his cavalry to Mitchell's Ford, where he received word from Lee that Pope's army had withdrawn from the Rapidan. Lee had personally climbed Clark's Mountain, that high hill from which the

---

MAP 9. POPE'S WITHDRAWAL BEHIND THE RAPPAHANNOCK

The situation at dark, August 20. When, on August 18, Pope became aware of Lee's plan to envelop his left flank, orders were issued for a rapid withdrawal beyond the Rappahannock. Movement of the trains started at once, the infantry and artillery following at dusk, with the cavalry protecting the rear and flanks. Sigel marched via Rixeyville and Jeffersonton to Sulphur Springs, but on the 20th was ordered downstream to take position on Banks' right; the map shows this movement under way. Banks, followed by McDowell, marched via Culpeper and Brandy Station to positions astride the railroad at Rappahannock Station. Reno forded the Rappahannock northeast of Richardsville, and at the time portrayed on this map was moving toward the Kellys Ford area.

Lee, knowing that a new plan must be formulated, rested his troops on the 18th. On the 19th and 20th he followed Pope to the Rappahannock. He has been joined by Fitz Lee's cavalry, while for the Federals a reinforcing division is on the way—Reynolds', which has disembarked at Aquia (Map 2), moved by rail to Falmouth, and is preparing to march to join Pope.

Confederates were able to look down on Pope's camps, and had seen the Blue columns, or at least the tell-tale evidence of marching troops in the long dust clouds, as Pope prudently withdrew from the pocket between the Rapidan and Rappahannock.

On the 20th of August numerous skirmishes occurred between Stuart's cavalry and the Blue squadrons of Buford and Bayard which were covering Pope's withdrawal. On that day an otherwise insignificant railroad building named Brandy Station gained prominence for the first time in the war, when Robertson's Confederate cavalry brigade tangled with Bayard's Union cavalry and drove them back across the Rappahannock after some spirited sparring. Brandy Station was a name that would make headlines in 1863, after Chancellorsville, when Pleasonton's Federal cavalry would for the first time treat Stuart's cavalry with unaccustomed roughness; but the Southerners had it pretty much their own way on this first of several occasions when the important crossroad of Brandy Station would provide the stage for cavalry combat.

Stuart's Raid on Pope's Headquarters

For the next two days Lee's infantry remained under cover while his cavalry felt Pope's line across the Rappahannock. Stuart gathered enough information to convince him that the Federals had no discoverable soft spots. On August 22 he asked Lee's permission to ride around the enemy right flank to cut the railroad line to Washington in Pope's rear and secure information that might be useful to the Commanding General in furthering his offensive plans.

With Lee's approval, Stuart at once gathered up Fitz Lee's and Robertson's brigades and started out with 2,000 troopers and several of Pelham's guns, leaving only two regiments on the south bank of the river. Crossing at Waterloo Bridge, the column rode swiftly to Warrenton and there took the road to the east, heading for Catlett's Station, on the line of the Orange and Alexandria Railroad. Stuart was now well to the rear of the Union army and, happy thought, in an excellent position

MAP 10. NIGHT OF AUGUST 22

Reinforcements are on the way to Pope at last. Reynolds' division, marching from Falmouth, has reached the vicinity of Kellys Ford. Porter's corps is disembarking at Aquia, and Heintzelman's corps is moving by transport to Alexandria; thence it will be shipped by rail to the Warrenton Junction area. That night McDowell's corps, pursuant to orders, marched to Warrenton.

Lee, having decided to swing wide around Pope's right flank, is sideslipping by echelon upstream. Jackson has moved first to Beverly Ford, then to Freeman's Ford, and is now opposite Sulphur Springs. He has crossed Early's brigade, which is isolated by a sudden rise in the river. For the Federals, one of Schurz's brigades was crossed at Freeman's Ford to attack Jackson's rear, but was driven back by Hood. There is considerable artillery fire, part of it being Lee's effort to convince Pope that a crossing is to be attempted below Waterloo.

Shortly after dusk Stuart, with seven regiments of cavalry, crossed at Waterloo Bridge, marched in column along the road past a burned woolen factory, and stopped for an hour near Warrenton to rest and water the horses. Then he went quickly on, following the route shown on this map, and raided Pope's headquarters near Catlett's Station. This occurred before midnight. Stuart retraced his route to Waterloo before daylight.

to retaliate for the humiliating blow to his pride in the undignified loss of his hat and papers.

Luck plays an important role in war and some generals have enjoyed more than their fair share. On close study, however, it will be found that the Lady confers her favors on those who by energy and boldness put themselves in the way of opportunity. Jeb Stuart belonged in this category. Pope did not. On the contrary, Pope's braggadocio, his harsh measures toward the Virginia country folk, and such inept and unmilitary policies as leaving his rear to take care of itself combined to make him one of the most universally despised Northern generals ever to move into Confederate territory.

In one respect only was Pope fortunate at the time of Stuart's raid on Catlett's Station. He was away from his headquarters when the jaunty Confederate and his two thousand cavalrymen paid him that surprise visit on the night of August 22. It was raining hard as Stuart and his brigades moved in from the west and prepared to wreak havoc on the supply trains of the Army of Virginia. They picked up a Negro "contraband" whose eyes rolled when he learned what was afoot, but who lost no time in telling all that he knew, including the exciting intelligence that the raiders were within shouting distance of Pope's headquarters and his trains were guarded by a single regiment of infantry.

The Federal camp, not expecting Confederate visitors, was lit up like an amusement park on a summer evening. Halting outside the lighted area, Stuart assigned missions: Fitz Lee's brigade to raid the camps and inflict all the damage possible; Engineer Captain Blackford with one of the regiments as escort to destroy the railroad bridge; Robertson's brigade to stand by in reserve. All outfits were to start simultaneously at the bugle call, whereupon the Rebel yell was to be sounded with such a roar as to scare the wits out of the completely unsuspecting Federal rear echelon.

The attack was literally a howling success. Even in daylight, with advance warning, two thousand wildly yelling troopers at the gallop, fanning out in every direction and disregarding all obstacles, can be a fearful thunderbolt. To receive such a greeting in a place of fancied security, on a dark and rainy night, when some of the officers were just sitting down to a late supper, was adding insult to injury and applying almost unfairly the important principle of surprise.

The affair went off beautifully for the Confederates, disastrously for the Federals. The Pennsylvania Bucktail Regiment, guarding the depot, was quickly overcome. Hundreds of mules,

CATLETT'S STATION ON THE MORNING AFTER STUART'S RAID

riding horses, and prisoners were rounded up, including several of Pope's staff officers. But the most rewarding of all the booty was the capture of Pope's complete file of orders and correspondence, plus his horses, tent equipage, and a dress uniform. The latter was presented to Stuart, who later paraded it to the delighted troops and then shipped it off to Richmond, where it was publicly displayed in the State Library as mute testimony to the unwisdom of Northern boastfulness. No wonder that Jeb Stuart, for whom such feats as this were all in the day's work, was the dashing idol of the South.

The success of Stuart's massive raid was tempered by only

one failure, blame for which did not rest with the Confederate cavalry. In the course of the destruction of the Union depot and camps a terrific thunderstorm broke on the wild scene, quenching all the fires that had been kindled and wetting down the railroad bridge so effectively that it refused to burn. Axes were applied, but as the rifle fire of defending Union infantry became increasingly punishing, the attempt was finally abandoned.

About the time the depot was captured, Captain Blackford heard the sound of an engine starting. A train was pulling out for Washington. The engineer refused to halt the train, whereupon Blackford, his horse trotting alongside the moving engine, fired into the cab and prepared to leap aboard to execute his own order. At that moment his horse stumbled, pitching him to the ground, as the train went merrily on its way. Blackford reported that it had proceeded out of control, although the skeptical reader may be justified in wondering just how the captain could be so sure that his pistol shot had found its mark, in view of the circumstances.

Just before daylight of August 23d, with a nearby creek rising rapidly and threatening to interfere with the withdrawal of his column, Stuart gave the order to retire. Recall and assembly were sounded, individual troopers rejoined their outfits, and with more than 300 prisoners and a gratifyingly large number of captured horses, mules, and wagons loaded with loot, the heavily encumbered brigade headed back for Waterloo Bridge via Warrenton.

A mounted messenger galloped ahead with the invaluable intelligence found among Pope's papers. Lee would soon know almost as much about the Federal plans and the expected reinforcements from Aquia Creek as Pope himself. Stuart had certainly turned the tables, with his sixty-mile march and humiliating descent on Pope's rear area.

And how, one may ask, did the absent General Pope react when the news reached him? Strangely enough, his official report estimated the raiders at a strength of only 300 troopers, while berating the Blue defenders for a disgraceful exhibition. It would be only natural for those caught napping to exaggerate the numbers of the invading horde of horsemen. The explanation might be that Pope, realizing the ridiculous position in which he found himself, tried to minimize Stuart's achievement in riding around the Union army with a large body of troops and without opposition or even hindrance.

At this stage there existed a situation most unusual in war. The opposing army commanders were in possession of each other's plans and orders. Both Lee and Pope intended to take the offensive, the difference being that one was ready while the other was not. Lee held the initiative and was sparring for an opening. But he was already behind in his schedule, in which the time element was all-important if he was to succeed in crushing Pope before McClellan should arrive on the Rappahannock.

The Stuart raid served a double purpose in throwing Pope badly off mental balance and in furnishing Lee with solid facts upon which he could act with confidence. He now knew Pope's dispositions, his strength, and how he planned to employ that strength. Even more vitally important, Lee knew that of McClellan's army, both Porter's Fifth and Burnside's Ninth Corps were on hand, with others coming up rapidly. With over 70,000 men already on the line of the Rappahannock or within supporting distance, and the remainder of McClellan's divisions ordered to his support, Pope would soon have 150,000 men under his command or within call. Against that large army Lee could count 52,000 men present, with only D. H. Hill's and McLaws' divisions and Hampton's cavalry brigade as reinforcements when they would arrive from Richmond. It was now or never, and Lee lost no more time in making his decision.

CONFEDERATE PILLAGE OF MANASSAS JUNCTION DEPOT

CHAPTER 6

JACKSON EXPLODES IN POPE'S REAR

THE retrograde movement of Pope's Army of Virginia from the Rapidan to the Rappahannock barrier, strategically sound and executed with little interference from the Confederates, served but to postpone the day of retribution which would soon reveal John Pope as an opponent no more capable of matching wits with the master, Robert E. Lee, than the succession of Union generals who preceded and would follow him in army command—until Grant.

Pope was now definitely on the defensive, dancing to the tune that Lee would choose to play. Nevertheless, his new line along the high east bank of the Rappahannock was skilfully constructed, with artillery and infantry strongly posted to deny to the Confederates the innumerable fords along the entire front. It should also be noted that he had successfully stalled off Lee's offensive probings almost—but not quite—long enough to enable McClellan, never known to move rapidly, to transfer the divisions of his Army of the Potomac from Harrison's Landing by the roundabout water route to Aquia Creek Landing and to dispatch several corps thence to the Rappahannock country.

"Dispute every inch of ground and fight like the devil till we can reinforce you. Forty-eight hours more and we can make you strong enough" wired the distraught Halleck on August 21. To which Pope, still confident, replied that he need not worry; "I think no impression can be made on me for some days."

That was what Pope thought, but Lee and Jeb Stuart had different ideas. The Catlett's Station raid was of course not the kind of "impression" Pope had in mind; still it was an unpleasant and fateful one that promised greater repercussions than the ordinary hit-and-run cavalry foray. The unfortunately loquacious general from the west again appeared to have said the wrong thing.

While Stuart was riding around Pope on August 22-23, Jackson, acting on Lee's instructions, was sideslipping to the west, feeling for a place to cross the river. Lee had made up his mind that Pope could not be whipped in his present strong position; main reliance would have to be placed on a maneuvering mass, capable of luring the opposing army out of position and strong enough to fight a pitched battle if it came to that. He reasoned that it would be a mistake to so maneuver that Pope could fall back in the direction of Fredericksburg, because there would be no fruits to gather from that tree; on the contrary, it would merely serve to unite Pope and McClellan, the very thing he was determined to prevent.

Jubal Early has a Rough Time

Unable to find any evidence of weakness on the left of Pope's line along the Rappahannock, Lee's efforts met similar frustration on the Federal right. Every ford that Stuart's cavalry investigated found alert Federal horsemen screening concentrations of infantry and artillery, evidence that Pope knew something about war of position and had done an efficient job of prevention.

At Beverly Ford Stuart had gone beyond mere reconnaissance and light skirmishing. Under a heavy Confederate artillery bombardment, his squadrons drove back a regiment of infantry and an artillery battery and immediately fanned out patrols in all directions to examine the terrain. Finding it unsuitable for an attack, and pressed by a large infantry force, Stuart withdrew.

Under continuing pressure from Lee to locate a feasible crossing further up the river, Jackson and Stuart continued their progressive movements to the northwest. Reaching the ruined bridge at Sulphur Springs, they at last found one ford that appeared to be undefended. The leading regiment dashed across and secured a bridgehead, while Early's brigade with two batteries crossed a short distance below and established a position on a ridge near the river's edge. (See Map 10.)

Night had now fallen and a heavy rain caused the river to rise rapidly as it invariably did. Jackson decided to bivouac his main body on the west shore, but the next morning sent Lawton's brigade to reinforce Early before the swollen river made further crossing impracticable. Although Jackson put pioneers to work rebuilding the bridge, while Longstreet's artillery kept up a brisk fire all along the line to divert attention, Early's isolated detachment would have been lucky to escape capture or destruction if the Federals had been sufficiently enterprising to discover the extent of its predicament. Jackson's calculated risk at Early's expense paid off, however, for no real attack was made by the Federals at any time.

Sigel's corps, further down the river in the direction of Freeman's Ford, could have made it mighty uncomfortable for Early, but his people had just finished an artillery duel with Longstreet's batteries and Sigel's thoughts were centered on defensive tactics at the moment. The crossing by the Confederates at Sulphur Springs conjured up in Sigel's mind the dire possibility that Lee's entire army might be on the move. Whereupon he informed Pope that his right flank was in danger of being turned and he thought it wise to withdraw his troops to a more secure location. Pope's reply was to order Sigel to hold his ground and let the enemy develop in the direction of Warrenton, whereupon Pope would come down on Lee and his whole army.

Early on the morning of August 23 Pope ordered Sigel to advance with his whole corps on Sulphur Springs "to attack and beat the enemy." Banks' corps was ordered to follow and support Sigel. The former was prompt to comply, but the latter was not, with the result that both corps became intermingled on the same road. Sigel's trains interfered with the troop movement, and things generally got pretty thoroughly fouled up. Running into some Confederate skirmishers near a small creek about half a mile from the Rappahannock, the advance regiment of Sigel's corps opened fire; whereupon the Confederates crossed the creek and burned the bridge. Apparently that was all Sigel needed to call a halt, so he bivouacked his entire corps about the middle of the afternoon and ordered the bridge repaired. This important undertaking required the rest of the day, during which the corps made no further effort to comply with Pope's order to "attack and beat the enemy."

In retrospect, the situation had its humorous aspects, even though Early's troops, apparently abandoned to their fate, did not see anything funny about it. The fact was that both Early and Sigel felt themselves to be in a dangerous spot and were anxious to get away from there. The difference was that Early had good reason to be nervous, while Sigel acted the timid soul when he could have gained an easy success if he had shown even a slight dash of the offensive spirit.

Pope reported the affair at Sulphur Springs as a determined attempt by Lee to cross a large force, which he said had been effectively repulsed. Apparently the Federal general had failed utterly to divine the intentions of his able opponent or even to consider the real significance of Jackson's maneuvers along the river.

Satisfied with the results secured, and knowing by that time that Stuart's raid on Pope's rear had been successfully concluded, Jackson relieved the tension of Early's force and permitted it, on the morning of the 24th of August, to return to the main body and the welcome food which had been denied them for most of the period of their isolation.

Jubal Anderson Early was one of many of Lee's generals who are appropriate subjects for dramatization or at least interested study, for his name crops up constantly in accounts of Civil War battles. He was a Virginian, 47 years of age, a strong and vocal opponent of secession, but, like Lee and many other Southerners, when it came to a matter of loyalty to State or Nation, he stuck with Virginia.

Entering West Point at the age of 16, he managed to achieve something of a record for the number of demerits earned, coming close to the two hundred maximum in two of the four years spent at the Academy on the Hudson. That was typical of "Jube," who was a nonconformist at heart, with a somewhat paradoxical attitude toward authority. He recognized the necessity for discipline, but tended to resist it from higher up, apparently because of a critical, inquiring nature that sought always to get to the heart of any matter. He was tall and angular, with a square jaw, dark eyes, and a luxuriant beard. Blunt in his speech, he was ready for a fight at the drop of a hat and he didn't always wait for the hat to fall, for the records at West Point include personal encounters in which Armistead and Joe Hooker either took on or were taken on by Jube Early at one time or another. Early's period at the Academy, incidentally, coincided with that of at least a dozen cadets who became prominent as general officers, including French, McDowell, Halleck, Hooker, Sherman, and Ewell.

After some skirmishes with the Florida Indians and a love

affair that turned out badly and left him a lifelong bachelor, Early resigned from the army, took up law and politics, and returned to the profession of arms long enough to play an unimportant role in the Mexican War. He did, however, become afflicted with rheumatism while in Mexico and it never left him, with the result that he developed a permanent stoop.

In the Battle of First Manassas, as a brigade commander with the rank of colonel, his brigade had the good fortune to be in the right place at the right time. That was the extreme left flank of the Confederate forces where, in conjunction with heavy attacks all along the front, Early drove into the Federal flank and rear at the psychological moment to tip the scales for Beauregard and against McDowell. The Union forces broke for Washington and "Old Jube," as his men later came to call him, was made a brigadier general on the spot.

Badly wounded at Williamsburg during the Peninsular Campaign, Early was out of action for some months, but returned in time to take the wounded Elzey's brigade under Ewell and put up an efficient performance at Cedar Mountain. There would be many subsequent occasions for Early to distinguish himself.

Lee "Shoots the Works"

The solution to the vexing problem of how to get at Pope appeared to Lee to be a wide flanking movement around the Federal right, well to the west of but parallel to the vulnerable Orange and Alexandria Railroad, the sensitive supply line to Alexandria upon which Pope had to depend for the necessities of military life. If Lee could thus draw him out of his present position into an instinctive reaction to protect his communications, Pope would have to march away from the oncoming Army of the Potomac and an opportunity might present itself to defeat him in the open.

It was a typically bold plan, the kind that appealed to Lee. It was also the sort of thing that delighted Jackson, whose sharp eyes glinted when the scheme was explained to him.

Jackson wanted to start early the following morning, but the more stolid and logistically minded Longstreet preferred to wait another day, to allow time for working out the details and provisioning the troops. Lee agreed with Longstreet.

The risks were great and he knew it. Only a general of Lee's caliber would venture to separate the two wings of his army by a gap of fifty miles, with a hostile army between them. Pope now outnumbered him by a considerable margin that would in all likelihood be widened at an increasing rate from day to day as more of McClellan's divisions landed at Aquia and moved inland to join Pope. Lee could of course yield the initiative and retire in the direction of Richmond, or he could attack Pope at once and put everything to the test in a knockdown encounter. Neither idea appealed to him. The plan that he did adopt was the only one that offered promise of decisive results, for his low opinion of Pope's ability, despite the defensive skill the Northern general had shown during the past few days, was such that he did not consider Pope's immediate strength superiority, or the greater risk of dividing his own army, to be particularly significant or dangerous.

Jackson and Longstreet were equally content with the roles assigned their respective corps. The former, with Stuart's cavalry to follow on the second day as a covering force, would on August 25 lead his three divisions, some 24,000 men, in one of his amazingly fast marches in a wide swing well beyond and around the Federal right, via Amissville, Salem, Thoroughfare Gap, and Gainesville, to Bristoe Station, where his force would cut the main railroad and, with luck, destroy the huge Federal warehouses at Manassas Junction.

Lee and Longstreet, with the rest of the army, about 28,000 men, would temporarily stay where they were, to hold Pope to the line of the Rappahannock with Old Pete's four divisions, demonstrating to the extent necessary to persuade the Federals that the Army of Northern Virginia was staying put. The greatest risk was that Pope would learn what was going on and act offensively to deal with Longstreet while Jackson was moving away from Lee. That however was a chance that had to be taken.

The monotonous, unavailing search for an unprotected crossing, as Jackson's men sideslipped to the left and the Federals kept pace with them on the opposite bank of the Rappahannock, was now over. The next move would be more to their liking as they moved into familiar country in one of those unfettered swinging half-lopes which in the Valley had earned for them the cherished designation of Jackson's "foot-cavalry."

On Sunday, August 24, Lee rode out to Jackson's command post at Jeffersonton to give him final instructions and discuss the route, the assembly area for the two wings of the army, and other important details. It was all clear in Lee's mind but he wanted to make certain that Jackson thoroughly understood his plan. Everything must go off like clockwork. Lee was so supremely confident on that score that he informed Jackson the two wings of the army would reunite in the vicinity of Manassas after, not if and when, Pope had been separated from the reinforcements marching to join him. Jackson was specifically told to march north behind the sheltering screen of the Bull Run Mountains to avoid detection, but not to bring on a general engagement. Lee was placing his money on the horse *Maneuver*, and Jackson was his jockey.

Jackson immediately made preparations to march at first dawn Monday, August 25, the troops stripped down to bare essentials, including a small amount of cooked rations. The men would not even carry their knapsacks. Wagon trains were to be limited to ammunition carts and ambulances. Live cattle would accompany the column, other items of food to be gathered from the countryside as they marched.

Jackson's rigorous rules for road marches placed him in a class by himself and way ahead of his time. McClellan considered 10 miles a day to be a creditable performance, but

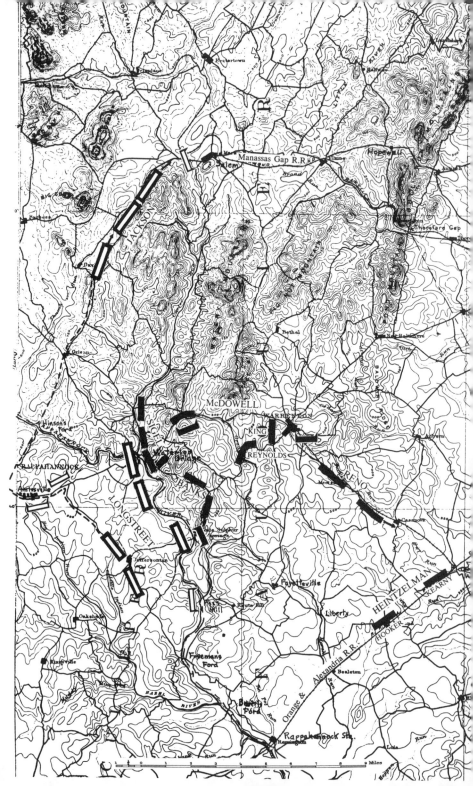

"Little Mac" was the antithesis of Stonewall in more respects than one.

Longstreet's guns replaced Jackson's along the Rappahannock under cover of darkness. Early Monday morning Jackson's column moved silently and swiftly up river to an unguarded crossing at Hinson's Mills, five miles west of Waterloo Bridge, where the troops splashed across on the first leg of an adventure that promised plenty of excitement. Meantime, Longstreet kept the Federals in place by demonstrating along the Rappahannock. His artillery played intermittently on the enemy positions across the river, Longstreet's infantry showed itself to the Federals, and Stuart's cavalry skirmished at the important fords.

Although Jackson's column circled widely around Pope's right, Federal observers noted the marching troops. Pope's headquarters, however, interpreted the information to mean that it was a move to the Shenandoah Valley on the part of a flanking column and that Lee's main body would shortly follow, headed for Front Royal. No troops were sent by Pope to dispute the march, not even a cavalry detachment to discover for certain whether the estimate was correct. All he did, apparently, was to speculate on what the move might mean.

By Monday evening Jackson's marching men had put 25

MAP 11. THE START OF JACKSON'S MARCH

The situation about dark, August 25. Jackson has departed from Jefferson-ton on his 50-mile march to Manassas, via Amissville, Hinson's Ford, Orlean; and at dark is approaching Salem. Longstreet is demonstrating noisily along the Rappahannock to hold Pope in place, and will follow Jackson in two days.

Pope, aware of Jackson's movement, but misinterpreting it, is beginning to get rattled. He has started his troops on a program of frenzied night marches, the pattern of which is confused, and which will continue in this manner until the armies are locked in their death struggle on the Manassas plains. Sigel, fearful of attack, and out of favor with Pope, is preparing to withdraw to Fayetteville. Reno, who reached Warrenton, is ordered back to Kellys Ford, and is on the way. Banks, ordered to Warrenton Junction, is enroute, via Sulphur Springs. Heintzelman's two divisions have detrained where shown. Porter's corps, after a leisurely march to join Pope, has halted at Deep Creek (not shown), 13 miles southeast of Bealeton.

dusty miles behind them and halted for the night at Salem, six miles west of Thoroughfare Gap on the Manassas Gap Railroad. At 9 p.m. Pope wired Halleck his opinion, as already stated, adding that he would send a reconnaissance party across the river Tuesday morning to find out whether the main body of Lee's army had in fact moved out. Most of the message, however, was devoted to a long dissertation on the low strength and poor condition of Banks' corps, the fact that Sigel was of no use to him and should be replaced, and that McDowell's corps was the only one that he could depend on to render effective service. It was obvious that Pope was rattled and devoting more attention to worrying about the condition of his army than he was to the pressing problem of how to deal effectively with the Army of Northern Virginia.

True to form, Jackson's men were not told where they were going, as their leader rode tirelessly up and down the column urging it forward. The general opinion was that they were returning to the Valley, a pleasant prospect indeed. That was also Pope's opinion, which made it almost unanimous. On Tuesday morning, August 26, however, as they resumed the march and passed through Salem, the head of the column turned to the right and headed for Thoroughfare Gap. That killed the Valley rumor, but it made no difference to the foot cavalry as they slogged along with complete confidence that "Old Jack" knew what he was doing.

Pope's Predicament

Back on the Potomac the Northern Capital was blanketed by the fog of war, that mysterious miasma which usually beclouds strategy that is compounded of divided counsel and the absence of mutual understanding, confidence, and cooperation. The members of the military team of Halleck, McClellan, and Pope, on whom Lincoln was now relying for results, were as far apart in their thinking as they were geographically, an absurd condition that should have been corrected long before the present crisis occurred.

The major responsibility was Halleck's. His was the ranking authority whose duty it was to give McClellan and Pope their instructions and to make his orders effective. Unfortunately Halleck lacked both the capabilities of a good field general and the intestinal fortitude to make vital decisions, impart them in concise and unmistakable orders, and then insist upon prompt and willing execution by the army commanders.

Seen in that context and with all the facts at hand, McClellan emerges as the dissident backfield member of the team, who purposely mistook or else interpreted to his own satisfaction the signals called by quarterback Halleck. Pope, the other backfield player, understood the team objective and was anxious to cooperate, but was not allowed to carry the ball until his interference should be in motion and able to guarantee the power that would make the play effective. One can sympathize mildly with Pope, the general who wanted to fight, but who, in conjunction with his military sins of commission, may be considered to have been a partial victim of circumstances. Although he was far from being a Man of Destiny, his army, but for McClellan, need not have suffered the disaster that was to engulf it at Second Manassas.

It is easy to be an armchair strategist after the event. But even a casual student of events is hard put to explain why the most obvious and fundamental steps were not taken by the Federal War Department in August 1862. Halleck had directed that the armies of McClellan and Pope be united. That implied that someone would have to command the consolidation. Nevertheless, Halleck neither took the field in that capacity, nor did he make it clear to either of the army commanders which one would direct the actions of the other's troops when they commenced to merge. He failed even to summon McClellan and Pope to a joint meeting with himself, at some convenient central point such as Manassas or Fredericksburg, to clear the air and lay down the law. "Old Brains," with all his intellect, legal knowledge, and reputed administrative ability, clearly lacked the decisiveness to jump into the arena, pound a few heads together, and exert the leadership that the situation demanded.

It is only necessary to read the telegraphic exchanges which passed between McClellan and Halleck during the afternoon and evening of August 24 to understand how uncertainty and lack of command unity was helping to nullify whatever constructive moves Pope might undertake, and indirectly to afford unwitting aid and comfort to the Confederate cause.

McClellan to Halleck, at 12 noon from Aquia Creek:

I telegraphed you at 6 a.m. this day that I had arrived here and respectfully reported for orders. I have heretofore received none, except to transfer my command to Aquia, and subsequently a telegraphic dispatch to come on in person as soon as I could.

* * * *

I regret to learn that General Pope last night abandoned Rappahannock Station without giving the slightest information to Morell and Sykes (Ed. note: two of McClellan's division commanders who had joined Pope's forces), who were within 6 miles of him. They discovered the fact accidentally this morning by means of a patrol they sent out. No certain directions can be given to those divisions until the position and intentions of Pope are ascertained, which can only be done through you.

Halleck to McClellan, 12:30 p.m.

Porter and Reno should hold the line of the Rappahannock below Pope, subject for the present to his orders. I hope by tomorrow to be able to give some more definite directions. You know my main object, and will act accordingly.

McClellan to Halleck, 9:40 p.m. from Falmouth.

Please inform me exactly where General Pope's troops are, that I may know what part of the Rappahannock is to be crossed from here and what transportation is necessary to supply the troops going to join him.

Up to what point is the Orange and Alexandria Railroad now available? Where are the enemy in force?

Halleck to McClellan: (hour not shown)

You ask me for information which I cannot give. I do not know either where General Pope is or where the enemy in force is. These are matters which I have all day been most anxious to ascertain.

Halleck to McClellan: (hour not shown)

There is nothing more to communicate tonight. I do not expect to hear from Pope before tomorrow. Will telegraph to you at Aquia. Good night.

This hint to McClellan that Halleck was tired and wanted to go to bed was ignored.

McClellan to Halleck, 12 midnight.

Are you in communication with Warrenton Junction and are Pope's forces in advance of Warrenton Junction?

Halleck to McClellan, 12:5 a. m.

General Pope did not retreat from Rappahannock Station, but advanced and attacked the enemy near Sulphur Springs and is now in pursuit. What we intend is to hold the line of the Rappahannock until all our forces can get together. Your operations are to be directed to this object. Kearny is at Warrenton Junction, but Pope is near Waterloo Bridge. There is no telegraph line to him.

In commenting on Pope's remissness in not keeping at least Halleck informed of the whereabouts of his major elements, McClellan undoubtedly had a legitimate gripe, which would have been unnecessary had the Union Army established a system of placing liaison officers on duty with corps, divisions, and particularly with flank elements, such as exists today. The routine nature of such a procedure in modern armies makes its absence in the Union armies of the Civil War stand out even more sharply by contrast. The Confederates used cavalry for the purpose, with marked success, but the Federals were uncommonly slow to learn from their opponents.

In striking contrast to the labored creaking of the ponderous machinery of the Federal high command, which strangely seemed to function at cross-purposes and in low gear, the quick, joyous reactions of the agile Confederate commanders to the almost conversational major decisions of General Lee are refreshing to contemplate. An unconscionable amount of time and energy was habitually expended by the Federal brass in sending long-winded compositions to one another. McClellan was the worst offender, but he was not alone. Conversely, while the Federal team would be engaged in the time-killing pastime of ex-, changing views on what to do, Lee and Jackson and Stuart would be making forward passes and end runs as Longstreet waited contentedly for the moment when he could carry the ball in one of his characteristic line plunges, to wrap up the ball game.

Pope's telegram of August 25 to Halleck is a typical illustration of the regrettable confusion that existed in the upper echelons of command in the Union armies at this crucial period. (Words have been italicized by the author, for emphasis.)

August 25th, 1862.

Major-General Halleck: Your dispatch just received. Of course I shall be ready to recross the Rappahannock at a moment's notice. You will see from the position taken that each army corps is on the best roads across the river. You wished forty-eight hours to assemble the forces from the Peninsula behind the Rappahannock, and four days have passed without the enemy yet being permitted to cross. I don't think he is yet ready to do so. In ordinarily dry weather the Rappahannock can be crossed almost anywhere, and these crossing-places are best protected by concentrating at central positions to strike at any force which attempts to cross. I had clearly understood that you wished to unite our whole forces before a forward movement was begun, and that I must take care to keep united with Burnside on my left, so that no movement to separate us could be made. This withdrew me lower down the Rappahannock than I wished to come. *I am not acquainted with your views, as you seem to suppose, and would be glad to know them so far as my own position and operations are concerned.*

I understood you clearly that, at all hazards, I was to prevent the enemy from passing the Rappahannock. This I have done, and shall do. I don't like to be on the defensive if I can help it, but must be so long as I am tied to Burnside's forces, not yet wholly arrived at Fredericksburg. Please let me know, if it can be done, what is to be my own command, and if I am to act independently against the enemy. *I certainly understand that, as soon as the whole of our forces were concentrated, you designed to take command in person,* and that, when everything was ready, we were to move forward in concert. I judge from the tone of your dispatch that you are dissatisfied with something. Unless I know what it is, of course I can't correct it. The troops arriving here come in fragments. Am I to assign them to brigades and corps? I would suppose not, as several of the new regiments coming have been assigned to army corps directly from your office. In case I commence offensive operations I must know what forces I am to take and what you wish left, and what connection must be kept up with Burnside. It has been my purpose to conform my operations to your plans, yet *I was not informed when McClellan evacuated Harrison's Landing,* so that I might know what to expect in that direction; and when I say these things in no complaining spirit, I think that you know well that I am anxious to do everything to advance your plans of campaign. I understood that this army was to maintain the line of the Rappahannock until all the forces from the Peninsula had united behind that river. I have done so. I understood distinctly that I was not to hazard anything except for this purpose, as delay was what was wanted.

The enemy this morning has pushed a considerable infantry force up opposite Waterloo Bridge, and is planting batteries and long lines of his infantry are moving up from Jeffersonville toward Sulphur Springs. His whole force, as far as can be ascertained, is massed in front of me, from railroad crossing of Rappahannock around to Waterloo Bridge, their main body being opposite Sulphur Springs.

John Pope, Major General

It is evident from the last paragraph of the foregoing dispatch that Pope was uaware of Jackson's flank march, which had been in progress for hours, or he would certainly have mentioned it. Pope's eyes were fixed only on the Rappahannock. His remark about being tied to Burnside's forces, "not yet wholly arrived at Fredericksburg," is at variance with Burnside's own report to Halleck of August 9, more than two weeks earlier, that his command of about 12,000 "effectives" had arrived at Falmouth and was "in position." It was a fact that by order of the War Department Burnside had brought his troops up from North Carolina without artillery, cavalry, ambulances, or even supply wagons, but the transportation shortage at least had been rectified by August 12, on which date Halleck wired Pope that Burnside was moving on that day to reinforce him, having received the required wagons from Washington. That would of course be Reno's division, consisting of twelve regiments of infantry, four batteries of artillery and two companies of cavalry, which left Burnside with only seven infantry regiments and six companies of cavalry to secure Fredericksburg, Falmouth, the Aquia Creek supply base, and fifteen miles of intervening country. Stuart's recent unimpeded cavalry swing around his right flank and rear apparently failed to suggest to Pope's mind the possibility that Jackson's fast-moving foot soldiers might try the same thing. Lee's plan was working out satisfactorily, with his opponent cooperating nicely.

On the morning of August 26, as Jackson's column proceeded eastward through the virtually unguarded Thoroughfare Gap, marching along the tracks of the Manassas Gap Railroad and over the Bull Run Mountain to the open country beyond, Stuart's cavalry took off along the same path at a fast pace to overtake the infantry, while Longstreet's corps (actually designated by Lee a wing, or temporary tactical grouping of assigned divisions, but essentially the same as a corps*) made

––––––

*The Confederate Congress had not yet authorized the organization of corps.

ready to follow Jackson's route as soon as Pope reacted to the new development. The reaction was slow in coming, for the Army of Virginia showed no sign of alarm nor evidence of movement all day long. Whereupon Lee gave the order to move, and Longstreet's men started their march, the entire wing bivouacking for the night at Orlean, about eight miles beyond Waterloo Bridge and a dozen miles short of Thoroughfare Gap.

Pope's Rear Again Exposed

Marching straight for Bristoe Station, his initial objective, Jackson's column passed through Gainesville, where Stuart caught up with him, and from there preceded and paralleled the infantry line of march as a covering screen until Bristoe Station hove in sight. The sun was setting when the advance elements reached their destination, Jackson's troops having marched 50 miles in two days, while Stuart's horsemen had covered the same distance since two o'clock that morning.

Jackson was now only five miles southwest of Manassas Junction, thirteen miles in rear of Pope's headquarters, and squarely on his road and rail communications to Washington. Munford's cavalry, sweeping ahead of Jackson's column, had gathered in the few enemy patrols encountered on the last few miles of the route, to guarantee that no word of the Confederate surprise should be relayed to Washington or Pope. No organized bodies of the enemy had been met during the two-day march of the infantry. It was almost unbelievable that 24,000 Confederates could circle a Federal army without detection, but it had been done.

Jackson could have taken the direct, shorter route along the Manassas Gap Railroad to Manassas Junction, but that would have left the Orange and Alexandria Railroad open for a quick rail movement to the north with a strong Federal force that could cause trouble. He therefore cut across country to Bristoe Station, where he could destroy the railroad bridge over that stream and use Broad Run as a barrier to hold off any threat

MAP 12. ACTIONS ON AUGUST 26

At 2 a.m. Stuart departed in Jackson's wake, with all the
Confederate cavalry, riding hard to overtake Jackson. By 4 p.m.
he had passed Jackson's divisions near Gainesville, and disposed
his brigades to protect the main approaches to Jackson's force,
as shown. Jackson bivouacked in the Bristoe area while Stuart
went on, accompanied by Trimble's brigade, to capture Manassas Junction. Leaving Anderson to watch the upper crossings over the Rappahannock, Longstreet followed Jackson at
4 p.m. After an eleven-mile march he bivouacked at Orlean.

The night of August 25-26 Sigel had sought safety at
Warrenton, reaching there at 2 a.m. McDowell moved up
King and Ricketts to cover the gap uncovered by Sigel's departure, King's artillery dueling with Anderson during the
day. Banks halted at Fayetteville. Reno, after a march of
two miles, halted at Warrenton Junction, near where Heintzelman's two divisions were still resting. Pope, hearing something
about Confederates at Manassas, sends a regiment to investigate.

from Pope while the stores were being uninterruptedly destroyed at Manassas Junction.

Galloping ahead to Bristoe Station, Munford's cavalry brushed aside a Federal cavalry detachment and mopped up a guard company of Blue infantry, at the same time hastily throwing obstructions on the tracks to block possible train movements in either direction. At that moment an empty train, returning to Alexandria from Warrenton Junction, roared up, crashed through the flimsy obstruction, and escaped. This was the first piece of bad luck the Confederates had experienced since leaving the Rappahannock. Washington would soon know something was afoot.

On the second attempt Hays' infantry brigade did a more thorough job of blocking the rails. Two more trains, also empties, following closely after the first, were derailed and set on fire. Pope's rail communication with Washington was now effectually cut.

Ewell's division, having led Jackson's column the full distance, bivouacked for the night near Bristoe Station and took over from the cavalry shortly after dark. With Jackson's rear temporarily secure against all but a Federal corps or larger, Stuart's horsemen marched the few intervening miles to approach Manassas Junction from the north while General Isaac Trimble with two infantry regiments moved up the tracks to take the depot from the front. Between them, Stuart and Trimble quickly gobbled up the depot against token resistance from the small defending garrison. By daylight of August 27 Jackson arrived with A. P. Hill's division and his own under Taliaferro, leaving the major part of Ewell's division at Bristoe, with several regiments of cavalry, to secure the rear.

As soon as Jackson had placed guards on the supply of liquor, the famished, ragged hordes of Confederates were turned loose on the huge warehouses, horse corrals, and other riches, to forage to their heart's content. The picture is one that defies the imagination. Having lived on meager rations for a long time, mainly the field corn plucked en route during the two-day march from the Rappahannock, the feast of plenty that was theirs for the taking at Manassas Junction was almost reward enough for the weeks of slim pickings that preceded their just completed historic achievement.

Many thousands of gaunt, grimy, unwashed, almost shoeless, hungry soldiers immediately proceeded to gorge themselves on the solid food and inviting delicacies that they found in such abundance. When they reached the point where not another morsel could be forced into already overloaded stomachs, they filled blanket rolls with more than they could carry, hoisted whole hams on their bayonet points, threw sacks of coffee across the saddles of their horses. Fat draft horses, and sleek riding horses were gathered in to fill gaps or replace animals that had given their all in the service of Stuart's hard-riding cavalry and Pelham's horse artillery. The wonder of it is that the whole outfit was able to weather the rare experience without foundering or being forced to sleep off a gastronomical orgy of such vast proportions. Neither is there a record of the envious disappointment with which Ewell's men, holding the fort at Bristoe Station, must have received the news of the good fortune of their comrades in the other two divisions.

MANASSAS JUNCTION IN 1862

Chapter 7

FEDERAL REACTION TO JACKSON'S RAID

JACKSON and Lee would have been highly gratified had they known how effective was the disruption of Federal communications resulting from the Manassas raid. The purpose of the Confederates was of course to sever Pope's lifeline, to deprive him of his source of supplies and reinforcements, to prevent the movement of troops, materiel, and food supplies from Alexandria; in short to render him—and his superiors in Washington—both blind and deaf.

There was, however, no panic either among the Union military personnel or the War Department. Possibly the full significance of the event, with all its potentiality for disaster, did not register at once. Still, the Confederates were between Pope and the Capital, only a few miles away, and it wouldn't have taken much to start a panic, if a twentieth-century type of fifth column, armed and sympathetic to the Southern cause, had been planted in Washington to exploit the opportunity.

118

Colonel Herman Haupt, the ubiquitous, efficient rail transportation chief for the Eastern armies, was undoubtedly the busiest man in the North at this time. Although he was accustomed to meeting and solving transportation crises, this one had occurred at the worst possible time, as he sweated to speed reinforcements to Pope's Army of Virginia. Given a little time, Haupt could justify his well-earned reputation for doing the improbable, but even he couldn't rebuild bridges in nothing flat. Neither could he recover for use at Alexandria Depot empty trains whose return trip from Pope's army found the railroad bridge down at Broad Run. But he strove mightily during the last few days of August, and without him the recovery from the effects of the raid, logistically speaking, might well have occurred too late to affect the campaign.

The Confederates are Coming!

Alexandria was the first to react on the evening of August 26, when the empty train that had crashed the barrier at Bristoe steamed into the station. Obviously the engineer couldn't have seen much as he dashed through to safety, so the Federal authorities weren't overly excited, believing it to be just another of Stuart's frequent cavalry raids. The excitement in Washington began to mount, however, when Herman Haupt forwarded to Halleck, about 9 p. m., an informative telegram from Manassas Junction, signed by Dispatcher McCrickett, which read:

> No. 6 train, engine Secretary, was fired into at Bristoe by a party of cavalry—some say 500 strong. They had piled ties on the track, but engine threw them off. Secretary is completely riddled by bullets. Conductor says he thinks the enemy are coming this way.

To this disturbing message Haupt added that the wire between Manassas and Warrenton (Pope's headquarters) had been cut, and that he had at Alexandria transportation for 1,200 men, who he suggested "might be sent to Manassas to protect the road while we repair it."

It was only a few minutes after sending the foregoing message that the dispatcher at Manassas closed his key and took off to escape capture. Haupt also passed that news on to Halleck, advising him that no more troops should be sent forward in cars. He proposed instead that they be sent by marching in order to provide better security for themselves and at the same time protect the rail communications.

Halleck's Frantic Order to Haupt

Halleck's inadequate, almost helpless reaction was to pass the buck frantically to the already overworked but capable Haupt in these words:

> General Smith, General Slocum, General Sturgis, or any other general officers you can find, will immediately send all the men you can transport to Bristoe Bridge or Manassas Junction. Show this order.
>
> H. W. Halleck,
> General-in-Chief

Haupt wasted two hours trying unsuccessfully to locate a general officer, advising Halleck at 11 o'clock that Cox was in Washington, Sturgis in the field, and Smith nowhere to be found. He didn't mention Slocum, but did locate two regiments of Cox's command and said he would next go to other camps "to drum up some more."

The upshot of Haupt's bird-dogging search was that he finally rounded up two more New Jersey regiments. Placing Brigadier General George W. Taylor, one of Slocum's brigade commanders, in command, Haupt loaded the four regiments and an artillery battery on cars, and sent them packing for Manassas Junction, with orders to seize and hold the Bull Run bridge.

Taylor Makes a Noble Effort

Taylor was an energetic fellow, but without the least idea what his raw troops were up against. The train was halted at a point above the Junction, the men were detrained and marched resolutely forward. Placing the battery near Bull Run, Taylor opened an annoying fire on the enemy in Manassas, crossed the bridge, and advanced to drive out the Confederate raiding party, as he vaguely understood them to be.

So far as Jackson knew, this might be a genuine threat. Taking no chances, he sent the better part of A. P. Hill's division to dispose of the brave but hapless Federals. When the Union troops realized the size of the determined force moving to cut them down, they suddenly turned and tried to

TAYLOR'S BRIGADE ENTRAINING, LITTLE KNOWING THAT THEY WERE HEADED FOR A MASSACRE.

escape. Taylor was killed, more than one hundred of his men killed or wounded, 6 guns and over two hundred men cap-tured. To add to their woes, the retreating troops ran into Fitz Lee, who with three regiments of Gray cavalry was returning from a reconnaissance to Fairfax Court House. That finished the Federals as an organization, although some individuals made their way back to Alexandria.

Pope's information at Warrenton had come from a fourth train whose engineer, sensing trouble ahead, jammed on the brakes as the train approached Bristoe Station and quickly backed away to safety. But Pope also accepted this intelligence as of little importance and took no action. The fact was that the Federal commander was fast reaching a stage which, to an objective observer, would suggest a state of bewilderment, although Pope himself believed he had the situation well in hand and was moving his chessmen around the board in clever fashion, all things considered.

Pope Operates in a Fog

Nevertheless, for three days, from the 24th to the 27th, as he shifted divisions here and there for reasons best known to himself, Pope had not the haziest notion of what the Con-federates were doing, so careful had been their preparations and so well masked the movements of both Jackson's and Longstreet's wings. As for Pope's cavalry, it might as well have been in Canada or elsewhere, for he had worn down Buford's and Bayard's regiments on inconsequential missions. Now, when they could have been usefully engaged on distant reconnaissance, he failed to assign them to that essential mis-sion, at least not in the early stages when information was needed the most.

While all this was going on behind the curtain of Federal ignorance that Lee had so effectively rolled down around three sides of the area occupied by the Union forces, just what was Pope's strength at sunset August 27, when Jackson's 24,000 men had finished making a shambles of his rear; and what were the positions and dispositions of the opposing armies?

It had finally penetrated Pope's consciousness, on the morning of August 27, that affairs had taken a more serious turn than he had at first supposed. Upon discovering that the strength of the Confederate force on his rear indicated far more than a mere raid, he had ordered up an infantry regiment and followed it with Hooker's entire division, which engaged Ewell in a brisk encounter that developed more fully the character of the Confederate opposition. Pope was now aware that Lee had, recklessly it seemed, divided his army. It appeared that his own Army of Virginia lay between the two Confederate wings. Exultantly, therefore, Pope concluded that Lee had worked himself into a dangerous position and that Jackson's exposed position presented him with "the only opportunity which had offered to gain any success over the superior forces of the enemy," as he stated in his official report.

"I determined, therefore," Pope's report continues, "on the morning of the 27th of August to abandon the line of the Rappahannock and throw my whole force in the direction of Gainesville and Manassas Junction, to crush any force of the enemy that had passed through Thoroughfare Gap, and to interpose between Lee's army and Bull Run. Having the interior line of operations, and the enemy at Manassas being inferior in force, it appeared to me, and still so appears, that with even ordinary promptness and energy we might feel sure of success."

Heavy Union Reinforcements Arrive

It was a reasonable evaluation, and the opportunity was even better on paper than Pope believed. For he now had at hand, under his immediate command, more than half again as many men as Lee; for the purpose of defeating each of the separated Confederate wings in detail his superiority was 3 to 1 against Jackson, as well as against Longstreet.

Pope's strength had expanded to approximately 77,000 men, his own army augmented by two two-division corps from the Army of the Potomac and Burnside's Falmouth troops, under command of Major Generals Fitz John Porter, Samuel P.

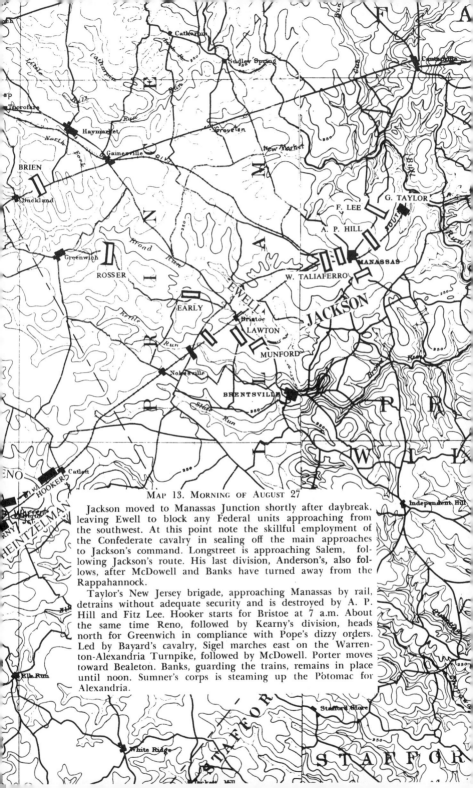

MAP 13. MORNING OF AUGUST 27

Jackson moved to Manassas Junction shortly after daybreak, leaving Ewell to block any Federal units approaching from the southwest. At this point note the skillful employment of the Confederate cavalry in sealing off the main approaches to Jackson's command. Longstreet is approaching Salem, following Jackson's route. His last division, Anderson's, also follows, after McDowell and Banks have turned away from the Rappahannock.

Taylor's New Jersey brigade, approaching Manassas by rail, detrains without adequate security and is destroyed by A. P. Hill and Fitz Lee. Hooker starts for Bristoe at 7 a.m. About the same time Reno, followed by Kearny's division, heads north for Greenwich in compliance with Pope's dizzy orders. Led by Bayard's cavalry, Sigel marches east on the Warrenton-Alexandria Turnpike, followed by McDowell. Porter moves toward Bealeton. Banks, guarding the trains, remains in place until noon. Sumner's corps is steaming up the Potomac for Alexandria.

Heintzelman, and Jesse L. Reno respectively, in addition to Reynolds' division of Pennsylvania Reserves and a brigade of Cox's Kanawha troops, which had been transferred from West Virginia and were awaiting transportation at Washington. Instead of being confronted by the superior forces of Lee's army, as he reported, his own strength exceeded Lee's by 25,000 men. The disparity was not nearly great enough to bother Lee; the difference between the two men being that Lee was not only the better general, but knew exactly what he was doing and precisely how to achieve the desired result.

When darkness fell on August 27, Jackson's force was concentrated at Manassas Junction, Ewell having broken off a sharp fight with Hooker's division below Bristoe Station and joined Jackson on the latter's instructions. Longstreet's wing was strung along the road from Salem to White Plains, the head of his column seven or eight miles to the west of Thoroughfare Gap.

Pope Plans to Crush Jackson

Pope issued movement orders to accomplish his purpose of crushing Jackson. By evening of August 27, his army was well north of the Rappahannock, moving by several different roads on Gainesville and Manassas Junction. That night the Federal troops were disposed as follows: Sigel's and McDowell's corps, in that order, with Reynolds' division attached, on the Warrenton turnpike, almost to Gainesville; Kearny's division and Reno's corps at Greenwich, south of Broad Run, and several miles to McDowell's rear; Hooker's division of Heintzelman's corps west of Bristoe; Porter's corps on the line of the Orange and Alexandria Railroad northeast of Warrenton Junction; and Banks' corps on the same rail line two miles back of Porter. Banks' orders were to guard the army trains, shepherding them to Manassas Junction or as far as the condition of the tracks and bridges permitted. When Banks reached Warrenton Junction, Porter's corps was under orders to proceed in the direction of Greenwich and Gainesville to support the spearhead corps of Sigel and McDowell in company with Heintzelman and Reno.

Buford's cavalry was operating west of the Bull Run Mountains, in the direct path of and only a few miles south of the head of Longstreet's column. Bayard's brigade was also reconnoitering in the vicinity of Thoroughfare Gap, which on August 28, he was directed by McDowell to occupy until Rickett's division could come up to relieve him and close the Gap.

When Pope finally learned, about dark on the evening of August 27, that the divisions of Ewell, A. P. Hill, and Taliaferro, Jackson's entire force were all at Manassas, he appears to have become so excited at what struck him as a glorious opportunity to bag the valuable prize that he lost sight of every other consideration. Whereupon he swung the order-changing department of his headquarters into high gear, sending orders to all the corps commanders that in effect threw into the discard the half completed movement by which a position was being developed that would face west on the line: Gainesville to the railroad crossing at Cedar Creek. The new plan was to concentrate the entire army in the Manassas-Bristoe area, but nothing was said as to what it would do on arrival. Pope probably expected to play it by ear, hoping to crush Jackson instead of Lee, if indeed he was capable of thinking in two dimensions at the same time, which one may at this stage be pardoned for doubting.

It is enlightening to read the revised march orders that Pope sent out by courier in all directions from Bristoe, to which point he had accompanied Hooker's division of Heintzelman's corps and witnessed the short but spirited engagement with Ewell's Confederate division. Pope's widely scattered corps commanders were all urged to move their forces expeditiously in the direction of Manassas Junction to support McDowell, temporarily in command of Sigel's corps as well as his own. McDowell was directed to proceed eastward from Gainesville and would presumably be the first to arrive at the Junction. It seemed to Pope, still optimistic, that all he had to do

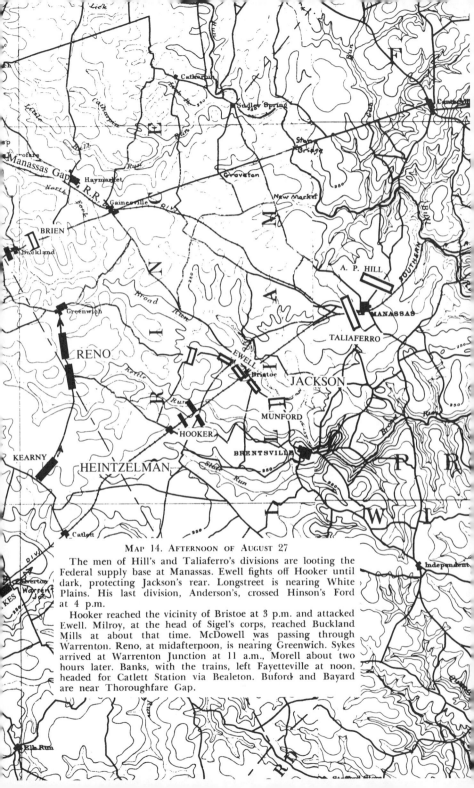

Map 14. Afternoon of August 27

The men of Hill's and Taliaferro's divisions are looting the Federal supply base at Manassas. Ewell fights off Hooker until dark, protecting Jackson's rear. Longstreet is nearing White Plains. His last division, Anderson's, crossed Hinson's Ford at 4 p.m.

Hooker reached the vicinity of Bristoe at 3 p.m. and attacked Ewell. Milroy, at the head of Sigel's corps, reached Buckland Mills at about that time. McDowell was passing through Warrenton. Reno, at midafternoon, is nearing Greenwich. Sykes arrived at Warrenton Junction at 11 a.m., Morell about two hours later. Banks, with the trains, left Fayetteville at noon, headed for Catlett Station via Bealeton. Buford and Bayard are near Thoroughfare Gap.

was converge on the wily Stonewall and "we shall bag the whole crowd"—a phrase that tickled his fancy, for he repeated it in practically all of the messages to his corps commanders that evening.

It would seem from these dispatches that the threatening position of Longstreet's divisions was being overlooked, for no mention is made of enemy troops other than Jackson's. If Pope remembered his morning telegram to Halleck, that Lee's main striking force was marching by the same road that Jackson had taken, and was even then within a few miles of Thoroughfare Gap, it is strange that he would order the whole army to proceed forthwith to Manassas Junction while turning its collective back on the approaching enemy main body.

Pope's last message to Halleck before Jackson's raiders cut the telegraph line was the long telegram of August 25 quoted in Chapter 6. In that dispatch he had admitted his ignorance of the strength of Lee's army, but did indicate that his opponent's intentions appeared to be directed towards his (Pope's) right. The next bit of information came from the train engineer who ran the gauntlet at Bristoe the night of August 26, news that gave no hint of the size or composition of the enemy force on Pope's rear. Then for four days not a word from the Army of Virginia, which first puzzled and then worried Halleck, who was at first not aware that the telegraph line had gone dead at Pope's end.

Pope was a busy general during the last few days of August, as events on the plains of Manassas hastened to a climax. Nevertheless one may be permitted to inquire why it was that communications between Pope's headquarters and the War Department at Washington were not routed through Falmouth when the direct wire through Manassas went out. Fitz John Porter was able to and did send frequent messages to McClellan at Aquia, through Burnside's headquarters at Falmouth, even after he came under Pope's command along the Rappahannock. Pope could have used that channel, with staff improvisation, had he wished. Perhaps it just didn't occur to him.

McClellan Muddies the Waters

Meanwhile, as division after division of McClellan's army was fed to Pope in successive installments from Aquia, McClellan and Halleck continued to bicker, as they had been doing ever since Halleck took over in Washington and began issuing orders to "Little Mac." With McClellan's arrival at Aquia on August 24, the interchange had taken on a different tone, however, for now McClellan saw his army slipping out from under him and wanted to know if Halleck intended to make good his promise that McClellan should command the two armies when they were joined. The war of nerves apparently didn't bother McClellan, but it was beginning to get under the skin of the harassed Halleck, who had plenty on his mind.

From Porter's messages, relayed through Burnside to Halleck and Lincoln, it began to look as though Pope was in trouble. Franklin's corps had reached Alexandria and Sumner's was at Aquia Creek. Maybe Pope would need both. So Halleck invited McClellan to come up to Washington to talk things over. He evidently managed to smooth McClellan's ruffled feathers, because the latter ordered Franklin to move his corps out toward Manassas Junction and summoned Sumner's to Alexandria to be in readiness to follow. Then the little general had second thoughts and regaled Halleck with reasons why both corps should be retained in the Washington defenses. The relationship between the General-in-Chief and one of his principal army commanders had developed owing to Halleck's pussy-footing, which had permitted the problem child to get completely out of hand at a most critical time. Halleck was now so dominated by his recalcitrant subordinate that his words and actions became almost childish. He couldn't seem to make up his mind how to solve what was after all a perfectly simple problem. The obvious solution was to send McClellan with his remaining corps to the theater of operations, take command of the combined armies himself, and make the necessary decisions in the field as required.

LONGSTREET'S MARCH THROUGH THOROUGHFARE GAP

CHAPTER 8

JACKSON OUTWITS POPE

NEWS travels fast through armies in the field; tradi-
tionally the ranks quickly learn through the grapevine
what is transpiring, and guess its probable meaning. The
troops grasped the significance of Pope's withdrawal to the line
of the Rappahannock, followed shortly by a rash of skirmishing
and an exchange of artillery fire between the opposing batteries stationed on either side of the river. Finally came Pope's
order to his divisions to march in the direction of Manassas.
None of this escaped the attention of the men who carried
the muskets; to many of them it brought forebodings.

"Events are fast approaching a crisis in this neighborhood,"
wrote Lieutenant Gillette in a letter to his father, postmarked
Warrenton Junction, Va., August 27, 1862. "The enemy have,
with their usual rapidity of action and daring, completely
surrounded our forces on the front, right and rear; leaving the
road to Alexandria across country the only one open. The

Rebels have burned the bridge in our rear over Broad River, thus cutting off exits that way. A heavy force goes up to dislodge the enemy and make a hole for us to get out of, when Bull Run will be the line of defense."

It was on that same day, August 27, that Pope reached the belated conclusion that enemy interruption of direct telegraph communication to Washington need not prevent him from sending reports to Halleck by way of Falmouth. At 1.0 o'clock in the morning, after a silence of four days, he got off a message to the General-in-Chief, several significant extracts of which are worth quoting:

> The enemy has massed his whole force at White Plains, with his trains behind him. A strong column penetrated by way of Manassas Railroad last night to Manassas, drove off a regiment of cavalry and one of infantry, and I fear destroyed several bridges. My position at Warrenton is no longer tenable. I am now moving my whole force to occupy the line from Gainesville to railroad crossing of Cedar Creek, on Alexandria and Central (Orange and Alexandria) Railroad, ... all forces now sent forward should be sent to my right at Gainesville. Whether the enemy means to attack us or not I consider doubtful . . . . I think it possible he may attempt to keep us in check and throw considerable force across the Potomac in direction of Leesburg. Under all the circumstances I have thought it best to interpose in front of Manassas Junction, where your orders will reach me . . . . You had best send a considerable force to Manassas Junction at once and forage and provisions, also construction corps, that I may repair the bridge and get the railroad trains to the rear.

It is clear from a careful reading of that message that Pope's information of the enemy was accurate in part, but his evaluation of their probable intentions, as of 10 a.m. August 27, faulty. Longstreet's corps was in fact within a few miles of White Plains, between Salem and Thoroughfare Gap, but instead of "a strong column" having penetrated to Manassas, it was Jackson's entire corps, almost half of Lee's army. It was not until that evening that the serious character of the Confederate movements was clear to Pope, at which time he issued orders that expose him as ignoring the opportunity to effectually seal off Thoroughfare Gap and prevent the junction of Longstreet's wing with Jackson's isolated force. Corps Commander McDowell had earlier appraised the situation correctly and sent Ricketts' division to occupy the Gap in time to have forced Longstreet to fight for the privilege of passing through the gate in the Bull Run Mountains. But Pope thought he knew better, failed to approve his subordinate's action, and thus played directly into Lee's hands.

Nevertheless Pope must be credited with reacting promptly and commendably in an effort to meet the radically altered conditions that confronted him. His orders to the scattered Union corps and divisions were based on a positive plan to concentrate against an implied threat to Washington, while at the same time cutting off the retreat of the "strong column" of the enemy at Manassas. The major weakness of his decision was that it rested on a foundation of hasty speculation that was somewhat premature.

The lack of adequate mounted reconnaissance during the past few days was being felt by the Federal commander, who apparently still had much to learn of that art from the Confederates. Pope had sufficient cavalry for the purpose but, in common with many of the higher commanders in the Union armies, either did not understand how to make effective use of the mounted arm, more particularly its great potential for gathering enemy intelligence, or else assumed that horses could keep going indefinitely without adequate care, feeding, and rest. At any rate, Pope was playing it half blind on August 27, making false moves, and heading for disaster.

The first phase of the Second Battle of Manassas had virtually been concluded with Jackson's accomplishment of his initial mission by the destruction of the Federal stores at Manassas and the cutting of the main railroad line in Pope's rear. Hooker's brush with Ewell's division at Bristoe Station was an episode of that phase, but without particular significance other than its effect on Pope, who rated it a successful effort to punish the bold Confederate raiders. The fact was that Ewell had voluntarily withdrawn to Manassas in conformity with Jackson's instructions to avoid bringing on a serious. engagement. The only reason Ewell had been stationed at Bristoe in the first place was to prevent interference with the job of demolishing the base at Manassas, and that condition he had fulfilled.

Pope's presence at Bristoe with Hooker gave him temporarily a front row seat from which he was able to observe to the north, late in the evening of August 27, the huge fires that lit the skies as Jackson's men put the torch to the Manassas stores that they were unable to carry away. By that time Pope had learned that Jackson's entire corps was in his rear and that Lee's army had thus been divided. He then convinced himself that if his army could be concentrated quickly he would be in position by morning to "bag the whole crowd," meaning Jackson, before Lee's main body should arrive.

To the serious student of the battle, who takes the trouble to war-game the campaign, gather up all the threads, and weave a meaningful pattern, the events of August 28 through September 1 appear strangely kaleidoscopic. The freewheeling manner in which Pope whipped corps and divisions back and forth, marching and countermarching in a dizzy whirl, must have seemed to his subordinate generals to have almost nightmarish characteristics.

It is no trick for an able lieutenant to lead a small, well-trained platoon of men in the field, quickly and efficiently, by voice control or simple signals, even in the presence of the enemy. But to try to do the same thing with a large number of army corps or divisions is another matter. It is something of a feat to put even a single division of 10,000 men into motion and cause it to reach its destination on time and in a formation to take on an opponent in combat. To achieve a similar result when one man is directing the movements of half a dozen army corps of several divisions each is no task for an amateur. Nor can even the most skillful general keep changing orders in midstream, as it were, and expect immediate and favorable reactions.

Today's veterans, experienced in the highly developed march techniques of recent vintage, such as the use of route markers, military police, motor patrols, radio contact and hovering helicopters, realize that Civil War communications were primitive by contrast, especially at night. Commanders in those days had to rely for the most part on mounted messengers who, as often as not, were unfamiliar with the country and frequently went astray, losing much valuable time. Pope was overly optimistic in assuming that he could countermand march orders, reverse directions, shift objectives at will, and still exercise close control over large, slow-moving bodies of troops while in motion. The mere fact that he tried to do so, expecting his crude methods to work, was a measure of his logistic immaturity, as well as that of the staff, who seem to have been anonymous, if indeed he had a staff and used it.

If Pope was aware of the importance of that cardinal rule of war known as the principle of simplicity, it evidently escaped his attention as he reeled off his series of successive march orders in frantic efforts to counter the sure, confident moves of that superbly coordinated team of Confederate generals, Lee, Jackson, Longstreet, and Stuart.

Assuming that Pope's corps and separate division commanders all received and complied with the night orders of August 27, the entire army would at daylight August 28 be converging rapidly on Manassas and Bristoe to swallow Jackson's three divisions which, according to Pope, were "between Gainesville and Manassas Junction." And so they were, as a matter of fact, but that was no guarantee that they would stay there to be gobbled up at will.

McDowell's own large corps of 18,500 men, which if effectively employed might have blocked Thoroughfare and Hopewell Gaps, delayed the advance of Longstreet's wing, and quite possibly ruined Lee's whole risky project, was instead directed to form the spearhead of Pope's lunge against Jackson. Pope could just as well have used a part or all of the corps commanded by Sigel, Heintzelman, Reno, and Porter as his attacking force while McDowell fought a delaying action with Longstreet. Instead of that, the whole army was ordered to fall upon Jackson, leaving no one to engage Longstreet.

McDowell's orders called for him to advance from Gainesville on Manassas with his right resting on the Manassas Gap Railroad, and his left "well to the east." Pope wanted McDowell to throw out a kind of net that would block Jackson's expected attempt to get away to the west.

Time was of course the vital element, whichever course Pope adopted. McDowell was certain to be in the unfortunate position of having to expose his rear to one wing or the other of Lee's army. Pope chose to ignore Longstreet and the larger half of the Confederate army, possibly in the belief (as he wired Halleck that morning) that Lee intended to cross the Potomac at Leesburg and therefore posed no immediate threat. There is no doubt that the Union general's mind was centered on bagging Jackson, to the exclusion of any other consideration, but most particularly that pertaining to the capabilities of his major opponent, General Lee.

Fitz John Porter's corps at Warrenton Junction was ordered to make an early start at 1:00 a.m. August 28, to reach Bristoe at daylight, without waiting for Banks corps to replace him as protector of the army trains. Porter was told, however, to send word to Banks, a few miles south of Warrenton Junction, to get a move on, while he marched north to reinforce Hooker for the advance to Manassas.

Reno's corps received orders similar to McDowell's except that his march would be from Greenwich direct to Manassas, while Kearny's division of Heintzelman's corps (the other being Hooker's) was to make a night march from Greenwich and report to Pope by dawn at Bristoe. Since Hooker's division was already there, he received no movement orders.

Pope's instructions to Banks were originally transmitted

to him through Porter, who may or may not have expedited the message, since everything Porter did or failed to do at this time subsequently became suspect. At any rate Pope repeated the instructions in a direct message to Banks on the morning of August 28, directing him to guard well the railroad trains that would all have been run back from Manassas Junction to Kettle Run, where the railroad was obstructed. Pope was going to be sure this time that the elusive Jackson should not add insult to the injury inflicted at Manassas, so he assigned an entire corps to protect what remained of his supplies. And it would appear that a couple of divisions was not too many, judging from the low opinion held by at least one brigade commissary officer in Banks' corps, who wrote home on August 27: "It need occasion no surprise to hear of the capture of a portion, at least, of the trains of General Banks' army. The teamsters invariably abandon their teams in the presence of danger, therefore making it an impossibility to save the train."

Jackson Escapes the Trap

Stonewall Jackson and his three divisions at Manassas were at dark on the 27th in a precarious position, to put it mildly. For most army corps a similar situation would be described as desperate. In two days they had marched sixty miles, on an arc of almost 270 degrees from their starting point on the Rappahannock, reached the virtually undefended rear of the Union army, destroyed its major base of supplies, uncovered the enemy's capital, and cut its communication with Pope's headquarters. Those were the favorable aspects. On the liability side, the rest of the Confederate army, marching to rejoin Jackson, was still 20 miles away. The bulk of Pope's 76,000* men, in a potentially favorable tactical position, was squarely on Lee's axis of advance, fully aware of Jackson's vulnerability

---

*Although Pope may have had 77,000 men a few days earlier, his losses from straggling, and from the fighting in the Manassas area, possibly reduced his available strength.

and confident that this time the elusive fox would be run to ground.

The affair at Manassas had gone off even better than Jackson had hoped, although he knew so well the capabilities of his men and the reliability of his division commanders, Ewell, Powell Hill, and Taliaferro, that it was no surprise to him that the mission had been accomplished so smoothly. Jackson had led them on this perilous adventure with supreme confidence that they could do the improbable. The men had been rewarded by the rich spoils and unaccustomed delicacies with which they had regaled themselves. They also had the extra satisfaction of having again outwitted and discomfited a Union army, this time under a commander who had made himself cordially hated in the South by his braggadocio, but even more by his punitive orders respecting civilians in the theater of operations.

Now it was up to Jackson to get his men out of the predicament which faced them. This would not be easy, for the element of surprise had disappeared. The enemy knew that Jackson was at Manassas with all his divisions, and that he was unsupported. The Federals were certainly not going to sit still and allow Stonewall to retire unscathed at his leisure.

Stuart's cavalry was functioning with its customary facility, watching all the roads radiating from Manassas, reporting Federal troop movements in that direction, and keeping the surrounding country under constant observation. Fortuitously, but not surprisingly for the enterprising Southern horsemen, a mounted messenger from Lee's position on the road to Thoroughfare Gap had successfully ridden through enemy-occupied territory to Manassas to advise Jackson of the progress of the main body. This was vital information, assuring him that Longstreet's corps was following the same route that his own column had taken and was not more than an easy day's march away.

Undisturbed by the certainty that Pope's army, or at least a portion of it, must even now be converging on Manassas,

MANASSAS JUNCTION AFTER JACKSON HAD VACATED IT

Jackson concluded that it would be tempting fate to remain any longer in his exposed position. There was but one sensible thing to do and only one direction to take: retreat along the roads leading north and northwest from Manassas Junction, and hole up somewhere to await Lee's arrival with Longstreet's wing. The only alternative, with but 24,000 men, would have been to attempt to punch his way through Bristoe Station and circle around to the west, in rear of the advancing Federal columns, to join Lee. That however would have the disadvantage of putting even greater distance between the two wings of Lee's army and would probably defeat Lee's purpose of fighting a general engagement with a united army to crush Pope before all his reinforcements arrived. Moreover, Jackson did not know enough about Pope's strength and dispositions to engage in such an uncertain venture.

Confident as always, Jackson had been sending mounted messengers from time to time to keep Lee informed of his position and the results that were being achieved. In none of the messages was there so much as a hint that his corps was in danger or even threatened. Consequently Lee was able to proceed with the execution of his design, with the assurance that his strategy held every promise of success.

The withdrawal of Jackson's three divisions northward from the flames of Manassas on the night of August 27-28 was reminiscent of his famous Valley maneuvers in the spring. With Stuart's troopers remaining behind to complete the work of destruction under orders to follow as rear guard protection for the infantry and artillery, Jackson started his divisions at intervals on three different roads. His plan had been carefully thought out with intent to deceive Pope as to his real purpose. Believing that when the Federals should reach Manassas and find the bird had flown, Pope would conclude that the Confederates had retreated in the direction they had come, Jackson calmly decided to add to Pope's bewilderment by doing the unexpected and adopting a typical Jacksonian strategem.

Three or four miles east of Gainesville, on the Warrenton Turnpike, the small hamlet of Groveton squatted on a crossroad, to the north of which the countryside was covered with groves of trees capable of concealing large bodies of troops. It was there that Jackson planned to hide his three divisions to rest from their strenuous labors and await Lee's arrival by the turnpike. With an eye to a defensive position in case Pope should take it into his head to attack, Jackson liked the looks of the rocky ledge known as Sudley Mountain (or Stony Ridge), that extended in a northeasterly direction about a mile north of Groveton. At its base ran an unfinished railroad that would serve nicely as a front line.

Toward that position Jackson directed his divisions. Taliaferro, accompanied by the corps trains, was sent up the Manassas-Sudley Road, starting sometime before midnight. Ewell moved up the Centerville road, crossed Bull Run at Black-

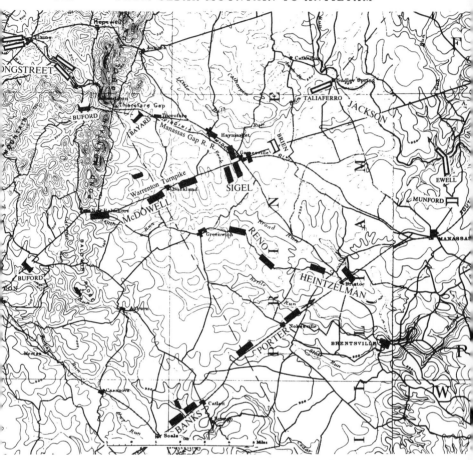

MAP 15. EARLY MORNING, AUGUST 28

During the night Jackson moved nimbly out of Pope's outstretched clutches. His troops are headed for the hideout which he has selected along the unfinished railway embankment (Map 17) north of Groveton. Taliaferro is already there; Hill, having feinted toward Fairfax, is turning west at Centerville, while Ewell is moving north from Manassas Junction. Longstreet is about to leave the White Plains area.

Heintzelman's corps is assembling at Bristoe. Reno is enroute to that point in compliance with Pope's plan to "bag the whole crowd." Porter's two divisions are moving along the Orange & Alexandria R. R. toward Bristoe. Sigel, breakfasting leisurely, does not leave Gainesville until midmorning, thus delaying his own divisions as well as McDowell's. Buford has spotted Longstreet's end run, but Pope apparently doesn't get the word (or doesn't believe what it means), for the cavalry is not operating directly under him.

burn's Ford, thence north along Bull Run, and turned west over the Stone Bridge towards Groveton. A. P. Hill was given the long route, with instructions to march to Centerville to mislead the enemy and throw another scare into Washington, then turn back along the Warrenton Turnpike to wind up at Sudley Church.

Although Jackson's general plan to transfer his corps from Manassas to Groveton accomplished its purpose without the knowledge of or interference by any Federal troops, with habitual reticence he refrained from informing his division commanders sufficiently to enable them to exercise more than a minimum of control beyond starting and stopping. As before Cedar Mountain and elsewhere, much was left to their imagination. Ewell, for example, was merely told that a guide would be furnished to lead him. But when the guide showed up with what appeared to be somewhat vague instructions, he took Ewell's division by a more roundabout road than had evidently been intended, for en route Jackson sent a staff officer to pull Ewell back in the proper direction; otherwise he would have followed Hill to Centerville. As it was, his division had to endure a march that was 6 or 7 miles longer than it need have been. Once again Jackson's reluctance to delegate authority had to be paid for in wholly unnecessary extra effort by troops who were by any standard deserving of greater consideration.

By noon on the 28th Taliaferro was concealed in the woods north of Groveton, and Ewell and Hill were nearing that rendezvous area. The cavalry was screening the movements, as shown on Map 15. Entirely unobserved by the enemy, and well before the converging Federal columns had reached Manassas, Jackson's tired men had gone into concealed bivouac north of the turnpike at Groveton and become lost to view as completely as though the earth had swallowed them up.

Jackson's Strategy

It is doubtful if Napoleon or any of the other great military leaders of history could have met the situation that faced Stonewall Jackson on the night of August 27 any better than he did. If his solution was not a perfect one, the burden is on the dissenter to prove otherwise. Consider the problem. Jackson had completed the first half of his mission, but it would be a hollow success if his isolation from the rest of the army were to pave the way for Pope to defeat the two Confederate wings separately, or to hold Longstreet off long enough to wipe Jackson out. Up to this time all that Pope had lost, other than clarity of strategic vision, were supplies and equipment that the wealthy North could replace from huge surpluses. Lee's major purpose, to defeat Pope in battle before McClellan's large army could join him in its entirety, was yet to be fulfilled. It would be fatal to Lee's hopes were Pope to interpose effectively between Jackson and Longstreet. Much depended on the ability of the Federal commander to take advantage of the golden opportunity afforded him, but of equal importance was the success or failure of Jackson's actions to minimize Pope's efforts to exploit what appeared to him to be the best chance ever offered to bag the elusive Jackson.

A perfectly natural, indeed the logical solution, would have been a rapid withdrawal to rejoin Lee's advancing main body. Certainly that would seem to have been the safest move that Jackson could make. Jackson, however, was not accustomed to think in passive terms, but rather how best to advance the Southern cause aggressively in conformity with Lee's broad plan of action. He did not wish to assume the defensive except to improve his immediate fortunes, yet he was fully aware of his vulnerability and the need for reducing it without impairing too greatly his capability to seize any opening that Pope's movements might give him to attack portions of the opposing army.

The selection of a position north of the Warrenton Turnpike, only twelve miles from Thoroughfare Gap, placed him in close proximity to, although not actually on the axis of advance of Longstreet's corps, and by now not over 5 hours' marching distance from the latter's oncoming divisions. The position was not only adequate for defense in itself, but lent itself admirably to the development of Longstreet's troops, on Jackson's right, with the turnpike as the dividing line, in case Lee should choose to bring on a general engagement in that place. Furthermore, it would serve to extend further the distance that McClellan's divisions would have to march in coming to Pope's aid, and finally, it concealed Jackson's position and intentions while at the same time providing him with an alternative route to retire further, if Lee's advance were unduly delayed, for the separate wings to joins hands by way of Aldie Gap, the northernmost pass through Bull Run Mountains.

Seen in that light, Jackson's solution was the perfect one, and the results to which it led were all that was needed to prove the soundness of his strategic thinking.

Longstreet at Thoroughfare Gap

Longstreet's corps of five divisions, commanded respectively by Major General Richard H. Anderson, and Brigadier Generals Cadmus M. Wilcox, James L. Kemper, David R. Jones, and John B. Hood, had left the Rappahannock on the afternoon of August 26, following the same route taken by Jackson. Longstreet's march was far more deliberate than Jackson's, however, for he took the better part of the two succeeding days to reach Thoroughfare Gap, covering in that time only half the distance that Jackson's corps had marched to reach Manassas in the same period of time.

The Bull Run Mountains, running north and south, are cut by four principal passes, Aldie Gap at the northern terminus, then Hopewell's Gap, Thoroughfare Gap, and the southernmost exit of New Baltimore. The one used by the Confederates, Thoroughfare Gap, was practically a mountain gorge, not long, but several hundred feet high, narrow and winding, with slopes that were rocky and steep. Although its passage could be negotiated swiftly by troops in a hurry, it was conversely susceptible to an obstinate defense by a relatively small force of a division or so, tactically well placed. At the very least the defenders could make it so expensive for even a

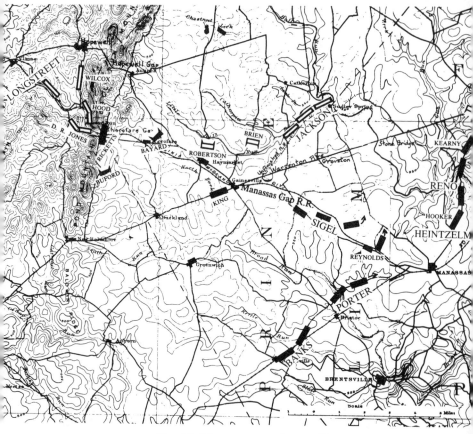

MAP 16. MIDAFTERNOON, AUGUST 28

Longstreet and Ricketts arrived on opposite sides of Thoroughfare Gap about 3 p.m. Longstreet started D. R. Jones' division through the gap, but met heavy resistance. After deploying Hood to the left, abreast of Jones, Longstreet started Wilcox's division toward Hopewell to circle around Ricketts' north flank. At this time Anderson (not shown) is passing through Salem, some 12 miles to the west. Jackson's command is concealed in the woods north of the unfinished railway above Groveton. Robertson and Brien are skirmishing around Haymarket. Fitz Lee is on the Little River Turnpike northwest of Fairfax (not shown) helping support the Federal delusion that Washington is threatened, with a regiment also near Centerville.

Fitz Lee's demonstrations helped fix Pope in his idea that Jackson was still headed northeast. At 4:15 p.m. he ordered his left wing to Centerville. Sigel and Reynolds, who were headed toward Manassas, hearing firing to the north, turned in that direction. King's division of McDowell's corps, bringing up the rear of the long columns coming from Warrenton, is still west of Gainesville, but will soon receive a changed order to continue toward Centerville on the turnpike.

greatly superior attacker that the latter would be likely to seek another and easier route over the mountains even at the risk of losing valuable time.

The leading elements of Longstreet's corps reached Thoroughfare Gap about midafternoon of August 28 to find the pass unoccupied by the Federals. Buford's cavalry had been reconnoitering the roads west of the mountain but had pulled back when McDowell sent Ricketts' division to take possession of the Gap. Even though Pope had disapproved the measure when McDowell first proposed it, the latter, to whose strength had been added Sigel's corps and Reynolds' division, all under McDowell's orders, decided to use his own judgment and sent Ricketts anyway.

As Longstreet approached from the west, Ricketts was belatedly moving in from the east. Receiving word from advance scouts that the pass was clear, Longstreet bivouacked his divisions for the night on the west side of the mountain, sending a brigade from Anderson's leading division to occupy the pass. Ricketts had arrived by that time and was in possession of the eastern exit. Longstreet would have to maneuver or fight, and the latter might promise a delay that could not be countenanced while Jackson remained unsupported.

Longstreet chose maneuver as the quickest and least expensive device. During the night, while the main body rested, General Wilcox with three brigades was sent four miles to the north to cross at Hopewell Gap, while General Hood took his brigades over a trail a short distance south of Thoroughfare Gap. The stratagem worked so successfully that Ricketts, to avoid attack from both flanks as well as the front, relinquished his hold on the eastern exit and by daylight had put plenty of distance between the mountains and Gainesville.

Thus McDowell's wise precaution in sending Ricketts to delay Longstreet and cover his own rear came to naught. Longstreet himself wrote later that if Ricketts' force could have been thrown against Jackson's right and rear instead of marching around him, and the Federals in front of Jackson had cooperated, such an attack, well handled, might have given the Confederates serious trouble before Longstreet reached the field. The flaw in that speculation was that neither McDowell nor Pope had any idea that Jackson was elsewhere than at Manassas Junction. Nor could Longstreet on August 28 have had any conception of the bewilderment into which the Federal commander had been thrown by Jackson's confusing in and out movements.

As Longstreet's troops debouched from the hills and headed down the road to Gainesville on the morning of August 29, still feeling no impulsion to speed because the messages from Jackson breathed a confidence that he was in good shape and fully able to take care of himself, all seemed quiet on the distant plains of Manassas, which were plainly visible as the men wound down the slopes of the mountain into open country. The peaceful quiet of the countryside gave no hint during the early hours of the morning that events were shaping, a dozen miles to their front, that would mean bitter fighting before the sun could reach the meridian.

The Cupboard Was Bare

The movements of the Federal divisions in response to Pope's night orders of August 27 to concentrate in the area of Manassas Junction were slow and uninspired. Much of the inertia was due to the mutual distrust of one another that characterized the relations between Pope and McClellan, whose army was being fed piecemeal to Pope as McClellan bickered with Halleck, Halleck straddled the issue of deciding which of the field commanders was to fight the pending battle, and Pope ran around in mental circles from which emanated hasty orders to all concerned based on incomplete military evaluations. At the very start Pope had irritated his new army by ill-advised, undiplomatic general orders; and his subsequent performance had done little to erase the pronounced unfavorable impression gained by his subordinates, in only a very few of whom, for his part, did he have any real confidence. The right climate for harmonious teamwork was wholly absent, and the fact showed up like a neon light as the Second Manassas campaign moved toward its climax. The army commander had not earned the confidence of his own corps commanders, while most, if not all of McClellan's generals, conscious of the latter's leadership qualifications even though they may not have admired his fighting ability, would naturally be slow to transfer their loyalty and allegiance to an untried leader under the anomalous conditions prevailing at the time.

Looking over the list of Union corps commanders present or on the fringes during the campaign of Second Manassas, there really wasn't much to stir martial enthusiasm. Franz Sigel represented in a sense the Lincoln Administration's concession to the German element in the army, but had little else to recommend him. Banks was somewhat better, but hadn't added anything to his reputation in the conduct of his semi-independent operations in the Shenandoah Valley. Irvin McDowell was the most capable of Pope's three corps commanders, a good solid soldier whose record had been tarnished by the opera-bouffé affair at the First Battle of Manassas, when he was so unfortunate as to be in command of the troops in the defenses of Washington, and was importuned by public opinion and against his better judgment to lead them into action before they had learned what it took to fight a real battle. Now that McDowell was again leading troops on the identical field, the memories of July, 1861 were still fresh in the minds of too many of his men to make them feel securely confident of his leadership.

Of McClellan's lieutenants, Reno and Heintzelman played it straight, conducted themselves in a soldierly fashion and fought their corps bravely. Fitz John Porter, however, a general who was probably as close to McClellan as was Burnside, acted in so cavalier a manner toward Pope, his superior officer, that after the battle he was ordered before a general court-martial and cashiered for failure to move his corps into battle as ordered. The Porter case later became a cause celebré, a subject of controversy for almost a hundred years.* On the written record alone Porter stands convicted on the score of his scathing and open condemnation of Pope and all his works in advance of the battle and on the inescapable fact that his Fifth Corps was held out of action for a long time although he was within short marching distance of the battlefield, received repeated orders from Pope to advance (all other corps commanders received the same kind of orders and obeyed them) to meet the enemy, and was faced with no more obstacles to compliance than were any of the other corps. Pope was later to comment that for his non-action in the presence of the enemy Porter had been likened to Benedict Arnold. Lincoln is quoted as having remarked to an intimate friend his conviction that McClellan wanted Pope to be defeated. Porter was a confidante of McClellan's and one of his favorites. All of which suggests the equation: things that are equal to the same or equal things, are equal to each other.

The darkness of the night of August 27 was one of the ex post facto alibis that Pope employed to explain the slow movements of his divisions toward Manassas Junction, where he hoped and expected to bring the career of Stonewall Jackson to a close. But Jackson's divisions marched unerringly and without difficulty in the same pitch darkness to their rendezvous at Groveton.

It was late on the morning of August 28 when the divisions of Hooker and Kearny reached Manassas Junction from Bristoe Station, to be joined shortly thereafter by Reno coming up from Greenwich. Although McDowell's two corps, his own and Sigel's, were supposed to be the first to arrive, it didn't work out that way, for one reason or another. Why McDowell's force was still at Gainesville is not clear, but it would seem that McDowell either did not act promptly on Pope's order

---

*In 1878, Porter obtained a new hearing before a Board of Officers, who reviewed the case in the light of testimony, including the Confederate reports, that was not available at the time of the original court-martial. The 1878 Board reversed in part the findings of the court-martial and Porter's rank in the Army was restored.

to march with his entire force at early dawn on August 28, or decided on his own to wait until Ricketts' division should return from Thoroughfare Gap. It is more likely, however, that McDowell did not concur in Pope's judgment, feeling that he would serve a better purpose by remaining poised at Gainesville, ready to move to Ricketts' support against the possible threat of Lee's main body following Jackson, or to start late in the opposite direction in compliance with Pope's order. In the light of history, McDowell could have been right, except that battles are not won when corps commanders act unilaterally or in contravention of instructions from their superiors, no matter how incompetent or inept the latter might appear to be.

Pope's arrival at Manassas to find the place empty of Confederates at noon of August 28 must have given him an unpleasant surprise, although he neglected to mention it in his report. Actually Jackson had cleared the area by 2:00 a.m. His reaction, however, was typical of the mercurial nature of his actions and orders throughout the campaign—ill-digested plans put into effect hastily and with the unjustified optimism that his alleged strategy seemed to generate; insufficient consideration of the logistics that army commanders simply cannot afford to ignore; woeful indifference to the necessary details of staffwork essential to proper execution of the army orders by subordinate commanders; thoughtlessly boastful letters to Halleck such as the one in which he had earlier written that he "could easily make the position of Gordonsville untenable." Following that sequence would come a change for the worse in the situation of his army, and then the cycle would start all over again.

The wheel started turning again when Pope reached Manassas and learned that Jackson had departed. Word came in that the enemy had been to Centerville and Groveton but had disappeared. Naturally, thought Pope, the brash Confederate was retreating along the Warrenton Turnpike. Still optimistic that Jackson could not escape him, fresh orders went out at 4:15 p.m., August 28, directing the army to march on Centerville, with McDowell's two-corps force to proceed along the Warrenton Pike. It was to be a kind of double envelopment that would catch Jackson between a Federal nutcracker, each arm of which was superior in strength to the fleeing fugitive.

Stonewall Jackson may only have seemed to possess certain of the qualities of a ball of quicksilver or a Mexican jumping bean, and his reputation for fast marches and deceptive maneuvers may have been merely a figment of the imagination with those hero worshipers who built the Jackson legend. The Unconvinced point to the Battles Before Richmond as confirmation, together with the still unexplained slowness of Jackson's march across Hooker's front at Chancellorsville—9 miles in 6 hours, or a rate of only 1½ miles an hour; and they explain that Jackson covered greater distances in less time than other commands only because he insisted on a ten-minute halt in each hour and could therefore demand, and receive, better results from rested soldiers.

The unbelievers have gone even further to topple Jackson from his high pedestal when they explain that General Bee was referring to Jackson in anything but a complimentary vein when at the First Battle of Manassas General Bee was reported to have rallied his faltering men near the Henry House by pointing to Jackson standing nearby "like a stone wall." On the contrary, they say, Bee was mad as a hornet because Jackson was slow in coming to his support and was heard to remark "Look at Jackson, standing there like a damned stone wall." The reader may take his choice as to which of the stories is correct, but so far as this writer is concerned, Jackson's fame as a general rests securely on facts, not fancies. There was nothing mysterious or mythical in his repeated exploits. He was just one of the smartest and hardest-working generals this country or any other country has ever produced. John Pope was fast finding that out.

THE FIGHT NEAR GROVETON ON THE AFTERNOON OF AUGUST 28—OPENING STAGES

CHAPTER 9

THE FIGHT NEAR GROVETON

UNTIL the late afternoon of August 28 the principal occupation of the more than 100,000 men presently comprising the armies of Lee and Pope had been marching and
bivouacking. For nearly a month elements of both forces had
been maneuvering for position while concentrating for a showdown battle. During that time the fight at Cedar Mountain
provided the only really bloody interlude between spurts of
mobile shadow-boxing. The footwork of the two contestants
in the aggregate had been nothing short of prodigious, but except for Cedar Mountain the casualties had been relatively
light.

The physically harmless phase of the campaign now came
to an abrupt end, as the larger half of Lee's army prepared to
move through Thoroughfare Gap and down the road to Gainesville to join Jackson, and the marching corps of the still
puzzled Pope moved hither and yon seeking the whereabouts
of gadfly Jackson.

Heintzelman's divisions under Hooker and Kearny, together
with Reno's and Stevens', both under Reno, were on the road
from Manassas to Centerville. Sigel's corps and Reynolds' division followed the Manassas-Sudley road. Porter's corps was still
south of the Manassas Railroad and seemingly content to remain there despite Pope's repeated orders to move up to the
Junction. The movements of McDowell's two divisions, King's
and Ricketts', are more difficult to trace, for several reasons,
one being the conflicting successive orders from Pope which
would have had McDowell moving in two directions at once;
the other, the fact that Ricketts' division had gone up the road
to Thoroughfare Gap and then down again, and was now somewhere between the Gap and Gainesville. McDowell himself,
riding alone from Gainesville to Manassas on the night of
August 28 to consult Pope with a view to clearing up the apparent misunderstanding about his corps' activities, managed
to get lost and was unable to recover his bearings until the
following morning.

King's division of McDowell's corps spent the night of
August 27 near Buckland Mills instead of in the Manassas
area, where it was supposed to be. Consequently it was near
the Warrenton Turnpike when Pope's afternoon order of
April 28 arrived to change the point of Federal concentration
from Manassas to Centerville. By pure chance, or perhaps it
should be called mischance, King's division was thus destined
to have the doubtful honor of drawing the first real blood in
the Battle of Manassas.

Jackson Lies in Wait

Carefully concealed in the woods north of the turnpike near
Groveton, Jackson's divisions rested and awaited developments.
Jackson was no longer the fox seeking cover, but more like a
crouched panther awaiting the arrival of its mate and ready to
spring on the back of any living thing that should come too
close to its lair.

The holed-up Confederates had received only a smattering

of information concerning the movements of the Federals which Stuart's troopers were able to pick up by contact. But a Confederate cavalry troop, operating with Taliaferro along the Warrenton Turnpike, captured a courier carrying a night dispatch from McDowell to Sigel and Reynolds that divulged Pope's plan to concentrate at Manassas Junction and furnished detailed information on the routes of the Union corps.

Colonel Bradley T. Johnson, one of Taliaferro's brigade commanders, picketing the side roads leading into the turnpike, collided with Reynolds' division on the Warrenton Pike and a short engagement ensued, with inconclusive results. Reynolds, assuming that Johnson's force was merely a reconnaissance detachment, turned off the road toward Manassas and kept on his way, unaware of the presence of Jackson's corps in the immediate neighborhood.

Jackson had established a temporary command post in the corner of a field not far from the turnpike. Stripped down to bare essentials, as his marauding column had been from the time it left the Rappahannock three days before, there was nothing in evidence to denote a corps headquarters; no train, no camp equipage, no cooking facilities, not even an ambulance—the corps trains and ambulances were parked near Sudley Church, but there was no surplus of baggage.

When Jackson used the word surplus, he meant not only peeling down to the skin, but cutting below the epidermis if that would help speed the march.

Decides to Pounce

Division Commanders Ewell and Taliaferro were close at hand by Jackson's order, so that immediate action could be taken whenever the situation might demand. All three generals were stretched out sleeping in the shade when Stuart's trooper rode up with the captured dispatch late in the afternoon of August 28.

What happened next was strictly in the Jackson tradition and quite different from the sequence of events one might expect from the normal general commanding. Jackson was an individualist who never followed the conventional pattern if a shorter way could be found. Getting to his feet, he quickly scanned the paper, roused Ewell and Taliaferro, and read Pope's dispatch to them.

There was no conference, no discussion on the best course to pursue, no questions asked and no suggestions invited. Jackson's mind instinctively reviewed the pros and cons. To allow King to pass now would be to interpose no opposition to Pope's concentration and might defeat the whole purpose of Lee's campaign. On the other hand, to attack prematurely could bring the Federal swarms buzzing about his ears before Longstreet arrived, and that too would thwart Lee's designs. It was indeed a fielder's choice, but Jackson never hesitated. When in doubt, attack, seemed the wiser course.

With that rapid mental estimate of the situation, almost an automatic reflex as it must have seemed to the two division commanders, Jackson remarked to Taliaferro, "Move your division and attack the enemy." Turning then to Ewell he employed only three words, "Support the attack." The two short sentences were more meaningful to those accustomed to Jack-

---

Map 17. THE FIGHT NEAR GROVETON ON THE EVENING OF AUGUST 28

Toward sunset of August 28, King's division of McDowell's corps was marching east on the Warrenton Turnpike, the four brigades being strung out over four miles. Jackson, concealed in the woods to the north of the unfinished railway, let Hatch's brigade go by, then attacked Gibbon's brigade. Gibbon moved promptly off the road to his left, and for an hour and a half slugged it out with a greatly superior force. He asked for help but got none, except from two of Doubleday's regiments. Hatch, to his right, did not return to see what was going on until the sounds of the fracas died out, while Patrick, some two miles toward Gainsville, (off the map to the left) was held in place by Confederate artillery and some cavalry lurking in the wings offstage. But Gibbon did quite well, with the powerful aid of his artillery battery which he placed on the high ground to his right. The fight, a bloody one, took place around the farm house and orchard of the Brawner farm. The woods through which the Federals advanced are now called Gibbon Woods.

General King, sick and riding in an ambulance (a 4-wheeled hack used by senior officers for personal transportation when they were unable to ride a horse) seems to have taken no active part in the battle, which was ended by darkness. King withdrew to the south during the middle of the night.

For a complete map of the Manassas battlefield see Map 19. The contour interval on this map is 40 feet, except that on significant portions the intervening 20-foot contours have been added to emphasize the ridges and draws.

son's taciturnity than any five-paragraph field order could possibly have been. Taliaferro and Ewell were told what to do but not how to do it. It was unnecessary to indicate the time of the attack, because Jackson was not in the habit of dealing in futures, and it was obvious that the place would be where-ever they found the enemy. Jackson himself would give the signal to launch the attack.

A.P. Hill's division was up at Sudley Church, guarding the Aldie road, and would not be engaged initially. Ewell's and Taliaferro's men were sleeping practically in formation. All they had to do was wake up and grab their muskets. By the time the officers' horses were saddled, long lines of infantry were moving toward the turnpike. When they reached a position in the woods from which to see the road, where they expected to find some trace of the Federals, none were to be seen. It was not until the lengthening shadows foretold the coming sunset that a Federal column was observed marching east in the direction of Centerville.

The Meeting Engagement on August 28

That would be King's division of McDowell's corps, heading for the Federal concentration point at Centerville, where Pope's latest faulty estimate had established Jackson's location. Furthermore, this outfit had fire in its eye, for the men of the Union army were sick to death of marching, marching, marching, and never seeming to get anywhere. Some real fighting would be a change for the better, and King's division was in the mood to mix it up with the enemy at the earliest opportunity. For that purpose at least two of King's four brigades, commanded by John Gibbon and Abner Doubleday, were ably led to carry the burden of the engagement that in the next few minutes would fall to their lot.

Divisions abreast, Taliaferro on the right, Ewell on the left, the Confederates were formed under cover with five brigades in the front line, under instructions to await the signal to attack, while Jackson himself, unaccompanied even by an orderly, rode forward into the open to observe the enemy column. Jackson's utter disregard of personal danger in establishing to his own satisfaction the basic facts upon which to predicate his actions and orders was never better illustrated than on this occasion. He was in high good humor, greatly relieved by the news that Lee and Longstreet would be up in the morning, and quite ready to show his hand to Pope.

Captain W. W. Blackford, an engineer officer on Jeb Stuart's staff, in whom the cavalry leader had great confidence, was for the time being with Jackson's corps in its Groveton hideout after delivering a dispatch from Stuart. Blackford with several companions had visited a nearby farmhouse to refresh themselves with a supply of buttermilk, only to find a couple of flankers from King's Federal division there for a similar purpose. Outnumbered, the Northerners had chosen to surrender. Blackford vividly describes Jackson at this moment:

> Soon after reporting to General Jackson my capture of prisoners and the presence of infantry in large force (Ed. Note: King's division), which information I had gotten from the prisoners, the head of their column appeared coming down the turnpike, with a heavy line of flankers out and everything in compact order. Jackson rode out to examine the approaching foe, trotting backwards and forwards along the line of the handsome parade marching by, and in easy musket range of their skirmish line, but they did not seem to think that a single horseman was worthy of their attention—how little they thought that this single, plainly dressed horseman was the great Stonewall himself, who was then deliberating in his own mind the question of hurling his eager troops upon their devoted heads.*

Hatch's brigade, the leading element of King's division, passed him on the turnpike as Jackson deliberated. He decided to let them pass, presumably to determine the extent of the Federal column, and it was only when Gibbon's brigade hove into view that he concluded the right moment had come.

------

*War Years with Jeb Stuart, by Lt. Colonel W. W. Blackford, C.S.A., c 1945, by Charles Scribner's Sons, New York. Page 120.

Satisfied with his close-up inspection of the enemy column, Jackson galloped back to the woods and informed Ewell and Taliaferro that they were free to attack.

The field for the encounter, north of the turnpike, was generally open, with Brawner's† farmhouse, an orchard, a patch of woods near the farmhouse, a few stacks of hay and a half-demolished worm fence affording the only available cover. The Southerners moved forward rapidly from their ridge position and the Federals, although surprised, just as quickly deployed to meet them. As the two lines approached one another, off to the west puffs of white smoke and the far-off detonation of artillery shells signalled the meeting between Longstreet and Ricketts at Thoroughfare Gap.

The fight between Jackson and King was fairly static, with both lines slugging it out practically toe to toe. Scarcely a hundred yards initially separated the two forces as the determined antagonists shot it out with neither side gaining or losing much distance. The available cover, however inadequate, was used by both sides, but the fighting was concentrated in a relatively small area and for the numbers engaged it was as sanguinary a battle as any that occurred during the war. Neither contestant was willing to call it a day, even when twilight made it almost impossible to see the target. At such close quarters, with no cover, the casualties mounted at a frightful rate, but in the obstinacy and sheer courage which marked the fight, neither side appeared able to gain a decision.

When the fight started, Gibbon had available only a single battery of six Napoleons against ten Confederate guns. Later in the engagement a second Union battery swung into action, doubling Gibbon's fire power to give him a slight artillery superiority, without which it is doubtful that his outnumbered infantry regiments could have held the field against the five Confederate brigades thrown against him. Taliaferro later reported that the Federal artillery was admirably served and "at

---

†Also spelled Browner and Brauner. Also known as the Douglass House.

one time the annihilation of our batteries seemed inevitable, so destructive was the fire."

Neither Side Wins

In several respects the opening engagement of the Battle of Second Manassas near Groveton was unique. Only five brigades, about 4,500 men, of Jackson's wing managed to get into the fight, while less than 3,000 of King's division, chiefly Gibbon's brigade of Wisconsin (soon to be known as the black-hatted Iron Brigade) and Indiana regiments, supported by two regiments of Doubleday's brigade, carried the entire burden for the Federals. The Confederates had the advantage of higher ground from which to launch their attack and, in addition, had time to form for attack on the unsuspecting enemy marching in column along the road and with flankers insufficiently extended to give warning of the concealed Confederates. King had been led by Pope's order to believe that Jackson was at Manassas, which of course did not excuse him from taking more effective precautions in enemy country, so the Confederate attack caught King's men completely by surprise.

Furthermore, the battle was fought in fading daylight, entirely by the troops who made the initial contact. No reserves were thrown in by either of the contestants, which would have been a normal expedient except for the rapidly increasing darkness that caused confusion, uncertainty as to the identity of nearby contingents, and loss of direction on the part of both infantry supports and artillery batteries attempting to shift position. The strange fact was that neither side attempted to execute a flanking maneuver, which would very likely, under the circumstances, have proven decisive for whichever commander had been able to manage it.

Finally, two of Jackson's generals were wounded in the action, Ewell and Taliaferro, which of itself was almost enough to swing the balance in favor of the Federals. They were the two division commanders who shared in the attack, and both were seriously wounded. "Old Baldy" Ewell lost his leg as the result of a shattered knee, was out of action for months, and thereafter had to be strapped to his horse or ride into battle in a carriage.

Aggregate losses exceeded 2,300 men out of about 7,500, an extremely high ratio of almost one-third, the Confederates suffering greater casualties than the Federals. Considering all factors, Gibbon's heavily outnumbered brigade covered itself with glory even though it was unable to claim a decisive victory. But the evidence clearly gives Gibbon the better of the argument, despite the fact that King's entire division, sometime during the night, pulled itself together and, leaving the field to the Confederates, resumed its interrupted march, but toward Manassas instead of Centerville. There wasn't much else for King's division to do, after putting up a heroic fight and suffering approximately 1,100 casualties.

Strategically the honors went to Jackson, who accomplished the purpose of his attack, which was to bring down upon him,

PART OF KING'S DIVISION AFTER THE FIGHT NEAR GROVETON

if possible, the whole of Pope's army in order to involve it in a general engagement before McClellan could join forces. Jackson had timed his successive moves shrewdly. He knew that Longstreet was only a few hours' march behind him and it now seemed tactically safe to show his hand. Jackson knew also that Pope's entire army was searching for him and it was a reasonable assumption that by morning, finally aware of his location as the result of King's battle at Groveton, Pope would throw into battle every division that could be rushed to the scene.

At 10:45 p. m., after the Groveton game was called on account of darkness, King sent off a message to McDowell, which must have reached Pope one way or another. In that dispatch he reported:

> From prisoners taken tonight there is no doubt that Jackson's main force is in our immediate front. Our position is not tenable, and we shall fall back toward Manassas, with the expectation of meeting forces sent to our support.
> If Ricketts should attempt to join us he might be cut off unless he falls back by the way of Greenwich. Prisoners report Jackson has 60,000 or 70,000 men.

In all probability King's warning reached Ricketts in a separate message during the night at Thoroughfare Gap and may even have influenced the latter's action in hastening his retreat after Longstreet maenuvered him out of position and forced him to head eastward on the Warrenton pike; or else Ricketts just naturally swung off to the south and away from the direct road to Centerville to avoid being caught between Longstreet and Jackson.

The interesting aspect of King's dispatch, however, is the Confederate prisoners' report on Jackson's strength. That was typical of the wily Jackson, whose soldiers were trained to feed misleading information to the enemy if captured. The accounts of his battles are full of similar episodes, in which his strength is magnified many times for his own purposes.

Earlier reports than King's on the affair at Groveton had reached Pope at Manassas, but the information was far from complete, for at 10 p. m., August 28, in a long telegram to Halleck, Pope's only reference to King's fight was contained in two sentences:

"Late this afternoon, a severe fight took place 6 miles west of Centerville, which was terminated by darkness. The enemy was driven back at all points, and thus the affair rests."

The message did not reach Halleck until 6:45 p. m., August 29, the following day, indicating how effective was the disruptions in communications caused by the Manassas raid. By the same token, however, it is not too flattering a commentary on the recuperative powers of Pope's signalmen.

McClellan a Dubious Ally

Meanwhile, since he had little else to occupy his attention back at Alexandria, McClellan relayed wild reports and rumors to Halleck in a way that seems almost reprehensible, in light of all the facts. This one was typical:

> Alexandria, August 28, 1862
> 10 p. m.

Major General Halleck
General-in-Chief, U. S. Army

Franklin's corps has been ordered to march at 6 o'clock tomorrow morning. . . .Colonel Waagner, Second New York Volunteer Artillery, has just come in from the front. He reports strong infantry and cavalry force near Fairfax Court House. Reports numerous, from various sources, that Lee and Stuart, with large forces, are at Manassas; that the enemy, with 120,000 men, intend advancing on the forts near Arlington and Chain Bridge, with a view to attacking Washington and Baltimore. I . . . think our fortifications along the upper part of our line on this side of the river very unsafe with their present garrisons, and the movements of the enemy seem to indicate an attack upon these works.

> Geo. B. McClellan,
> Major-General.

McClellan always had a penchant for at least doubling in his estimates the actual strength of the enemy, so it was perfectly natural for him to accept the figures given him as valid, without the slightest effort at verification. But to play the alarmist in such a manner, and on such flimsy evidence, reflects no credit on an officer in his position. One cannot escape the conclusion that McClellan was acting with almost Machiavellian intent in his war of nerves with the harried and indecisive Commander-in-Chief, and in an effort to do what he could with safety to humble his rival, Pope.

Federal Confusion

Pope's field generalship, which had been reasonably effective on the Rapidan and Rappahannock positions, had notably deteriorated as soon as the war of position was changed by Lee's strategy to a war of maneuver. Pope's habit of jumping to conclusions on the basis of insufficient and frequently inaccurate intelligence, together with his consistent wishful thinking, led him to issue a succession of individual march orders to the scattered elements of his army. Thus he had them shifting back and forth until his corps and division commanders must have begun to wonder whether Pope had any idea at all what he was doing. First there was the order to concentrate at Manassas. Next came the change order which made Centerville the objective. And still later he made a shift in the direction of Groveton.

The result was almost universal lack of confidence in the general commanding. Pope himself had only a vague general idea as to the positions of his several corps at any given moment and, conversely, they never knew just where to find him. His troops were leg-weary from marching and countermarching. The Army of Virginia, to put it bluntly, was not in good shape to fight a coordinated battle against an aggressive opponent who knew his business.

The receipt of King's 10:45 p. m., dispatch started again the old familiar cycle in Pope's mind. Jumping to the immediate conclusion that McDowell's corps (King and Ricketts) had intercepted Jackson's retreat and that now he, Pope, had finally pinned the elusive Confederate between two major elements of his own army, Pope lost no time in ordering an early morning attack to wind up the business, as he thought.

Proceeding happily on the assumption that all parts of his army were just where his earlier orders had directed, which unhappily was far from the fact, Pope ordered McDowell's wing (which included Sigel and Reynolds) to hold its ground at all costs to prevent Jackson's retreat to join Lee, advising McDowell that "at daylight our whole force from Centerville and Manassas would assail him from the east, and he would be crushed between us."

Kearny's division at Centerville was ordered to move forward cautiously during the night along the Warrenton Turnpike, drive in the Confederate pickets and keep in close contact with the enemy main body until daylight. At that time Kearny was to make a vigorous assault that would be supported by the divisions of Hooker and Reno.

Porter's corps, which Pope thought was at Manassas Junction, was ordered to move on Centerville at dawn, so that Porter's strength, two divisions made up mostly of Regulars, could be added to the blow to be aimed at Jackson's force in the morning.

That was the night when McDowell was making his personal journey to Manassas to see Pope, who had moved his headquarters elsewhere. As stated, McDowell lost his way in the darkness, and remained out of touch with both army headquarters and the troops under his command, including his own corps (King and Ricketts), Sigel's corps, and Reynolds' division.

Pope might just as well have "shot an arrow into the air" so far as that half of his plan was concerned which directed McDowell from the west to block Jackson's supposed retreat while the rest of the army attack him from the direction of Centerville-Manassas. For there were no Federal troops except Buford's wearied cavalry brigade and Ricketts' retreating division between Jackson at Groveton and Longstreet at Thoroughfare Gap, since the lost McDowell had not received Pope's order and of course could not comply. Finally, since Sigel, Reynolds, King, and Ricketts were a part of McDowell's command, all were perforce obliged to make their own decisions as to what steps to take in the fluid situation, until McDowell should again be in touch with them.

Toward morning of August 29 Pope learned that his plan has miscarried and that the divisions of King and Ricketts were retiring to Manassas Junction and Bristoe respectively. It must have dawned on him that the road which Longstreet would use to join Jackson was now wide open; therefore it would be necessary to defeat Jackson quickly before the rest of the Confederate army completed its advance to reinforce him.

As it happened, Reynolds' division and Sigel's corps were that night south of the Warrenton Pike and not far from Groveton, which fitted nicely into Pope's plan of attack for Friday morning, August 29. Pope thereupon sent supplementary orders direct to Sigel, shortly before dawn, "to attack the enemy vigorously at daylight and bring him to a stand if possible." And to Fitz John Porter, still in the vicinity of Manassas Junction, about 3:00 a. m. went an order "to move upon Centerville at the first dawn of day."

In the welter of messages that Pope so freely dispatched to his subordinate commanders during the hectic rat race by which he desperately sought to counter the Confederate moves, at no time does there appear to have been any carefully conceived or coordinated plan of action. The messages were mostly fragmentary and incomplete, in virtually every case simply directing the corps commanders concerned to march on a designated point at a specified time. If Pope had a definite plan in his mind other than to move enough troops between Lee and Washington to protect the Capital, following the fright thrown into the Federal camp when Jackson interposed his corps in Pope's rear, he failed utterly to transmit it to his generals.

The state of mind of those subordinate commanders is not difficult to imagine. A good soldier is trained to obey orders, but he doesn't have to like them. The army commander had by this time managed so thoroughly to confuse the issue that it became a serious question whether Pope's army would be able to hold together in a serious test of arms, even against an opponent of lesser strength.

JACKSON'S POSITION AS SEEN FROM GROVETON

CHAPTER 10

THE MAIN BATTLE OPENS

TO AVOID the topographical indigestion that might result from an effort to compare the two battles fought at Manassas, or Bull Run, it would be well to exclude for the time being all thoughts of First Manassas, July 1861, particularly the familiar historic place names. While both engagements were fought on the same Plains of Manassas southwest of Centerville, the 1862 battle, once the two armies were locked in combat, was rather less fluid and certainly more professionally conducted than the 1861 encounter.

The stream itself, Bull Run, played a minor role in the Battle of Second Manassas, except as a terrain feature for reference purposes. The 1862 battle was fought six to eight miles west of Centerville and three miles east of Gainesville, astride the Warrenton Turnpike, in the area about Groveton, where the opening engagement between Jackson and King occurred on the evening of August 28.

The battlefield was singularly free of obstruction that might hamper the movements of troops. The gently rolling ground, criss-crossed by a network of roads and country lanes, made it convenient for lower commanders to shift their units about and for the troops themselves to execute their tasks with a better understanding of the purpose.

It is a mark of good generalship when a commander maneuvers his opponent into a position that forces him to fight on terrain chosen by the former. Stonewall Jackson had commanded a brigade at First Manassas and knew the ground well. He also had in Captain Jed Hotchkiss a peerless, indefatigable map maker, and it may safely be assumed that the two of them had not overlooked the matter of topography when they were doing their homework along the Rappahannock earlier in August, in preparation for Jackson's wide sweep to reach his prearranged target on Pope's rear, the Manassas depot.

That however should not have afforded the Southerners any great advantage, for McDowell was in command of the Union forces at First Manassas and it is a fact that Pope, to whom the area was unfamiliar, relied heavily on McDowell's presumed knowledge of the terrain during the second battle. The major difference was of course the relative ability of the opposing commanders to utilize their knowledge to advantage.

It would be interesting to know just when Jackson chose the position north of Groveton to which he adjourned his corps on the night of August 27-28, when Manassas Junction became too hot, literally and figuratively, for him to hold. But, regardless of when the decision was made, he certainly moved to the new area with speed and precision, as though he had long planned it that way and then executed the movement virtually as an automatic reflex.

The position that Jackson selected was an ideal one for the Confederates, from every standpoint. It was not only strong for defensive purposes, but possessed strategic value of vital importance to Lee's whole campaign. For it must be remembered that the success of the Confederate plan depended on bringing Pope to battle before the armies of McClellan and Pope could join forces in overwhelming strength. Examined in that light, Jackson's decisions and actions were admirable in themselves, but even more so in the highly successful way by which they were fitted into Lee's plan of campaign.

Single handedly Jackson had first conducted his 24,000 men on a gruelling sixty-mile march around and to the rear of Pope's army to destroy his base of supply and cut his communications. Then he tarried at Manassas Junction just long enough to fool Pope into thinking that he had the venturesome Confederates in the bag. With exquisite timing, neither too soon nor too late, Jackson next faded back to a concealed position as the Union commander rushed the scattered elements of his army back and forth in a wild fox chase that compounded Pope's confusion and wore down the energy and morale of his equally bewildered troops, while the wily quarry and his own weary men caught up on their sleep in the woods above Groveton.

Still timing his actions on a split-second schedule, Jackson's knowledge that he was in the ideal spot for the purpose, that Lee and Longstreet were by that time only a few hours' march away, and that the time had come to let Pope know where he was so that the latter would do the expected, Jackson attacked King's division of McDowell's corps on the evening of August 28.

It couldn't have worked out better for the Confederates. Call it luck that Pope's confusion and bad guesses prevented McDowell from conceivably ruining the operation for Lee. The point is that Pope *was* confused, McDowell *did* get lost that night, Porter *did* drag his heels, Federal coordination and control *was* deficient. Furthermore, Lee and his principal lieutenants had developed to a fine art the ability to weigh military factors, to appraise the capabilities, probable intentions, and actions of their opponents, and to act quickly and as a rule unerringly on the conclusions to be drawn. It is beside the point that the Confederate moves were so often terribly risky and overly audacious and should by all the rules of warfare have resulted in their own defeat and destruction. For their very boldness and unexpectedness exploited the element of surprise, that most useful principle of war which, when efficiently introduced, could and usually did negate the best laid plans of a less competent but stronger opponent.

The Stage is Set

With the coming of daylight August 29, the Plains of Manassas became the stage for the enactment of another great drama starring the North and the South. All the actors were on hand for the play except Lee and Longstreet, who had been but briefly delayed by the temporary incident at Thoroughfare Gap, which in fact had no ill effect on the Confederate timetable.

Jackson's three divisions, now reduced to about 20,000 men, had resumed their Groveton position, after the surprisingly tough and sanguinary fight with King's Federal division the preceding evening, along the eastern base of Sudley Mountain or Stony Ridge, which extended in a 2-mile long arc to the northeast from the vicinity of Sudley Church to a point on the unfinished railroad north of Brawner's. The Confederate line ran behind the unfinished railroad bed along which Jackson's skirmishers were posted to warn the main body of danger in time for the troops, under cover in the direction of the ridge, to form up for defense or attack.

A.P. Hill's division held the left of the line, its flank strongly anchored on a rocky hill that faced northeast and commanded the road to Aldie Gap. Part of Hill's position included a belt of timber about five hundred yards in width, which afforded concealment but offered a poor field of fire, and to that extent was the weak point of Jackson's position. To offset that disadvantage, Hill's troops were disposed in depth, deployed in three successive lines, with half of the division strength assigned to the third, or reserve line. (Map 18.)

Jackson's center was held by two brigades of Ewell's division, now commanded by Lawton, occupying a single line. Ewell's other two brigades, under Early, were detached to guard the right rear of Jackson's position from a wooded knoll overlooking the Warrenton Turnpike, where they could serve the dual purpose of securing the right flank and watching for Longstreet's approach from Thoroughfare Gap.

Jackson's right, in front of Early, was held by Taliaferro's division, now commanded by Starke, also disposed in three lines with half of the division in the third line.

Overall, Jackson's defensive position was approximately two miles in length, supported by 40 guns, and with both flanks secured by Stuart's cavalry, one brigade being at Haymarket to maintain communication with Longstreet, the other well out toward the enemy to watch the roads in the direction of Manassas and Centerville.

Jackson's mission was now to wage a strictly defensive battle against the vastly superior force that Pope could amass to crush him. The odds that confronted him were terrific; it would take every thing the Confederates had to prevent disaster if the Federals should succeed in exploiting their overwhelming superiority in manpower and artillery. Nevertheless, Jackson's position was a strong one, by nature and troop disposition, for the unfinished railroad afforded a succession of dirt embankments and cuts that were made to order for infantry on the defense.

Pope's Glasses Still Clouded

Pope's third plan to catch Jackson before he escaped, following the abortive lunges in the direction of Manassas and Centerville, both of which were countermanded in mid-air, was as hastily conceived as the first two, and based on equally incomplete intelligence.

Compounded partly of his own lack of judgment and partly of just plain bad luck, the conclusion to which Pope quickly leaped when word arrived of King's fight at Groveton was that the latter had run into the head of Jackson's column retreating on the turnpike in the direction of the Gap. Apparently no other possibility entered the consciousness of his single-track mind; the news seemed to him to confirm the accuracy of his earlier evaluation and he immediately triggered orders for a dawn attack in which McDowell with Ricketts' and King's divisions would prevent Jackson from getting away while the rest of the army demolished him in a converging attack from the east and south.

Pope lacked vital information. McDowell had gotten lost during the night, with the result that Ricketts and King were forced to act on their own. Ricketts' report to McDowell on the action at Thoroughfare Gap disappeared in thin air, and King decided to move on to Manassas, and hence out of circulation, when he found that no one else seemed to care what became of him. Thus McDowell's temporarily leaderless corps, instead of blocking Jackson's supposed route of departure, had vacated the area and removed all possible hinderance to the fast approaching junction between Lee's two wings; for when Ricketts learned of King's departure, it was perfectly natural for him to follow suit, being already on his way in a rather dense fog of war of his own.

So far as Pope's knowledge went, he was all set to achieve his goal of erasing Jackson, who was, he thought, struggling desperately to escape the net. Longstreet must still be west of Bull Run Mountains, and anyway, Pope may have figured that his campaign to date hadn't placed him in too favorable a light in the eyes of the North, and he had better do something worth reading about pretty quickly to remove the possibility that the Administration in their impatience might send McClellan galloping out to take his place.

So the attack orders went out late in the evening of August 28. Sigel's corps of three divisions would attack in conjunction with Reynolds' single division, supported by Heintzelman's two-division corps and Reno's two divisions. McDowell's corps and Porter's, two divisions each, were directed to reverse their direction and push on to Gainesville to make certain that Jackson should not escape. Banks' corps would continue its job of protecting the army trains.

The brief direct order to Porter to change direction and

shoot for Gainesville preceded a lengthier joint dispatch to McDowell and Porter:

> HEADQUARTERS ARMY OF VIRGINIA,
> Centreville, August 29, 1862.
>
> Maj. Gen. FITZ JOHN PORTER:
> Push forward with your corps and King's division, which you will take with you, upon Gainesville. I am following the enemy down the Warrenton turnpike. Be expeditious or we will lose much.
>
> JNO. POPE,
> Major-General, Commanding.

Pope then penned a weird document to McDowell and Porter, that same morning of August 29. Since become famous, or perhaps infamous, as the "Joint Order," its contents raise a serious question as to the state of Pope's mental apparatus at that stage of the proceedings:

> HEADQUARTERS ARMY OF VIRGINIA,
> Centreville, August 29, 1862.
>
> Generals McDowell and Porter:
> You will please move forward with your joint commands toward Gainesville. I sent General Porter written orders to that effect an hour and a half ago. Heintzelman, Sigel, and Reno are moving on the Warrenton turnpike, and must now be not far from Gainesville. I desire that as soon as communication is established between this force and your own the whole command shall halt. It may be necessary to fall back behind Bull Run at Centerville to-night. I presume it will be so, on account of our supplies . . . .
> If any considerable advantages are to be gained by departing from this order it will not be strictly carried out. One thing must be had in view, that the troops must occupy a position from which they can reach Bull Run to-night or by morning. The indications are that the whole force of the enemy is moving in this direction at a pace that will bring them here by to-morrow night or the next day. My own headquarters will be for the present with Heintzelman's corps or at this place.
>
> Jno. Pope,
> Major-General, Commanding.

The order exuded uncertainty and wishful thinking, gave misleading information, directed an offensive while implying that it would end in a withdrawal, and finally closed on the one thing that Pope was sure couldn't be criticized—the occupation of the line of Bull Run. It was indeed a pathetic piece of writing which couldn't help but confirm Porter's already well-established, adverse opinion of John Pope. The order speaks for itself and little purpose would be served by pointing out its obvious defects, misinformation, and omissions.

The receipt of the joint order late in the morning found Porter's Fifth Corps near Dawkin's Branch, a tributary of Broad Run, with twin forks running south from their source just north of Manassas Gap Railroad. Porter had received Pope's earlier message and already reversed his snail-like movement toward Centerville, so that his arrival at Dawkin's Branch placed him about three miles from Gainesville, the objective assigned by Pope.

McDowell had caught up again with his divisions near Manassas Junction, where he discussed with Porter the joint order that had just arrived from the commanding general. It was decided, because of the exhausting marches of Ricketts and King and the latter's fight at Groveton, that McDowell's divisions would follow Porter on the Manassas-Gainesville Road, and so it was arranged.

As the column inched its way toward Gainesville, McDowell rode on ahead to join Porter. On the way a courier handed him two messages from cavalry brigadier John Buford, who had been keeping in touch with Longstreet's advance and was now observing from the vicinity of Gainesville:

> Headquarters Cavalry Brigade
> August 29, 1862. 9:30 a. m.
> General Ricketts:
> Seventeen regiments, one battery, and 500 cavalry passed through Gainesville three quarters of an hour ago on the Centreville road. I think this division (Ed. note: Buford apparently includes Bayard's Brigade in this refer-

ence) should join our forces, now engaged, at once. Please
forward this.

> JOHN BUFORD,
> Brigadier General.

> Headquarters Cavalry Brigade
> August 29, 1862.

(General McDowell):

GENERAL: A large force from Thoroughfare Gap is
making a junction through Gainesville up the Centreville
road with the forces in the direction of the cannonading.

> JOHN BUFORD,
> Brigadier General.

Immediately after reading Buford's informative dispatches,
McDowell joined Porter on a small rise of ground near the
head of the latter's halted column at Dawkin's Branch. The
two generals, looking in the direction of Gainesville, could
see clouds of dust rising above the treetops, a sure sign of
marching troops, and no doubt the advance elements of Longstreet's wing moving east on the Warrenton Pike to join Jackson. No enemy troops were visible in the open country to the
west and there seemed to be no reason why Porter should not
move rapidly forward to strike the marching enemy columns
in flank.

Stuart Employs an Artful Dodge

Stuart's cavalry, according to General Lee's official account
of the situation on Longstreet's front on August 29, reported
that a large enemy force was approaching the Confederate
right flank from the direction of Bristoe, in reacting to which
three brigades under Wilcox—Pryor's, Featherston's, and Wilcox's, were sent to reinforce Jones' division on the right of
the line. Lee added that the supports were not needed, however, since the enemy merely fired a few shots in the direction
of the Confederates and then withdrew. The shots referred
to evidently came from the skirmishers thrown across Dawkin's Branch from Porter's corps.

Stuart's report also mentions the brief but bloodless long-

MAP 18. THE SITUATION UP TO ABOUT 12:30 P.M., AUGUST 29

After the fight with King on the evening of the 28th, Jackson deployed his divisions behind the embankment of the unfinished Independent Line of the Manassas Gap R.R. Along Stony Ridge this made an ideal fortification, for the bank was steep and high for a half mile, being composed of large chunks of rock blasted out, and with a deep ditch in rear from which the earth fill was made. To the immediate north, dense woods afforded excellent cover while the ground to the south was relatively open and gave a good field of fire. The "Deep Cut," 600 yards southwest of where the embankment crosses Sudley Road, was to be the scene of some very heavy fighting. Today this spectacular vestige of an old battlefield is deep in the woods but is still sought out by souvenir hunters, many of whom are equipped with metal detectors. In 1862 the strength of the position must have contributed greatly to the successful Confederate defense, perhaps more than has been appreciated.

Early on August 29 Schurz's division and Milroy's brigade began a series of piecemeal attacks on the left and center, respectively, of Jackson's line, which were repulsed. Gregg's brigade of Hill's division was in position near another railroad cut, which is sometimes confused with the "Deep Cut." While Sigel was making his sporadic assaults in the morning, Reynolds' division and two brigades of Schenck's division are moving westward south of the turnpike. As shown on Map 19, they will soon receive fire from the vicinity of Brawner's farm. This contact will be with the leading elements of Hood's division of Longstreet's command, which is coming up from Thoroughfare Gap. Reynolds and Schenck did not know this at this time.

Jackson has moved Early's and Forno's brigades to the west, across the pike, to watch for Longstreet and block any Federal threat from the direction of Gainesville.

range contact with Porter's corps by a portion of the Confederate cavalry. The cavalryman remarked with obvious satisfaction that, while awaiting the expected approach of the enemy corps, he kept several detachments dragging brush down the road from the direction of Gainesville in a ruse to deceive the enemy. Recalling that McDowell and Porter had observed dust clouds to the west and believed that they indicated the approach of the Confederate main body in their direction, it may well be that Stuart's stratagem proved to be a significant element in diverting an offensive Federal move on the southern flank.

In any event, the actions of both McDowell and Porter were definitely influenced by the signs of dust. Ex post facto, the stories told by McDowell and Porter differed materially from what they had agreed upon at their conference. McDowell, who was senior to Porter, later testified that he directed Porter to advance to the attack at once, and that he would lead his own corps directly north on the Sudley Springs Road, to add his strength to the battle that had been raging intermittently beyond the turnpike for some hours between Jackson and the Federal divisions under Sigel and Reynolds.

It is important, in light of the subsequent court-martial which found Porter guilty, to note that the conference between McDowell and Porter at Dawkin's Branch took place late on the morning of August 29, when Longstreet's wing was coming up on the Warrenton Turnpike, Jackson's right flank north of the pike was in the air until Longstreet deployed, and for the time being a terrain vacuum existed that Porter's corps was in position to fill if he had done nothing more than briskly obey Pope's order to move on Gainesville.

Violent Clashes

Pursuant to Pope's orders, shortly after sunrise Sigel's corps on the right, with Reynolds' division on the left and somewhat to the rear, deployed for action as the Federal artillery opened on Jackson's stronghold along the unfinished railroad northwest of Groveton. As the Union skirmishers marched warily forward, Jackson's troops also moved up to their firing positions, to await the attack. For several hours the Federals jockeyed for position but, except for a succession of sharp skirmishes, a large-scale attack was held up until the leading divisions of the Union corps of Reno and Heintzelman, Reno's own and Kearny's, could come up to extend the line to the north in the direction of Bull Run and Sudley Church. The delay was of incalculable advantage to the Confederates, for whom every hour of additional time brought that much closer the fortunate moment when Lee's army would be reunited on the field of battle.

Pope established his field headquarters at noon on Buck Hill, a short distance north of the Warrenton Turnpike–Sudley Springs crossroad, from which eminence his field of vision included a large part of the battlefield. The situation looked good to the army commander, who had, as he thought, issued orders that would soon result in a happy solution to the problem that had been vexing him for several days. So far as he knew, Longstreet was still far removed and, if his divisions acted expeditiously, the firm of Jackson and Company would shortly be dissolved.

By early afternoon the Federal divisions assigned to this zone were all up, dispositions for battle completed, and the troops ready to engage in the serious fighting that Pope had hoped would begin at daybreak. Kearny and Hooker of Heintzelman's corps held the right of the line. Behind Hooker was Reno, then Sigel's corps astride the turnpike, and on the extreme left stood Reynolds, south of the Warrenton Pike and southwest of Groveton.

Sigel held the center of the line. His men had been involved during the morning in sporadic but fairly severe fighting, carrying out Pope's instructions to hold Jackson in position till Heintzelman and Reno could reach the scene from Centerville. Reynolds' division, operating on Sigel's left, about 1:00 p. m. was briefly in contact with Longstreet's leading elements without realizing they were from Longstreet's wing, following which he moved back to Chinn Ridge.

Reynolds was in a state of some uncertainty as commander of an independent division attached to McDowell's corps. Theoretically he was acting under McDowell's orders, but that peripatetic general seemed to be all over the field, hard to locate, and apparently acting as Pope's roving deputy-at-large, without a recognizable portfolio. A message that Reynolds sent to Pope's Chief of Staff, Colonel Schriver, at 3:30 in the afternoon, shows how far communication and control had deteriorated:

> Colonel: General Sigel is moving on Gainesville down the pike, with my right near Groveton. My left toward the railroad.
> I do not know where anybody is but Sigel. Please let me hear from you.
>
> John F. Reynolds,
> Brigadier-General, Comdg.

Two of Sigel's divisions (his corps was composed of three divisions under Schenck, von Steinwehr, and Schurz, with Milroy's independent brigade attached) bore the brunt of the morning attacks over a broad front, and were roughly handled by the defending Confederates, protected as the latter were by the railroad cuts and embankments. Never a particularly aggressive fighter, Sigel's customary procedure seemed to be to look for reasons why immediate battle for his troops should be deferred. This time he had no choice in the matter, but true to form reported to Pope, about noon, that his line was weak, Schurz' division and Steinwehr's had been badly cut up, and ought to be pulled out of the line to recover. Pope was aware that Sigel was a weak reed and could not be strongly relied on, but without any other troops at hand there were no replacements, so Sigel was told to stay put. Feeling perhaps that his subordinate's morale could stand a little boosting, Pope confidently informed him that McDowell and Porter were even then moving in on Jackson's right flank (which of course was premature and inaccurate despite Pope's orders), and would quickly relieve the pressure on Sigel. That was pretty helpful medicine, thought Pope, who then rode the line to pass the same good word on to Reno and Heintzelman.

Jackson Takes Punishment

From about 1:30 to 4:00 in the afternoon, Pope's divisions launched piecemeal but vigorous attacks against Jackson's intrenched position all along the line. Artillery roared continuously and there was scarcely a time when an infantry attack was not in progress at one point or another. Yet there was no directing genius to coordinate the brave but successive advances of the Union divisions, or to take advantage of any favorable opportunity which might offer, as would certainly have been the case if Lee, or Jackson, or Longstreet had been directing the Federal effort in place of Pope.

In fairness to Pope it may be contended that his battle plan was sound enough had it been properly executed. Pope could say that the frontal attacks by Sigel, Heintzelman, and Reno were directed as a pivot for the purpose of fully occupying the attention of Jackson's corps, which Pope believed to be the only force at that time on the field, while the corps commanded by McDowell and Porter represented the maneuvering mass that was ordered to press the attack against Jackson's flank to assure the victory.

That was fine on paper, except that it underestimated the ingenious battlefield capabilities of Lee and his chief lieutenants, allowed no margin of safety in case any part of the plan failed to work, and completely overlooked the necessity of using the auxiliary arm, the cavalry brigades of Buford and Bayard, for close-in reconnaissance and counter-reconnaissance when the two armies met on the battlefield. Even after giving the devil his due it must be concluded that Pope himself has to bear the major responsibility for the Union defeat at Second Manassas, with however a very powerful assist from a reluctant corps commander by the name of Fitz John Porter. All of which is getting a bit ahead of the story while forming impressions

MAP 19. SITUATION FROM 2 TO 5 P.M., AUGUST 29

By 2 p.m. Schurz's two brigades, which had been making piecemeal attacks, were exhausted and were pulled out of line. Hooker's division, moving west from Centerville, is coming in to relieve Schurz, while Hatch (King's division) and Ricketts are marching up from Manassas. At 3 p.m. Grover's brigade of Hooker's division is ordered to attack in conjunction with Kearny. Grover makes the attack on time, but Kearny does not move until after 5 p.m. Nevertheless Grover succeeds in penetrating Lawton's line at "The Dump"—a 50-yard gap in the embankment. After forcing his way through two of Jackson's lines, Grover is forced by Confederate reserves to withdraw, having lost heavily.

In the center, Reynolds and Schenck are aware of the threat in their front near Brawner's, and are withdrawing, Reynolds to Chinn Ridge.

Longstreet, having learned of the presence of a Federal unit of unknown size (Porter) to his right front, has moved Wilcox's division to strengthen his south flank.

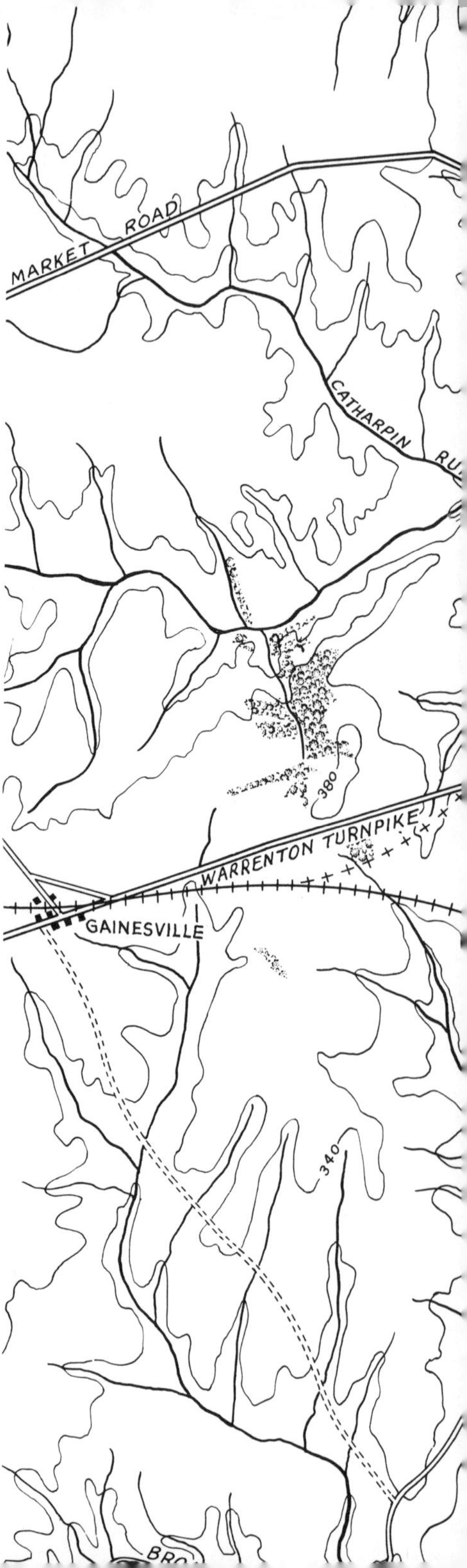

that cannot help but force themselves on one's consciousness as the play progresses.

With three full corps, reinforced by a separate division plus an independent brigade, in line from Bull Run on the right to a point half a mile south of the turnpike and about a mile west of Groveton on the left, Pope's attacking line covered a good three miles of front with a strength of about 33,000 men. The line paralleled Jackson's along the unfinished railroad and overlapped it slightly at either end. The Federal offense therefore mustered twice as many men as Jackson had available to stave them off, but Pope would need the additional 26,000 of McDowell's and Porter's corps if he was to have any success in dislodging Jackson's obstinate fighters.

Pope in person took command of his army for the afternoon phase on August 29. The possibility of turning Jackson's left in conjunction with McDowell's expected flank attack on the Confederate right prompted him to order Heintzelman to make an all-out effort, since Sigel's hand had been played out in the center without result, although one of his attacks through a patch of woods had created a temporary gap in the Confederate line which the Federals were unable to exploit. Reno was directed to attack concurrently on his front, while Sigel would be given a respite for the time being.

A.P. Hill's Light Division, which held the left of Jackson's position, was one of the best, if not the best fighting division in the entire Confederate Army. It would need all its courage and determination this day to withstand the violent attacks made on it by the divisions of Kearny, Hooker, and Reno. Fortunately for the fiery Ambrose Hill, the Federal divisions made their attacks successively, a tactical defect which one might suppose to have been a military policy of the Federal corps and army commanders, judging from the consistency with which they adhered to that policy in so many battles during the first half of the war.

The intention however had been for all three divisions, Kearny, Hooker, and Reno, to attack simultaneously, which in a sense contravenes the statement made in the preceding paragraph. But something more positive than intentions is necessary to put driving force into the unpleasant task of marching troops into a hail of antagonistic shells and bullets. It was the higher command echelons, superior to the individual division and brigade commanders, which somehow failed to provide the essential ingredient of minute-by-minute coordinating control on the battlefield.

Jackson's massed artillery on the north flank poured a galling fire into Kearny's division on the right, to prevent his advance, while Hooker and Reno moved disjointedly but impetuously into the attack, the Confederate skirmishers falling back rapidly to the railroad embankment as the Blue masses pushed resolutely forward through the underbrush.

Hill's veterans met them with heavy volleys of musketry that set fire to the dry underbrush, but still the determined Federals came on, in spite of losses. This was Hooker's division, and "Fighting Joe" was at his best as a division commander. The no-man's land between the two forces quickly disappeared as the on rushing brigades ate up the intervening distance to engage in hand-to-hand combat. A gallant Federal charge penetrated Hill's line, took possession of the railroad at that spot, and drove the Confederates out. But only for a moment. Then the defenders' second line came forward at a run and it was the Union's turn to retire. Hooker's men fell back, re-formed, and again rushed forward to repeat their earlier success. Once again Hill's supports drove them out, and so it went at close quarters for some time.

Inevitably, when a supposedly irresistible force meets an immovable body, the mobile element loses out, and so it was with the stout-hearted brigades of Hooker and Reno. Despite the protecting railroad embankment for the Confederates, and the rolling ground which afforded partial cover for the advancing Federals, the slaughter was terrific on both sides and could not be sustained indefinitely. The local victory would fall to that commander who would throw in his last reserve at

WHERE GROVER ATTACKED

In 1863 Union soldiers find the unburied skeletons of Grover's dead in front of "The Dump," the opening in the unfinished railroad embankment which the brigade penetrated on August 29, 1862.

the psychological moment. That commander was the red-haired, red-shirted Hill, and his ace-in-the-hole was Pender's brigade, which crossed the railroad and hit Hooker's weary men at an angle that sliced through the ranks with sufficient fresh force to turn the tide. The still unwounded Federals broke for the rear.

But Hooker also had an unused reserve, Grover's brigade, which he now threw into the swirling fight. Grover had been watching the battle all along and done some thinking. When his turn came, he told his men to advance at a walk until the Confederates opened fire, when they would make one rush, halt and deliver a single volley, and then cover the remaining distance in a second rush to drive the attack home with the bayonet.

Grover had already formed four of his regiments in two lines, with the fifth in the lead, and had reconnoitered the ground over which he was to advance. His direction of attack ran through a copse into a 50-yard gap in the railroad bank, called "The Dump." One volley, one irresistible rush, and Grover's force poured through The Dump and into the woods beyond. They kept right on going, and Lawton's second line at that point was swept away. The Confederates were in real trouble, but help was at hand. Stonewall Jackson, who always seemed to see what was going on, observed the impetuous Federal charge and took prompt steps to neutralize it. Pulling a brigade from another part of the line nearby, which was not in action at the moment, he threw it at the victorious Federals and the extra weight of the fresh troops in turn caught Grover's men in the flank. It was more than they could manage, weakened as they were by heavy losses sustained in the assault. Grover fell back, fighting gamely, through the woods, and rejoined his division, leaving 25 percent of his men on the field as casualties.

The fighting spirit of the men of both sides had been deeply stirred in this first major clash of the Manassas battle that involved large forces of either army. Memories of First Manassas played a part, undoubtedly, for many of the officers and men had fought over this same ground in July 1861. There were old scores to be paid off; the Federal troops animated by the urge to erase the memory of the wild panic that had seized so many of the raw Union levies in their first defeat of the war; the Confederates equally determined to show that they could repeat the performance. It was a knock-down, drag-out affair from beginning to end, lasting from mid-morning to dark, up and down the line, in fragmentary encounters without at any time developing into a general engagement involving all the troops in contact.

The casualty lists grew longer by the hour, but neither side showed the slightest evidence of giving up. Dead bodies cluttered the railroad bed where the close-in encounters mostly took place. The afternoon phase was mainly A.P. Hill's battle, with assists when needed from Lawton's (Ewell's) neighboring division, for it was on Hill's front that the driving attacks

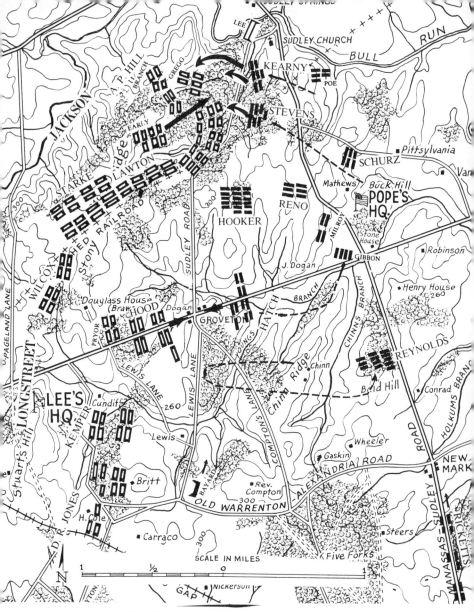

MAP 20. SITUATION FROM 5 TO 8 P.M., AUGUST 29

About 5 p.m. Kearny and Stevens made a heavy attack on the left of A. P.
Hill's division, bending it back on the center. Hill, assisted by Early's brigade,
succeeded in restoring his line, but he had a close call. By nightfall his troops
were in their former positions. At the same time, Reynolds again advanced
westward but by 7 p.m. had once more pulled back to Chinn Ridge and Bald
Hill. Meanwhile McDowell's corps continued to advance north on the Manassas-
Sudley Road. Pope, imagining that Jackson was in retreat, ordered the leading
division of McDowell's corps. Hatch's, to hasten west along the turnpike in
pursuit. Hatch lost no time; he collided east of Groveton with Hood, ordered
by Longstreet to move east along the pike. Darkness ended the resulting bitter
fighting. To the south, Porter (see Map 19) is still static near the head of
Dawkins' Branch.

by Hooker's and Reno's divisions were directed. The Light Division had lost heavily; thousands of its members were down to their last cartridge. Federal marksmen from wooded cover kept up the firing pressure unceasingly so that resupply of ammunition was a hazardous undertaking.

At 4 o'clock, almost as though by unanimous consent, occurred a lull in the booming of artillery guns and the clatter of musketry fire that had been practically continuous for more than six hours. But not for long. Pope had ordered a fresh attack by Kearny and Reno, again directed against the left of Jackson's line where Hill's undefeated but badly depleted Light Division had already withstood the driving attacks of Hooker and Reno. Five Federal brigades, shoulder to shoulder, charged through Confederate gun fire, captured the railroad in their zone, and pushed Hill's exhausted men steadily backward several hundred yards within their own lines. The critical moment had arrived; Jackson's line was bent back on the center; if supported in depth the Federal attack could be decisive.

Sometime earlier the brigades of Early and Forno, of Lawton's (Ewell's) division, posted on the extreme right of Jackson's line near the Warrenton Turnpike, had been relieved of their vigil by the arrival of Longstreet's leading division. They had then rejoined their own outfit in the center and were ready for business. Jubal Early seemed marked by destiny to be Johnny-on-the-spot at critical junctures, particularly when a counter-attack was called for. His troops had turned the trick at First Manassas; and now they would do it again.

Summoned by the hard-pressed Hill in a desperate effort to stave off disaster, Early's reinforced brigade came charging through the weakened Confederate line with leveled bayonets. Kearny's Federals had by this time lost some of their impetus and cohesion. These fresh, determined, onrushing Confederates threw the Union troops into confusion, cold steel had its customary effect on morale, and the attackers turned about and fled to shelter, with Early's avengers in hot pursuit.

The final Federal attempt to break Jackson's line had failed as did the first four. Pope made no further effort on August 29 to destroy Jackson, and the battle ended on that front with both Federals and Confederates occupying the same general positions between the turnpike and Bull Run each held when the serious fighting had started early in the afternoon.

Meanwhile, King's division of McDowell's corps, now commanded by Brigadier General Hatch (King was still sick and had to be relieved), had completed its march up the Sudley road from Manassas Junction and was led into the line on Reynolds' left. As they were taking position, however, McDowell pulled them out, having just received a message from Pope that the enemy was falling back and he wanted Hatch's division to pursue down the Warrenton Road. The day was almost spent, but the division responded enthusiastically, quickly got under way, and ran smack into a reconnoitering Confederate column (one of Longstreet's divisions) coming from the opposite direction. Both outfits were somewhat surprised at the unexpected meeting. They engaged in a spirited and extended exchange in the gathering dusk and then called it off for the day. Ricketts' division, following in trace of Hatch, was assigned to a position in reserve, north of the turnpike, as Hatch, after his brush with the enemy, moved into the Union line on the left of Sigel's corps.

Most of the fighting on the 29th was north of the turnpike between Jackson's corps on the one side and the Union corps of Sigel, Reno, and Heintzelman on the other. Both armies lost heavily in killed and wounded, but neither could claim a victory, although Jackson was clearly entitled to the honors of the day for having maintained his position in the face of repeated and heavy Federal attacks. Now he was no longer isolated and alone, for Lee and Longstreet had arrived on the field along toward noon, when Longstreet's divisions, as they came up, filed off the road in successive increments and were fed into an extension of Jackson's line, astride the turnpike and to the south of it.

Pope Still in the Dark

Pope, wholly unaware that Lee's army had been reunited and now confronted him in its entirety, and still operating under the delusion that only Jackson's wing opposed him, was as determined as ever to knock him out by means of the flank attack that he had earlier in the day directed Porter and McDowell, working together as a unit, to mount.

In pursuit of that objective, the hopelessly optimistic commander of the Army of Virginia sent Porter this order:

> HEADQUARTERS IN THE FIELD,
> August 29—4:30 p.m.
>
> Major General Porter:
> Your line of march brings you in on the enemy's right flank. I desire you to push forward into action at once on the enemy's flank, and, if possible, on his rear, keeping your right in communication with General Reynolds. The enemy is massed in the woods in front of us, but can be shelled out as soon as you engage their flank. Keep heavy reserves and use your batteries, keeping well closed to your right all the time. In case you are obliged to fall back, do so to your right and rear, so as to keep you in close communication with the right wing.
>
> John Pope,
> Major-General, Commanding.

Unfortunately for Pope's hopefully ambitious plan, Porter's corps was not where he thought it was, advancing steadily on Gainesville, but instead was halted in place, still east of Dawkin's Branch, doing nothing much but marking time where it had been all day. Porter himself was back at Bethlehem Church, near the tail of his column and not much over a mile west of Manassas Junction. It was about 6:30 p.m. when he received the above message, rather late in the day to initiate an attack under the circumstances as Porter understood them. Nevertheless, and probably chiefly for the record, he ordered Morell's division to prepare to attack, but cancelled the order as soon as he found that the entire division was ready to move.

The messages sent to Morell were couched in language that could hardly be said to breathe a martial ardor; on the contrary they were wholly defensive in language and intent, and clearly reveal Porter's purpose to "let George do it":

(Received by Morell about sunset August 29, 1862)
General MORELL:

I wish you to push up two regiments, supported by two others, preceded by skirmishers, the regiments at intervals of 200 yards, and attack the party with a section of a battery opposed to you. The battle works well on our right, and the enemy are said to be retiring up the pike. Give the enemy a good shelling when our troops advance.

F. J. PORTER,
Major-General, Commanding.

To Morell:

Give the enemy a good shelling without wasting ammunition, and push a party over to see what is going on. We cannot retire while McDowell holds his own.

F. J. P.
August 29, 1862.
(Received about dusk)

General MORELL:

Put your men in position to remain during the night, and have out your pickets. Put them so that they will be in line, and on rising will be in position to resist any attack. I am about a mile from you. McDowell says all goes well, and we are getting the best of the fight. I wish you would send me a dozen men from that cavalry.

F. J. PORTER,
Major-General.

Keep me informed. Troops are passing up to Gainesville, pushing the enemy. Ricketts has gone; also King.

The Pope-Porter Controversy

The case of Pope versus Porter is an interesting story that would take half a dozen chapters to tell. All the details were aired during the subsequent court-martial trial in November, 1862, which found Porter guilty of disobedience of orders and cashiered him out of the Army. Suffice it to state that Porter had a very low opinion of Pope, expressed himself freely on the subject in letters to McClellan and Burnside while he was under Pope's command, and gave only lip service to the latter's orders from the time he was detached from the Army of the Potomac for service with Pope's Army of Virginia. On the other hand, Pope's orders to Porter on April 29 were written without knowledge of the true situation on Porter's front. Longstreet's wing had moved into position in front of Porter, but Pope didn't know then that Longstreet had arrived, and assumed that the road to Gainesville was open and Porter was simply reluctant to act.

Porter's contention was that Pope's orders called only for McDowell and himself to advance on Gainesville, establish contact with the three corps moving on the same objective along the Warrenton road, and halt for further orders; and that the instructions were based on the assumption that Jackson was retreating and Longstreet had not arrived. The fact that the last two assumptions were both incorrect, in Porter's opinion exonerated him from culpability, for he maintained that Longstreet's whole corps was in fact then in position and greatly outnumbered him, particularly after McDowell took his corps up the Sudley road in a modified compliance with Pope's evident wishes.

The controversy is somewhat beclouded by varying reports as to the actual hour when Longstreet's divisions filed on the field to connect with Jackson's line on the turnpike. Confederate testimony is to the effect that the head of the main body reached Groveton at 10:30 o'clock, which would mean that a minimum of two additional hours must have elapsed before the following divisions, even in part, had closed up, moved off the road and advanced in line to the ridge position indicated.

Every corps of the Army of Virginia except Porter's responded with alacrity to the opportunity to finally close with the foe. The mere fact that Longstreet's column was advancing doesn't exonerate Porter from the charge that he made no effort whatsoever to even find out by a reconnaissance in force whether his fears were well founded or groundless, but supinely sat on his hands east of Dawkin's Branch, with only a handful of skirmishers on the west side of the stream, and permitted the Confederates to occupy the key position south of the turnpike without the slightest effort to beat them to it.

Unfortunately for Porter's reputation as a soldier, his dispatches to Burnside at Fredericksburg, during the very time that his orders called for his advance into action, reveal his attitude of mind. The messages that follow seem almost to chortle with delight that Pope had gotten himself into difficulty, and apparently assume that Burnside would feel the same way about it. But they are not likely to prejudice the average reader in Porter's favor any more than was the case with the members of the courtmartial who later tried and found him guilty.

FALMOUTH, VA., August 29, 1862—5:15 p.m.
General H. W. HALLECK, General-in-Chief:

The following message has just been received (from General Porter):

Bristoe, August 29, 1862—6 a.m.
General Burnside:

Shall be off in half an hour. The messenger who brought this says the enemy had been at Centreville, and pickets were found there last night. Sigel had severe fight last night; took many prisoners. Banks is at Warrenton Junction; McDowell near Gainesville; Heintzelman and Reno at Centreville, where they marched yesterday, and Pope went to Centreville with the last two as a body guard, at the time not knowing where was the enemy and when Sigel was fighting within 8 miles of him and in sight. Comment is unnecessary. The enormous trains are still rolling on, many animals not having been watered for fifty hours. I shall be out of provisions tomorrow night. Your train of 40 wagons cannot be found. I hope Mac is at work, and we will soon get ordered out of this. It would seem from proper statements of the enemy that he was wandering around loose; but I expect they know what they are doing, which is more than any one here or anywhere knows.

Just received the following order:

Headquarters Army of Virginia,
Near Bull Run, August 29, 1862.

Major-General Porter:

General McDowell has anticipated (intercepted) the retreat of Jackson. Sigel is immediately on the right of McDowell. Kearny and Hooker march to attack the enemy's rear at early dawn. Major-General Pope directs you to move upon Centreville at the first dawn of day with your whole command, leaving your trains to follow. It is very important that you should be here at a very early hour in the morning. A severe engagement is likely to take place and your presence is necessary.

GEO. D. RUGGLES,
Colonel and Aide-de-Camp.

A large body of enemy reported opposite. I am preparing and will hold the place (Fredericksburg) until the last. The only fear I have is a force coming from Manassas Junction.   A. E. BURNSIDE,
Major-General.

FALMOUTH, VA., August 29, 1862—1 p.m.

Maj. Gen. H. W. HALLECK, General-in-Chief, and
Maj. Gen. GEORGE B. McCLELLAN, Alexandria:

The following just received from Porter, 4 miles from Manassas, the 28th, 2 p.m.:

All that talk of bagging Jackson, &c., was bosh. That enormous Gap (Manassas) was left open and the enemy jumped through, and the story of McDowell having cut off Longstreet had no good foundation. The enemy have destroyed all our bridges, burned trains, &c., and made this army rush back to look after its line of communication and find our base of subsistence. We are far from Alexandria, considering this moving of transportation. Your supply train of 40 wagons is here, but I can't find them. There is a report that Jackson is at Centreville, which you can believe or not. The enemy destroyed an immense amount of property at Manassas—cars and supplies. I expect the next thing will be a raid on our rear by way of Warrenton by Longstreet, who was cut off.

F. J. Porter,
Major-General.

This is the latest news.

A. E. BURNSIDE,
Major-General.

STARKE'S BRIGADE FIGHTING WITH STONES NEAR THE DEEP CUT

CHAPTER 11

LEE'S ARMY IS REUNITED

LEE'S battles had in common one significant characteristic that was strangely lacking on the part of most of his opponents. That was the mobility of his army, an expression of the commanding general's uncanny, almost instinctive ability to maneuver his divisions in such a way as to have them in the right place at just the right time to make their presence felt most effectively. That same trait was one of the secrets of Napoleon's victories, but Lee repeated the performance so often and with such uniform success that it is a question whether he may not have surpassed the great Corsican at his own game.

Time and space factors were available for adaptation by all generals, not many of whom, however, were so fortunate in execution by their subordinates as Lee. The complete and mutual understanding that existed between Lee and his chief lieutenants was a unique requisite to the effective application of the time and space factors; with it Lee mastered the art of shifting his corps and divisions with a strategic competence that made his Federal opponents appear as rank amateurs.

Not often was his supreme confidence in Jackson, Long-street, and Stuart misplaced. Their individual capabilities, widely as their characters and personalities may have differed, when added to the superb leadership of Lee himself, combined to generate a mighty force that has few parallels in warfare. Without that combination, Lee's stature as a field commander could scarcely have risen to the eminence associated with his name.

Lee knew his generals like a book, their strong and weak points, and every facet of their characters, as well as the most effective way to adapt their several characteristics to his own plans. They in turn had learned to respect and admire him as a man and leader, whose judgment could be relied on and who exercised his authority with supreme tact and consideration. Such a team was a tough combination to lick, as one Union general after another had learned to his sorrow and humiliation.

A Risky Confederate Venture

Lee's plan of campaign, that led to Pope's disaster at Second Manassas, was unbelievably bold; could even be called a reckless adventure that offered only a slim chance of success. Yet it was well on its way to fruition as Jackson completed its first phase by throwing Pope into a dizzy whirl on August 27-28. Notwithstanding Pope's setback, the danger to Lee's army would continue to be critical until it could be reassembled to present a united front against Pope's ever-increasing strength.

The almost casual, unruffled manner in which Lee and Longstreet brought the main body of the Confederate army through Thoroughfare Gap to join Jackson's isolated wing at Groveton revealed a calm confidence in the joint Confederate ability to safely effect the reunion. It likewise implied an almost contemptuous disregard of Pope's capability to prevent it.

Pope's forces, chiefly through his own neglect, offered only negligible opposition to Longstreet's advance. Ricketts' well-intentioned but token resistance at the eastern end of the pass through Bull Run Mountains turned out to be a half-hearted measure, directed by corps commander McDowell on his own volition and without orders from or even the knowledge of the army commander, who was so obsessed with the idea of bagging Jackson that he seemed to have forgotten about Longstreet.

After Ricketts, maneuvered out of position the evening of August 28, had moved rapidly away from the Gap to make his way back to Bristoe, the Federal cavalry under Buford was all that stood between Longstreet and Jackson except an 8-mile road march. Although the Confederates in the Gap heard the sounds of battle between Jackson and King, the music struck Lee as a reason for rejoicing rather than a cause for worry, in the sense that it was convincing evidence that Jackson's divisions were nearby and apparently quite able to take care of themselves. Had the reaction been otherwise there can be no doubt that Longstreet's force would have been ordered to push ahead without a halt, in a night march to Jackson's support.

Early on the morning of August 29 the Confederate divisions resumed their journey, passing through Haymarket and Gainesville, near which latter point Buford was keeping the road under observation and from where he sent his 9:30 message to Ricketts (see page 176). As Longstreet's reinforcements neared the battlefield, Sigel's corps was attacking Jackson's position from the east and the pace of Hood's leading Confederate division accelerated as the noise of battle grew louder. In fact Hood moved so fast that he outdistanced the divisions in rear, so that Longstreet had to slow him down.

The evidence points to the arrival of Hood's division, preceded by part of Stuart's cavalry, in rear of Jackson's line about 10:30 or 11:00 o'clock in the morning. As succeeding units came up they were turned off to right and left of the turnpike, deployed and moved forward. When the entire corps (less Anderson's rear-guard division, with the trains, which came up later) had arrived and formed up on the right of Jackson's line, the Longstreet order of battle from left to right was as follows: Hood's two brigades (on either side of the turnpike) with Evans' independent brigade in support on the turnpike, Kemper's small division, and D. R. Jones' division. Wilcox's three brigades, in column formation, were disposed on the north side of the turnpike on Hood's left rear, apparently as corps reserve. Jeb Stuart with Robertson's cavalry brigade moved out to Jones' right, a half-mile south of the Manassas Gap Railroad, to cover the army right flank, while Fitz Lee's brigade covered Jackson's north flank. (See Map 19 which, however, shows situation later, after Wilcox had moved to the south flank.)

The entire Confederate line now covered a front that extended for a distance of almost five miles, from Jackson's left in the vicinity of Sudley Church to Longstreet's right on the Manassas Gap Railroad, not including the cavalry, which operated still further out on each flank. The line was shaped like a V, the apex pointing west, affording an excellent opportunity to emplace artillery on a commanding elevation where the two wings joined about half a mile north of the turnpike near the bed of the unfinished railroad. There Longstreet massed a heavy concentration of guns, so placed as to enfilade the open spaces along the front line in either direction. The afternoon was enlivened by an artillery duel which continued for several hours, to inflict material damage on the unprotected troops of both sides.

The movement of Longstreet's corps into a position that should long before have been preempted by Porter's and McDowell's two corps, according to Pope's plan, was accomplished without Federal opposition, for the reason that Porter was cooling his heels on the far side of Dawkins Branch

THE MANASSAS-SUDLEY ROAD, LOOKING NORTH
The Stone House is seen to the right. Heavy fighting occurred in this area.

and McDowell was getting ready to march north on the Manassas-Sudley Road, some 2½ miles to the east.

Battlefields are usually marked by one or more terrain features of particular tactical value to the troops that first take possession. North of the turnpike it was the Stony Ridge line in front of which ran the unfinished railroad. When he first arrived Jackson occupied that position and could not be budged from it by the most intense Federal attacks. South of the turnpike the key was still another stretch of high ground called Stuart's Hill, probably a prolongation of Stony Ridge, studded with woods and extending almost due south for several miles from a point near the turnpike, to the Manassas Gap Railroad and beyond. On the northern extremity of Stuart's Hill, several hundred yards south of the turnpike, Lee established his field headquarters and from that central point prepared to direct the battle.

Longstreet Counsels Delay

Porter's failure to seize the tactically important ridge south of the turnpike, upon which were situated the Munroe (or

Monroe) and Cole houses, gave Longstreet an opportunity that he was quick to seize. As it happened, no offensive measures were attempted by the Federals against Longstreet's position, in consequence of which Lee was persuaded by Longstreet to bide his time on the premise that Jackson, while battling fiercely, was not in serious trouble, and there would come an opportunity to decisively employ the massive army reserve of four divisions (five when Anderson arrived) after the Union divisions were given the privilege of wearing themselves out in repeated attacks. Although Lee's anxiety to assist the embattled Jackson was understandable, his desire to press for a conclusion, now that a general engagement seemed inevitable, was influenced more by the belief that every hour of delay would bring more of McClellan's divisions to bear on the outcome. At the same time, however, the presence of Longstreet's 30,000 men now (August 29) gave him 50,000 to Pope's approximately 65,000* actually on the field, instead of an army of 100,000 or more, which could so easily have been at Pope's command except for McClellan's consciously dilatory execution of Halleck's orders. The knowledge that the opposing forces were now on practically even terms undoubtedly was a factor in Lee's decision to delay the immediate commitment to action of Longstreet's wing.

Lee Defers to Longstreet

As Pope shifted the weight of his attacks from Jackson's center to his left, where A.P. Hill's division was about to carry the major burden of the defense, Lee watched the battlefield and deliberated. Uncertain as to the extent of Pope's reinforcements from McClellan's army, and reluctant to bring on a general engagement between the Federals and his own entire army until the relative strengths and dispositions were more accurately determined, Lee discussed with Longstreet the question whether the time was not ripe for the right wing,

---

*These totals take into account probable losses up to this point, and for Pope the absence of Banks' corps from the field. It is assumed that R. H. Anderson is "present," his division being between Gainesville and Haymarket.

now in position, to attack down the turnpike to assist in relieving the pressure on Jackson's somewhat depleted ranks.

Longstreet demurred, adhering to his firmly established tactical conviction that it was more profitable to maneuver his troops into a position that would force the enemy to attack from a less advantageous position. Beside which, he said, he had not yet had time to study the ground to his front, and until he could do so, it were better to refrain from what might prove to be a premature effort.

Returning from his reconnaissance, Longstreet expressed himself in favor of further delay, in support of which he described the terrain as unfavorable, adding that the Federal line extended a long way to the south of the turnpike, and heavy reserves might well be coming up from the direction of Manassas. As Lee and Longstreet talked, a courier arrived from Stuart to report a Federal column marching up from Manassas and another, estimated as an army corps, moving up the Manassas-Sudley Road. That seemed to confirm Longstreet's fears, and it was then that Lee ordered Cadmus Wilcox's division over from Longstreet's left to reinforce D. R. Jones on the extreme right.

Lee continued to wait, while Longstreet again rode off to reexamine the situation in light of the new information. When he returned the second time, Jackson had arrived at Lee's command post to bring the Commanding General up to date on his own situation. Lee again indicated to Longstreet his opinion that an attack was indicated, but Longstreet advised still further delay until the intentions of the Federal troops that were advancing could be determined. It might be expected that Jackson, who up to now had done most of the work and taken all the losses, would support Lee's opinion, but whether from pride or because to be taciturn was strictly in character, he offered no comment, and soon left the conference to get back on the job where the noise of battle was increasing up Sudley Springs way.

A few moments later Stuart himself rode up and confirmed

the approach of a Federal corps, presumably McDowell's. Impatient at Longstreet's continued unwillingness to commit his divisions to action, Lee mounted Traveler and rode forward to look the situation over for himself. After an hour or so he was satisfied that the Confederate line was secure, that the Federals reported by Stuart did not pose an overwhelming threat, and that his original idea of a strong attack along the turnpike held excellent promise, including the possibility of splitting off the approaching Union reinforcements. The discussion with Longstreet was resumed, but the latter remained obdurate in opposing an attack.

It was an interesting picture—Lee in his quiet, firm way indicating a positive wish that Longstreet should get going—Longstreet just as firmly sticking to his guns in favor of a defensive attitude, for the time being. Two men of strong character, neither of whom was convinced by the other; surely a commentary on the way in which Lee dealt with his chief lieutenants, each according to his character. Lee knew Longstreet too well to insist on action against Old Pete's considered judgment. Yet it was not a sign of weakness on Lee's part, simply a realization that the results that he wanted would not be forthcoming at the hands of an unwilling general. Nevertheless, as Douglas Southall Freeman has observed, the seeds of the failure at Gettysburg were planted on August 29, 1862, when Lee permitted Longstreet to differ with him, and Longstreet in turn realized the extent of his safety in opposing the judgment of his commanding general.

Hours had passed since Lee had first indicated his wish that Longstreet attack, and the afternoon of August 29 was nearly spent. Longstreet suggested that there would now be insufficient daylight to initiate an offensive, and proposed instead that he institute a reconnaissance in force down the turnpike to develop the situation preparatory to a possible concerted Army attack the following morning. Lee reluctantly approved, so about sunset Hood's division moved out, ran into Hatch's (recently King's) Federal division, and late at night withdrew with a number of prisoners to its original line. The effect on Longstreet was to convince him that the Federal strength was such as to preclude success in an early morning attack, even though R. H. Anderson's division and the reserve artillery had reacned the field during the day to give Longstreet five divisions under his immediate command. Old Pete had made up his mind that an active defense was the correct prescription and he was going to do it his way so long as Lee continued willing to defer to his subordinate's judgment.

On the record it would seem that Lee's original plan of campaign, to cut Pope off from McClellan's reinforcements before their arrival and then crush him with more nearly equal strength, had been somewhat modified when he learned how many of McClellan's divisions had already reached Pope since the latter's retrograde movement from the line of the Rappahannock to counter Jackson's threat to his rear. The battle urge which in the presence of the enemy at Groveton led Lee to advise Longstreet to attack was a temporary adherence to the original conception, but his readiness to go along with Longstreet's defensive psychology indicated a revision of his basic thinking. Now it became Lee's policy to again depend rather on maneuver than offensive fighting to defeat his stronger opponent, as evidenced by his early morning dispatch of August 30 to President Davis, in which he said; "My desire has been to avoid a general engagement, being the weaker force, and by maneuvering to relieve the portion of the country referred to (the Rappahannock frontier). I think if not overpowered we shall be able to relieve other portions of the country, as it seems to be the purpose of the enemy to collect his strength here. . . . . ."

Little if anything can be proven by speculating on who was right, Lee or Longstreet, insofar as an attack by Longstreet's wing on the afternoon of August 29 was concerned. At the very least it would have taken much of the pressure off Jackson, whose left was bent back upon itself and came perilously close to being broken by Heintzelman and Reno. It might also have resulted in throwing Pope into a complete state of confusion, for even at that late hour he was still unaware that Longstreet's wing had joined Jackson and continued to believe that Jackson's three divisions were all that faced him. Finally, a well-supported drive down the turnpike might very well have driven a wedge through Pope's fluid position, to catch his supports coming up to attack Jackson and possibly also to hit McDowell's two tired divisions as they plodded north on the Manassas-Sudley Road. As for Porter, who played the timid soul on this occasion, and was scarcely acting in character as a part of McClellan's army (or was he?), it is not unlikely, considering his attitude on that day, that an "I told you so" reflex would have led him to seek safety in a retrograde movement.

Longstreet's fear that his own force might be overwhelmed if he attacked was of course unfounded in view of Porter's reluctance to engage. There were in fact no Federal troops whatever directly in front of Longstreet, between the turnpike and the Manassas Gap Railroad, a two-mile wide frontage, except Reynolds' lone division, and Reynolds' position was wide open on both flanks. Sykes and Morell of Porter's corps had not even deployed south of the railroad, and McDowell was leading the divisions of Hatch and Ricketts up the Manassas-Sudley Road, which was a good 2½ miles distant from Longstreet's front line.

From Longstreet's standpoint, to be sure, Porter's corps was a potential threat to the security of his own line and could have caused the Confederates a lot of trouble had Porter chosen to act aggressively. Longstreet could not have anticipated how supinely Porter would act. In his estimate of the situation he would naturally assume that so large a body of Federal troops would be utilized to the best advantage. Porter's two divisions happened to be so disposed that by moving rapidly straight to the front they could, assuming a quick overthrow of Drayton's brigade, have moved easily around and behind Longstreet's right flank.

That would not necessarily have had fatal results for Longstreet, who preferred the defensive and was far more adept than Porter in his tactical reactions and in shifting brigades and divisions on the battlefield. Longstreet's strength at the moment was three times that of Porter, and even if the latter had committed his corps to a flank attack, his major contribution to the Union cause would in all probability have been to disrupt Confederate plans for their successful counterattack on the second day. That, however, would have been military teamwork of a high order, to which Fitz John Porter was not disposed to contribute, with John Pope calling the signals.

McClellan Fiddles While Pope Burns

While Pope's army fulfilled its ill-fated destiny on the Manassas plains, 20 miles from Washington as the crow flies, a disgruntled McClellan kept sending a steady stream of telegrams to Halleck from Alexandria, where he remained in an unhappily anamalous position as the titular commander of an army that was fast melting away from his control.

Halleck for several days had been importuning McClellan to speed the two corps of Franklin and Sumner to Pope, while McClellan sought every excuse and expedient to hold them in Alexandria. Whether that additional strength would have been effectively employed by Pope or not is beside the point, which was that the General-in-Chief, the official head of all the armies, had ordered them to be sent, and it was not McClellan's prerogative to circumvent Halleck's direct and increasingly peremptory orders to that effect.

Illustrative of McClellan's attitude are the following telegraphic exchanges from noon to early evening on Friday, August 29, when the Groveton battle of the first day was at its height.

> HEADQUARTERS ARMY OF THE POTOMAC,
>   August 29, 1862—12 m. (Received 12.8 p.m.)
> Maj. Gen. H. W. HALLECK, General-in-Chief:
>   Your telegram received. Do you wish the movement of Franklin's corps to continue? He is without reserve ammunition and without transportation.
>   GEO. B. McCLELLAN,
>   Major-General.

HEADQUARTERS ARMY OF THE POTOMAC,
Alexandria, Va., August 29, 1862—12 m.
(Received 12.50 p. m.)

Major-General HALLECK, General-in-Chief:

Have ordered most of Twelfth Pennsylvania Cavalry to report to General Barnard for scouting duty toward Rockville, Poolesville, &c. If you apprehend a raid of cavalry on your side of river I had better send a brigade or two of Sumner's to near Tennallytown, where, with two or three old regiments in Forts Allen and March, they can watch both Chain Bridge and Tennallytown. Would it meet your views to post the rest of Sumner's corps between Arlington and Fort Corcoran, where they can either support Cox, Franklin, or Chain Bridge, and even Tennallytown? Franklin has only between 10,000 and 11,000 ready for duty. How far do you wish this force to advance?

GEO. B. McCLELLAN,
Major-General, U. S. Army.

———

WASHINGTON, D. C., August 29, 1862—3 p. m.

Major-General McCLELLAN, Alexandria, Va.:

Your proposed disposition of Sumner's corps seems to me judicious. Of course I have no time to examine into details. The present danger is a raid upon Washington in the night-time. Dispose of all troops as you deem best. I want Franklin's corps to go far enough to find out something about the enemy. Perhaps he may get such information at Annandale as to prevent his going farther; otherwise he will push on toward Fairfax. Try to get something from direction of Manassas, either by telegram or through Franklin's scouts. Our people must move more actively and find out where the enemy is. I am tired of guesses.

H. W. HALLECK,
General-in-Chief.

———

WASHINGTON, D. C., August 29, 1862.

Major-General McCLELLAN, Alexandria, Va.:

I think you had better place Sumner's corps as it arrives near the fortifications, and particularly at the Chain Bridge. The principal thing to be feared now is a cavalry raid into this city, especially in the night-time. Use Cox's and Tyler's brigades and the new troops for the same object if you need them.

Porter writes to Burnside from Bristoe, 9.30 a. m. yesterday, that Pope's forces were then moving on Manassas and that Burnside would soon hear of them by way of Alexandria.

General Cullum has gone to Harper's Ferry, and I have only a single regular officer for duty in the office. Please send some one of your officers to-day to see that every precaution is taken at the forts against a raid; also at the bridges.

H. W. HALLECK,
General-in-Chief.

————

HEADQUARTERS ARMY OF THE POTOMAC,

August 29, 1862—5.25 p. m. (Received 5.38 p. m.)
Maj. Gen. H. W. HALLECK, General-in-Chief:

Before receiving the President's message I had put Sumner's corps in motion toward Arlington and the Chain Bridge, not having received any reply from you. The movement is still under your control in either direction, though now under progress, as stated. I think that one of two alternatives should be fully carried out.

GEO. B. McCLELLAN,
Major-General.

————

WASHINGTON, D. C., August 29, 1862—7.50 p. m.
Major-General McCLELLAN, Alexandria, Va.:

You will immediately send constructing trains and guards to repair railroad to Manassas; let there be no delay in this. I have just been told that Franklin's corps stopped at Annandale, and that he was this evening in Alexandria. This is all contrary to my orders; investigate and report the facts of this disobedience. That corps must push forward, as I directed, protect the railroad, and open our communications with Manassas.

H. W. HALLECK,
General-in-Chief

August 29, 1962.

Major-General HALLECK, Washington, D. C.:

I have directed General Banks' supply trains to start out to-night, at least as far as Annandale, with an escort from General Tyler.

In regard to to-morrow's movements, I desire definite in- ·structions, as it is not agreeable to me to be accused of disregarding orders when I have simply exercised the dis- cretion you committed to me.

GEO. B. McCLELLAN,
Major-General.

If General Franklin was in Alexandria this evening I know nothing of it, but will inquire.

––––––

Pope Claims a Success

The Confederates, during the heavy fighting on Jackson's front on Friday afternoon, had pushed their line ahead of the unfinished railroad in several places, and Hood's scrap with Hatch's division on the turnpike ended late in the evening with the former's division parked some distance ahead of Long- street's ridge line. During the night, however, it seemed best to Lee to pull the advanced units back to their former position, which resulted in what looked to the Federal troops in contact to be a wholesale withdrawal. That in any case was the way Pope chose to interpret the movements, and he so advised Halleck in an early telegram, which interestingly said nothing about the arrival of Lee and Longstreet, on which sub- ject Pope may still have been uncertain, unbelievable as that may sound.

HEADQUARTERS OF BATTLE,
Near Groveton, Va., August 30, 1862—5 a. m.

Major-General HALLECK, General-in-Chief:

We fought a terrific battle here yesterday with the com- bined forces of the enemy, which lasted with continuous fury from daylight until dark, by which time the enemy was driven from the· field, which we now occupy. Our troops are too much exhausted yet to push matters, but I shall do so in the course of the morning, as soon as Fitz John Porter's corps comes up from Manassas. The enemy is still in our front, but badly used up. We have lost not less than 8,000 men killed and wounded, but from the appearance of the field the enemy lost at least two to one. He stood strictly on the defensive, and every assault was made by ourselves. Our troops behaved splendidly. The battle was fought on the identical battle-field of Bull Run, which greatly increased the enthusiasm of our men. The news just reaches me from the front that the enemy is retreating toward the mountains. I go forward at once to see. We have made great captures, but I am not able yet to form an idea of their extent.

I think you had best send Franklin's, Cox's, and Sturgis' regiments to Centreville, as also forage and subsistence.

I received a note this morning from General Franklin, written by order of General McClellan, saying that wagons and cars would be loaded and sent to Fairfax Station as soon as I would send a cavalry escort to Alexandria to bring them out. Such a request, when Alexandria is full of troops and we fighting the enemy, needs no comment.

Will you have these supplies sent without the least delay to Centreville?

JNO. POPE,
Major-General.

THE ACTION AT 4 P.M., AUGUST 30, AS SEEN FROM HENRY HILL

CHAPTER 12

THE CLIMAX

Withdrawal of the Confederate lines to their initial battle position as a stronger one upon which to receive the expected, and hoped-for, attack by Pope's army on Saturday, August 30, was misinterpreted by the Federal commander to mean that Jackson declined to take further punishment and preferred to retire from the field. Dawn reconnaissances by Federal parties found that the Confederates had in fact relinquished their advanced lines, which when coupled with similar reports by two of his corps commanders, McDowell and Heintzelman, confirmed Pope in his optimistic appraisal and stirred him to lay plans for a vigorous pursuit.

At 3:00 o'clock in the morning, Porter received Pope's latest order to bring his command immediately to the field of battle. This time he responded with alacrity, possibly in the belief that he had already carried his indifference to orders too far, especially if his information of the evening before was correct, that the battle was going well for the Federals in the area of the turnpike and to the north. His prompt compliance with the new directive meant that there would be no Union troops opposing Longstreet's divisions in the direction of the Manassas Gap railroad, but that was Pope's concern, not his. Without losing any time, he started north on the Sudley Road and upon arrival at the center of the army position reported to Pope in person for instructions.

Pope's latest strategic brain-child, compounded as usual of grossly insufficient knowledge of his opponent's dispositions and strength and his own wishful thinking, played directly into Lee's hands. With his customary skill at interpreting the advantages of terrain and its utilization for the benefit of his own forces, Lee had set up for Pope's reception a vise-like set of jaws, at whose hinge stood the mass of his reserve artillery, with a clear field of fire to front and flanks. The Warrenton Turnpike, natural avenue of approach, led through the center of the position, and it was quite probable that troops advancing on either side of the road would tend to gravitate in that direction, and thus funnel directly into the very place Lee wanted them, and from which he could inflict the heaviest damage. Pope's contribution to the Confederate desideratum, by the act of weakening his own left to bring Porter's two divisions to the center of his planned attack, was as a result quite pleasing to General Lee. The fact was that Pope still acted as though he had only Jackson to deal with, that the latter was now retreating, and that Porter would be of no earthly use to him way down there on Dawkin's Branch.

Strange as it may seem, Pope thought Jackson might get away from him and at the same time Lee was worrying lest Pope fall back in the direction of Washington and escape the destruction that the Confederates had in store for him. On August 29 Lee had discussed with his lieutenants what measures they might take to encourage the Federals to attack if Pope should stall for time. In fact, Lee's fear of Pope's possible withdrawal was so well defined that he made plans that evening to resume the march next day by way of Sudley Ford and the Little River Turnpike to get between the Federals and Washington to prevent the very thing he feared. On the other hand, Pope maintained later that because he was short on rations he had no choice but to attack on August 30 or fall back to meet up with his supplies. In substance, then, it appears that Lee was mighty anxious for Pope to attack, while Pope was equally anxious to do so, but with no intent to accommodate Lee.

Lee Awaits Pope's Next Move

Saturday, August 30, started out hot, with a hint of rain to come. The Confederates rested on their arms, leaving the initiative to the Federals, who spent the morning in preparation for another go at their obstinate opponents, who the day before had seemed so determined to retain for themselves every foot of the terrain they had acquired. The Confederates could clearly see from their own lines the vast troop movements by which the Federals were rearranging themselves for the new attack. Jackson was especially intrigued by the amount of marching that took place in the enemy zone during the morning, much of it seeming to indicate a shift of emphasis to the south and away from his own left, where A. P. Hill still held the line, but with far fewer fighting men than the number with which he had thrown back twice his own weight on Friday.

Jackson is reported to have made the observation that appearances indicated the unlikelihood of an attack that day, but he decided to wander over to Lee's headquarters to compare notes. There he found Lee already discussing the outlook with Longstreet and Stuart, and considering what steps might be taken to needle Pope into action if that should be needed.

Generally speaking, the morning passed quietly, except for a sharp exchange of gunfire on the north flank, where a Confederate battery took appropriate steps to discourage several enemy guns from becoming too venturesome, and an infantry exchange when several regiments of Ricketts' division ran into a hornet's nest and were given a lively time. Pope's sketchy reconnaissance during the morning had failed to discover Confederates where they had been the day before. From this he jumped to the erroneous conclusion that Jackson had withdrawn and was retreating toward Thoroughfare Gap. What had actually happened was that Gregg's brigade had pulled back to replenish ammunition, then returned to its former position. Had Pope made an effort to confirm his hasty impression by consulting his front line troops, Ricketts for one could have assured him that the Confederates were still very much in evidence.

Pope's Inadequate Reconnaissance

Pope's sorry reconnaissance on his north flank was duplicated on the south flank. Where Hatch and Hood had collided on the turnpike on the evening of April 29 Pope again found no Confederates, which seemed to confirm his belief that Jackson had in fact pulled out. Pope still hadn't learned that Longstreet was on hand. Had the Federal commander pushed his reconnaissance a few hundred yards farther he would have been unpleasantly surprised to find Longstreet's corps ready and waiting where Pope was sure there were no enemy troops at all. Without exaggeration, it may be doubted that there was ever in the history of American armies a better example of inadequate reconnaissance.

By noon Pope's plan of action had matured, and orders went out for all commanders:

> HEADQUARTERS.
> Near Groveton, August 30, 1862—12 m.
> SPECIAL ORDERS
>   NO. ——
> The following forces will be immediately thrown forward in pursuit of the enemy and press him vigorously during the whole day. Major-General McDowell is assigned to the command of the pursuit.
> Major-General Porter's corps will push forward on the Warrenton turnpike, followed by the divisions of Brigadier-Generals King and Reynolds. The division of Brigadier-General Ricketts will pursue the Hay Market road, followed by the corps of Major-General Heintzelman. The necessary cavalry will be assigned to these columns by Major-General McDowell, to whom regular and frequent

reports will be made. The general headquarters will be somewhere on the Warrenton turnpike.

By command of Major-General Pope:

GEO. D. RUGGLES,
Colonel and Chief of Staff.

In preparation for further heavy work, Pope wired McClellan, Halleck, and any others that he could think of, to rush extra artillery ammunition to him. Halleck in turn telegraphed Banks, at Manassas Junction, in charge of Pope's trains, advising that ammunition would be sent as soon as possible, but meantime "Cannot you send him some from Manassas?"

Banks' reply to Halleck was a gem, indicating as it did the low state to which Pope's system of communication and supply within the army had fallen:

> Manassas Junction, Va.
> August 30, 1862—1.45 p.m.

Major General Halleck, *General-in-Chief:*

Your dispatch received. There is artillery and other ammunition in my train near Centerville, Sixteen wagons went up last night. I have many more wagons on the road now near this place, which can be moved directly to him if I knew where to send them.

Please inform me.

N. P. BANKS,
Major-General, Commanding.

Halleck took time to reply to the helpless Banks, advising him that Pope's headquarters were at Groveton that morning, and adding, with what must have been a wry smile: "You can judge best from the firing where he is now. The enemy this morning was said to be falling back toward the mountains."

Halleck Tries to Reassure Pope

Ineffectual as his efforts to date had been to expedite through McClellan the prompt transfer to Pope of the divisions of the Army of the Potomac as they debarked at Aquia and Alexandria, Halleck must be credited with making strenuous efforts in that direction. Predicated on the unwarranted assumption that

McClellan was following orders and had already sent Franklin's corps to Pope, Halleck telegraphed the latter in the afternoon:

> Washington, August 30, 1862—2.p.m.
> Major-General Pope:
> Yours of 5 a.m. is received. All matters have been attended to. Thirty thousand men are marching to your aid.
> Franklin should be with you now and Sumner tomorrow morning. All will be right soon, even if you should be forced to fall back. Let your army know that heavy reinforcements are coming.
> Yours, truly,
> H. W. HALLECK,
> General-in-Chief.

But Franklin was at that moment still a long way from Bull Run. He had gone only so far as Annandale, a mere 5 miles from Alexandria and a good eighteen miles from the battlefield. McClellan, who was applying the curb bit, gave Halleck the lame excuse that Franklin was unable to get transportation for his extra ammunition, implying that it was all the fault of the quarter-masters. Halleck expressed his dissatisfaction in a caustic message to McClellan:

> I am by no means satisfied with General Franklin's march of yesterday. Considering the circumstances of the case, he was very wrong in stopping at Annandale. Moreover, I learned last night that the Quartermaster's Department could have given him plenty of transportation if he had applied for it, any time since his arrival at Alexandria. He knew the importance of opening communication with General Pope's army, and should have acted more promptly.

On receipt of the last message McClellan capitulated, directed Franklin to proceed, and ordered Sumner to "march immediately to the relief of General Pope." About the same time he informed Halleck that Couch's division had arrived in part, that the remainder would soon be there, and requested instructions as to the disposition of the additional reinforcements. Halleck replied that Couch should be immediately sent to Pope, and directed McClellan to send transports to Aquia to bring Burnside's command up to Alexandria as well.

Halleck, apparently not trusting McClellan to impress on his corps commanders the urgency of the situation, made still another effort to rush aid to Pope:

August 30, 1862—2.10 p.m.

Major-General McClellan,
Alexandria, Va.
Franklin's and all of Sumner's corps should be pushed forward with all possible dispatch. They must use their legs and make forced marches. Time now is everything. Send some sharpshooters on the trains to Bull Run. The bridges and property are threatened by bands of Prince William Cavalry. Give Colonel Haupt all the assistance you can. The sharpshooters on top of cars can assist in unloading the trains.

H. W. HALLECK,
General-in-Chief.

If it was any satisfaction to McClellan, his protracted delay in sending Franklin and Sumner to join Pope, which should have given the Army of Virginia 30,000 more rifles and close to a 2 to 1 superiority over Lee on the field of Bull Run, had withheld the vital reinforcements just long enough for Lee's army to achieve the victory that sent Pope's divisions reeling back in defeat that very afternoon.

Brigadier General Jacob D. Cox, commanding the Kanawha Division, having made a well-regulated move from West Virginia and finally succeeded in reassembling his division at Alexandria, was now occupying a position at Upton Hill, west of Annandale, from which point his cavalry patrols reconnoitered the country to the front and on both sides of Fairfax Court House. As Pope was about to initiate his alleged pursuit of Jackson on the afternoon of August 30, Cox reported to his superior, McClellan, that all was quiet and no enemy were reported in the country about Fairfax Court House.

The impression prevailed in Washington at this time that Pope was doing all right, but could use the additional troops to clinch the matter. Still there were plenty of wild rumors floating about, as there always are when a major battle impends or is occurring, and it was not beneath the dignity of certain major generals to speed all such on their way for the benefit of others.

General Banks, who was playing a sedentary role as guardian of the army trains at Manassas Junction and Centerville, had plenty of time on his hands while his fellow corps commanders were marching and fighting. Judging from the pages of the Official Records, Banks improved his time by penning messages to all and sundry, including President Lincoln, as though he were an official war correspondent charged with responsibility for disseminating all the news that came his way. One particular telegram to McClellan, on the morning of August 30, was typical:

> There was a camp rumor as I came in from Bristoe that Jackson had moved toward Alexandria. Col. J. S. Clark, one of my aides, who has been out to the front, reports that Jackson has fallen back about 5 miles toward the mountains. He judges mainly by the sound of the guns. There has been an entire change of position, I judge. A scout reported to me at 10 a.m. that Jackson was at Gainesville with about 30,000. He said he saw and knew him. My corps is moving up from Bristoe. No enemy near.

Pope Has Misgivings

Pope's private thoughts on the morning of this third day of battle were somewhat less optimistic than his orders to pursue the "retreating" Confederates indicated, if his subsequent official report is to be accepted as entirely objective. Therein he presents a dismal picture of the condition of his army on the morning of August 30, stating that the troops were "greatly exhausted by marching and fighting almost continuously for many days," but without mentioning the fact that much of the countermarching was for the reason that the army commander himself was operating in a fog of war more or less created by his own ineptitude.

Pope also declared, in his ex post facto bill of particulars, that the War Department failed to speed rations and forage to the army from Alexandria, with the result that his men and horses had but little food for two days and were consequently in a weakened condition for further marching and fighting. The fact that Lee's army managed to live and fight at considerably greater distance from its supply base was disregarded, as Pope sought for alibis.

Porter's successful effort to keep his corps from participation in the battle and in so doing to deprive Pope of a possible victory over Jackson on the 29th became increasingly disloyal, almost treasonous, the more Pope thought about it, and his dark mood was not brightened by the continuing failure of McClellan's two corps, Franklin's and Sumner's, to come to his support. "It was not until I received this letter (referring to Franklin's slow pace in coming to his support) that I began to be hopeless of any successful issue to our operations; but I felt it to be my duty, notwithstanding the broken-down condition of the forces under my command, to hold my position," he wrote.

In spite of such forebodings, Pope prepared to renew the engagement on August 30, although it is difficult to understand his mood of the moment, if he was honest in so describing it, when at that time he was under the impression that his opponent was actually marching away from the battlefield. "Every indication during the night of the 29th and up to 10 o'clock on the morning of the 30th, pointed to the retreat of the enemy from our front." Those are Pope's own words, and his 12 noon pursuit order was issued in that belief. It may well be asked, in view of the fact that the Confederate line was again exactly where it had been all during the previous day's fighting, what kind of scouting and patrolling Pope's army had undertaken between the night of August 29 and midday of August 30. Pope had castigated Porter for failing to initiate a reconnaissance in force the previous day, to ascertain whether the Confederates were in such strength as Porter claimed, without corroborating evidence. Now the shoe was on the other foot, but Pope kept very quiet on that aspect of the situation.

There was one additional incident that occurred that Saturday morning which centered about whipping-boy Porter and, compounding that general's other sins of omission and commission, was duly recorded in the evidence introduced at Porter's later trial by court-martial. Porter's corps of two regular divisions had been reinforced by a brigade of Sturgis' division, dispatched from Washington, which gave it a strength of about 11,000 men. As Porter's troops were marching up in the early morning from Dawkin's Branch to join the center of Pope's army, Griffin's brigade of Morrell's division and Piatt's brigade of Sturgis' division missed a turn in the road and shortly found themselves with division commander Morrell himself at their head in Centerville, some miles east of the battlefield.

When Piatt discovered that his brigade was headed away from the battlefield, he reversed his brigade's direction of march and rejoined the army in time to participate in the action. Griffin's brigade, however, in company with Morrell, remained at Centerville all day, within hearing of the battle and without making any move to join its own outfit in the fight. "On the contrary," wrote Pope bitterly, "the brigade commander made requisition for ten thousand pairs of shoes on one of my aides-de-camp who was at Centerville in charge of the headquarters train." Was it possible that Porter had authorized the side jaunt? If so, it was not inconsistent with his freely written expressions as to how he really felt about his superior officer.

The Attack is Launched

Between 12 noon and 2:00 o'clock the Federals moved forward to what purported to be a pursuit but which at once became an attack, on a 3-mile front which extended from the Warrenton Turnpike near Groveton on the left, to Bull Run near Sudley Church on the right. The Confederates were fully prepared and waiting along their prepared position of the previous day, on a line that was 4 miles in length, and which consequently overlapped the attackers by a mile or more on Longstreet's southern flank.

Porter's corps on the Federal left, Heintzelman's on the right, moved forward abreast, under Pope's instructions to push forward generally along the turnpike, which to observers indicated that the main effort would be made against the Confederate center. This was what the doctor (Lee) ordered, or rather hoped for, as the Federals obligingly advanced directly toward the point where Lee had massed the weight of his artillery.

Preceded by the usual skirmishers and followed by great numbers of guns and heavy concentrations of reserve troops, the imposing Federal mass advanced in three waves at approximately 100 yards distance. McDowell's corps was given the mission of direct support for the two leading corps, Hatch's division backing up Porter on the left, Ricketts' division to follow Heintzelman on the right. Pope's ephemeral "pursuit" proved to be so shortlived, however, in view of the Confederates' failure to cooperate, that hasty improvisation by the lower echelons was necessary to adapt the forward elements to the unexpected situation.

Skirmishers from both Porter's corps and Hatch's division almost at once came in contact with Jackson's line in the Groveton woods north of the Pike and the main bodies immediately deployed for combat. Somewhat misled by the woods, Hatch swerved to the north, losing contact with Porter, whose right brigade complained that Hatch failed to lend support as ordered. But Hatch had his hands full, what with the heavy woods and Confederate volleys from behind the railroad, and there was nothing much that he could do about it.

The corps commanded by Sigel and Reno constituted the third echelon under Pope's plan for the advance, Sigel on the left, Reno on the right, both north of the turnpike. Reynolds' division, covering the army left on the south side of the turnpike, was in fact the only Federal force actually facing Longstreet's corps, but McDowell and Pope in their ignorance chose to transfer Reynolds to the north side just prior to the Confederate counterattack, in spite of Reynolds' reports that he

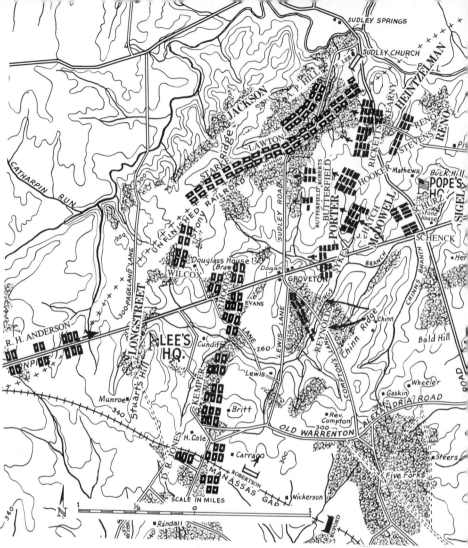

MAP 21. SITUATION FROM NOON TO 2 P.M., AUGUST 30—
POPE'S "PURSUIT" OF JACKSON

Shortly after noon Pope issued another order for pursuit. Heintzelman was directed to move on the road running north to Sudley Springs, thence via the old Haymarket-Sudley Road. Porter, reinforced by Hatch, was to pursue via the Warrenton Turnpike, while Reynolds covered the left flank. Sigel, Reno, and Stevens were to be in reserve.

Lee awaited Pope's move, placing 18 guns on the high ground near Jackson's right flank, and adjacent thereto was S. D. Lee's artillery battalion. (Artillery not shown.) With the arrival of R. H. Anderson, Lee's force is complete.

Porter had marched north from the head of Dawkins' Branch early that morning. As his troops commenced to deploy, Roberts' brigade of Morell's division became engaged about 2 p.m. in the woods near Groveton. It soon became evident that Jackson was not retreating. Reynolds, who had gone on a personal reconnaissance far to the front, was fired upon west of Lewis Lane. He conveyed this information to Pope's headquarters. Butterfield has command of the two brigades (his own and Roberts') of Morell's division which are present on the field. Morell himself with the remainder of the division is at Centerville.

was in contact with enemy infantry in the woods on his front!

Only the tread of thousands of feet, the rumble of gun carriages and the creaking of harness broke the uncanny silence on the field where yesterday had resounded the roar of guns and the cries of the wounded. There was something ominous about it, and it is to be doubted that many of the troops believed that they were engaging in a merry chase of retreating Confederates. Those who may have accepted Pope's pursuit order at face value were soon to be disillusioned.

Here and there, from behind protective cover, an occasional Confederate head popped up to get a better look at the impressive scene as the Union lines swept forward. It was just the sort of picture that Civil War artists loved to paint, but other thoughts were passing through the minds of Jackson's men, who it seemed were again to be the principal target of the stubborn Unionists, as they had been all the preceding afternoon.

The advancing lines were allowed to come forward without a shot or sound from the waiting Confederates. Suddenly an authoritative signal was given and the artillery at the center of the line opened fire with a crashing roar that brought Jackson's men at the double to their fighting positions. At once the attackers poured a hail of bullets into the woods in front of them, and the fight was on.

The sweeping bursts of artillery fire staggered the Blue front line, but the attack had been mounted in depth and the lines in rear pushed steadily ahead, ignoring losses. It soon became apparent that the Federal advance was aimed at Jackson's right center, where the divisions of Lawton and Starke held forth, with the Stonewall brigade, of First Manassas and Valley fame, as part of Starke's division.

Longstreet's line, mostly south of the Warrenton Turnpike, appeared to have been left out of Pope's calculations entirely, as though it didn't exist. Improbable as it may seem, that Longstreet's 30,000 men had been on the field for 24 hours without Pope's knowledge, no evidence can be found to dis-

prove such an opinion. On the contrary, the dispositions that
Pope made for attack on the second day, completely ignoring
the southern sector, are confirmatory, unless Pope is to be
charged with complete tactical ignorance.

Longstreet's desire to get a close-up view of the attack and
to prepare for his own participation in the battle caused him to
ride forward to his front line while the fight raged along and
to the north of the turnpike. In his own words: "I reached a
point a few rods in front of my line on the left of the pike
where I could plainly see the Federals as they rushed in
heavy masses against the obstinate ranks of the Confederate
left. It was a grand display of well-organized attack, thoroughly
concentrated and operating cleverly. So terrible was the on-
slaught that Jackson sent to me and begged for reenforce-
ments. About the same time I received an order from General
Lee to the same effect."

Porter's troops were evidently anxious to show that they
could fight as well as relax, when the spirit should move them.
Composed largely of Regular troops, they had demonstrated
their combat ability on the Chickahominy in the Peninsular
campaign. As the spearhead of the August 30 attack, they appear to have aroused Longstreet's admiration as they pushed
doggedly ahead in determined attempts to penetrate and overwhelm the right and right center of Jackson's line behind
the unimproved railroad, although the official reports of several general officers of other Federal corps, contiguous to
Porter's zone of advance, were somewhat less complimentary.
Sigel, for example, criticised Porter for masking his own
troops and bunching in the open, as well as having retreated
before he need have, with the excuse on the part of several
regiments that they were out of ammunition.

The pressure of Sykes' Regulars on the left and a part
of Morell's division under Daniel Butterfield on the right
(Morell himself was calmly passing the time in Centerville,
as previously noted) carried the aggressive Federals almost
to the railroad bed at a point a mile north of Groveton

THE STONE HOUSE

Famous landmark dating from the 18th century. It and the Dogan house at Groveton are the only Civil War buildings standing today on the field of Second Manassas. Young's Branch is seen in the foreground.

and west of the Groveton-Sudley road. The Stonewall Brigade, ranks badly thinned by casualties taken the previous day, fought grimly to hold their position, as the attackers pressed relentlessly forward until the two lines were only a few yards apart, when it became a hand-to-hand struggle.

After a time Jackson's old division ran out of ammunition, but still the men refused to give up. Instead they seized rocks from the railroad embankment and from that vantage point hurled them at their opponents. The effect of such non-lethal but unpleasant weapons on the Federals has not been recorded, but the fact remains that the "Deep Cut," where the last-ditch stone throwing occurred, marked the farthest advance of Porter's corps and the Stonewall Brigade was credited with turning the Federals back. It is more reasonable to assume, however, that Lee's reserve artillery, massed only a short distance off, had the range of Porter's advanced units, took them in flank, and made the place too hot to hold.

When Porter's corps was repulsed and driven back, the Confederates figured the time had come to do a bit of attacking themselves. With their advance the whole battle line north of the turnpike became seriously engaged. Ricketts' Federal division was pulled out from support on the right and sent around to strengthen the line threatened by Porter's withdrawal. (Map 22.) Sigel's corps, backing up Porter's position, took the Confederate blows with stubborn resistance, as Ricketts came up to help. For several hours the battle continued between Pope's army and Jackson's smaller force plus Hood's division. The latter was in position astride the turnpike and became engaged when Porter retired, with a view to speeding his departure. Porter's troops retreated in good order, were halted farther back, re-formed and after a while were returned to the battle and, according to Pope, rendered distinguished service.

Longstreet's Tactical Judgment Vindicated

From the moment Longstreet had come on the field, about midday August 29, his tactical sense, as well as his confirmed predilection for the active defense, told him that it would be the part of wisdom to put off the commitment of his divisions until the psychological moment should arrive when he could deliver a devastating blow to produce the decisive result that Lee sought. Longstreet was a determined, even stubborn, character, but a rugged fighter when the chips were down. What he wanted, and insisted upon almost to the point of occasional insubordination, was that the conditions should be as nearly right as possible before he would consent to throw his divisions in.

The extent to which the troops of his colleague, General Jackson, were forced to suffer while his own remained unengaged, seemed not to enter his mind. Repeated urging by Lee, short of direct orders, failed to budge him. Let's wait some more, was the burden of his song, even when Jackson's line cracked ominously. At Second Manassas it turned out that Longstreet would withhold the weight of his counter-

attack with impunity, but when the performance was repeated at Gettysburg the following summer, Lee lost the
battle to Meade.

Longstreet laid his plans carefully. His divisions were alert
and waiting for the moment when all of Pope's divisions should
be committed and many of them had reached the stage where
they may be said to have been fought out. The battle on
Jackson's front had gone on and on for hours. His own division
had narrowly escaped defeat in fending off Porter's corps.
Stephen Lee's reserve artillery had been in action all morning on the high ground in front of Jackson's right; it was
that battalion which was largely instrumental in turning back
Porter's early attack. Ewell's division on Jackson's center had
had little to do, but A. P. Hill's on Jackson's left, weakened by
its severe fight on August 29, faced odds and came close to
breaking.

It was then that Jackson, unaccustomed to admitting that his
corps needed help, swallowed his pride and sent to Lee for
support from Longstreet. Lee immediately ordered Old Pete
to send a division to Jackson's aid on the left. "Certainly," responded Longstreet, even though he was confident that the
artillery would halt the Federal attack with their guns. Longstreet's instinct, and what he could see with his own eyes from
his vantage point at the center of the army line, told him
that the advanced guns, with the ability to deliver a plunging
enfilade fire, could stop the attackers in their tracks long before he could get the supporting division into position to be
of help.

The artillerymen had their own observers forward on the
ridge in rear of which their 18 guns stood ready, horses
hitched, waiting only to be unleashed. The Federal attacking
line, now aimed toward the left center of Jackson's position,
marched with its exposed flank within easy gun range, offering
a target that occurs but once in a lifetime for the average
gunner.

At just the right moment the teams galloped forward to

the crest and opened fire with shattering effect. The attack melted away. Lee messaged Jackson to inquire if he still wanted reinforcements. Jackson took his time in replying, to make certain that the artillery had in fact done more than hold the Federals in check. As soon as he was convinced by what Lee and Longstreet had already observed, that the disruption of Pope's second and third waves had left the front line unsupported and that the leading attackers, finding their supports escaping from the deadly gunfire, had promptly followed suit—Jackson withdrew the request. Almost at the same moment, his men, sensing instinctively that the tide had turned, dashed out in pursuit.

Lee Counterattacks

The climactic moment had arrived! It was what Longstreet, long on patience but a terrific fighter when aroused, had been waiting for. The enemy had been repulsed, his reserves had been thrown in and driven back, his whole force was probably in a state of confusion and must not be allowed to recover. It was the psychological moment to hit them hard while off balance, with everything the Confederates had.

Lee saw the golden opportunity at the same time. An order was sent to Longstreet to counterattack immediately with his whole force of five divisions, including that of R. H. Anderson, who had been assigned to the reserve since his arrival. Longstreet had however anticipated Lee's action and already ordered the advance, shortly before 4:00 p.m.

Now the V-shaped Confederate vise was about to close on the disordered ranks of Pope's army. The lines swept forward, Longstreet's right bearing northeast as his center and left headed directly east. At the other end of the line, Jackson's right would move straight ahead while his left bore southeast. There was naturally some confusion, with Longstreet's fresher divisions making better time against lesser initial opposition, except on the turnpike, than Jackson's men, who had been defensively engaged at close quarters for several hours. Indeed

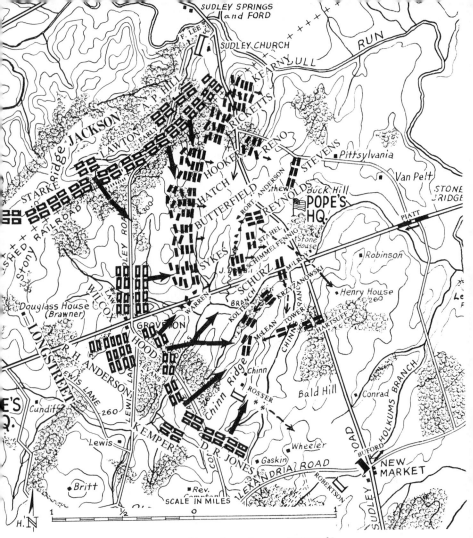

MAP 22. SITUATION FROM 4 TO 5 P.M., AUGUST 30—
THE CONFEDERATE COUNTERATTACK

Hood's division crushed Warren's brigade of Sykes' division, as the latter was withdrawing. Similarly Lieut. Col. Robert Anderson's brigade, the rear element of Reynolds' division, caught in motion while Reynolds was shifting to the north side of the pike, was destroyed. However, the severe fighting caused Hood's units also to lose their cohesion. These elements drifted south-east, encountering McLean's brigade of Schenck's division, near Chinn House. At this point Kemper's division took over the attack from Hood, advancing against McLean, Tower, and Hartsuff. D. R. Jones began to come up on Kemper's right, extending Longstreet's lines and strengthening the Confederate counterattack.

North of the turnpike Pope's divisions were retiring toward the Sudley Road, except for Sigel's division, which moved to the high ground about J. Dogan. As soon as Reynolds reached the north side of the pike his division was faced about and directed toward the Henry House plateau to reinforce Pope's left flank. Similarly, the one serviceable brigade of Reno's division, and the brigades of Koltes and Krzyzanowski of Sigel's corps, were started toward the Federal left.

Pope's "pursuit" has become a retreat.

only a small part of Jackson's force actually took part in the early stages of the pursuit.

Reynolds' division, at first posted on Chinn Ridge*, had been moved to the north to support Porter's attack on Lee's center, leaving that important terrain feature unoccupied. Chinn Ridge, a prominent landmark and obviously a key position on that part of the field, protected Henry House Hill, on the next ridge to the east, and should have been held at all costs. For Pope to order Reynolds elsewhere was the height of folly, although typical of the Army Commander's tactical handling of his battle. Reynolds was complying with Pope's order to cross to the north side of the turnpike when Longstreet struck. Two of Reynolds' brigades had completed the move, but the third, commanded by Lieut. Colonel Robert Anderson, was caught in motion and wrecked.

Despite the disconcerting set-back there was no evidence of a Federal rout. The heavy pressure of Longstreet's impetuous advance against the Union left caused Pope to order a wholesale shifting of divisions to meet the threat of an envelopment. Sigel first sent McLean's and Milroy's brigades to Chinn Ridge, followed soon after by Koltes and Krzyzanowski, who took position somewhat to McLean's right. Finally came Tower with his own and Hartsuff's brigades. McLean's and Milroy's brigades of Sigel's corps, and Tower's brigade of Ricketts' division offered strong resistance to Longstreet's determined effort to effect a penetration west of Chinn Ridge. The Confederates had to fight for all of their gains, but with five divisions in line, fired with the hope of a solid breakthrough, the advantage lay with Longstreet, who made the most of it. When Longstreet's advance seized Chinn Ridge to threaten Henry House Hill, a short distance to the northeast, Porter, Reno, and Reynolds were all rushed to the latter historic ridge in a desperate effort to prevent the Confederates from rolling up the entire left flank of Pope's army.

_____

*Most Confederates and some Federals mistakenly called Chinn Ridge "Bald Hill." The latter, a somewhat smaller knob, lay east of and was probably masked from the west by Chinn Ridge.

Moxley Sorrel, a staff officer who later became Longstreet's chief of staff and was one of the officers sent by the corps commander to urge his divisions into a speedy pursuit of the retiring Federals, described the exciting affair thus:*

> The easy, rounded ridges ran at right angles to the turnpike, and over these infantry and artillery poured in pursuit. The artillery would gallop furiously to the nearest ridge, limber to the front, deliver a few rounds until the enemy were out of range, and then gallop again to the next ridge. And thus it went on until black darkness stopped operations—the enemy defeated at all points and hastening back to the Potomac. Many prisoners, guns, colors, small arms, and large quantities of stores and equipment fell into our hands.

Cavalry Combat

Jeb Stuart, upon whom Lee relied almost exclusively to keep him informed on troop dispositions of his own as well as the enemy divisions, was not one to remain on the sidelines if opportunity offered to put his troopers and horse artillery into action. Longstreet's counterattack provided just such an opportunity, one that fitted the role of horse cavalry in the pursuit and harassment of a retreating opponent.

When Longstreet's divisions moved forward in the assault that broke the back of Pope's army, Stuart managed to get hold of four batteries, Stribling's, Roger's, Eshelman's, and Richardson's. Detaching Colonel Tom Rosser from his cavalry regiment, Stuart put him in temporary command of the artillery contingent and turned him loose on Longstreet's right to enfilade the Union lines. Rosser's detachment, supported solely by horse cavalry, moved to positions near the Chinn House from which point the Confederate guns caused consternation in the unstabilized Union ranks with their raking enfilade fire. Displacing forward by battery as the Federals fell back, Rosser shortly found his leading guns near the Wheeler House, half a mile in front of Longstreet's advancing line.

------

*Recollections of a Confederate Staff Officer, by Brig. General G. Moxley Sorrel, C.S.A., © 1958 by McCowat-Mercer Press, Jackson, Tennessee.

While Rosser with his artillery was having a field day on Longstreet's extreme right and in front of his infantry, Robertson's cavalry brigade, with Munford's regiment in the lead, engaged Buford's Federal cavalry in a spirited mounted fight near Lewis' Ford. Robertson had moved his brigade up to the Lewis house in order to be in position to circle the Union rear at Stone Bridge if the opportunity should occur. The opposing cavalry were near enough to hear each other's commands. Buford's brigade, in column of regiments, moved forward at the trot. Munford charged at the gallop, passed through the first Union line, encountered the second, and a fierce hand-to-hand struggle ensued, in which Munford, greatly outnumbered, was driven back. Soon, however, the two remaining regiments of Robertson's brigade came up, whereupon the Union cavalry in turn retired, leaving 300 prisoners in Confederate hands. It was one of the handsomest mounted engagements of the war to date, according to eye-witnesses, and as such received glowing reports at the hands of Munford, Rosser, and Stuart, all of whom seemed rather pleasantly surprised at the unaccustomed spirit shown by the heretofore reluctant Union cavalry.

Pope's Last Stand

The losses were heavy on both sides as Longstreet's scythe relentlessly cut a wide swath in its curving northeasterly attack. A mile and a half the Confederates advanced, but there was no penetration and no outflanking, and Pope's divisions still held possession of the Warrenton Turnpike as the Union left was folded slowly but surely back toward the field of First Manassas. Several Confederate brigades south of the pike made repeated charges to carry the Henry House Hill, bitterly defended by Reynolds' brigades under Meade, Seymour, and Anderson, in company with one of Sykes' brigades and other assorted troops. The famous landmark of First Manassas might be called Pope's Last Stand at Second Manassas, for it was there that Longstreet's spear was blunted long enough for darkness and a handful of hard-fighting Federal brigades to save Pope from complete rout and to permit the rest of the

MAP 23. THE FEDERAL COLLAPSE. SITUATION FROM 6 TO 8 P.M., AUGUST 30

Chinn Ridge fell before the continued attacks of R. H. Anderson, Kemper, and D. R. Jones, and the fight for Henry Hill began. Anderson was extending the Confederate right flank.

Reynolds' division, defending Henry House Hill, drove the Confederates west of Sudley Road. But on Pope's right, his units withdrew to the high ground east of Sudley Road, followed by Jackson's troops. Pender and Archer struck Ricketts and Stevens near Pittsylvania (Carter's house), driving them back from this ridge. Early and Branch turned east and advanced unopposed to Pittsylvania. Robertson's reinforced cavalry drove Buford across Lewis Ford.

Franklin's corps (not shown), having marched from near Alexandria west to Cub Run at 6 p.m. could go no farther, the turnpike being choked with units and individuals trudging to the rear. Franklin withdrew to Centerville. Pope now ordered a general retirement. After dark troops continued to pour east through the defile at Stone Bridge. The battle was over.

army to retreat, across Bull Run at the equally famous Stone Bridge and the nearby fords, to the temporary safety of a defensive position at Centerville.

Bull Run for the first time during this campaign now attained greater prominence than a mere geographical reference point of no tactical significance. Except for a few places where it could be forded with some difficulty, the famous Stone Bridge on the turnpike to Centerville became the bottleneck through which Pope's retreating army for the most part had to pass. The stream was fifty to sixty feet wide, with vertical sandstone bank on the east side, some 20 or 30 feet high in the

STONE BRIDGE OVER BULL RUN

vicinity of Stone Bridge, thus constituting a real obstacle. The bridge itself, part of which had been reconstructed, was less than 19 feet in width, but it was possible for the troops to march in two files on one side while artillery and wagons simultaneously used the other half of the bridge. That is, under conditions of discipline and control, which in a retreat are usually lacking. Fortunately for Pope's army, the victorious Confederates had equally expended their energies, and Reno's rear-guard discouraged any real effort on Longstreet's part to turn the retreat into a rout, so that the withdrawal was in fact effected with virtually no interference by the victors.

The battle of August 30 came to a close only when the shades of night were drawn, by which time Longstreet's men were winded by their energetic pursuit and his units, becoming intermingled during the race, required time to become unshuffled. At the same time it started to rain, which served to dampen martial enthusiasm. Pope's army had taken a licking, that was certain, and the army commander decided to throw in the sponge, while putting as good a face on the matter as possible.

Pope's Army Retires to Centerville

At 8 o'clock that night, almost as soon as the shooting ended, Pope sent written instructions to the corps commanders "to withdraw leisurely toward Centerville," the route each corps was to follow being indicated in the orders. Reno's two divisions were designated as a rear guard to cover the retirement. An order was sent to Banks at Bristoe Station to bring the army trains to Centerville after destroying the railroad trains and such other stores as had not already been transferred therefrom to the army wagons. Banks was specifically told to leave no ammunition behind, and to take along all of the sick and wounded for whom transportation could be found.

The retirement was somewhat inaccurately reported by Pope to have been made quietly and in good order, without interference from the Confederates, who made no effort to press the pursuit. Pope himself rode back to set up his headquarters at Centerville, from where, at 9:45 p.m., he wired the bad news to Halleck.

> CENTREVILLE, August 30, 1862—9:45 p.m.
> Major-General HALLECK, General-in-Chief:
> We have had a terrific battle again to-day. The enemy, largely re-enforced, assaulted our position early today. We held our ground firmly until 6 p.m., when the enemy, massing very heavy forces on our left, forced back that wing about half a mile. At dark we held that position. Under all the circumstances, both horses and men having been two days without food; and the enemy greatly outnumbering us, I thought it best to draw back to this place at dark. The movement has been made in perfect order and without loss. The troops are in good heart, and marched off the field without the least hurry or confusion. Their conduct was very fine. The battle was most furious for hours without cessation, and the losses on both sides very heavy. The enemy is badly crippled, and we shall do well enough. Do not be uneasy. We will hold our own here. The labors and hardships of this army for two or three weeks have been beyond description. We have delayed the enemy as long as possible without losing the army. We have damaged him heavily, and I think the army entitled to the gratitude of the country. Be easy; everything will go well.
> JNO. POPE,
> Major-General.
> P.S.—We have lost nothing; neither guns nor wagons.

Whistling in the dark and figuratively shrinking from the unpleasant duty of reporting another failure instead of the victory which Washington had been led by earlier dispatches and other miscellaneous intelligence from various sources to expect, one can sympathize to some extent with the dejected general whose initial boasting just prior to the campaign would now be thrown back at him from every direction.

The distortions in his dispatch, including the part where he speaks of being greatly outnumbered and reports the troops "in good heart," were in the McClellan tradition and had come to be routine on the part of Union army commanders, but the latter portion of his message is the one that stands out, particularly the absurdly inaccurate postcript. Poor Pope, a recognized failure in his trial of strength with an opponent whose apparent invincibility had seemingly again been confirmed, and torn between dashed hopes and the feeling that he had been double-crossed by the unfriendly, uncooperative McClellan, said nothing in this message about success being snatched from him by Porter's action in absenting his corps from the battle at the crucial moment. That would come later.

Right now he sought vindication, although doubtless feeling deep down that he was fighting a losing cause. The rather pathetic effort to ward off a scathing rebuke from Halleck brings to mind a friendly dog, expecting punishment, as he extends his body close to the ground and advances toward his master with an appealing look in his hurt eyes.

Halleck had to think over the nature of his reply, which reached Pope the following day, as his army took up its defensive position at Centerville. He was probably touched by the tragedy of Pope's situation and rates an accolade for the diplomatic manner in which he tried to put heart into the Army of Virginia through its commander.

WASHINGTON, August 31, 1862—11 a.m.

Major-General POPE:

My Dear General: You have done nobly. Don't yield another inch if you can avoid it. All reserves are being sent forward. Couch's division goes to-day. Part of it went to Sangster's Station last night with Franklin and Sumner, who must be now with you. Can't you renew the attack? I don't write more particularly for fear dispatch will not reach you. I am doing all in my power for you and your noble army. God bless you and it.

Send me news more often if possible.

H. W. HALLECK,
General-in-Chief.

Porter Briefs his Boss

As he had been doing ever since his corps was detached from the Army of the Potomac for duty with Pope's army,

Fitz John Porter dutifully reported in a letter to McClellan the events of the battle of August 30 and its aftermath. Whether its contents, in whole or in part, were passed on to Halleck is doubtful, but it is quite likely that a McClellan supporter in the cabinet, or other official with a pipeline to the President, was duly informed of at least the implications in some of Porter's comments written late at night after the retreat of August 30.

Enclosing for McClellan's examination copies of his recent orders from Pope's headquarters, Porter told how four of his brigades had hit the center of Lee's line and been overpowered because they were not supported on the right. Beyond praising the efforts of his own divisions and remarking that the Pennsylvania Reserves under Reynolds had done beautifully, the long letter made no reference to Heintzelman, Reno, Sigel, or McDowell, the inference being that the army might have won if Porter's attack had been supported and if the others had done as well as Reynolds.

The sneering tone of the letter, the subjects selected for inclusion therein, the innuendoes, and the sarcastic way in which the writer gleefully prophesied the further humiliation of the hated John Pope, may well have been the determining factor in bringing the military career of the author to an ignominious end by action of a general court-martial.

The case against the "brash braggart from the west," who had had the temerity to encroach on George McClellan's territory, was building to its climax, as what can only be viewed as the Porter-McClellan cabal drove a few more nails into Pope's coffin. A careful study of Porter's strictures on Pope, which later served as evidence against himself, even today would raise the temperature of any objective person who still believes in such qualities as loyalty to a cause and fair treatment to colleagues on the same team.

A few selected extracts from Porter's letter are sufficient to show its defeatist character:

We were driven from the field, and here we are, after marching all last night, strongly located in a position which, if the enemy shells, will cause slaughter; but I do not believe he will attack, but get in our rear, and compel us to attack him in a well-selected place. The men are without heart, but will fight when cornered. Today General Pope asked the question of the Government if arrangements had been made to protect Washington in case the army met with a disaster. He said to us (chief of corps present), when the reply was received, that he was glad the Government had decided the question for him, but we were to fight wherever the enemy was—meaning we were not to return to Alexandria, etc., as all forces were coming to us. I believe the decision was a general disappointment, except to him. . . . Pope says there are political considerations which control, not the safety of the army; but our men will not fight with heart when they know, if wounded (as we cannot retain the field against present odds), they are to be left to the care of the enemy. Pope sent in a flag today to get our wounded. . . . Our wagons are gone, and our artillery and cavalry will not soon be movable. We have taken very few prisoners (some 400). In return we have left all our killed and most of our wounded in their hands. . . . Lee is here; Jackson is not now here. The enemy are massing to turn us. I expect to hear hourly of our rear being cut and our supplies and trains (scarcely guarded) at Fairfax Station being destroyed, as we are required to stay here and fight.

As the defeated Army of Virginia was making its way back to Centerville and being redisposed in the intrenchments there, McClellan kept up his barrage of telegrams to Halleck, with the latter beginning to show signs of nervous exhaustion and an increasing disposition to transfer his command responsibilities to McClellan or any one else strong enough to halt the rapid deterioration of the military situation.

Early on the evening of August 31, McClellan wrote Halleck that he had been informed there were 20,000 stragglers from Pope's army between Centerville and Alexandria and that he had sent all of Gregg's cavalry to endeavor to drive them back to their regiments.

At 10:25 the same evening this telegram went forward:

I am ready to afford you any assistance in my power, but you will readily perceive how difficult an undefined position, such as I now hold, must be. At what hour in the morning can I see you alone, either at your own house or at the office?

Geo. B. McClellan,
Major-General.

One of Halleck's aides replied that the General-in-Chief had gone to bed but that he was directed to inform McClellan to come to see Halleck any time in the morning (Sept. 1) that suited his convenience. Meantime, Couch's division had reached Alexandria and was en route to Centerville, and Burnside was instructed to embark his troops for Alexandria as rapidly as possible.

To add to the worries of the high command, Colonel Haupt, the transportation chief, wired Assistant Secretary of War Watson from Alexandria Depot that "a large portion of the nurses who came over last night were drunk and very disorderly. . . . They are much in the way. Can you not place a guard on Long Bridge? We are now using cars to bring back nurses, who are satisfied with the experience of one night, and are skedaddling back again."

It appeared that Halleck either couldn't get to sleep Saturday night, August 31, or had second thoughts about McClellan's messages, because at 1:30 Sunday morning he wrote the general to "make arrangements to stop all retreating troops in line of works or where you can best establish an outer line of defense," adding that his news of Pope was up to 4 p.m., at which time Pope "was all right," and that it was necessary that he wait for more definitive information before he could order a retreat. The message closed with the statement: "Give me all additional news that is reliable. I shall be up all night and ready to act as circumstances may require. I am fully aware of the gravity of the crisis and have been for weeks."

By 10:30 Sunday morning Halleck was growing so anxious

to see McClellan that he sent him an urgent message to come quickly. At the conference that ensued, Halleck must have urged McClellan to do something about Porter, for at 5:30 p.m. McClellan sent a belated appeal to the uncooperative corps commander couched in the following language:

> Major-General Porter, Centerville, Commanding Fifth Corps:
> I ask of you for my sake, that of the country, and of the old Army of the Potomac, that you and all my friends will lend the fullest and most cordial cooperation to General Pope in all the operations now going on. The destinies of our country, the honor of our arms, are at stake, and all depends now upon the cheerful cooperation of all in the field. This week is the crisis of our fate. Say the same thing to my friends in the Army of the Potomac, and that the last request I have to make of them is that, for their country's sake, they will extend to General Pope the same support they ever have to me.
>
> > Geo. B. McClellan,
> > Major-General.

In the interim between receipt by Porter of the foregoing appeal on the evening of September 1 and his reply the next morning, the action at Chantilly had taken place, without Porter's corps being engaged. By that time Pope was so thoroughly deflated that there was no longer any reason for Porter to continue his verbal offensive against the army commander, so his communication to McClellan was all sweetness and light, with somewhat hypocritical overtones:

> FAIRFAX COURT HOUSE, September 2, 1862—10 a.m.
> General George B. McClellan, Washington:
> You may rest assured that all your friends, as well as every lover of his country, will ever give, as they have given, to General Pope their cordial cooperation and constant support in the execution of all orders and plans. Our killed, wounded, and enfeebled troops attest our devoted duty.
>
> > F. J. PORTER,
> > Major-General, Commanding.

THE FEDERAL RETREAT

CHAPTER 13

POPE MAKES A BRIEF STAND

SUNDAY morning, August 31, Pope called his corps commanders together to receive his orders for the posting of their troops on the somewhat higher ground in the Centerville area, where six roads converged to a point five miles east of the recent Bull Run battlefield. Franklin's corps of 8,000 men, much smaller than expected, had arrived during the night, and 11,000 troops of Sumner's corps were close by and should be up by the end of the day.

According to Franklin's official report, his divisions reached Centerville Saturday afternoon, August 30, after he had detached one of the brigades of Slocum's division with a battery of guns to guard the point where the Little River Turnpike joins the Warrenton Pike between Centerville and Alexandria. Passing through Centerville without stopping, the balance of Slocum's leading division had advanced three miles in the direction of the Bull Run battlefield and crossed Cub Run, when Franklin rode up to find Slocum, his division formed across the road, endeavoring to stem a massive tide of retreating men, horses, guns, and wagons, "all going pell-mell to the rear in an indiscriminate mass," as Franklin described it. Slocum expressed the opinion that it was as bad as the Bull Run retreat of 1861. There was no stopping the majority of the frantic horde, but Slocum's officers did manage to herd about 3,000 of them into a nearby yard; the rest ran to the rear as one man; nothing could stop them." All of which indicated that at least one corps commander disagreed with Pope's statement that the army withdrew quietly and in good order.

The ordered dispositions at Centerville were as follows: Porter on the right, north of Centerville, with Franklin next on the left; then Sigel south of Centerville, with Reno on his left and rear. Behind the four corps on the semicircle covering the crossroad and facing west, Heintzelman was posted, east of Centerville, as army reserve. McDowell was stationed 2 miles to the east on the Centerville—Fairfax Court House Road. That accounted for all but Sumner and Banks, who were on the way but had not yet come up, and the cavalry brigades under Buford and Bayard, whose horses had been so badly used up that Pope no longer had any cavalry that could be effectively employed. Banks' assignment would be on the north side of Bull Run, covering the bridge on the Manassas-Centerville Road, while Sumner would move immediately upon arrival to a position between Centerville and Chantilly, which latter place he would occupy in force.

From right to left, under Pope's defensive plan, the army would be disposed along a seven-mile front, on commanding ground, covering all approaches from the direction of the enemy. Assuming a prompt distribution of the troops as indicated, and since Lee's tired soldiers were not supermen, there might still be a chance for the Army of Virginia to turn the tables on the Army of Northern Virginia, *if* Pope should prove capable of providing the necessary leadership and *if* his officers and men retained any respect for or con-fidence in their leader.

It was still raining that Sunday morning, the streams were rising, the dirt roads fast becoming paths of soft muck, and the Stone Bridge over Bull Run had been destroyed. Dead bodies of men and horses, Blue and Gray alike, cluttered the scene of the recent battle in company with broken fences, trampled fields, and the usual flotsam and jetsam of discarded equipment, broken rifles, upturned wagons, and other memorabilia of a fiercely fought battle.

The Confederates Close to Exhaustion

Lee's united army, reduced in numbers by some 9,000 killed, wounded, missing and captured, was not far from being at the end of its string, despite its decisive victory over Pope's larger army and the indomitable spirit of the ragged veterans who had just added one more glorious page to the battle history of the Confederacy. Lee's ammunition was down to the danger point. His food and supply problem had become acute. The effect of the windfall that Jackson's depot raid had acquired had by now worn off. A resurvey of the situation was indicated.

Fitz Lee's cavalry, which had been reconnoitering to the east, reported the arrival of Pope's reinforcements at Centerville, including the corps of Franklin and Sumner and the divisions of Cox and Sturgis. Lee was fully conscious of the fact that his troops had not been able to pursue the retreating Federals, in consequence of which it was reasonable to assume that Pope would not be likely to keep running, but would occupy the most logical nearby position from which to oppose any further effort on Lee's part to drive for Washington. That would probably be the road center at Centerville, where the Confederates had worked hard the previous year to construct impregnable defenses that could still be useful.

Lee rode out through the rain Sunday morning with Stonewall Jackson for a personal survey. A short distance beyond Bull Run his party came under the fire of Federal pickets, indicating the possibility that Pope had come to a halt and proposed to bicker further with his victorious opponent.

Reverting to his heretofore highly succeessful reliance on maneuver, Lee decided that he would once again move to circle Pope's right in the hope of striking his line of communications to Washington and thus pry him loose to finish the job of winding up his military career. Jackson's corps, worn out though it was by this time, unfortunately occupied the logical position on the north flank from which to make the attempt. "Good, good," was all that Jackson remarked when Lee gave him the mission; there is no record, however, that his soldiers used the same polite 4-letter words to express *their* reactions.

With Fitz Lee's cavalry covering the column, Jackson's three divisions slowly took off in the direction of Sudley Springs, where they would cross Bull Run, move north to the Little River Turnpike and follow that road toward Fairfax Court House, while the rest of Stuart's cavalry made a demonstration on the Warrenton Pike east of Bull Run. Longstreet's corps was detailed to remain where they were to bury the dead and remove the wounded, and then follow Jackson's route. For Confederate route, see. Map 25.

During the afternoon, after Jackson's corps had departed, Lee was again riding over the field when he suffered a painful accident. Wearing coveralls to protect him from the rain, while he was dismounted his horse shied at a sharp noise nearby. Lee grabbed for the bridle, caught his foot in a fold of his unaccustomed garb, and was thrown to the ground, breaking the fall with both arms. A sprain of one wrist and a broken bone in the other hand required splints, forcing him to take to an ambulance for transportation. The usual rumors reached the Northern papers, which reported Lee to have been wounded in the battle, several imaginative accounts going so far as to give the precise details.

The Battle of Chantilly (Ox Hill)

With A. P. Hill's division in the lead, the long column started out, weary, hungry, soaking wet from the continuing rain, and slipping crazily in the narrow, muddy road. The unhappy foot soldiers, showing little resemblance to a victorious army on parade, can scarcely be said to have put their hearts into the renewed march, so that progress was painfully slow. The troops bivouacked for the night at Pleasant Valley, along the Little River Turnpike near Cub Run, still several miles from Pope's rear, which now for a change was being guarded almost as strongly as his front and all other portions of the army's anatomy. Longstreet's divisions were equally apathetic as they took to the road, spending the night on the west side of Bull Run.

Jackson resumed the march on the morning of September 1, by which time the rain had ceased, but the roads were still muddy, the hunger of the men unsatisfied, and the rate of march continued slow. It was mid-afternoon when the head of the column passed through Chantilly, which boasted a fine old mansion on the turnpike about four miles due north of Centerville and the same distance west of Germantown. The Confederates were marching east along Little River Turnpike (now U.S. 50). with A. P. Hill's division again in the lead, followed by Jackson's division (under Starke) and Ewell's division (under Lawton). The troops moved in double column, half the brigades off to the right of the road and the others to the left, leaving the road itself for artillery, wagons, and couriers. This method of marching, used often by both sides, was usually more pleasant for the men, who thus traversed meadows instead of tramping in a cloud of dust. More important, it provided a tight, closed-up formation from which deployment could be effected quickly to the front or either flank.

The terrain was rolling, the low ridges running generally at right angles to the road. Pastures and fields of grain, with occasional clumps of woods, lay on either side of the highway. About four miles east of the hamlet of Chantilly was a ridge called Ox Hill which, like the other low ridges in this area, intersected the highway roughly at right angles. To the casual traveler Ox Hill is scarcely to be distinguished from the rest of the terrain, though it is nearly 100 feet higher than the other ridges in this area. As may be seen from the map, it is crossed by the Ox Road coming in from the north. At the point where Ox Road intersects the turnpike, an unnamed road runs south to the Warrenton Turnpike.

The battlefield of Chantilly, or Ox Hill, lies immediately south of Little River Turnpike, and on both sides of the unnamed road mentioned above. There was a narrow clearing along the pike adjacent to the crossroads, from which the wooded slopes of Ox Hill extended south for some 400 yards to an open field nearly a half-mile wide and deep, part of which was in corn. A rail fence bordered this field on the north, and the trace of the unfinished branch of the Manassas Gap Railway ran roughly along its southwestern edge.

Confederate skirmishers moving south of the column, along the railway bank, reported that the Federals in considerable strength were coming up from the general direction of Centerville. Though Jackson did not know it, an inhabitant of the Chantilly-Ox Hill area, a man named Campbell, had gone south to report to Pope near Centerville that the Confederates were moving in strength along Little River Turnpike toward Fairfax Court House. They had advanced to the point, Pope thought, where it began to look like a serious effort to turn the Federal right flank at Centerville. He thereupon prepared to meet the new situation and to fight a general battle if that should become necessary. Hooker was detached and sent to Fairfax with instructions to take command of all the troops in that vicinity and move them to Germantown, while McDowell's corps was sent in the same direction to form on Hooker's left. Stevens' reinforced division of Reno's corps was dispatched in the direction of Ox Hill with part of Heintzelman's corps in support.

Stevens' guide, Campbell, led the column off to the northeast of the Warrenton Pike, following an obscure wagon track through the woods. A battery of field artillery and Kearny's division followed. The leading units emerged into the clearing across the unfinished railroad southwest of the Reid house, the battery being placed in firing position on a low knoll in that vicinity. The battery began to shell the woods to the north, where smoke puffs from the muskets of Jackson's withdrawing skirmishers were seen.

When Jackson became aware of the threat on his flank he at once deployed his divisions, facing south, on either side of the road running south. The brigades began to advance slowly through the woods, the left of the line being refused to give flank protection.

At Jackson's direction A. P. Hill peeled off Branch's brigade, followed by Brockenbrough's, to move through the woods on the right of Lawton, to feel out the enemy. From the firing it appeared that the Federals were in greater strength on that flank. After advancing 400 yards below the turnpike the men came to a rail fence, with the clearing beyond—from which they received small arms and cannon fire. The two brigades halted along the fence, while three more brigades came up to their support. The Confederates placed a battery in position on the high ground near Stuart's house, on the pike, but it was unable to fire because the woods to the south of the highway prevented the gunners from seeing the cornfield in which the battle was raging.

After watching the action for a time from the knoll where his Federal battery was firing, Stevens concluded that he could gain nothing by remaining in position, but must attack. About 4:30 p.m. he formed his division, now reduced to some 2,000 muskets, in a column of brigades, and leading them in person, he charged toward the rail fence where the Confederates were in position. As he climbed over the fence Stevens was killed. About this time a tremendous thunderclap exploded and a torrential rain descended in the mens' faces. In a short time many of the soldiers on both sides could not fire, their powder being water-soaked. Nevertheless the fighting grew heavier, and somewhat confused, both sides taking considerable losses.

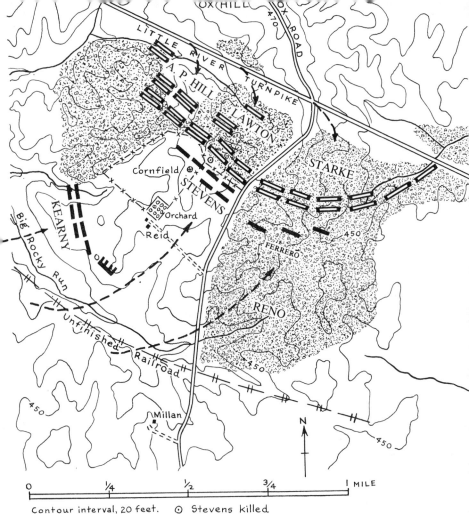

Contour interval, 20 feet. ⊙ Stevens killed
⊕ Kearny killed
x—x—x rail fence

MAP 24. THE BATTLE OF CHANTILLY (OX HILL), SEPTEMBER 1, 1862

Showing the early stages of the engagement. Shortly after arriving on the southern edge of the clearing Stevens' division charged up to the rail fence behind which the Confederate line was forming. At this point Stevens fell, and heavy firing drove his regiments back to a line approximately even with the Reid house (then owned by Ballard). Meantime Ferrero's brigade advanced through the woods on the right, driving back Starke's division.

Kearny came up at the head of his leading brigade, and attempted to get Stevens' leading regiments to resume the attack while his own troops joined on the left. Riding forward alone into the cornfield, Kearny was killed. But rain and darkness had already virtually ended the fighting. The Federals withdrew southward to the Centerville-Fairfax pike, their mission of flank protection accomplished; Pope's defeated army was able to continue its withdrawal unmolested.

Lee remained on the field, preparing to turn north on Ox Road toward Leesburg, starting his projected invasion of Maryland.

Today the battlefield is unmarked, and little changed from its appearance in 1862. The Reid (Ballard) house is still there, as is the Millan house.

During Stevens' charge, the Confederate lines on the east of the side road fell back. But there were no fresh Federal units on hand to exploit this success. The fighting in the edge of the woods, the loss of their commander, and the heavy rainstorm demoralized Stevens' units, so that Kearny, who came up about this time, was unable to get them to move

MAJOR GENERAL ISAAC I. STEVENS,
Killed at the Battle of Chantilly.

forward again in support of his leading brigade, Birney's. Kearny was informed by one of the regimental commanders at the south end of the field that his men were out of ammunition and that the enemy were in the cornfield a few yards ahead. Despite this warning, Kearny, in a rage, rode forward alone to reconnoiter. In a moment the nearest Federals heard some firing, from which they concluded that Kearny was dead or captured. Soon the heavy rainfall and gathering darkness took the starch out of everyone, so that the fighting was not renewed.

The mercurial John Pope apparently had had one of his better moments when he moved that afternoon, with a surprising show of resoluteness, to counter the threat of the new Confederate flanking maneuver in the direction of Fairfax Court House. The possibility of just such an attempt as Jackson made had been foreseen, for as early as 3 a.m. Pope had ordered the newly arrived Sumner, whose corps was the last detachment from the Army of the Potomac to come up, to send a brigade of infantry to reconnoiter the Little River Road beyond Germantown. His subsequent troops dispositions were initiated hours before Jackson's slow moving column hove into sight. The Confederates' last view of their enemy had been a confused mass of men and vehicles all trying to cross the Stone Bridge at once, in what many accounts have described as a disorderly rout. Hence the discovery that Pope's divisions were no longer retreating, but on the contrary were moving against them with obviously aggressive intent, must have come as an unpleasant shock. Although the two Federal divisions that had blocked Jackson were greatly outnumbered, the fierceness of their attacks and the fact that the violent storm and darkness discouraged further conflict combined to convince the Southerners that further efforts were potentially too costly to undertake.

It was chiefly the divisions of Stevens and Kearny which had stopped Jackson in his tracks in the relatively short but deadly encounter in the vicinity of Ox Hill. Although Longstreet had come up late in the day at the head of his column, insufficient daylight remained for his corps to develop for action. Therefore the engagement ended in a stalemate. Later that night the Federals withdrew in the direction whence they had come, having accomplished their mission of protecting the north flank of the retreating main column

The importance of the action lay in the fact that the stiff Federal resistance at Ox Hill prevented Lee from achieving the crowning success that would otherwise have been his as an aftermath to the second Confederate victory at Bull Run, in the form of a final humiliation for the despised Pope; while the latter, acting with surprising resilience, had shown his teeth instead of his tail in warning Lee that he had better let well enough alone. The Federals lost about 1,000 men and the Confederates 500. But for the North it was an expensive battle, resulting in the loss of two of its best division commanders, Stevens of Reno's corps and Kearny of Heintzelman's.

The Death of Stevens and Kearny

Isaac I. Stevens, graduate of West Point at the head of the class of 1839, was an officer of sound judgment, unusual intelligence, great strength of character, breadth of vision, and a soaring ambition, who had left the Army in 1853 because he felt that it afforded insufficient scope for his energies. Accepting an appointment as Governor of Washington Territory and ex-officio Superintendent of Indian Affairs, he proceeded to build a reputation for solid achievement second to none in that period of transformation of the western frontiers. Among other distinguished accomplishments, he had led an expedition to explore a railroad route to the Pacific, in the course of which he traveled over 2,000 miles through an almost trackless wilderness, examining a belt of territory some 200 miles wide through virgin country. Upon completion of the survey he predicted the feasibility of spanning the continent upon three main railroads, filing a comprehensive report that was a model of conciseness and far-reaching vision.

Stevens' energy, fairness, and resoluteness resulted in treaties with the Indians that brought 100,000 square miles of land under government ownership. In discharging his responsibilities in that field he had occasion at one time to declare martial law in two counties and personally caused the Chief Justice of the Territory, who had in Stevens' judgment exceeded his legal authority, to be arrested in his own courtroom and imprisoned till the close of a war growing out of a mutiny by revolting Indians.

The attack on Fort Sumter brought Stevens back into the

service of the Union, where his many talents were recognized as he rose rapidly from colonel to brigadier general, and then, in July 1862, to major general of volunteers. As a division commander in Reno's Ninth Corps, in the Northern Virginia Campaign, his horse was shot from under him and half of his command became casualties in the Battle of Second Manassas. In the action at Chantilly, Stevens caught the colors falling from the hands of a wounded color bearer, led his division into the heaviest fire of the advancing enemy, crossed the rail fence into the edge of the woods and fell, shot through the head, with his hand still firmly clenching the national colors.

In Pope's official report Stevens was singled out as having "distinguished himself in the most conspicuous manner during the battle of the twenty-ninth and thirtieth of August," and it was subsequently stated by an authority believed to be reliable that "at the very hour of his death the President and Secretary of War were considering the advisability of placing Stevens in command of the Army in which he was serving." Whether the story is true or not, Stevens was a general who was undoubtedly marked for high command had he lived.

Major General Phil Kearny, a colorful character who first gained fame as an Indian fighter in the pre-war army, and lost his left arm at Churubusco in the Mexican War, had fought as a division commander in Heintzelman's Third Corps of the Army of the Potomac throughout the Peninsular Campaign, and in the Battle of Second Manassas against Jackson's wing on August 30-31.

Supporting Reno at Chantilly on September 1, he led his division with great gallantry, as always, holding the reins of his horse between his teeth as he swung his saber with one hand. In the premature darkness caused by the severe thunderstorm, Kearny had recklessly ridden forward alone to reconnoiter in the cornfield, not knowing the exact position of his front line, and being exasperated with what he thought was the slowness of some of the leading units to advance. Sud-

denly he came upon a Confederate regiment, part of Thomas'
brigade, one of whose officers called upon the Union general
to surrender. Instead Kearny wheeled his horse and galloped
rapidly in the direction of his own lines, lying close to his
horse's neck after the fashion of Indians, whose equestrian
tricks he knew so well. A well-directed volley caught him
squarely in the rear, killing him instantly.

His body was carried into the Confederate lines and the

THE DEATH OF MAJOR GENERAL PHILIP KEARNY

word reached Ambrose Hill, an acquaintance in the old Army. "Poor Kearny," remarked Hill as he identified the body, "he deserved a better death than that." Under a flag of truce, the mortal remains of one of the Union army's best fighting generals were quietly carried to the Federal lines for appropriate disposition.

The affair at Chantilly, in which only a relatively small part of Pope's army succeeded in turning back Lee's final attempt to exploit his cleancut victory west of Bull Run, convinced the Confederate commander that the Union army not only was not running away, but still had some fight left in it. Furthermore the position at Centerville had its advantages and, since the Confederates themselves had labored to strengthen the works the preceding year, they were fully aware that the defenses could not easily be breached. The latest Confederate turning movement had been thwarted, and it seemed to Lee that it would be a most difficult matter for his tired troops to gather in any more fruits except by means of another major engagement, which he was not prepared to demand of them. Human endurance can be stretched to extraordinary lengths under stress of battle, but sooner or later a physical reaction sets in that nothing but rest can overcome. That extra something, a reserve of energy called up from the untapped resources of the spirit, had already been expended. As for the cattle, the living embodiment of Civil War commissary stores, they and the mules seemed to have lost interest in life and could not be persuaded to stir even when tempted by the abundance of captured hay and corn, but only lay dejectedly on the ground.

Lee's decision not to press the advance would have been good news to Pope, a badly defeated general whose earlier boldness and will to fight had by this time completely evaporated. All Pope wanted now was to get back safely to the defenses of Washington. From his new headquarters at Fairfax Court House he reported to Halleck on September 2 that "we had another pretty severe fight last night, in which Reno's and

Heintzelman's corps were engaged," and expressing the fear that the enemy "will again turn me as soon as he brings up his forces again." As Pope composed his message, it is not hard to sense his depressed state of mind:

> I will give battle when I can, but you should come out and see the troops. They were badly demoralized when they joined me, both officers and men, and there is an intense idea among them that they must get behind the intrenchments. The whole force I had for duty yesterday was 57,000 men, exclusive of Couch's.
>
> The straggling is awful in the regiments from the Peninsula. Unless something can be done to restore tone to this army it will melt away before you know it. . . . The enemy is still in our front. It is his undoubted purpose to keep on, slowly turning our position so as to come in on our right. You had best decide at once what is to be done. The enemy is in very heavy force and must be stopped in some way. . . .
>
> If you knew the troops here and their condition I think it would be well. You had best look out well for your communications. The enemy from the beginning has been throwing his rear toward the north, and every movement shows that he means to make trouble in Maryland.
>
> Wherever I have attacked him he is in greatly superior force. I would attack today, but the troops are absolutely unable.
>
> JNO. POPE
Major-General, Commanding.

It was all over; nothing remained for Halleck to do but tell Pope to come on in to the defenses of Washington, which he did in a politely cryptic telegram that for all practical purposes placed the defeated general and his routed but still sullenly defiant army under the command of General McClellan.

> Washington, D. C., September 2, 1862.
> Major-General Pope, Fairfax Court House, Va.:
> You will bring your forces as best you can within or near the line of fortification. General McClellan has charge of all the defenses, and you will consider any direction, as to the disposition of the troops as they ar-

rive, given by him as coming from me. Do not let the
enemy get between you and the works. It is impossible
for me to leave Washington.

H. W. HALLECK,
General-in-Chief.

After the fight at Chantilly, Lee discontinued the pursuit
and turned his thoughts toward an invasion of Maryland,
paying no further attention to his recent antagonist except to
direct Stuart's cavalry to engage in harassing tactics with the
double purpose of making it as unpleasant as possible for the
defeated army and to cover such movements of his own army
as he proposed shortly to initiate.

Brigadier General J. D. Cox, commanding a brigade at
Upton's Hill, was directed to cover the last stages of the retrograde movement of Pope's army to Alexandria and vicinity,
when the march from Centerville was resumed on the morning
of September 2. In the absence of further pressure from the
Confederates, the better led and disciplined divisions were
gradually restored to some semblance of order, but thousands
of stragglers had to be rounded up between the scene of the
late battle and the Washington fortifications.

To the best of the War Department's knowledge, the danger
to the Capital was still acute and there was no assurance that
Lee's army, flushed with victory, might not still drive around
or through Pope's apparently disorganized mass of troops in
an attempt to capture Washington. So real was the fear that
orders were issued to promptly ship all ordnance to New York
and, by direction of the President himself, to immediately
organize all clerks and employees of the Government into companies and to arm and supply them with ammunition for the
defense of the Capital.

Masses of freshly recruited Union soldiers were milling
around in Washington, many of them completely new to
soldiering. One of the more articulate among them, Private
Robert G. Carter, Company H, Twenty-second Massachusetts
Volunteers, who graduated from West Point after the war and
subsequently earned a Congressional Medal of Honor for ac-

tion against the Indians, described the excitement and confusion in the Capital occasioned by Lee's victory at Bull Run:*

> Monday afternoon, September 1, 1862. We move tonight with two days' rations. The enemy are at Fairfax Court-House, ten miles from here. The battle Saturday was 'nip and tuck,' I could hear the cannonading all day long. To-day, the wounded are coming by the road; some shot through the arm, leg, or hand. I have talked with them, and they all say that McDowell is a traitor, and should be shot as one. . . .
>
> The river is obstructed with shipping; the wharves groan beneath the weight of army paraphernalia; long trains of cars creep through the mass of humanity, and artillery now and then, with its deafening rumble, adds to the din, while a dense cloud of dust hangs above all the town, blinding the eyes and choking up the respiratory organs of every visitor of this modern Babel.
>
> All the restaurants have been closed by the authorities, and infantry patrol every street. All the hotels and boarding-houses were crowded beyond comfort, and hundreds of officers go about the street disconsolate, vainly seeking for a place to lay their heads.
>
> Of course the 'secesh' element is jubilant. Delight upon the countenances of rebel sympathizers too plainly marks their long-nurtured hopes of deliverance from the 'Yankees,' and the bitter experience of former delinquents only checks the full expression of disloyalty.
>
> There has been continual anxiety all the morning relative to the engagement now going on in the vicinity of Centreville. It is 12 o'clock, and there is a lull in the cannonading, which has been very severe up to this hour. On every hill from Fort Ellsworth to the city, and on many of the roofs of the houses, crowds were observed listening to the distant cannonading. The 'secesh' families kept their houses closed, and occasionally would partially open their doors, and with dark and scowling features peer up the street, as if anxiously expecting Jackson.

A faint idea of the state of the military defenses of Washington, if the Confederates had chosen to make an effort to cap-

---

*Four Brothers in Blue, © 1913 by R. G. Carter, Washington, D.C.

ture it after Second Manassas, is reflected in Carter's further comments on the incidents of that night which came under his personal observation:

> There were about 4,000 men in all, mostly recruits, and on that muddy, rainy night, it was a scene I shall never forget; those men all mixed up, trying to get arms; everything was helter-skelter, and order and method were beyond looking for. It was a regular mob, and when you consider that the commanding officer gave us to understand that we were going to aid our regiments and that they were retreating, you can conceive of the whole arrangement somewhat; and remember, too, that not one of us had ever put on a belt, buckle, cartridge-box or cap pouch.

Pope Hopes to Retain Command

Arriving at Ball's Crossroads, Pope reported to Halleck that by morning September 3, all of his troops would be in camp within the intrenchments and that the enemy showed no signs of making further attacks. Then, after a day's rest, Pope began to take account of stock and to speculate on what was in store for Major-General John Pope, late of Manassas, Virginia and points south and west. Halleck's last message had been far from reassuring, so Pope tarried at Ball's Crossroads, putting off the evil hour when command should pass to McClellan. Taking up his pen, he put out an indirect feeler, through a friend in the War Department, to ascertain how far McClellan's authority extended and to suggest again that Halleck exercise command in person.

Getting no satisfaction through indirect channels, Pope tried a new approach direct to Halleck, to whom he made the suggestion that the army should attack again with fresh troops "while the enemy is weakened and broken down." But Pope was finished, his ideas no longer worthy of even a polite brushoff, although Halleck did extend the courtesy of a reply, in which he made it plain that McClellan was in command, would exercise general authority over all the troops, and directing Pope, as soon as all his troops had come within McClellan's jurisdiction, to report in person at Halleck's headquarters. It was the army's unique way of saying, in effect, come on over and get the axe.

Pope, however, seemed to have a fairly tough hide and, although it was clear to every one else that he was going down for the third time, he submitted on September 4 a proposal for a reorganization that would give him an army of about 50,000 men with a lot of new regiments, organized into four corps under Banks, McDowell, Reno, and Hooker. That gratuitous suggestion was not even given the dignity of an acknowledgment, instead of which Halleck informed Mc-Clellan that Pope was to be relieved of command.

Querulous letters kept flowing from Pope to Halleck, while McClellan issued orders direct to Pope's former subordinates, completely ignoring the crestfallen commander of the erstwhile Army of Virginia. It finally dawned on Halleck that the decent thing to do would be to end Pope's suffering, which was accomplished by a terse order, dated September 5, which simply said: "The Armies of the Potomac and Virginia being consolidated, you will report for orders to the Secretary of War."

Exit John Pope!

McClellan's Comeback

The last days of August and the first few days of September afforded many anxious moments for the amateur strategist in the White House. President Lincoln had brought Halleck in from the west to provide, as he hoped, unity of command and a coordinating force that might accomplish for the Union what separate army commanders seemed incapable of achieving—a cleancut victory over the enemy.

McClellan had failed in his Peninsular Campaign, following which Pope had been given his chance with the Army of Virginia, into which were fed the several corps of the Army of the Potomac as they arrived from the James River. Halleck, however, proved unable to handle the situation, which degenerated rapidly to the point where Lee's army, with 50,000 more men, might well have destroyed Pope's Army of Virginia, broken the defenses of Washington, and conceivably dictated a negotiated peace from the national capital.

McClellan's hostility to Pope, coupled with his callous readiness to do everything possible, by whatever means, to facilitate the downfall of his military rival, was a shocking thing in Lincoln's view. Despite McClellan's resistance to Halleck's efforts to speed the forces of the Army of the Potomac to reinforce Pope at Manassas, enough of them had joined Pope to enable him to defeat Lee's separate wings in detail if the Union Commander had been enough of a field general to employ his augmented army effectively.

The anomalous position in which McClellan found himself, with his own army pulled out from under his control and nothing to take its place until he was finally placed in command of the Washington defenses, was an unhappy one for the little Napoleon, who continued to regard himself as the only general who could "save the country." McClellan was a determined character, however, and lost no opportunity to advance his own cause, whether it be by chipping away at Pope or feuding with Halleck.

As the Battle of Second Manassas mounted in fury, Lincoln watched developments anxiously. Direct information from Pope's headquarters was nonexistent. The President daily visited the telegraph office to read the sparse items of news that came in from other sources, chiefly Porter's biased telegrams to Burnside, and the reports which the indefatigable Colonel Haupt sent in a steady stream to the War Department from Alexandria. The latter were fragmentary in character, however, and could furnish only certain pieces of the jigsaw puzzle. Impatient to learn more, Lincoln finally wired McClellan on August 29 to inquire if he had any news of Pope. It was McClellan's reply to that telegram that badly shocked the President, for McClellan took it upon himself to offer advice, suggesting that one of two courses should be followed, either concentrate all available forces to establish connection with Pope, or "leave Pope to get out of his scrape" as best he could and use all other available troops to secure the Capital against attack.

Pope's wire of 5 a. m. Aug. 30 (pp. 211-12) suggested that he had won a partial victory and would make it a total one the following day. That sounded encouraging, and Lincoln's spirits rose. Unfamiliar with Pope's habit of wishful thinking and inadequate generalship, Lincoln can scarcely be blamed for accepting at face value a battlefield report that in actuality was founded on a complete misconception of the real facts.

The hopes that Pope raised in Washington were dashed the following day, when the news of the Union army's defeat arrived, followed by other reports which recorded the progress of the retreat in the direction of Washington. But it was not until after Pope had obliquely invited Halleck to order his army back into the defense of Washington and Halleck had obliged him, that McClellan was placed in command of the defenses and all troops therein. As usual, Halleck waited until a critical situation had become a fait accompli and then made it official; Old Brains simply lacked the ability to exercise the functions of general-in-chief and to direct events with a firm hand.

The cocky McClellan now believed the Administration had turned to him because he was the man of destiny who would save the country. Nothing could have been farther from the truth. Lincoln had become convinced that McClellan wanted Pope to be defeated, no matter what the cost to the country, and that he had passively, if not actively, contributed to that result. On the other hand, Lincoln knew also that McClellan was a skilful organizer and that no other general officer was better able to whip the troops into fighting trim, even though he was not a fighter himself. The President's decision was therefore in the nature of a temporary expedient to carry the country through a crisis, with no intent to allow Little Mac to again lead the army in a field campaign. The proof of the latter statement is found in the fact that command of the Army of the Potomac was offered to Ambrose E. Burnside

when Lee a few days after Manassas moved into Maryland, and
it became evident that another campaign was imminent.

McClellan's hold on the imagination and affection of his
army was amazing. It is said that when the disheartened and
dejected troops were threading their way back to the Washington defenses from Centerville on September 2, McClellan
rode out from Alexandria with a single staff officer to meet
them. Catching the first glimpse of the familiar figure on horseback, some of Porter's men raised a cheer. The magic word
passed swiftly down the line and—but let's hear what happened,
in the words of Captain William H. Powell of the 4th
Infantry:*

> Captain John D. Wilkins, of the 3d Infantry, came run-
> ning toward Colonel Buchanan, crying out:
> "Colonel! Colonel! General McClellan is here!"
> The enlisted men caught the sound! Whoever was awake
> aroused his neighbor. Eyes were rubbed, and those tired
> fellows, as the news passed down the column, jumped to
> their feet, and sent up such a hurrah as the Army of the
> Potomac had never heard before. Shout upon shout went
> out into the stillness of the night; and as it was taken up
> along the road and repeated by regiment, brigade, divi-
> sion, and corps, we could hear the roar dying away in the
> distance. The effect of this man's presence upon the Army
> of the Potomac—in sunshine or rain, in darkness or in
> daylight, in victory or defeat—was electrical, and too won-
> derful to make it worthwhile attempting to give a reason
> for it.

"The army is now better contented than it was," wrote
Lieut. Gillette to his parents on September 8. "General Mc-
Clellan, their idol, is restored to command. He is, in the opinion of all soldiers, the only honest and skilful leader we have
had. None other can replace him in the affection of the men.
To take from an army the leaders it loves and to substitute
those who are to them unknown or disliked, is to defeat that
army at once. I firmly believe that had General McClellan's

---

*Battles and Leaders, Vol. II, P. 489.

plans been uninterfered with by politicians and people at home who never know what they are gabbling about when they speak of field and camp movements, the rebellion would have been crushed. . . .

"I have twice narrowly escaped capture or death at Catlett's Station, when General Pope's train was destroyed, and at Manassas where the Commissary, his depot, and stores were all captured. Such dangers will not likely occur again, as any other General than Pope would try to protect his rear. With General Pope the rear is the unsafe place, the front is all bluster and brag and noise. The rear is the battleground. How we got out of Va. I can't tell. No one has confidence in General Pope."

CHAPTER 14

SECOND MANASSAS—AN APPRAISAL

THE Campaign of Northern Virginia, which ended in a Confederate victory at Second Manassas on August 30, 1862, was a ringing defeat for the Union primarily because Lee outgeneraled Pope. But to rest content with that statement is to oversimplify the case. The difficulty in uncovering the significant contributing causes lies partly in the fact that Mc-Clellan's subsequent resumption of command of the Army of the Potomac, and Lee's unsuccessful invasion of Maryland, culminating in the bloody battle of Antietam, followed later by Fitz John Porter's trial by court-martial, all tend to focus attention on the newsworthy events that grew out of Pope's defeat and were therefore effects rather than causes.

Still another roadblock to a clear understanding of the 1862 campaign is the natural confusion caused by the fact that two important battles were fought on the same stage, although under different commanders and in successive years, both being given their place in Civil War history as the Battle of Bull

267

Run (North) or Manassas (South). It's much the same thing as trying to sort out the history of England under the reign of a king named Henry, or James, or Charles, with the dubious assistance of an unhelpful Roman numeral.

About the only similarity between the two battles, aside from the duplication of place names and locale, was the denouement—the retreat of the Union forces to the questionable security of what was called the defenses of Washington. But even in that final act of both dramas there was a marked difference, for in July 1861 the return to the capital was a panicked rout, while in September 1862 the retreat was conducted in reasonably good order with the exception of a minority of undisciplined, badly led units, most of whom deserved better of their commanders.

While the statement may be said to beg the question, there is good reason for emphasizing the fact that it was the army commander, John Pope, rather than the Army of Virginia, who lost the battle of Second Manassas, just as Ambrose Burnside was defeated at Fredericksburg the following December, and Joseph Hooker at Chancellorsville in May 1863. In all three cases the respective Union armies were composed of excellent material, whose regiments, brigades, and divisions were with the normal exceptions capably led by experienced field commanders, whose names and shining records are second to none in the memories of a grateful republic.

The basic statistics of the campaign, excluding what may be called the preliminary round at Cedar Mountain on August 9, between only a part of each of the two armies under Lee and Pope, are of themselves an interesting commentary. Pope's combat strength was at all times in excess of the numbers available to Lee, from the date when the fully assembled armies faced one another across the Rappahannock, following the Federal withdrawal from an untenable position in the pocket between the Rapidan and the Rappahannock; while in the latter stages, on the plains of Manassas, his strength was progressively augmented by arriving units from McClellan's Army of the Potomac, until the ratio approached 8 to 5 in his favor on or about August 26, leaving out of consideration some 30,000 additional troops within supporting distance, plus the residue of Burnside's force at Fredericksburg, and the troops assigned to the Washington fortifications. Pope's difficulty lay in the fact that he failed to utilize effectively his preponderance of manpower, whereas Lee and his lieutenants fully employed the lesser Confederate strength and made it count at the right times and places.

Relative Strengths and Casualties

The number and character of the casualties sustained in the campaign are also significant. For while Pope threw into the action at Groveton and Manassas over 70,000 men, excluding Banks' corps with the trains, against Lee's approximately 55,000, the Confederates suffered fewer losses than the Federals, as disclosed by the official records:

	Killed	Wounded	Missing or Captured	Total
Union	1,746	8,445	4,258	14,449
Confederate ...	1,554	7,747	119	9,420

Thus it is seen that the Union forces sustained losses of 20 percent of their strength as against 17 percent for the Confederates. On the other hand, the attacker is usually more badly hurt than the defender and retreating troops frequently take severe punishment during their retrograde movement. It would therefore seem that the principal conclusions to be drawn from the casualty figures are that a lot of bitter close-in fighting took a heavy toll of both armies, and neither side held a monopoly on either *individual* bravery or small-unit combat aggressiveness.

In evaluating a campaign or battle in which the fighting ability of the men in the ranks is essentially the same for both armies, and there is comparable competence as well as incompetence in a cross section of the officer leadership up to and including division commanders, the problem narrows down to the relative capabilities of a handful of individuals on each side, the corps and army commanders.

It was so in this campaign, which, as stated before, cannot be dismissed as simply Lee's victory over Pope. There were too many collateral factors that influenced the result, even though in the final analysis the superior Confederate strategy and tactics were decisive in overwhelming the Union general who lacked the ability either to employ to advantage the forces available or to exploit the opportunities offered him by that great exponent of the calculated risk, Robert E. Lee.

Lee and his three lieutenants, corps commanders Jackson and Longstreet, and cavalry commander Jeb Stuart, formed a team combination that resembled a well-oiled, smooth-running piece of machinery that in this campaign was beautiful to contemplate. On the Union side a far different picture was presented. Pope had as corps commanders in his own Army of Virginia Generals Banks, Sigel, and McDowell, not one of whom could be called outstanding; augmented by Heintzelman and Fitz John Porter from McClellan's army (with Franklin and Sumner hovering offstage in the wings) and Reno from Burnside's corps. Heintzelman and Reno were reliable, competent generals, and Porter was highly regarded by the professional officers, but his attitude at Second Manassas made him more of a liability than an asset to Pope. There was no counterpart to Stuart, for the Federal cavalry was parceled out to the corps commanders in an inefficient, extremely wasteful manner, with one brigade to each of the three corps commanded by Banks, Sigel, and McDowell.

McDowell may be regarded in part as a victim of circumstances, commencing with the first Battle of Manassas in July 1861, into which he was pushed unwillingly by public opinion in the Northern States, before the troops under his command knew what it was all about. From then on, somewhat unjustly, he was charged with the responsibility for that Union fiasco, nor did his subsequent military activities serve to erase the initial impression. His tactical judgment was sound enough, but he seemed to be fated, when things went wrong, to be in the limelight, such as the occasion when he became lost during the Second Manassas campaign and spent an entire night, at a critical moment, trying to recover his bearings and resume his place at the head of his two-corps command. The enlisted men, no doubt, blamed him for the seemingly uncoordinated and fruitless marches to which they were subjected by Pope's futile efforts to trap Jackson's divisions. At Second Manassas he broke out a weird type of headgear that resembled an inverted basket, but which failed to arouse admiration on the part of the men of his corps, many of whom were veterans of First Manassas and vividly recalled what had happened there under McDowell's army command. There is no question, certainly, that his troops progressively held McDowell in such low regard as to cause a number of them to freely express the harsh opinion that he was a traitor and that "thousands of the men firmly believed that their lives would be purposely wasted if they obeyed his orders during battle."*

In comparing the top leadership of the opposing armies, and by assigning a scale of values based on prior and subsequent individual performance from the vantage point of history, the Confederates so far outscore the Federals that a privileged, perceptive forecaster would have been reasonably safe in predicting the outcome at any given time after contact on the Rapidan in mid-August.

Federal Strategy

President Lincoln and Secretary Stanton had made a wise decision, in the best military tradition, when they moved be-

---

*On September 6, 1862, less than a week after the Second Battle of Manassas, General McDowell wrote President Lincoln requesting that a Court of Inquiry be appointed to investigate fully and without limitation his conduct as a general officer. The requested court was convened in Washington, heard testimony for sixty-seven days, from November 21, 1862 to February 23, 1863, with the result that the charges of treason, drunkenness and military incapacity were fully refuted and McDowell given a clean bill of health. The testimony which was taken during the court covers almost 300 printed pages in Volume XI, Part I, of the Official Records.

latedly to achieve unity of command by consolidating the independent forces of Fremont, Banks, and McDowell into a single army. Of even greater importance was the appointment of a general-in-chief as directing head, to coordinate from Washington the activities of all the Union armies in the vast theater of war that extended from the Atlantic ocean to the Missouri River and from Pennsylvania to the Gulf of Mexico.

From a strategic standpoint, the wisdom of recalling McClellan's Army of the Potomac from the James River, where it constituted a sword of Damocles hanging over the capital of the Confederacy, is open to serious question. It is inconceivable that the order would ever have been issued had McClellan not convinced the Washington administration, by his interminable stalling, that he lacked a fighting heart and kept insisting on unattainable conditions that might never be fulfilled.

Had Grant been in command rather than McClellan, it is almost certain that Lincoln would not have interfered, for three years later Grant ended the war by his operations in forcing the capitulation of Petersburg and Richmond from the very same lines south of the James River that the Army of the Potomac occupied in 1862, whence it was recalled under McClellan. The major difference was that McClellan talked more than he fought, whereas Grant reversed the process.

Having embraced the principle of unity of command and extended it to consolidate the eastern armies for what was conceived as a decisive campaign against Lee's Army of Northern Virginia, all that remained was to implement the strategic plan. Lincoln now had his general-in-chief in the person of Henry W. Halleck, and his two army commanders in Pope and McClellan.

Where the President failed was not so much in the strategy as in the selection of the men charged with its execution. For after Halleck was put in the top military spot and the plan approved, the military hierarchy was not interfered with, despite McClellan's intemperate charges, alibis, and critical letters from which it was made to appear that the Administration did little but throw obstacles in the way of the self-appointed savior of his country.

Fortunately Lincoln's place in history does not have to be judged on his lack of success in choosing winning generals in the years 1861, 1862, and the first half of 1863. Still, he should not be criticized too greatly so far as his selection of Halleck, Pope, and McClellan is concerned, for the two first named had indeed shown evidence of potential success in the west; while McClellan had initially done very well in West Virginia against the then relatively unknown Robert E. Lee, and had without question subsequently performed a great service in organizing and whipping into shape a magnificent weapon in the form of the Army of the Potomac.

All three Federal generals were to prove unequal to the tasks assigned them, although it will never be known whether any one of the three might have succeeded under different circumstances. A strong leader in place of Halleck should have been able to achieve a more prompt consolidation of the two armies had he cracked a few heads and taken command in person. A general such as Hancock, or Reynolds, or Couch would have cooperated where McClellan obstructed. A more competent general in Pope's place would not have run his army ragged, but rather have held it together and maneuvered it in a manner to expedite the junction of the two armies (as Halleck planned it) before Washington, preparatory to launching a coordinated offensive with every chance of success.

Pope's original mission was complicated and difficult. His initial instructions, it will be recalled, were to cover Washington, assure the safety of the Shenandoah Valley, and operate on the enemy lines of communication in the direction of Gordonsville and Charlottesville, for the purpose of drawing Lee away from Richmond and thus assisting McClellan in a renewal of the latter's attempts to capture Richmond. Pope's mission, therefore, was both defensive and offensive, a difficult task for the best of generals, and an almost impossible one for a man of Pope's limited capacities; particularly when he was first required to assemble three independent corps under only average corps commanders and in enemy territory at that, and then to weld them into a single, cohesive organization virtually in the presence of the enemy.

The newly appointed army commander was still in Washington, issuing manifestoes and orders at a remote distance from his as yet unconsolidated corps, when Halleck changed the strategy by ordering McClellan to bring his army back to the Aquia Creek-Fredericksburg area to join with Pope's army. That killed the idea that Pope had been considering, to advance on Richmond from the west, at a time when McClellan proved slow in taking the initiative by attacking the Confederate capital from the east and south. At the same time it accomplished one part of Pope's initial four-point mission by drawing Jackson's augmented wing from Richmond to Gordonsville, and thus dividing Lee's army. However, Lee detached Jackson only when he was satisfied that McClellan was moving north and that Richmond was safe for the time being.

In effect, what Halleck did by modifying the Federal plan was to discard the nutcracker scheme whereby Richmond would be attacked from two sides. By so doing he yielded the initiative to Lee, who quickly grasped what looked like a favorable opportunity to defeat Pope before the two Federal armies could effect a junction. The transfer of the Army of the Potomac from the James to the area between Fredericksburg and Washington also automatically canceled a second section of Pope's four-point mission, that of covering Washington, or should have, leaving him free to address himself to the remaining two parts, which were to secure the Shenandoah Valley and operate against Gordonsville and Charlottesville.

When Pope finally joined his army in the field, some weeks after assuming command, he decided to concentrate at Culpeper and proceed from there to the Rapidan and then on to Gordonsville. While he was in the process of attempting to execute that plan, Stonewall Jackson moved to prevent the concentration of Pope's army. The Battle of Cedar Mountain ensued, after which Pope completed his concentration and occupied the line of the Rapidan, while Lee came up from Richmond and the Army of Northern Virginia was again intact, facing Pope on the other side of the river.

Time for the Federals was a-wastin'. The picture had vastly changed, and Pope was now strictly on the defensive, as Lee probed for weak spots and the reinforcements from McClellan's army were moved sluggishly and reluctantly to the place where Little Mac would have to relinquish them. It was during this transition period that Halleck slipped badly in his unwillingness to take command in person or to clear the air by positive orders with respect to the chain of command. McClellan's divisions were fed piecemeal to Pope as they arrived, initially from Aquia Creek and later through Alexandria, but Halleck weakly temporized so that both Pope and McClellan were unsure as to the exact status of the newly arriving troops, with the terrific loss of morale that such indecision assured.

Pope and McClellan held each other in low esteem to begin with, so that Halleck's lack of firmness only served to compound an already difficult situation. Added to Pope's other problems, one cannot help but sympathize with the unfortunate general at that particular period. Nevertheless, Pope rose to the occasion, went on the defensive in deference to Halleck's orders not to advance beyond the Rapidan, and swiftly extricated his army from its untenable position in the narrow V strip of land between the Rapidan and the Rappahannock. He was lucky to have his cavalry capture a copy of Lee's order for a turning movement against his left flank; an advance notice of the Confederate leader's plan of action which galvanized Pope into his immediate retirement to the Rappahannock and forced Lee to revise his own tactics. On the north bank of the Rappahannock Pope took up a strong position from which Lee decided that he could not drive him by frontal action.

And it was there, on the line of the Rappahannock, that Pope's hopeful star began to decline. Now confronted by Lee's

entire army, he didn't know how soon the Army of the Potomac would come to his support. Again the fault lay more
with Halleck and McClellan than with Pope, who was promised by the former that if he held for two days he would have
plenty of reinforcements. Halleck should have directed Pope
to fall back, as far as Bull Run if need be, but to prevent at
all costs any move by Lee to get through or around him. The
main job now was to concentrate the Union armies, and the
surest means to that end would have been for Pope to facilitate
the junction by continuing his progressive retrograde movement until the integration of all the available divisions, Pope's,
McClellan's, Burnside's, and those in the Washington defenses,
was complete. Every other consideration was at that stage secondary in importance, in view of Lee's demonstrated skill at
the game of wartime chess and his obviously offensive intentions.

With Lee's second and successful attempt at a flanking movement, this time against the Federal right, Pope's real troubles
began. Stuart's large cavalry raid on Pope's rear at Catlett's
station, which exposed Pope to ridicule for his stupidity in
advertising a policy of looking to the front and letting the
rear take care of itself, failed to teach the Federal commander
a lesson. Pope made no effort to strengthen his rear echelon,
with the result that Jackson's three division corps, accompanied
by Stuart's two cavalry brigades, repeated Stuart's performance,
cut the Federal communications, destroyed the huge supply
depot at Manassas Junction, and laid the groundwork for the
Confederate battlefield victory on August 30.

Pope's Blunders

The last few days of August were sad ones for John Pope.
Nothing seemed to go right, which should not have surprised
him, because he himself was so bewildered by Lee's audacious
maneuvers that he blundered repeatedly, to the great advantage of the Confederates. From the moment that Lee divided
his army to send Jackson on his wide swing around the Union
army, Pope seemed to lose whatever judgment and mental bal-

ance he may have possessed. If Lee was waging psychological warfare in an effort to lead Pope on to commit his army to a general engagement before being fully reinforced by McClellan's army, he succeeded admirably.

Pope's lack of qualification for army command was revealed in what seems to have been an incredible disregard of the fundamental principles of war, notably those having to do with security, simplicity, and economy of force, although he managed at one time or another to violate the other six as well. His indifference to the importance of security was the major contribution to his ultimate defeat, however, since each successive blunder started a chain reaction which progressively increased the distrust of his subordinates in the competence of the commanding general.

While the military dictum that attack is the best defense may be true under appropriate circumstances, it does not mean that ordinary precautions can be disregarded, particularly against opponents who were experts in taking advantage of every opening. Pope's employment of his cavalry for other than courier service was practically non-existent; as a matter of fact the three brigades that he had in the Army of Virginia were attached respectively to the three organic corps, and there is no evidence that Banks or Sigel utilized their services to advantage. It would have been infinitely better if the cavalry had been concentrated under John Buford, an excellent commander, as a weapon of opportunity under army command, similar to the superb manner in which Stuart's cavalry was employed for the Confederates. Nevertheless, it was Buford, reconnoitering west of Bull Run Mountains under McDowell's orders, who first encountered Longstreet at Salem, caused him several hours' delay, and reported his advance as he moved through the gap and Gainesville to Groveton. That was all that the small Federal cavalry force could hope to accomplish without infantry support, which Pope had no intention of furnishing.

Because of the dissipation of the Federal cavalry strength in uncoordinated movements under the direction of the several corps commanders, Jackson was able to lead 24,000 men completely around Pope's right on a sixty-mile march, to come up squarely on his rear without encountering a single Federal; and then, after cutting the railroad to Alexandria and setting fire to the depot at Manassas, march his divisions a few miles farther into temporary hiding north of Groveton; while Pope, having no idea as to where Jackson had disappeared, played hare and hounds with his own troops in a frantically frustrating effort to catch the elusive Confederate.

Seldom in the history of war has an army been so badly handled as was the Army of Virginia, during the two days of Pope's ineffectual maneuvers to bag the cool, assured Stonewall Jackson and his men. To make matters worse, all Pope could think about was the seemingly golden opportunity which Lee had offered him to defeat one half of the Confederate army while the other half was believed to be too far away to prevent. Jumping to false conclusions appears to have been Pope's stock-in-trade, for the last thing that Jackson contemplated was retreat, and Pope's generalship was so inadequate that he was able to plan in only one dimension, if indeed his jerky actions can be said to have been based on any considered plan whatsoever.

It was undeniably true that Lee took a frightful risk when he permitted Pope to interpose his larger army between Lee's two wings; under all the rules of warfare the Confederate commander should have been badly punished for doing so. But, as usual, Lee reckoned on the character of his opponent, as well as the relative mobility of the two armies. Lee felt reasonably secure in the knowledge that Pope's army, marching historically about 6 to 10 miles a day, could never hope to catch Jackson, whose 25-mile per day marching capability should easily enable him to step nimbly away from Pope's outstretched clutches. The history of Second Manassas proves that Pope was not the general who could take the measure of so doughty a combination as Lee, Jackson, Longstreet, and Stuart.

Pope's greatest error, among the many that he committed, was his failure to seal Thoroughfare Gap with sufficient strength to delay Longstreet's approach march long enough to allow the Federal army to crush Jackson. He had enough strength to accomplish the purpose, even without further reinforcements, but when his ineffective field generalship is studied, one wonders whether his battle tactics would have succeeded in doing any more than force Jackson to utilize his carefully planned escape route by way of Aldie Gap, to rejoin Lee on the west side of Bull Run Mountains.

McDowell made an effort to block the Gap on his own, but Pope overruled him to negate the attempt, which probably would not have succeeded anyway, with only Ricketts' division in action. However, had Pope planned his strategy more efficiently, McDowell's corps of two divisions, with Buford's cavalry brigade attached, *might* have turned the trick, the imponderable being the unpredictable Jackson, who was still foot loose and fancy free. But Pope had in addition 39,000 men in the corps of Heintzelman, Sigel, Reno, and Porter, a total of eight divisions. If Pope could have brought his total strength to bear at this time, he would have outnumbered Jackson 3 to 1. Or if he had even allowed McDowell to use his full corps to block Longstreet at Thoroughfare Gap, he could still have outnumbered Jackson by better than 2 to 1. Intelligently employed, the military facts of life would seem to have made it almost a certainty that Jackson would have been prevented from making his escape, the only alternative being his destruction or capture.

The cold fact of the matter is that Pope lost his head when Jackson fastened on his rear. Practically every one of his subsequent impressions was based on incomplete or inaccurate information and false presumptions on his own part. First he ordered his entire army to converge on Manassas to bag Jackson, while he forgot all about Longstreet. Next, when Jackson slipped away from Manassas, sending A. P. Hill by way of Centerville, Pope changed the order of march of his separated corps and directed them all to go to Centerville. Finding no Confederates there, he jumped to the conclusion that Jackson was retreating to join Lee. so Pope started the army down the Warrenton Turnpike after him, only to find that Jackson wasn't retreating after all, but had taken up a defensive position north of Groveton.

Still thinking in his narrow mental groove, Pope ordered an attack in the continued belief that only Jackson's corps was in front of him. In the meantime, however, Longstreet had come up, extended Jackson's line, and Lee's concentrated army was ready. The battle of August 29, with Pope still unaware of Longstreet's presence, resulted in Pope's misconception that the Confederates had had enough and were retreating. So he ordered a *pursuit* for the following morning.

With the two armies now on approximately even terms, although the advantage of numbers still remained substantially in Pope's favor, Lee allowed Pope to batter his men against Jackson's defensive positions until the opening occurred which an experienced general like Lee was sure to exploit. Longstreet's counterattack turned the tide, Pope's nerve was gone, his army retreated, and the Second Battle of Manassas passed into history.

Steele sums up Pope's failure in succinct fashion:*

> Pope did not "receive just impressions and estimate things and objects at their real value" (quotes are from Napoleon's Maxims). He did not form right conclusions; and with each new report he changed his mind concerning the situation and issued new orders. He wore his men out with marching and countermarching, and destroyed their confidence in himself with vacillating and contradictory orders. He never had a true conception of the situation from the time when he learned of Jackson's movement northward, until he reached the fortifications of Washington with his beaten army. He never discerned the opportunity presented him to destroy the two fractions of Lee's Army separately.

---

*American Campaigns, Steele.

Pope's Apologia

The disillusioned architect of his army's misfortune, who after Second Manassas was relegated to a remote northwestern post for the rest of the war, wrote his own account of the campaign at a later date. In it he made a great point of the fact that his wagon trains and supplies were carefully guarded so that none of the trains or mules were lost, as though that was a signal achievement. Actually, the neutralization of Banks' entire corps to guard the army trains leaned as far in the opposite direction as his earlier lack of judgment in using but a single regiment for the purpose. If Jackson, having burned Manassas Junction, had chosen to do so, he could probably have destroyed the trains in spite of Banks. After the Confederates withdrew to Groveton, with only Fitz Lee's small cavalry brigade available to raid Banks, a single infantry brigade would have been sufficient to guard the trains. As it was, Pope deprived himself of strong infantry reserves at the critical moment and at the critical point.

Division commanders Kearny and Stevens, both of whom were killed at Chantilly, as well as Generals Schenck, Tower, Reynolds, Milroy, Hooker, and Buford, were singled out for commendation, but Fitz John Porter was roundly castigated for his failure to attack the enemy right flank on the afternoon of August 29, an action which in Pope's words "would have been conclusive." "For this action (failure) or non-action," wrote Pope, "he has been on the one hand likened to Benedict Arnold, and on the other favorably compared to George Washington. . . . Porter's case is the first I have ever known, or that I find recorded in military history, in which the theory has been seriously put forth that the hero of a battle is the man who keeps out of it."

In attempting to explain his conduct of the campaign, Pope was far from convincing, or even concise. There is no admission of failure on his part, the thought being conveyed that his army lost the battle because it was outnumbered and that a worse fate was avoided through the skilful use of maneuver. In view of the historic facts, Pope would have been wiser to remain silent, but this was his explanation:

> To confront with a small army greatly superior forces, to fight battles without the hope of victory, but only to gain time by delaying the forward movement of the enemy, is a duty the most hazardous and the most difficult that can be imposed upon any general or any army. While such operations require the highest courage and endurance on the part of the troops, they are unlikely to be understood or appreciated, and the results, however successful in view of the object aimed at, have little in them to attract public commendation or applause.
>
> At no time could I have hoped to fight a successful battle with the superior forces of the enemy which confronted me, and which were able at any time to outflank and bear my small army to the dust. It was only by constant movement, incessant watchfulness, and hazardous skirmishes and battles, that the forces under my command were saved from destruction, and that the enemy was embarrassed and delayed in his advance until the army of General McClellan was at length assembled for the defense of Washington.
>
> I did hope that in the course of these operations the enemy might commit some imprudence, or leave some opening of which I could take such advantage as to gain at least a partial success. This opportunity was presented by the advance of Jackson on Manassas Junction; but although the best dispositions possible in my view were made, the object was frustrated by causes which could not have been foreseen, and which perhaps are not yet completely known to the country.

The really sad part of the whole unfortunate business was that Pope admitted defeat and initiated his retirement to the Washington defenses without any necessity for retreating. It was Pope's spirit, not that of his army, which had been broken. He didn't realize it, but the Confederates had been just as badly hurt as his own troops, if we except the 4,000 odd men listed as captured or missing, and they could be written off as an expendable byproduct in view of the relative strength of the two armies.

Although pushed back by Longstreet's counterattack, the Federals still held Henry House Hill, a key position, when the fighting ceased, and despite the lurid accounts of the rush across the Stone Bridge, Pope's army for the most part retired on order of their commanding general. It is not beyond the realm of probability, in the opinion of students of the battle, that had Pope shown a determination to hold on the line of Bull Run, or later in the Centerville position, the military factors were such that any further Confederate advances might very well have been repulsed, for Lee's men were exhausted and quite ready to call it a day when August 30 came to an end. In such an event, Second Manassas would have been recorded in the history books as a stalemate, for it is unlikely that Lee would have tarried long in that vicinity, with 30,000 or more fresh troops under Franklin and Sumner prepared to do battle as the spearhead of a counteroffensive under the personal direction of McClellan.

Confederate Strategy

To fully appreciate the genius of Robert E. Lee, the quality of whose leadership was superior to that of any other general of the Civil War, North or South, it is necessary to put oneself in his position and study all the circumstances upon which his decisions and actions were based at the time of whatever campaign is under scrutiny.

McClellan's Peninsular Campaign in the summer of 1862, which culminated in the Seven Days' Battles before Richmond, afforded Lee his first opportunity as an army commander. Although the end result was defeat for the Union in McClellan's failure to take Richmond, in the course of which Lee himself made a few mistakes, he also learned much about his own generals and those on the enemy side, knowledge that he would put to excellent use in the campaigns that followed.

Thoroughly conscious of the North's great superiority in manpower reserves and industrial sinews, Lee adopted a military strategy based on boldness, rapidity of movement, flexibility in maneuver, and the widest possible reliance on the calculated risk; a policy that took the fullest advantage of Washington's sensitivity on the subject of the defense of the Northern capital. His knowledge of the character and ability of many of the more prominent Northern generals was unique, but it was his shrewdness in anticipating their probable reaction to a given situation, and acting boldly on such military evaluations, which contributed so greatly to the series of successes enjoyed by his Army of Northern Virginia from the day he took command until his first decisive repulse at Gettysburg on July 3, 1863.

When McClellan's Army of the Potomac withdrew from before Richmond to its position on the James River, and Lee learned that a new Union army under General Pope was being assembled in the Culpeper area, he faced a new situation whereby he would shortly find his army in the defenses of Richmond confronted by 100,000 men under McClellan on the James, and an army of as yet unknown strength under Pope to the west of Richmond. At best he would be outnumbered 2½ to 1, a numerical disadvantage that could be overcome only through the exercise of superior generalship, bold offensive maneuvers, and maximum employment of the element of surprise with the minimum number of mistakes by the Confederates. In other words, Lee had to depend on fast footwork and lightning jabs to keep his heavier opponent off balance with the least practicable punishment to himself.

McClellan's lethargy convinced Lee that he could safely release Jackson's two divisions, later reinforced by a third, A. P. Hill's Light Division, to occupy. Pope's newly constituted army while Longstreet's corps tarried at Richmond until McClellan's intentions became clear. The latter's departure by installments was soon appraised for the withdrawal that it actually was. Whereupon Lee detailed the divisions of McLaws and D. H. Hill to hold the Richmond fort while he, with Longstreet's divisions, joined Jackson for the purpose of destroying Pope's army, before the Army of the Potomac could complete its movement and reconcentration in support of Pope.

The assembly of the Army of Northern Virginia under cover of Clark's Mountain, without Pope's knowledge, was the forerunner of a plan to cross the Rapidan, turn the Federal left, and break Pope's army between the two rivers, a plan that was foiled when Stuart's adjutant was captured with a copy of Lee's orders and Pope withdrew his army to a strong defensive position along the high north bank of the Rappahannock.

Lee followed, probed the enemy line to develop a weak spot, without success, and at length hit upon the audacious plan of sending Jackson's corps on a wide swinging movement around Pope's right to get on his rear.

Having wasted five days in a fruitless effort to find a weak spot in Pope's armor, and having also learned that reinforcements from Burnside's force at Fredericksburg and a portion of McClellan's army from the Peninsula had joined Pope to give him a strength that Lee accurately estimated at about 70,000 men, Lee realized that no more time could be lost. Nevertheless, his decision to split his army into two wings of 24,000 and 30,000 men respectively, and to send Jackson with the smaller number to cut Pope's rail communications and spread confusion in his rear, was as dangerous a risk as any general has ever taken.

The opportunity to defeat one's opponent in detail is eagerly sought after by troop commanders, but here was General Lee voluntarily dividing his army to offer Pope the very chance that most generals would give their eyeteeth to seize. The Confederate leader's opinion of the Federal army commander must have been very low and his confidence in his own lieutenants extremely high to so seriously jeopardize the very existence of his own army.

Lee was not one to write wordy reports or to record in letters the details of his plan of action. His telegrams to President Davis during the latter days of August were short and to the point, and wholly devoid of speculation. It is of interest that in only one dispatch did he give any indication of his intentions. That was on the morning of August 30, a few hours before Pope was defeated and started retreat to Centerville, at which time Lee wrote the President that his opponent had been drawn from the Rappahannock by Jackson's maneuver and had thus far been deceived as to the purpose of the flank march. He then made the surprising statement: "My desire has been to avoid a general engagement, being the weaker force, and by maneuvering to relieve the portion of the country referred to (evidently meaning the line of the Virginia Central railroad, his main supply route)."

It would seem from the foregoing that Lee may have had second thoughts on the subject of exterminating Pope, which had certainly been his hope at the start of the campaign. Lee's progress had however been badly retarded by the delays encountered at the Rapidan and then along the Rappahannock, which should have given the Federals the additional time needed to bring McClellan up in strength. Avoidance of a general engagement could only be achieved if Pope were forced by Jackson's activities to withdraw from the Rappahannock, which in turn would mean narrowing the gap between the two Federal armies and could thus defeat the object of crushing Pope's army *before* the Army. of the Potomac arrived.

Actually the effect on the Federals of Jackson's brilliant achievement in cutting the Orange and Alexandria Railroad in Pope's rear, and destroying the army supply base at Manassas Junction, need not have been serious, for the reason that there were ample additional supplies at Alexandria, and Haupt's efficient transportation corps could repair the break in the railroad in a few days' time. The impact of the raid was largely psychological; Pope's greatest trouble was caused by his own errors of omission and commission. To the extent, then, that Lee predicated his otherwise militarily unwise venture in dividing his army on the confident belief that bold execution of the Confederate strategy would throw Pope into a tactical tailspin, he was justified in his decision. The fact that the plan succeeded, even though it led to the general engagement that Lee informed Davis he wished to avoid, is after all the best evidence that he was right in taking his great gamble.

Holding Longstreet's corps temporarily south of the Rappahannock to keep Pope occupied while Jackson circled his army was sound procedure under the circumstances and considering the actors in the drama; and Longstreet's follow-up march to Jackson's support was not unduly delayed. Nevertheless, in that phase also of Lee's operations the fates were kind, with Pope's generous assistance, for the latter made not the slightest effort to prevent the junction of the two Confederate wings.

Finally, it will have been noted, when Lee's army was safely reunited at Groveton, that Lee played it conservatively, formed his lines for defense, and counterattacked only when it became apparent that Pope's army was ripe for a knock-out blow. It is true, of course, that in the heat of battle on the afternoon of the 29th, when Jackson's wing was taking severe punishment and came close to breaking, Lee urged Longstreet to attack. But the fact that Longstreet preferred to wait and Lee did not insist rather suggests that the latter was persuaded to delay because his policy at that time was fundamentally one of watchful waiting. Had Longstreet attacked then, he might have caught McDowell's corps marching up the Manassas-Sudley Road; but Pope was still thinking in offensive terms that day and in retrospect it appears that the counterattack of August 30 was timed more effectively then than would have been the case earlier, before Pope gave up hope and suffered the psychological defeat that engulfed his mind on the night of August 30.

JACKSON'S TROOPS CROSSING THE POTOMAC AT WHITE'S FORD

CHAPTER 15

LEE INVADES MARYLAND

THERE were rumors afloat in the Confederate ranks, even before the action at Chantilly, that Lee's next move would be to cross the Potomac, to carry the fight to enemy territory. Many were of the opinion that the order had already been issued and the march for Edward's Ferry begun, when on September 1 Jackson led his divisions north through Sudley Springs, only to turn right instead of left when the head of the column reached the Little River Turnpike leading through Germantown to Alexandria.

The speculation of the men in the ranks was well-founded. The area of Virginia over which the armies had ranged in recent weeks had been pretty thoroughly drained of supplies, whereas Maryland and Pennsylvania offered a rich territory not only for restocking Lee's army with food and clothing, but with much other needed materiel as well, such as livestock, and especially riding and draft horses as replacements for Stuart's cavalry and the artillery.

While it served Lee's purpose admirably to keep official Washington in suspense and fearful for its safety, he had no intention of going the whole distance to the capital. Although he had not succeeded in destroying Pope's army, he had so clearly crippled it that after Second Manassas it ceased to exist as an organization, its constituent elements being absorbed into the Army of the Potomac.

It is one of the measures of Lee's superior talents as an army commander that he would not take foolish risks; what appeared to less able generals as audacious ventures were in Lee's mind calculated with an eye to the relative capabilities of his own army and that of his opponent, with particular emphasis on the abilities of the Union commander as Lee himself evaluated them. Also there must be potential gains commensurate with the risks for the latter to be taken. He was too shrewd a strategist to push his luck too far; consequently his plans did not at any time contemplate an attack on the Washington fortress.

The gratifying results of his campaign against Pope had however exceeded Lee's expectations. Starting out with the hope that he could inflict a crushing defeat upon that hated general, the plan was altered, by Pope's stubborn opposition on the Rappahannock, to become a campaign of maneuver; and was again modified to launch a successful counteroffensive when the opportunity was offered by the failure of Pope's battle tactics. Lee felt that the brilliant Confederate victory deserved to be exploited, in fact it had to be, or the enemy would recover his balance, renew his strength, and make ready to stage a new offensive on Virginia soil. The Army of Northern Virginia could not afford to stand still or rest on its laurels. It must either go forward to press the advantage just gained at Second Manassas, or pull back to refit.

There was considerable justification for optimism in Confederate circles. Much had been accomplished in the three
months that had elapsed since Lee took command. At the
start, McClellan had been within sight of Richmond, Jackson was facing greatly superior odds in the Valley, and the
Federals controlled all of West Virginia and the North
Carolina coastline; the initiative rested with the North and
everywhere the pressure had thrown the Southerners on the
defensive. Now all that had been changed. Richmond was
saved, the Valley cleared, the Army of the Potomac had
withdrawn to Washington, Pope's army had been defeated,
virtually all of Virginia and most of West Virginia cleared
of enemy troops. The Confederates had seized and now held
the initiative, with Washington rather than Richmond in
fear for its very existence.

Invasion of the North had been in Lee's mind for some
time. He believed it would have international implications
in creating an atmosphere favorable to the Confederacy in
England and France, an extremely important factor in view
of the strong Federal naval blockage of Southern ports. The
presence of his army in Maryland might swing that doubtful
State into the Confederate column. It would also be most
helpful if the Northern countryside should take over the
burden of sustaining his 50,000-man army for a time. Finally,
the morale of the army had been given a lift by its recent
victory, its confidence in its leaders and itself was at a high
pitch, and neither must be allowed to decline.

Nevertheless, Lee knew perfectly well what the great exertions of the summer had done to his army. The losses before Richmond and at Manassas had been heavy. A number
of his better generals had been killed or wounded. His
divisions were admittedly not in condition to invade, as Lee
stated in a letter to President Davis: "The army is not
properly equipped for an invasion of an enemy's territory.
It lacks much of the material of war, is feeble in transportation, the animals being much reduced, and the men are poorly

provided with clothes, and, in thousands of instances, are destitute of shoes."

Again, however, it was desirable to take a calculated risk. The advantages of a successful invasion, in Lee's judgment, outweighed the disadvantages. The possibility existed that the Baltimore and Ohio Railroad could be destroyed, which would be a disaster of some magnitude to the Northern armies. If all went well, the Confederates might even push on into Pennsylvania to cut the Pennsylvania Railroad, in which event the supply route to the west via the Great Lakes would remain as the only connecting link between East and West. There was indeed great promise in an invasion. And so the die was cast and the orders issued.

Two routes were open to Lee. He could take the sheltered roadway by way of the Shenandoah Valley, or the more exposed approach east of the Blue Ridge Mountains. The second would be quicker and, being closer to Washington, more likely for that reason to have greater psychological impact on the North. Practical benefits might accrue as well, in causing the Administration at Washington, if sufficiently alarmed, to make hasty, ill-advised decisions.

McClellan Resumes Command

McClellan's resumption of command was far from being the result of a universal belief that he was the man of the hour, whose leadership of the Union armies of the East would restore their fallen fortunes and carry them forward to victories. By and large that may have been the attitude of the rank and file of the Federal soldiers, as demonstrated by their spontaneous enthusiasm when he rode out into their midst as they trudged dejectedly back to the capital. They knew, as did their Confederate opponents, that they had fought with as much bravery and determination as Lee's men, but they were also well aware of the incompetent generalship which had brought about their defeat. It was their conviction that Pope and McDowell had not given them the chance for victory which, rightly or wrongly, they believed with all their hearts could be theirs under General McClellan.

Lincoln and the members of his cabinet however viewed McClellan in a very different light and were in better position than the army to appraise his attitudes and actions in the light of the overall situation. There were some members of the cabinet whose objections to "Little Mac" were based largely on political considerations, but his record of achievement in the purely military spheres, unimpressive as it was, overshadowed the political implications. Secretary of War Stanton and Secretary of the Treasury Chase were more vocal than the rest in their opposition to McClellan's restoration to power. In Chase's view, it was a matter of life or death for the government, while Stanton, who by virtue of his position had a more intimate knowledge of the day-by-day military situation, worked desperately on his colleagues to convince them that only disaster could be anticipated if McClellan were again to be given a command of any importance.

That McClellan was a controversial national figure is to put it mildly. The historical accounts vary widely as to how it actually came about that he was in the top military spot when the Army of the Potomac moved out from Washington to counter Lee's invasion of the North. Lincoln himself had been at no pains to conceal his growing distaste for McClellan as a fighting commander, believing that he had rendered the country a distinct disservice by his lack of cooperativeness with Pope's army and his superiors in the War Department. On the other hand, the President's custom of keeping his ear to the ground and talking freely with military visitors from the Army, regardless of rank, enabled him to keep his finger on the army pulse, so he knew how strongly the troops felt about McClellan. Consequently, when affairs reached the point where civilian clerks were pressed into service and armed to repel the imagined attack on Washington, and it became apparent that the armies were floundering in an almost leaderless morass of uncertainty, Lincoln concluded that all personal feelings must give way before the critical emergency should dissolve into irretrievable disaster.

Burnside's refusal to accept the post left no general of sufficient experience in army command, in Lincoln's opinion, to turn to except McClellan. It is perfectly clear, however, that the President's decision was to put McClellan in command only of the troops *in the defenses of Washington*. He had no intention of allowing the general to lead the army into the field or to fight a battle, and said so, without any reservations, to a number of intimates. The idea was to use McClellan's genius for organization to again whip the army into a sound state of organization and thus gain time to figure out who would take over when it became necessary to wage a campaign. "If he can't fight himself," said Lincoln, "he excels in making others ready to fight."

Lincoln's decision, then, was to place McClellan in charge of the Washington defenses, and it was made on his sole responsibility in spite of the opposition of a majority of the Cabinet. When on September 2 the President announced the decision at a Cabinet meeting, it is said that Stanton, trembling with rage that his advice was being disregarded, burst out with the statement that no such order had been issued by his authority. To which the President, putting aside for once his gentle manner, remarked curtly that the order was his own and he would be responsible for it to the country.

Interestingly enough, the one-sentence order: "Major-General McClellan will have command of the fortifications of Washington and of all the troops for the defense of the capital" was the *only* formal order that McClellan received from the War Department until, early in November, six weeks after the battle of Antietam, he was again relieved from command, this time for good. A gesture in the direction of officially creating a new field army was made by the War Department on September 3, when Halleck was directed to "prepare an army to take the field." But Lee's invasion of Maryland had so soon created a new crisis that, insofar as the chain of command was concerned, all administrative considerations were of necessity shelved in face of the needs of the moment.

McClellan was not the man to act coyly in such a situation, and so it came about that he assumed limited command as ordered, got busy, ignored Pope, absorbed the Army of Virginia into the Army of the Potomac, and then marched at the head of that unofficial army to meet Lee. All this was without specific orders; but on the other hand it was not repudiated by Halleck or the War Department. There are times in the affairs of men when unilateral action by one individual may be the only answer, and this appears to have been one of those times.

McClellan's first action, on receipt of Halleck's written orders confirming the President's oral statement to the general on the morning of September 2, was to ride out to show himself and to receive the plaudits of those of the army who felt so disposed. His second was to bring order to the defenses and restore a sense of discipline, which was effected simply by telling the experienced corps and division commanders what they were to do.

Three corps, Heintzelman's Third, Fitz John Porter's Fifth, and Sigel's Eleventh, were assigned to the fortified line on the Virginia side. Sumner's Second Corps, Burnside's Ninth, and Mansfield's Twelfth covered the city on the Maryland side. The Sixth Corps under Franklin and the First, shortly to be commanded by Hooker, had not yet been reshuffled and were consequently in a semi-state of reserve. In numbers of bodies the eight corps exceeded 100,000 men by a substantial margin, seemingly more than enough to protect Washington and defeat Lee's 50,000 at the same time. In addition, 26,000 other troops, including newly arrived contingents and the regular garrison, manned the remaining forts that ringed the city, with 120 field pieces and 500 heavy guns in position to provide a powerful deterrent to a possible enemy attack. As it turned out, an attack on Washington was never seriously undertaken or even planned at any time during the war.

Among McClellan's notes that were published in the Century Magazine shortly after his death, he referred to the concern with which in early September 1862 he viewed Halleck's insistence that the Federal garrison of some 12,000 men at strategic Harper's Ferry be kept there. Although outside of his jurisdiction, McClellan felt strongly that the post should be abandoned and the troops brought to Washington to augment those already within the defenses. It was typical of "Little Mac" that his overriding theme of bringing every available man under his own wing was again foremost in his mind, but the reasons given on this occasion were that the garrison was isolated, could not be expected to avoid capture or destruction if attacked, and if Harper's Ferry should be occupied by the Confederates the matter would be of little consequence since his army, if successful, could easily effect its recapture.

Halleck gave McClellan's views a brusque brushoff, terming them erroneous. He refrained from using the word gratuitous, which he might very well have done, since McClellan's responsibilities were specifically limited to the defenses of the capital, and Halleck had informed him in no uncertain terms, on several occasions, that he was not to command troops beyond the line of demarcation. Furthermore Halleck had stated that the general who would command the troops when they should move had not yet been selected. He might as well have saved his breath so far as McClellan was concerned, for the latter coolly proceeded with his own plans, which included the assumption of field command without Halleck's specific approval.

The ironic factor involved in McClellan's belief that Harpers Ferry should be abandoned was yet to be disclosed. As will appear later, that vital position loomed importantly in Lee's thinking, so that its influence on the forth-coming battles would be tremendous. Had McClellan been clairvoyant, he would have foreseen that Federal possession of Harpers Ferry was the very thing that led Lee to divide his army, and barely escape destruction as a result. As it turned out, advance reinforcement of the garrison at Harpers Ferry by the Federals might have proven to be the decisive factor, by holding that strategic area just a few hours longer, in utterly destroying the separate wings of Lee's army instead of recording the Battle of Antietam as a stalemate.

Theater of Operations

In the summer and early fall, the Potomac River is easily fordable at many points, so that presented no problem. There are only three streams of any military importance that empty into that great river on its north side; in order, from east to west—the Monocacy River, Catoctin Creek, and Antietam Creek.

It is the Blue Ridge Mountains, however, that present the most significant terrain feature in the Maryland theater of operations, which was shortly to serve as the stage for the next trial of strength between Lee's army and whatever opponent should emerge from the confusion in which the Union forces were presently confounded. These mountains cross Maryland in parallel ranges, in almost a north-south direction, separated by a fertile valley from six to eight miles wide and about fifteen miles long on the Maryland side. The easternmost range is known as Catoctin Mountain (an extension of Bull Run Mountains), which has a narrow, low, razorback characteristic from the Potomac north to the Hagerstown-Frederick Road, beyond which it rises steeply to an altitude of about 1700 feet where it merges with South Mountain in closing the wide valley between the two ranges.

Catoctin Mountain can be negotiated by marching troops without difficulty, but South Mountain to the west offers a stern military obstacle all the way to the Potomac. Its crest towers above 1500 feet, and it can be crossed only at the passes, of which the most important are Turner's Gap, Fox's

Gap, Crampton's Gap, and the gap where the Potomac passes through the range.

Three miles west of South Mountain is the northern, eight-mile-long extension of the most western range of the Blue Ridge Mountains. Known as Elk Ridge, it too has a crest of 1,000 feet that frowns down from Maryland Heights on Harpers Ferry, where the Potomac and Shenandoah Rivers join forces on the far side. Its northern terminus, with but a single gap intervening, levels off in a cluster of foothills a few miles to the east of the village of Sharpsburg, then a crossroad community which nestled in the arc made by the Potomac as it winds its looping course toward Harpers Ferry. Antietam Creek passes Sharpsburg a mile or so to the east as it flows toward the Potomac. Between South Mountain and Elk Ridge lies Pleasant Valley, a well-named, narrow corridor between towering ridges that if properly used by able generals could, and did, play an important role in the tactics employed by the opposing forces.

The theater of operations for the coming campaign included thickly wooded farming country, with frequent clearings and dirt roads running in all directions on either side of the mountains. Several turnpikes existed, of which the two most important were the old National Road from Hagerstown through Boonsboro that crossed South Mountain at Turner's Gap and the road through Crampton's Gap, both of which led to Frederick.

The principal railroad was the Baltimore and Ohio, which from Baltimore crossed the Monocacy River at Frederick Junction, turned south to the Potomac, and followed that river around the nose of Catoctin Mountain to Harpers Ferry, where it crossed the river on its way through West Virginia to the west.

Lee Crosses the Potomac

Without waiting for the reinforcements that had been dispatched from Richmond on Lee's request to President Davis, the Confederate army on September 3 started out on its new

MAP 25. LEE'S INVASION OF MARYLAND

Showing the routes of Lee and the Federal corps during the period September 1-9, inclusive. Lee crossed the Potomac September 5-7, and the head of his column reached Frederick on the 7th. McClellan, now commanding the Federal forces, moved out cautiously from within the forts surrounding Washington during the period September 4-7, and marched toward Frederick on the three, then the four routes. By this time Lee had reached Frederick and was planning his next move.

and exciting adventure into enemy territory. Moving west in the direction of Leesburg, to cross the Potomac at shallow White's Ford, thirty miles upriver from Washington, the bands blared forth with "Maryland, My Maryland," as the column headed for Frederick City, Lee's first objective thirteen miles north of the river. There he hoped to rally to the Confederate cause the people of Maryland, thousands of whose sons were already serving in the armies of the South.

Dirty, unshaven, ragged, and barefooted as so many were, the Confederates were lighthearted and cheerful as they swung along the invasion route. Three fresh divisions under Lafayette McLaws, Daniel H. Hill, and John G. Walker, together with Wade Hampton's cavalry brigade and the reserve artillery, caught up with the column on the way, adding 20,000 additional troops to Lee's army. Most of these units crossed the Potomac at Cheek's Ford, at the mouth of the Monocacy River, several miles above White's Ford. But to Lee's disappointment, even with these reinforcements he could count no more than 50,000 in all, for his stragglers duplicated the experience of Pope's army after Second Manassas, and in such numbers as to nearly offset the gain in strength from the newly arrived contingents from the capital.

By September 7 the entire army was across the Potomac, had disrupted traffic along the Chesapeake and Ohio Canal, paralleling the Potomac River, and looked forward to the early breakup of the Baltimore and Ohio Railroad, which latter was one of the major purposes, or at least scheduled byproducts of the invasion. The previous day Lee had issued his proclamation to the people of Maryland, but neither the invitation nor the presence of Confederate troops on their soil had the desired effect, for Maryland remained loyal to the Union. It was Lee's first setback, and it made the invasion an even more hazardous affair with respect to communications, although there is no reason to believe that Lee made any change in his schedule, despite the chilly reception from the inhabitants.

Lee's Plan of Campaign

Major General John G. Walker, commanding one of the three reinforcing divisions, has left an interesting account of his reception when he reported to General Lee upon his arrival in the vicinity of Frederick on September 8. The Commanding General evidently had confidence in Walker's judgment and discretion, for he told him that his division would probably be ordered on detached service during the campaign and it was therefore necessary that he know its "ulterior purposes and objects."

"Here," said Lee, tracing with his finger on a large map, "is the line of our communications, from Rapidan Station to Manassas, thence to Frederick. It is too near the Potomac, and is liable to be cut any day by the enemy's cavalry. I have therefore given orders to move the line back into the Valley of Virginia, by way of Staunton, Harrisonburg, and Winchester, entering Maryland at Shepherdstown.

"I wish you to return to the mouth of the Monocacy and effectually destroy the aqueduct of the Chesapeake and Ohio Canal. By the time that is accomplished you will receive orders to cooperate in the capture of Harper's Ferry, and you will not return here, but, after the capture of Harper's Ferry, will rejoin us at Hagerstown, where the army will be concentrated. My information is that there are between 10,000 and 12,000 men at Harper's Ferry, and 3,000 at Martinsburg. The latter may escape toward Cumberland, but I think the chances are that they will take refuge at Harper's Ferry and be captured."

Lee seems to have been more loquacious than usual on that occasion, if Walker did not embellish the account by antedating some of the facts, because the commanding general is reported as having gone to some length to divulge his entire plan of campaign, even to the extent of explaining why he felt that he was safe in executing his plans without fear of interruption by the Federals.

"McClellan is an able general but a very cautious one. His army is in a very demoralized and chaotic condition, and will not be prepared for offensive operations—or he will not think it so—for three or four weeks. Before that time I hope to be on the Susquehanna."

"In ten days from now," Lee continued, "if the military situation is then what I confidently expect it to be after the capture of Harper's Ferry, I shall concentrate the army at Hagerstown, effectually destroy the Baltimore and Ohio road, and march to this point," placing his finger at Harrisburg, Pennsylvania. "That is the objective point of the campaign. You remember, no doubt, the long bridge of the Pennsylvania railroad over the Susquehanna, a few miles west of Harrisburg. Well, I wish effectually to destroy that bridge, which will disable the Pennsylvania railroad for a long time. After that I can turn my attention to Philadelphia, Baltimore, or Washington, as may seem best for our interests."

Parenthetically it may be noted at this point that Walker's division, in carrying out Lee's instructions, made an effort to destroy the aqueduct near the mouth of the Monocacy River, but found its construction to be such that neither by the use of picks or crowbars could his men make any impression on the solid granite structure, and the drills available to his engineers were too dull to pave the way for blasting. Consequently that part of his mission had to be written off as a failure.

Special Orders No. 191

At Frederick, on September 9, Lee issued the now famous order to his army, the purpose of which was to take Harpers Ferry out of Federal control and at the same time advance the main body of the army to Boonsboro, a reconcentration point that was subsequently changed in order to halt D. H. Hill's division of 5,000 men at South Mountain, while Longstreet's corps continued on to Hagerstown. It was a copy of this order, carelessly dropped in Frederick, that was picked up by a Union soldier when the Federal Twelfth Corps reached there at noon on September 13. The premature disclosure of the whereabouts and planned movements of Lee's army, the inadequate use to which McClellan put the information thus fortuitously acquired, and the later fact that Lee himself attributed his loss of the Battle of Sharpsburg (Antietam) to the incident of the "Lost Dispatch," gives to Special Orders Number 191 a significance greater than that of any single event in the entire campaign.

Special Orders }   Headquarters, Army
   No. 191   }   of Northern Virginia.
                                     September 9th, 1862.

The army will resume its march tomorrow, taking the Hagerstown road. General Jackson's command will form the advance, and after passing Middletown, with such portions as he may select, take the route toward Sharpsburg, cross the Potomac at the most convenient point, and by Friday night take possession of the Baltimore and Ohio Railroad, capture such of the enemy as may be at Martinsburg, and intercept such as may attempt to escape from Harper's Ferry.

General Longstreet's command will pursue the same road as far as Boonsboro, where it will halt with the reserve, supply, and baggage trains of the army.

General McLaws, with his own division and that of General R. H. Anderson, will follow General Longstreet; on reaching Middletown he will take the route to Harper's Ferry, and by Friday morning possess himself of the Maryland Heights and endeavor to capture the enemy at Harper's Ferry and vicinity.

General Walker, with his division, after accomplishing the object in which he is now engaged, will cross the Potomac at Cheek's Ford, ascend its right bank to Lovettsville, take possession of Loudoun Heights, if practicable, by Friday morning, Keys' Ford on his left, and the road between the end of the mountain and the Potomac on his right. He will, as far as practicable, cooperate with General McLaws and General Jackson in intercepting the retreat of the enemy.

General D. H. Hill's division will form the rear guard of the army, pursuing the road taken by the main body. The reserve artillery, ordnance, and supply trains, etc., will precede General Hill.

General Stuart will detach a squadron of cavalry to accompany the commands of Generals Longstreet, Jackson, and McLaws, and with the main body of the cavalry, will cover the route of the army and bring up all stragglers that may have been left behind.

The commands of Generals Jackson, McLaws, and Walker, after accomplishing the objects for which they have been detached, will join the main body of the army at Boonsboro or Hagerstown.

Each regiment on the march will habitually carry its axes in the regimental ordnance-wagons, for use of the men at their encampments, to procure wood, etc.

By Command of General R. E. Lee,
R. H. Chilton, Assistant
Adjutant General.

Major General D. H. Hill, Commanding Division.

The preceding reprint, quoted in McClellan's official report, shows that it was the copy sent to General D. H. Hill, whose division was assigned to form the army rear guard. From that fact stemmed a historic controversy among the surviving Confederate generals as to where the responsibility rested for the loss of the order. Hill always maintained that he never received a copy directly from Lee's headquarters, the implication being that it was dropped by a staff officer en route. However the loss came about, its vital effect on Lee's first invasion of the North is a matter of history.

The gratifying outcome of Lee's calculated risk in dividing his army as a prelude to defeating Pope in the latter days of August was fresh in the Confederate leader's mind. Although he had a greater respect for McClellan, he was also familiar with his opponent's uniformly cautious attitude and believed that a repetition of his own strategy in the present case would allow sufficient time for the detached portions of his army to accomplish their mission and reunite with the main body in ample time to forestall what otherwise could be an extremely dangerous situation.

Longstreet and Jackson each reacted in his accustomed manner when Lee first discussed his plans with them at Frederick. Jackson was enthusiastic at the prospect, remarking that it was about time that he pay his friends in the Valley another visit. Longstreet, however, who in his own written account of the campaign said that when Lee first proposed the Harpers Ferry division as a project for a special force under Longstreet himself, he objected to dividing the army at that stage. He argued that the troops were not yet in condition to undertake any more marching in enemy country than was absolutely necessary, that the Federal army was *not* as disorganized as it had been pictured, and that it would certainly come after them. Since Lee was anxious to take Harpers Ferry, and found Jackson equally in favor, Longstreet's objections were ignored.

The movement order was issued on Tuesday, September 9. In it Lee mentions Friday morning as the time when the separate detachments under McLaws and Walker were expected to be in position on Maryland Heights and Loudoun Heights, respectively, to prevent a possible escape by the Federal garrison until Jackson's corps of three divisions could come in from the west to close the trap. Jackson was given three days, until Friday night, September 12, to travel a circuitous sixty-mile route, capture the Federal garrison at Martinsburg, and close the escape route of the Harpers Ferry garrison to the west. Upon completion of the converging movement of the three detachments, Jackson as the senior would automatically take command of the whole, but it will be noted that the two-division force under McLaws was given the mission of actually capturing the troops at Harpers Ferry.

The importance that Lee ascribed to the seizure of Harpers Ferry may be judged by his action in sending six of the ten divisions in his army, including two of Longstreet's, on that diversionary mission, leaving but four divisions with the main body, three of them in Longstreet's corps, and D. H. Hill's separate division. Walker's division was small, mustering only about 2,000 men, but even so, less than half the army would be forced to contend with McClellan's Union army if things should go wrong. On the other hand, both Confederate wings would be sheltered by the high mountain ranges, and could unite rapidly in either direction via Martinsburg. If worst came to worst, the entire army could retire via Harpers Ferry to the safety of the Shenandoah Valley, a defensive contingency to which Lee's psychology did not particularly lend itself under the circumstances.

McClellan Moves to Counter Lee

As soon as it became apparent that the Confederate army was committed to operations in Maryland and cherished no designs on the city of Washington, the unofficially reconstituted Army of the Potomac moved warily out from the defenses of the capital to regain contact.

The anomalous position in which Halleck had placed McClellan did not seem to faze the latter, who proceeded to take charge of military affairs as fully as though he had been given carte blanche by the War Department. The situation was unique, since neither the President, the Secretary of War, nor the General-in-Chief, wanted to restore McClellan to field command, but were prepared to hand the reins to another general in his stead. Nevertheless McClellan acted on his own authority, leaving his superiors, however they may have felt about it, to acquiesce passively. After all, when the house is on fire, the owner is not likely to throw obstacles in the path of the fireman, even though he may not think well of him.

Lee's army had faded from the vicinity of Washington, commencing on the third of September, and it looked as though they would cross the Potomac. When the probability became a certainty, McClellan progressively redisposed several corps in positions at Rockville, Tennallytown, Offutt's Cross-roads, and Leesboro, holding those of Heintzelman, Porter, and Sigel within the lines at Washington. General Pleasonton, given command of the cavalry, was ordered out on September 6 to establish and maintain contact with the enemy cavalry. The army was organized into two wings and a center column under Burnside, Sumner, and Franklin; and Banks was assigned to command the defenses of Washington. On September 7, by which date all of Lee's army had crossed the Potomac, McClellan opened field headquarters at Rockville and prepared to follow Lee.

Now that McClellan had relieved in a measure the nervous strain under which the indecisive Halleck had been laboring, the General-in-Chief revived his accustomed fears for the safety of the capital. In the current circumstances he expressed the belief that Lee would double back across the Potomac to come in on McClellan's left rear, which would again place Washington in jeopardy. McClellan was cautioned to make haste slowly, which in the light of Little Mac's record to date might be termed gratuitous advice. It may be doubted, however, that McClellan would now pay any more attention to Halleck than he had heretofore.

Cavalry Skirmishes

The Army of the Potomac was preceded in its advance by an entirely different cavalry team than the one which had served with Pope in the Virginia campaign. In that campaign three brigades, a total of fourteen regiments, had been attached to the three corps of the Army of Virginia, each brigade commander being responsive to the orders of his corps commander. By the end of the campaign the horses were so broken down by the excessive demands made on them that for all practical purposes the organizations concerned had become inoperative, for the time being at least.

McClellan put together a group of cavalry regiments, from his former army and elsewhere, in an organic division under the command of Brigadier General Alfred Pleasonton, a dapper little horseman who was an old dragoon, knew how to use cavalry in its proper role, and proceeded to do so. He divided his division into five brigades, each under a colonel except the First, which was commanded by a major. Each of the brigades was composed of two regiments except the Second, which had four; that one was commanded by Colonel John Farnsworth, a fine young Regular who was destined to die in a fruitless charge at Gettysburg ten months later. Pleasonton counted twelve regiments in his division, none of which had participated in the Manassas campaign.

Moving out as a body, the Federal cavalry quickly fanned

out over the Maryland countryside to scout the fords and seek out the enemy cavalry, which was similarly dispersed over a wide area, screening Lee's army. Initial contact was made September 7 at Poolesville. Thereafter, for three days, frequent skirmishes occurred between opposing detachments, as the Federals pushed westward toward Lee's main body in the Frederick area.

The Confederate cavalry under General J. E. B. Stuart, after crossing the Potomac at Edward's Ferry, had swung off to the right and were disposed along a line twenty miles in length, with Munford's reduced brigade on the right at Poolesville, Wade Hampton's in the center at Hyattstown, and Fitz Lee's on the left at New Market. Stuart established his headquarters at Urbana, a central point from which roads radiated to the several brigade command posts to the front, and to army headquarters at Frederick.

Sugar Loaf Hill, an isolated ridge five miles southwest of Urbana, which rose to a height of 700 feet to dominate the surrounding area, was an excellent observation point from which the Confederates could watch the roads which McClellan's army would have to use in coming to Lee's position. Pleasonton marked this prominent landmark as his objective and made strenuous efforts to take it, driving Munford's defending brigade out of Poolesville in the process. But Stuart's cavalry cordon managed its counter-reconnaissance mission with such skill that McClellan was unable to learn what Lee was up to in the early stages of his advance.

For several days, Stuart's troopers had an easy time of it until the Federal cavalry pressed closer, when the skirmishing became more brisk and the Union infantry began to add their weight of numbers. It would only be a matter of a few days before McClellan's superior strength would be felt and Lee would have to decide whether to meet the challenge east of the mountains.

During the peaceful period before the Union infantry in strength forced the Confederate cavalry screen to withdraw, the fun-loving Jeb Stuart at Urbana organized one of those dances which he enjoyed almost as much as a saber charge. There were plenty of attractive Maryland girls in the vicinity, and Stuart's staff lost no time in rounding them up. The merriment was at its height when the report came in that enemy cavalry was attacking the Confederate pickets. Buckling on their swords and taking a hasty farewell, Stuart and his officers assured the ladies the interruption would be temporary and please to wait. The business of discouraging the over-zealous Federal patrols having been accomplished, the dancing cavalrymen returned as promised, the party was resumed, and a good time was had by all.

Frederick City Changes Hands

The Army of the Potomac moved slowly forward at the rate of only six miles a day for the first few days, reflecting Halleck's "go-slow" policy. Each of the three columns was assigned a different route on parallel roads that diverged more widely to cover a broad front as Washington faded into the background. Burnside's right wing, which included the First Corps under Hooker and the Ninth under Reno, marched on the Brooke-ville-New Market Road. The center under Sumner, including his own Second Corps and Mansfield's Twelfth, advanced along the Rockville-Frederick Road. Franklin's left wing, composed of his own Sixth Corps and Couch's division of the Fourth Corps, followed the Offutt's Crossroads-Seneca Road. Porter's Fifth Corps would later be reassigned to McClellan's army to constitute the reserve, but for the time being it was held in Washington. In all, McClellan had seventeen veteran divisions at his disposal, some 90,000 men altogether. This gave him almost a two-to-one superiority over Lee, which, however, it was not in McClellan's nature to admit. As usual, he over-estimated Lee's strength by more than one hundred per cent, insisting that the number of Confederate troops exceeded his own by a large margin.

On the morning of September 10 Lee's Army of Northern Virginia, pursuant to Special Orders No. 191, resumed the

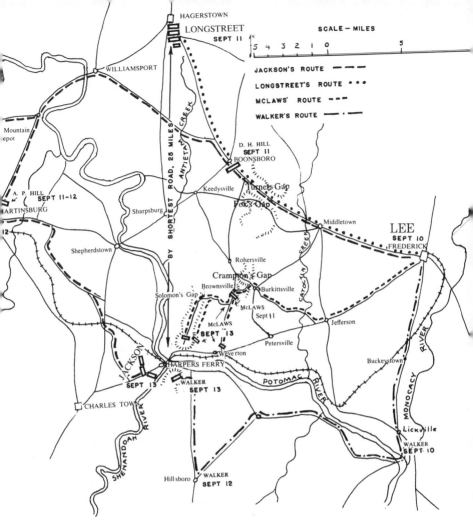

MAP 26. CONFEDERATE MOVEMENTS, SEPTEMBER 10-13

The marches of the elements of Lee's army shown on this map were made in conformity with his plan to capture Harpers Ferry with a part of his force, then concentrate at Boonsboro, later changed to Hagerstown, for the continuation of the advance on Harrisburg. The divisions left Frederick on the 10th; Longstreet, with Anderson's, Hood's, D. R. Jones', and D. H. Hill's divisions, and Evans' brigade, set out for Hagerstown. D. H. Hill, acting as rear guard, was dropped off at Boonsboro. Jackson, with J. R. Jones', Lawton's, and A. P. Hill's divisions, marched on Harpers Ferry via Boonsboro-Williamsport-Martinsburg. Lawton and J. R. Jones on the 11th went to North Mountain Depot, on the Baltimore and Ohio R.R., which they captured, then joined A. P. Hill at Martinsburg on the 12th. Walker marched south from Frederick on the 10th, crossed the Potomac, and moved on Loudoun Heights via Hillsboro. McLaws marched to Burkittsville, thence over the pass to Brownsville. Here he divided his force, part remaining near Brownsville, the other portions moving on Maryland Heights by the three routes shown. McLaws was reinforced by R. H. Anderson's six brigades. On the evening of the 13th the forces were in the positions shown on the map. For a detailed picture of the capture of Harpers Ferry, see Map 30.

march in accordance with the mission assigned to the several fragments, Jackson's corps in the lead and moving west on the Boonsboro road. As division after division crossed Catoctin Mountain, Stuart's cavalry screen, still skirmishing here and there with the aggressive Federal cavalry, prepared to follow, covering the rear.

Pleasanton informed McClellan of the Confederate departure, whereupon the march tempo of the Union army was stepped up. On September 12 and 13 the leading elements of Burnside's right wing and Sumner's center column entered Frederick.

Union Lieutenant Gillette described the attitude of the people of Frederick toward the brief Confederate occupation in a letter to his parents:

> Sept. 13—Frederick, Md.
> The Confederates evacuated Frederick last evening.
> The charm is broken, Jackson's last raid has done away with "My Maryland" forever. The time of their stay was like a Sabbath on which no business is done and when people go about quiet and subdued. Not a welcome was given the soldiers who expected an uprising (referring to Lee's hope that his invasion would rally the Marylanders to the Confederate cause). The Secessionists were anxious that they should leave. Union men refused positively to sell their wares. The rebels met icy coldness where they expected genial warmth and gratitude.
>
> Maryland is all right, as I always said she was. The North should give her credit for it. Now there is general rejoicing and Union flags out on all houses.

Quoting a Union lady of Frederick, Gillette contrasted the relative discipline of the opposing armies:

> In manners, in the conduct of soldiers and the discipline, these bundles of rags, these cough racked, diseased and starved men excel our well-fed, well clothed, our best soldiers. No one can point to a single act of vandalism perpetrated by the rebel soldiery during their occupation

of Frederick, while even now a countless host of stragglers are crawling after our own army devouring, destroying or wasting all that falls in their devious line of march. God knows I have no need to praise Confederate forbearance, but the fact that we are confronted by an army perfectly under the control and discipline of tried and experienced officers is incontrovertible. It accounts for the excellence of their fighting, and the almost powerlessness of our own army.

TURNER'S GAP, LOOKING SOUTHEAST ALONG BURNSIDE'S ROUTE OF ADVANCE

CHAPTER 16

THE BATTLE OF SOUTH MOUNTAIN*

AS THE Confederate columns debouched from the shallow passes over Catoctin Mountain, only the most phlegmatic in the ranks would have been unimpressed by the imposing sight of the long, towering South Mountain range that reached skyward at a distance of seven miles across the intervening valley to the west. To the men in Jackson's corps, thoughts of their own Shenandoah Valley would be uppermost, for this fertile Maryland valley as well as the bordering mountains had a familiar look, except that this Northern valley was closed in at its upper end where the two mountains merged in a graceful, lofty horseshoe curve.

General Lee would not fail to note the scenic grandeur, on this his first invasion of Northern soil. But the esthetic features

―――――
*Known in the South as the Battle of Boonsboro.

would quickly be subordinated to the military implications as
he contemplated the possible developments of the next few
days. The bastion of South Mountain might well prove to be
a shield against McClellan's oncoming army, now that he was
committed to the Harpers Ferry diversion. It had been his
expectation, when he crossed the Potomac, that the Federals
would relinquish Harpers Ferry rather than permit the garrison to be sacrificed, but Halleck had decided otherwise.

Lee was taking a huge gamble by dispatching divisions in
all directions, dividing his army into four separate parts, and
offering an enterprising opponent the opportunity to destroy
him on the installment plan. That is, if McClellan should be
alert enough to discover what great risks Lee was taking, and
quick enough to take advantage of the opening. Lee did not
believe that McClellan would react that speedily; on the contrary, he was confident that Jackson would quickly take
Harper's Ferry and rejoin the main body in the Hagerstown-
Boonsboro area before the Union army could or would do
anything about it. And it would in all probability have worked
out just as Lee planned had it not been for the "lost dispatch," which so completely changed what had started out as
a promising invasion to a near disaster at Antietam.

McClellan Learns of Lee's Plans

The 27th Indiana Volunteers, a regiment of the First Division of Mansfield's Twelfth Corps, Army of the Potomac,
reaching Frederick on the morning of September 13, bivouacked in the same field that had been occupied the evening
before by D. H. Hill's division, the rear guard of Lee's army.
A few minutes after the regiment had stacked arms, First
Sergeant John M. Bloss and Private B. W. Mitchell reported
to their regimental commander that Mitchell had just picked
up an order signed by Colonel Chilton, General Lee's Chief
of Staff, which had been wrapped around three cigars.

The order was immediately taken to General A. S. Williams,
the division commander, whose Adjutant General, Colonel
Pittman, had known and served with Colonel Chilton before

the war. Pittman stated that the signature was authentic. The important document was rushed to General McClellan.

The excitement at army headquarters caused by this unexpected windfall can only be imagined. For once McClellan was galvanized into prompt action. The news was almost too good to be true! Orders were quickly dispatched to the several corps commanders and within a matter of hours the army was ready to resume the march. The left column was directed to force the South Mountain pass at Crampton's Gap in an advance on Rohrersville, the center and right columns were to proceed through Turner's Gap on the Middletown-Boonsboro Road in the direction of Hagerstown.

McClellan was now in the enviable position of knowing exactly where all elements of Lee's army were, what course each had been instructed to follow, and the exact timetable for each. Through the almost criminal carelessness of an unknown Confederate staff officer, Lee at one stroke was deprived of the advantage of surprise, and lost the initiative gained by his invasion of Maryland. To his opponent he must have appeared to be a veritable sitting duck, ripe for the kill. From the viewpoint of the Federals, Lee had taken one calculated risk too many, with Jackson's force of four divisions in the vicinity of Harpers Ferry south of the Potomac, separated from Lee and Longstreet by twenty-five miles and a broad river; and with the five Confederate divisions on the Maryland side of the Potomac divided into three parts, each part a half-day's march from either of the others. (See Map 26.)

Such an opportunity to defeat an enemy in detail has rarely occurred in the history of war. It remained to be seen whether McClellan was enough of a general to turn the opportunity to his own advantage.

McClellan's plan of maneuver contemplated the seizure of the principal passes through South Mountain, followed by the occupation of Pleasant Valley. If the plan succeeded, the left wing under Major General William B. Franklin would take Rohrersville, cut off, destroy, or capture the two Confederate divisions under McLaws on Maryland Heights, and relieve the garrison under Colonel Miles at Harpers Ferry. As McClellan phrased it in his evening order of September 13 to Franklin: "My general idea is to cut the enemy in two and beat him in detail."

In spite of the great good fortune that had come to the Union commander in the form of a copy of Lee's orders, his chronic incapacity to move with alacrity led him to defer the starting time for the movement until the following morning. Why he failed to order a night march, which would have brought his army to the gaps by daybreak, is hard to understand. His army was relatively fresh, time was all-important, and possession of the passes over South Mountain would enable him to effectively dominate the situation. Although McClellan did not know it, Lee had no intention of defending them until he learned that the Army of the Potomac was closing in. All the mountain passes were in fact McClellan's for the taking, with only Stuart's light cavalry force to be brushed aside. But the Union commander allowed the afternoon and night of September 13 to pass before he moved, a delay which was to be a godsend to the Confederates.

Today's students of the two separate struggles for the South Mountain gaps, and certainly the Confederate generals who defended them in September 1862, have been puzzled as to why McClellan made his main effort through the pass leading to Hagerstown, assigning twelve divisions to that mission and only three to the reduction of Crampton's Gap, seven miles to the south. Possession of Lee's march table for the scattered troops of his army had given McClellan as much information as the Confederates themselves had, and his announced plan was to cut Lee's army in two. It would seem logical for McClellan to have reversed missions, sending a small corps to engage Longstreet at Boonsboro while the Federal main body was marched through the lower pass at Crampton's. That was the more direct route, which not only would have encouraged the Harpers Ferry garrison to hold out till relieved, but more

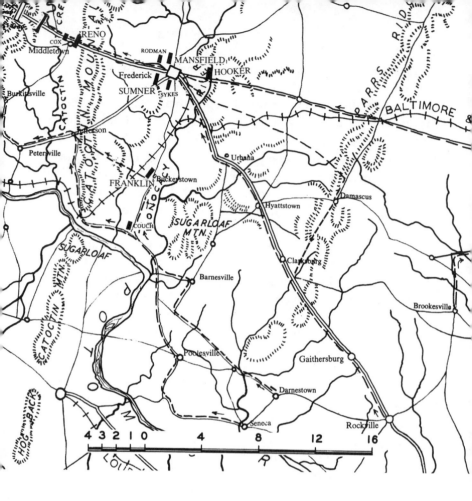

MAP 27. FEDERAL MOVEMENTS, SEPTEMBER 10-13

Showing the routes of advance of the several corps during the period. The troop positions are those for the night of September 13, with routes forward to Fox's and Turner's Gaps and Crampton's Gap. Porter's corps was not united until September 16. On the night of the 13th Sykes is at Frederick; Morell has started north from Arlington and has reached Leesborough, a few miles north of Washington.

The Confederate situation for this date is shown on Map 26.

certainly would have achieved the object of cutting the Confederate army in two.

McClellan may have reasoned that if he should take his army too close to the Potomac, Lee might somehow pull his divisions together and sideslip to the east in the direction of Washington, which would again cause a near-panic among the civilians at the capital. Or, he may subconsciously, or even consciously, have still harbored resentment because of his alleged cavalier treatment at the hands of the War Department, compounded by Halleck's rejection of his earlier recommendation that Harpers Ferry be abandoned. It was not beyond the realm of possibility that the general who had suggested to the War Department that Pope be allowed to "get out of his scrape as best he could" might harbor similar thoughts about Harpers Ferry. Also it is probable that, according to his custom, he estimated Lee's strength at twice its actual size and based his tactics accordingly. However McClellan may have figured it, the results fell woefully short of an effective exploitation of the glorious opportunity that was afforded him to whip the invader to the point of impotence if not final destruction.

The Action at Crampton's Gap

Franklin's Sixth Corps, followed by Couch's division of the Fourth Corps, reached Burkittsville, a small town at the base of South Mountain near the eastern end of Crampton's Gap, about noon on September 14. There the advance guard encountered the Confederates posted on both sides of the mountain road, protected behind stone walls and fence lines, with artillery sited above the junction of the two roads leading into the pass. Franklin assigned Major General Henry W. Slocum's division to a position on the right, Major General William F. Smith's division on the left, whereupon the two divisions, on a frontage of about 2,000 yards, advanced promptly to the attack.

Colonel T. T. Munford, temporarily in command of Robertson's brigade of General Stuart's cavalry division, had played a prominent part in screening the southern flank of Lee's army before Frederick and in delaying the forward movements of Pleasonton's Federal cavalry. It was now Munford's task to hold Crampton's Gap as long as possible, in company with similar action by D. H. Hill's rear-guard division at Turner's Gap, seven miles to the north.

Munford had been given a man-sized job, which was in effect to block the advance of a major element of McClellan's army with a mere handful of men, initially two small Virginia cavalry regiments aggregating less than 300 troopers. In addition, he was expected to hold the Brownsville Pass, two miles south of Crampton's. His only artillery support consisted of Chew's battery and several guns each from three other batteries, all of which were posted halfway up the mountain in positions to cover both Crampton's and the Brownsville Pass.

As Munford's small rearguard fell back through Jefferson and Burkittsville before the Federal advance, to take position on either side of the mountain road, Mahone's infantry brigade of R. H. Anderson's division, a part of McLaw's force charged with the capture of Maryland Heights, was called back across Pleasant Valley to Munford's support.

About 3 o'clock on the afternoon of September 14 Slocum and Smith advanced to the attack. In overwhelming numbers the Federals pressed their advantage, and although Munford's combined infantry-cavalry-artillery command fought every step of the way and held Franklin's corps to a slow and painful advance for three solid hours, the weight of numbers of the determined Federals proved too much for the defenders. Munford retired slowly up the mountain, his force dwindling steadily. When near the crest, his line broke. At that moment reinforcements from McLaw's division, Semmes' and Cobb's brigades, hastened up from Pleasant Valley. But the rout, once started, could not be stemmed. The entire Confederate force, original defenders and reinforcements alike, retreated in disorder into the valley below, the infantry to Brownsville, the cavalry to Rohrersville. Losses amounted to several hundred on each side, including a sizable number of prisoners, several colors, and at least one gun captured by the attackers.

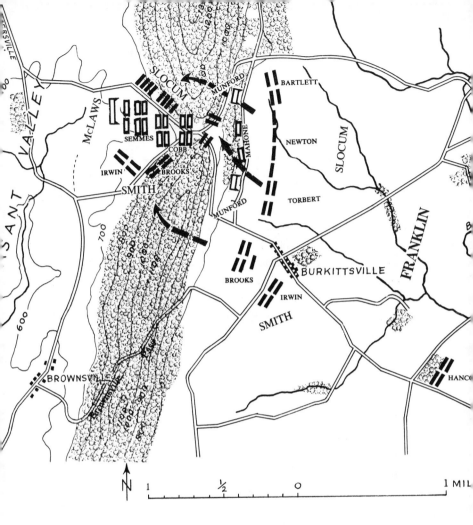

Map 28. Battle of Crampton's Gap
Showing the positions of Franklin's forces when they launched their attack
at 3 p.m. on Sunday, September 14; and the positions they reached at about
5 p.m. The initial Confederate dispositions only are shown; the cavalry retreated toward Rohersville, the infantry toward Brownsville.

The gateway to Pleasant Valley was now open and South Mountain breached at the lower pass. Events at that point were moving according to McClellan's plan, but General Franklin failed to follow up his initial success. A dispatch from McClellan, at one o'clock on the morning of September 15, directed him to occupy the road from Rohrersville to Harpers Ferry, take possession of Pleasant Valley, open communication with the Federal garrison at Harpers Ferry, and then join the main body of the Union army at Boonsboro, which McClellan said he would attack the following day.

Franklin's reply at 8:50 a.m. indicated that the enemy was drawn up in line of battle across Pleasant Valley and that the cessation of firing at Harpers Ferry made him suspect that it had already been captured by the Confederates. If so, he added, he would need reinforcements before he could attack. Two hours later, he sent McClellan a second message to the effect that the Confederates then had two lines of battle across the Valley, in a very strong position, and since he was "outnumbered two to one" he felt that he was not justified in attacking.

The accuracy of Franklin's observations as to the relative strength of the enemy and his own corps of three divisions is open to doubt, but in view of McClellan's own habit of vastly overestimating his opposition, Franklin was simply following the leader's example. Be that as it may, Franklin did *not* attack. He merely held his force in position until Lee moved his troops behind Antietam Creek; the Sixth Corps then followed, to join McClellan's main body on September 17, two days later, on the line of the same creek east of the town of Sharpsburg.

McClellan's Main Body Moves West

The Federal troops of the center column under Major General Edwin V. Sumner, his own Second Corps and Mansfield's Twelfth, were united at Frederick on September 13 with Major General Ambrose E. Burnside's right wing, composed of Hooker's First Corps and Reno's Ninth. This large force of twelve divisions, four times as strong as Franklin's left wing, was given the task of seizing Turner's Gap, through which ran the old National Road from Frederick to Hagerstown. Passage of the gap would bring McClellan's main body into contact with Lee and Longstreet, who according to Lee's dispatch should have with them only three of the nine Confederate divisions of Lee's army, not counting Stuart's cavalry division; the other six being engaged in the Harpers Ferry adventure. Preceding the infantry-artillery column were three brigades of Pleasonton's cavalry division, one brigade having been detached to cooperate with Franklin at Crampton's Gap, and another sent on reconnaissance in the direction of Gettysburg, 30 miles to the north.

The fortunes of war, however, were not to smile exclusively on the Union army. McClellan's delay in moving his army out from Frederick until the morning of September 14, eighteen to twenty hours after digesting Lee's order, to a large extent nullified the rare military advantage afforded him in the knowledge of his opponent's troop dispositions and intentions. Had he gone beyond the mere dispatching of advance elements on the night of September 13, Lee would have been deprived of the time necessary to plug the two mountain gaps with infantry and artillery in support of the thin cavalry screen. McClellan's army could have been through the passes and spreading out in the valley beyond before the Confederate units ordered back to South Mountain could have reached it.

It so happened that when Lee's lost dispatch was handed to McClellan during the morning of September 13, a citizen of Frederick who was secretly a Southern sympathizer, was at McClellan's headquarters and of course picked up the startling news of the disclosure of Lee's plans. As soon as he could get away without arousing suspicion, the volunteer spy rode hard to South Mountain to advise Stuart, who in turn immediately relayed the intelligence to Lee at Hagerstown.

Longstreet's presence at Hagerstown rather than Boonsboro had been brought about as the result of a rumor that Federal troops were coming down on Hagerstown from Pennsylvania. The word had gotten around that Lee's first attempt in the direction of Pennsylvania had so alarmed the authorities in Harrisburg, the capital city, that Governor Andrew G. Curtin hastily called up 50,000 militia and wired President Lincoln for help to secure the State against the expected Rebel invaders. In reply, the War Department pulled Major General John F. Reynolds away from his regular assignment with troops and dispatched him to stiffen the backbones of the raw volunteers. Although the rumor had no foundation in fact, Lee decided that he could protect McLaws' operations in the vicinity of Maryland Heights more effectively from the road center at Hagerstown, twelve miles north of Boonsboro. In addition, that position would facilitate the reconcentration of his army after Harpers Ferry fell, and would afford him, as well, greater flexibility of maneuver in carrying out the later phases of the invasion.

D. H. (Harvey) Hill's Confederate division, the army rear guard, had been left at Boonsboro to block the anticipated retreat of the Harpers Ferry garrison up through Pleasant Valley and to assist Stuart in holding Turner's Gap. Hill had managed, as a result of a somewhat critical temperament and occasionally grumpy attitude toward others, to antagonize a number of his colleagues among the general officers. Like many others, then and now, he hated administrative chores to such an extent as to sidestep his responsibilities in that direction. Another weakness was an apparent lack of assurance in making decisions when not in combat, although in battle he was to grow in stature with experience. Hill had clashed with Stuart on several occasions because he had spoken contemptuously of the cavalry arm, and the relations between the two generals were far from cordial. There may have been no significance in that fact insofar as Hill's sense of duty was concerned, but for some reason he left the defense of the gap largely to Stuart's cavalry. Meanwhile Hill remained at Boonsboro, keeping an eye on what he considered his principal mission, and in that respect neglected his additional responsibility at Turner's Gap.

When Stuart reported to Hill that the cavalry was being pushed back to South Mountain by the advancing Federals, the rear-guard commander made a gesture of support by sending one of his brigades under Colonel A. H. Colquitt to support Stuart at the Gap, while at the same time another brigade, Garland's, was alerted but not dispatched. The rest of Hill's division remained at Boonsboro, three miles from Turner's Gap. Colquitt moved his brigade to the eastern face of the mountain and there, in the darkness of the night of September 13, he looked down into the broad valley between South and Catoctin Mountains. As far as the eye could see, innumerable enemy camp fires indicated that the Federals were in vastly greater strength than the two cavalry brigades which Stuart had reported as the only troops that had been pressing him. This startling intelligence was likewise quickly forwarded through Hill to Lee.

Thus by midnight of the 13th the situation had been drastically altered. Lee knew that a copy of his orders had fallen into McClellan's hands. Harpers Ferry had not yet capitulated as expected on September 12. The Confederate army, widely scattered, was an easy prey for an aggressive adversary. It was now clear to Lee why the Army of the Potomac seemed to be moving with unaccustomed celerity, a matter that had been puzzling him for some hours.

The Confederate strategy would have to be changed, and at once. The ambitious plan to move into Pennsylvania must be shelved, temporarily at least. Lee's earlier idea, not to defend the passes of South Mountain in order to lure McClellan farther from his base of supplies, had now lost its attraction, coupled as it was with the timetable upset caused by the prolonged delay in capturing Harpers Ferry.

Having lost the initiative through no fault of his own, and through sheer luck so far as McClellan was concerned, Lee reacted with customary firmness in the face of adversity. His situation had suddenly become so critical that he began to think seriously of the wisdom of calling the whole program off and returning to Virginia. His orders and dispositions for the next two days were planned and executed with that possibility in mind.

The immediate requirement was to meet the Federal threat by delaying McClellan's advance through South Mountain, and to safeguard the status of that portion of his own army that remained in Maryland. For it must be remembered that Stonewall Jackson's corps and Walker's division were by this time south of the Potomac, carrying out their instructions to throw a net around Harpers Ferry prior to taking it over in conjunction with McLaws' force, which was operating from the Maryland side of the river.

By midnight September 13, Harvey Hill had received from Lee confirmatory orders to cooperate with Stuart in holding the passes at Turner's Gap and vicinity, which included three crossings: the National Road through Turner's Gap; Fox's (Braddock's*) Gap, where the old Sharpsburg Road crossed the mountain a mile to the south; and still another gap a mile to the north, where a second road led to Hagerstown. Hill was informed that Longstreet's troops, the divisions of D. R. Jones and John B. Hood, would be sent back from Hagerstown the following day to add their strength to the defense of the passes.

The Fight at Turner's Gap

The morning of Sunday, September 14, was bright and clear. The Union troops, advancing on all the roads leading west to the South Mountain gaps, were in a cheerful mood. Their favorite general was again leading them, Lee's army was retiring before them, and this time they would be fighting to drive the brash invader from their own Northern soil.

Pleasonton's cavalry had the preceding day driven the Confederate cavalry back into the mountains, but Pleasonton, after making a reconnaissance up the mountain, concluded that as

---

*So named as the route followed by General Braddock and Colonel George Washington on their march to Fort Duquesne (Pittsburgh) in the French and Indian War.

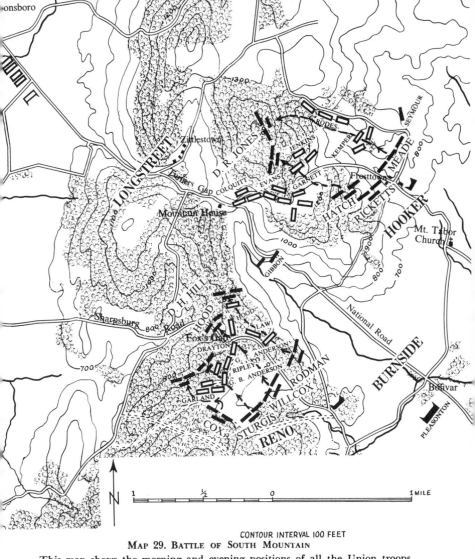

CONTOUR INTERVAL 100 FEET

MAP 29. BATTLE OF SOUTH MOUNTAIN

This map shows the morning and evening positions of all the Union troops engaged. Only the initial Confederate positions are shown. Actually the units were committed successively. Wise's field, where Reno was killed, is the small clearing just above the word "Gap" in Fox's Gap.

the enemy position was too strongly held, it would be wise to let the infantry and artillery catch up before attacking.

At Pleasonton's request, Brigadier General Jacob D. Cox, in command of the Kanawha division of Reno's corps, assigned Scammon's brigade to join the cavalry in storming the pass. Suspecting that his entire division might be needed, Cox personally brought his other brigade, under Colonel George Crook, to follow Scammon, who about 9 o'clock in the morning had reached the foot of the mountain and started to make the ascent on the old Sharpsburg Road.

The right wing of the Union army advanced with corps abreast, Reno's Ninth and Hooker's First, which together totaled seven divisions, moving in the lead in columns of divisions on parallel roads. When Reno was advised that Cox's division was on its way up the mountain, he sent word that the entire Ninth Corps, three additional divisions commanded respectively by Willcox, Sturgis, and Rodman, would support the attack. Two batteries of twenty-pounder Parrott guns were placed near the turnpike to cover the advance from a position that enabled them to effectively reach the enemy guns near the crest.

Scammon's brigade proceeded in a deployed formation to the left of the Sharpsburg road with the mission of turning the enemy right. The going was not too difficult for the first mile or so, across cultivated fields, but when, farther up, the slope became steeper and more wooded, the troops found it necessary to halt frequently to recover their wind. As they neared the crest, Hill's Confederate infantry opened fire, while at the same time a battery poured in canister and case-shot from a still higher position. The Southerners, protected by portions of a stone wall paralleling the rough country road that connected the Sharpsburg road with the old National turnpike, were apparently there to stay; it would take cold steel to drive them out. The Federals were in the mood, so, with Crook's column in close support, the attacking line fixed bayonets and advanced with loud cheers.

The regiment on Scammon's left, the Twenty-third Ohio, was commanded by Lieutenant Colonel Rutherford B. Hayes, later a President of the United States. Hayes' regiment, moving through the woods, was given the task of outflanking the enemy. Unseen by the Confederates, Hayes passed the crest and came in on their right and rear as the other regiments of his brigade charged frontally. The fight was close-in and vicious, both sides losing heavily, but Scammon's men were not to be denied the fruits of their laborious climb. The combined troops of D. H. Hill and Stuart fought doggedly and bravely. It was not until Confederate General Garland, whose brigade was defending Fox's Gap, was killed that the Confederates broke and yielded the crest on that part of the mountain to the victorious Federals of Cox's division. Even then Hill's men fought on, attempting in repeated counterattacks to recover the lost ground, but without success. Finally, about noon, both sides had lost so many men in the hand-to-hand combat in the woods, and were so exhausted by their continuous efforts over the entire morning, that a lull in the battle occurred, almost as though by mutual consent an unspoken truce had been declared until both contestants should receive reinforcements to enable them to again be at each other's throats.

Hill Gets a Reprieve

General D. H. Hill, charged by Lee with the responsibility of holding Turner's Gap as long as possible, had foolishly relied on Jeb Stuart to inform him of the tactical features of the mountaintop and neglected to even visit the Gap until the early morning of September 14. His first shock upon arrival was to learn that the peripatetic Stuart had ridden down to see how things were faring at Crampton's Gap. The second shock, when he and Colquitt rode along the crest on a reconnaissance, occurred when they distinctly heard the rumble of artillery carriages and the voices of Federal officers giving commands on the road leading up to the crest. Colquitt's brigade was the only one of the five brigades in Hill's division that was at hand, although Garland's was climbing fast. Hill concluded that his entire division, if present, would not be strong enough to block the Federals, but his uncertainty was so marked that all he did was to order up G. B. Anderson's brigade and direct one regiment of Ripley's brigade to move to the next pass north of Turner's Gap, leaving the balance of Ripley's and all of Rodes' small brigade to continue the watch at Boonsboro. Consequently, when Cox attacked shortly after 9 o'clock, Hill had only two brigades in line to receive him, but those two did their best for three hours, and their best was extremely good.

It was not until late in the morning, when Garland's brigade was shattered, losing 200 men as prisoners in addition to a large number of killed and wounded, that Hill could bring himself to the point of abandoning the Boonsboro part of his mission. Finally he sent word to Rodes and Ripley to bring their brigades up the mountain. But it would be mid-afternoon before they could arrive and then it might be too late, since Hill had no idea when Longstreet had left Hagerstown nor how long it would take his two divisions to cover the 12-mile march to the foot of the mountain. While Hill was gloomily dwelling on the critical situation in which he found himself, welcome aid came from an unexpected source—the enemy, in the person of General Burnside.

Burnside Takes Charge

General Burnside, commanding the Federal right wing, and General Reno, Ninth Corps commander, met at the foot of the mountain for a brief conference. Hooker's First Corps had not yet reached the field, but Reno's corps was on hand, and Willcox's division had already joined Cox, forming on his right and extending across and to the north of the old National Road leading through Turner's Gap. In the process Willcox had lost many men from Confederate direct and enfilading artillery fire.

Burnside now took command of the battle and directed Reno to send the remaining two divisions of the Ninth Corps, Sturgis' and Rodman's, to join Cox and Willcox, but not to make a general attack until Hooker's corps had arrived and was well on its way up the mountain in the zone north of the

Hagerstown Turnpike. It was this reprieve which proved such a boon to D. H. Hill's thin line of defense at the summit, but it is doubtful if either Burnside or Reno had the remotest idea that their delay would forfeit the opportunity for Cox and Willcox with their superior numbers to sweep the top of the mountain clear of Hill's three depleted brigades.

A Thrilling Spectacle

David L. Thompson, Company G, 9th New York Volunteers, an articulate enlisted man in Burnside's corps, recorded his impressions of the eye-filling scene as the Army of the Potomac crossed the broad valley between Catoctin and South Mountains.

That day—the 14th of September—we crossed the Catoctin range of mountains, reaching the summit about noon, and descended its western slope into the beautiful valley of Middletown. Half-way up the valley's western side we halted for a rest, and turned to look back on the moving host. It was a scene to linger in the memory. The valley in which Middletown lies is four or five miles wide, as I remember it, and runs almost due north and south between the parallel ranges of Catoctin and South Mountains. From where we stood the landscape lay below us, the eye commanding the opposite slope of the valley almost at point-blank. An hour before, from the same spot, it had been merely a scene of quiet pastoral beauty. All at once, along its eastern edge the heads of the columns began to appear, and grew and grew, pouring over the ridge and descending by every road, filling them completely and scarring the surface of the gentle landscape with the angry welts of war. By the farthest northern road—the farthest we could see—moved the baggage wagons, the line stretching from the bottom of the valley back to the top of the ridge, and beyond, only the canvas covers of the wagons revealing their character. We knew that each dot was a heavily loaded army wagon, drawn by six mules and occupying forty feet of road at least. Now they looked like white beads on a string. So far away were they that no motion was perceptible. The constant swelling of the end of the line down in the valley, where the teams turned into the fields to park, gave evidence that, in this way, it was being slowly reeled along the way. The troops were marching by two roads farther south. The Confederates fighting on the western summit must have seen them plainly. Half a mile beyond us the column broke abruptly, filing off into line of battle, right and left, across the fields. From that point backward and downward, across the valley and up the farther slope, it stretched with scarcely a gap, every curve and zigzag of the way defined more sharply by its somber presence. Here, too, on all the distant portions of the line, motion was imperceptible, but could be inferred from the casual glint of sunlight on a musket barrel miles away. It was 3 o'clock when we resumed our march, turning our backs upon the beautiful, impressive picture—each column a monstrous, crawling, blue-black snake, miles long, quilled with the silver slant of muskets at a "shoulder," its sluggish tail writhing slowly up over the distant eastern ridge, its bruised head weltering in the roar and smoke upon the crest above, where was being fought the battle of South Mountain.*

Burnside's Weight Begins to Tell

During the midday breathing space of several hours thus afforded Hill, the two remaining brigades of his division, Ripley's and Rodes', scaled the mountain and were fed into the defensive line, Ripley to the south, Rodes to the north of the turnpike. Longstreet also, approaching Boonsboro with the divisions of D. R. Jones and John B. Hood, would reach the crest in the nick of time to redress the balance late in the afternoon and prolong the battle until far into the night.

With the arrival of Sturgis' and Rodman's Federal divisions at the scene of action, the Ninth Corps commander, Reno, took over from Cox in a continuation of the attack on the Sharpsburg Road leading through Fox's Gap. Major General Jesse L. Reno, graduate of the Class of 1846 at West Point, age 39 and a Virginian by birth, had fought in the Mexican War and distinguished himself with Burnside in the latter's successful invasion of North Carolina, which led to the capture of Roanoke

_____

*Battles and Leaders of the Civil War.

Island in early 1862. In the Battle of Second Manassas he had again conducted himself in a manner to win the unstinting commendation of General Pope, who seemed to take a rather dim view of so many of the other corps and division commanders who served under him in that ill-fated campaign.

By the time Sturgis and Rodman were in position, McClellan had arrived and was in consultation with Burnside and Reno at Pleasonton's command post, on a central knoll in the midst of the curving hills on the south slope of the mountain. The conference resulted in a decision to press the attack in the direction of the Mountain House, west of the turnpike, a key position which commanded the road through Turner's Gap at its most sensitive spot. Before the coordinated corps attack could be launched, however, Longstreet's reinforcements had come up. The combined divisions of Hood, Jones, and Hill pitched into Reno's divisions. The fight was bloody and prolonged, swirling back and forth without a decision for several hours.

Just before sunset, General Reno came forward to the front line to see what was holding up progress toward the summit objective—the Mountain House. As he exposed himself to get a better view, an enemy bullet found its mark and he fell, mortally wounded, the highest ranking officer of either army to lose his life in this battle. As he was being carried to the rear, Reno managed with his last breath to gasp out a final message to his men: "Tell my command that if not in body, I will be with them in spirit." One of his fellow officers has recorded the opinion that "the hero's body was small, but his spirit was mighty."

The head of Hooker's corps reached Mount Tabor Church about the middle of the afternoon, pausing while the corps commander looked over the terrain. His three divisions, led by Generals Meade, Hatch, and Ricketts, all veteran commanders, were successively deployed as they arrived, Meade on the right, Hatch on the left, and Ricketts, last to come up at about 5 o'clock, in rear as reserve. The right of Meade's line was posted about 1½ miles beyond the old National Road. Three roads were available for the ascent, partly through woods and partly over farm lands, the two country roads (other than the turnpike) winding through ravines or depressions between the rounded mountain peaks which towered several hundred feet above the turnpike on either side.

MAJOR GENERAL JESSE L. RENO, KILLED AT FOX'S GAP

Advancing abreast, Meade and Hatch soon encountered the Confederates, when the battle became general all along the line east of the turnpike. Pushing steadily forward and upward, Meade's division succeeded in turning the Confederate left. Soon the first ridge, which commanded the pass on both sides of the mountain, was in Federal hands. Gibbon's brigade of Hatch's division was then sent directly up the turnpike in a brisk engagement which forced the Confederate center back to the crest; at that point reinforcements braced the line, but Gibbon managed to hold his gains.

Longstreet Moves to Hill's Support

On receiving the news from D. H. Hill late in the evening of September 13 that McClellan's army was present in strength in the valley east of South Mountain, Lee at Hagerstown called Longstreet to his tent to inform him that on the following morning he would have to take his two divisions back to the mountain to support Hill. Longstreet demurred, on the premise that the proper strategy was to adhere to the original plan not to hold the passes. Old Pete argued that it would be better to retire to Sharpsburg where the army could be reunited in safety, but Lee insisted that the order be carried out so that McLaws' two divisions on Maryland Heights would not be jeopardized.

As Longstreet's column on September 14 plodded along the dusty road to Boonsboro, the sounds of furious fighting on the mountain heights came clearly to the ears of the men. When they neared Boonsboro a dispatch rider galloped up to Lee, riding as usual at the head of the column, with an appeal from Hill to hurry Longstreet's reinforcements if the crest was to be held against a greatly superior Federal force. Shortly after three o'clock, when the head of the column reached the foot of the mountain and began the ascent, Hood's Texas brigade strode by and spied General Lee sitting on his horse beside the road, watching the troops breaking from column into extended order for the climb.

"Give us Hood," they shouted. Lee nodded his head in acquiescence, a reaction that twentieth century military men might have some difficulty in understanding. But Lee, who knew his soldiers, appraised their apparent lack of discipline sympathetically. Their division commander, John B. Hood, one of the South's best fighting generals, had been placed under arrest by Longstreet back at Manassas for insubordination in connection with a wrangle between General N. G. "Shank" Evans and himself over some captured Federal ambulances, which had been claimed by both parties to the controversy. Hood had been permitted to accompany his division on the march into Maryland, but without command authority, and now that his men were again going into battle they wanted their trusted leader at the helm. Acting on the spur of the moment, and without consulting Longstreet, Hood was summoned by Lee, his status of arrest suspended until after the battle, and the restored division commander rode to the head of his troops with their cheers ringing in his ears.

Longstreet's reinforcements arrived barely in time to prevent a repetition of the Confederate rout at Crampton's Gap. Hill's five brigades had been fighting all day to hold off two Union corps with a strength of seven divisions, and they had about reached the limit of endurance. Hill's right had been turned, but the line had somehow been restored further up the mountain. Several hours later Hooker's troops were massed to turn Hill's left, where Rodes' undersized brigade was fighting stubbornly against overwhelmingly superior strength. Daylight was almost gone before Longstreet's divisions under D. R. Jones and Hood, with Evans' brigade attached, tuckered by their tiring march from Hagerstown and the climb to the top of the mountain, moved into position for the relief of Hill's exhausted troops. Longstreet immediately took charge of the defense and, even before he had examined the terrain, sent back word to Lee that South Mountain could not be held. Nevertheless the Confederates, strengthened by Longstreet's divisions, hung on until night brought an end to the bitter fighting. All the troops, on both sides, were more than ready to flop down on the ground for some blessed rest, no matter what the next day should demand of them.

About the time the battle on the heights ended, two more Union corps, Sumner's and Mansfield's, the latter under the temporary command of the senior division commander, Brigadier General A. S. Williams, reached the eastern base of the mountain and went into bivouac. McClellan's army was now fully concentrated, but when the Federal skirmishers up on the crest moved forward at daylight, September 15, to feel out their opponents, they discovered that the Confederates had withdrawn during the night, leaving their dead and wounded behind.

Some 5,000 casualties, including those missing and captured, represented the cost to both armies of the engagements at Crampton's and Turner's Gaps. That was the penalty the Confederates had to pay for delaying McClellan's army for twenty-four hours; it was McClellan's price for gaining the passes too late to save Harpers Ferry or to cut Lee's army in two as planned. The Union casualty reports show losses of 533 at Crampton's and 1,813 at Turner's for a total of 2,346, practically all killed or wounded. The Confederate reports, as usual incomplete and unofficial, group South Mountain and Antietam as one and are virtually impossible of separation. Douglas Southall Freeman placed the Confederate killed and wounded at some 1,800 at Turner's Gap only, exclusive of Garland's brigade, the greater part of which was captured. Adding the losses at Crampton's, it may safely be assumed that the aggregate of losses at South Mountain for Lee's troops exceeded 2,500. Since the Union strength was far greater than the Confederate, the percentage of loss of the Southerners was consequently substantially higher than that of their opponents, a rather unusual occurrence because the Confederates had the advantage of a stronger position and the defense normally inflicts greater damage on the attackers than it receives.

It is an intriguing picture that presents itself in studying the Confederate maneuvers at this stage of Lee's campaign. With a small force of only two divisions, barely one-fifth of the manpower of his army, General Lee bivouacked at Hagerstown with supreme confidence as McClellan, with an army almost twice as large as the entire Confederate invading army, moved west in pursuit. With his right arm, so to speak, Lee reached out to gather in Harpers Ferry and safeguard his line of supply to Virginia. With his left arm, when he learned that McClellan's unaccustomed rate of march posed a threat to his own safety, Lee straight-armed to bar his opponent's passage of the mountain gaps long enough (he hoped) to assure the fall of

Harpers Ferry and enable him to reconcentrate his full strength farther west, probably in the Sharpsburg area.

It would be a close thing, but the Confederate leader figured all the angles and, as happened time after time on other battlefields such as Richmond, Second Manassas, Fredericksburg, Chancellorsville, and Gettysburg, his precision timing brought the desired results. Invariably, in taking his calculated risks, Lee counted on the inability of his opponent to match his own mental agility and the quick reactions, to his orders, of his subordinates and their brigades and divisions. In the case of the Battle of South Mountain, it was McClellan's tardiness in forcing the gaps rather than superior Confederate battle proficiency that gave Lee the vital extra time that he needed. From his standpoint, the strategic gains outweighed the losses, without which it is more than probable that he would have retreated to Virginia without fighting the Battle of Antietam.

HARPERS FERRY AND, TO THE LEFT, MARYLAND HEIGHTS

CHAPTER 17

THE HARPERS FERRY DIVERSION

WHAT happened at Harpers Ferry in mid-September 1862 is reminiscent of the favorite strategy of American Indians on the warpath in frontier days. Every reader of "westerns" or confirmed movie-goer is familiar with the Red Man's preferred method of attack, in which a horde of almost naked savages, hideous in their brilliant war paint, would race their ponies in wide circles around the objects of their attack, shooting arrows and firing rifles until the defenders were softened for the kill.

Lee's plan for the investment by encirclement of the Federal garrison at Harpers Ferry followed that pattern. He sent close to 30,000 soldiers, almost 60 percent of his army, to make certain that the overwhelming Confederate superiority should force the capitulation of the relatively small garrison without loss of time. For it would prove a losing gamble if McClellan should surprise Lee by closing in on his scattered divisions before they could reassemble as an operational army.

Lee's timetable as set forth in Special Orders No. 191 of September 9 called for the occupation of Maryland Heights and Loudoun Heights by McLaws and Walker respectively by Friday morning, September 12, at which time Jackson was expected to be at Martinsburg, in position to prevent the Federals from escaping in that direction. If all went smoothly, the sideshow should be concluded so that the traveling Confederates would be able to rejoin Lee at Hagerstown or Boonsboro before the Union army could interfere.

The strategic importance of Harpers Ferry, which changed hands periodically during the Civil War, lay in the fact that its possession was essential to that army, Union or Confederate, whose operations included the use of the Shenandoah Valley either for offensive or defensive purposes. It was a sensitive area, located at the confluence of the Shenandoah and Potomac Rivers, where the Baltimore and Ohio Railroad, so vital to the North, crosses the Potomac.

Squatting at the base of the Blue Ridge Mountains, which tower a thousand feet above the Potomac to look down directly from that imposing height on the little town, Harpers Ferry does not strike the observer as the best place to fight a battle. The small community nestles in the angle formed by the two rivers, which in conjunction with the massive bluffs hem it in on all sides except the west, where the lesser but still formidable Bolivar Heights provide access to the town. Loudoun Heights loom rocky and steep directly to the east on the far side of the Shenandoah River and the lofty Maryland Heights complete the impressive picture across the Potomac as the northern arc of the mountain perimeter. (See Map 30.)

Harpers Ferry is only 18 miles west of Frederick by the most direct road, but Lee's orders required Jackson's three divisions to take a long, roundabout, sixty-mile march through Middletown, Boonsboro, Sharpsburg, across the Potomac and through Martinsburg in order to dispose of the Federal detachment reported to be at the latter place, to intercept escapees from Harpers Ferry, and to approach that town from the west. With

McLaws' two-division command blocking the escape route to the north from his position on Maryland Heights, and with Walker's division closing the route to the east from Loudoun Heights, the 11,000-man Federal garrison at Harpers Ferry would have the choice of surrender or death.

The Federal garrison, under command of Colonel Dixon S. Miles, included two regiments and several additional squadrons of cavalry, a dozen or more regiments of infantry, and about six batteries of artillery, but formal defenses were practically nonexistent. Several pseudo-forts on Maryland Heights and lines of rifle pits and earthworks here and there on Bolivar Heights made a pretense of fortifications that were scarcely worthy of the name. There were no Federal troops on Loudoun Heights. Miles had disposed 7,000 men on Bolivar Heights, manning a curving line about a mile and a half long from the Potomac to the Shenandoah; 2,000 on Maryland Heights; and about 1,800 to guard bridges and other points on the rivers and the fringes of the town itself.

Brigadier General Julius White was in command of the small Union force of 2,500 men at Martinsburg. Exercising his discretionary authority, on receipt of word that the Confederates were approaching from the north on September 12, he moved his detachment to Harpers Ferry, raising the strength of the garrison there to approximately 13,000 men. Normally White would by reason of rank have assumed command of the combined forces, but since Colonel Miles had specific orders from General Halleck, White's position became largely that of an observer. Halleck was seriously intent on holding Harpers Ferry. On September 7 he had telegraphed Colonel Miles to advise him that McClellan's army was in motion and emphasizing the importance of holding the town as long as humanly possible.

McLaws First to Arrive

To Lafayette McLaws, whose division had reached Manassas from Richmond too late to take part in that recent battle, Lee assigned the leading part in the three-way undertaking to reduce Harpers Ferry. With "Dick" Anderson's division added to his own, under McLaws' command, the latter was instructed to take the road from Middletown to Harpers Ferry and by Friday morning, the twelfth, to seize Maryland Heights "and endeavor to capture the enemy at Harpers Ferry and vicinity." The topography being what it was, Maryland Heights seemed to be the key to the tactical success of the overall mission. It so dominated Harpers Ferry that with the Confederates occupying the mountain peak on the Maryland side and Loudoun Heights in Virginia, the town would be next to untenable for the defenders. Nevertheless, McLaws' two divisions would be exposed in rear to a possible sudden appearance of a strong Union force approaching through the mountain gaps from the east. It therefore behooved him to work fast and carefully in discharging his difficult double mission of attack in one direction while guarding his rear from another.

McLaws started from Frederick early on the morning of September 10, with less than a twenty-mile march ahead of him; but his movements were slow, requiring two days to cover about twelve miles. Thursday night, September 11, found him encamped at Brownsville, at the western exit of the South Mountain pass of the same name, some six miles north of the Potomac where it passes the base of Elk Ridge, a tall mountain range whose southern extremity was known as Maryland Heights. Possibly McLaws preferred not to reach his objective too early lest he stir up a Federal hornet's nest prematurely and thus risk the escape of the garrison at Harpers Ferry before Jackson and Walker could reach their designated positions to close the circle. (See Map 26.)

From his bivouac at Brownsville, the mountain peak from which McLaws had been directed to eject the Federal occupants loomed as a formidable obstacle from which plunging fire could be expected from the Union guns that would certainly be located on Maryland Heights. McLaws reasoned that the best approach would be to scale the heights by way of Solomon's Gap, four miles north of Maryland Heights and only two or three miles from his present camp. Once having gained the ridge, he would proceed south along the crest, following a mountain road that he was told led directly to the Federal artillery position.

Having thus decided, McLaws split his command into two parts, Kershaw's brigade supported by Barksdale's to follow the mountain road, while the remaining eight brigades would be disposed in Pleasant Valley in a central position that would enable them to challenge any enemy who might cross South Mountain. The latter force would at the same time block the valley route against troops from the Harpers Ferry garrison who might attempt to escape in that direction.

McLaws himself led the advance of his main body to the Potomac, which was reached by nightfall, September 12, in the vicinity of Weverton. This small town at the southern extremity of South Mountain, derived its significance chiefly from the fact that the road from Harpers Ferry along the north bank of the Potomac, the Baltimore and Ohio Railroad, and the Chesapeake and Ohio Canal all pass that point in the narrow space between the river and the mountain. Kershaw concurrently climbed the mountain, but the route was so rough and steep and full of boulders that he found it necessary to halt for the night about a mile from his objective.

Saturday morning, September 13, Kershaw's two brigades pushed forward along the ridge, Barksdale working around the precipitous eastern face of Maryland Heights to outflank the enemy, whose outposts had already been driven in. One of Barksdale's companies opened fire at close range, which seemed to disconcert the Federals. In any event, they started down the mountain and were promptly joined by the entire force of the defenders, so that by mid-afternoon all of Maryland Heights was in the hands of the Confederates, most of the Union troops returning to the town of Harpers Ferry. The Federal troop commander, Colonel Ford, claimed later that he abandoned the position on order of Colonel Miles, who denied that he had issued any such order. There was no doubt that the Federals had failed to put up a vigorous defense and the evidence seemed to point to Ford as the culprit. The result was that McLaws was able to take Maryland Heights with ease, while Colonel Ford was later tried and convicted on a charge of neglect of duty.

The dramatic collateral features of the Confederate investment of Harpers Ferry and its influence on the Battle of Antietam, which turned Lee back into Virginia, will appear later in the narrative. At this point, however, it is of interest to note that military strategists have enjoyed speculating on what might have resulted had Miles made a more serious effort to hold Maryland Heights, the dominant terrain feature in the area. It is reasonably certain that 10,000 Federals on that side of the Potomac could have prevented McLaws from accomplishing his mission, but Miles' instructions were to hold Harper's Ferry as long as possible, which obviously would be impossible if he should transfer the bulk of his troops to the other side of the Potomac. By adhering strictly to his orders, even though Maryland Heights was evacuated with untimely speed by a none too courageous colonel, the resistance offered by the Federals in the town made it necessary for Lee's converging columns to tarry in the vicinity of Harpers Ferry several days longer than Lee had planned, with almost disastrous effect on the Confederate fortunes.

While McLaws on September 13 was completing the first half of his mission by taking possession of Maryland Heights, Walker without opposition occupied Loudoun Heights and Jackson arrived with the leading elements of his corps to the west of Bolivar Heights. Much work was still to be done, however, before the attack could commence. Pioneers must cut paths along the mountain tops, so that the guns could be placed to deliver maximum fire on the town below. Communications must be established between Jackson's force, which included the divisions of A. P. Hill, A. R. Lawton, and John R. Jones, and those of McLaws and Walker across the Potomac and Shenandoah Rivers. The cordon around

Harpers Ferry must be made tight in Jackson's zone, which meant disposing troops in a wide arc paralleling the Federal rifle pits and earthworks from the Potomac to the Shenandoah. All of which took time, so that it was not until the afternoon of September 14 that Jackson was ready to advance his troops to Bolivar Heights preparatory to signaling the order for the converging, coordinated artillery bombardment to open simultaneously from the two mountaintops and from his own position west of the town.

During the time that Jackson was making his preparations and trying with indifferent success on September 14 to establish flag signal communication with McLaws and Walker across the two rivers, McLaws was having his troubles. While getting his artillery into position for the second part of his mission, the capture of Harpers Ferry, things began to pop at the northern end of Pleasant Valley, where Semmes' and Mahone's brigades had been posted in a dual mission to protect the road taken by Kershaw to reach Maryland Heights, and to guard the passes through South Mountain. It was Semmes whose alert reconnoitering discovered that there was no Confederate infantry in position to secure Crampton's Gap. On his own authority Semmes dispatched several regiments of Mahone's brigade with a battery to occupy the gap. From then on events moved rapidly, as recounted in Chapter 16.

McLaws heard the firing on South Mountain and rode back with Jeb Stuart to investigate. As they neared the western exit of Crampton's Gap, they met General Cobb, who in some excitement informed them of the loss of the Gap and the rout of the Confederates, who were even then streaming down the western side of the mountain. McLaws was at that moment in a very difficult position. It was impossible for him to hold off the Army of the Potomac, if the Federal troops now in the Gap should prove to be the advance elements of McClellan's army. Furthermore, the brigades of Semmes, Cobb, and Mahone would probably be quickly cut

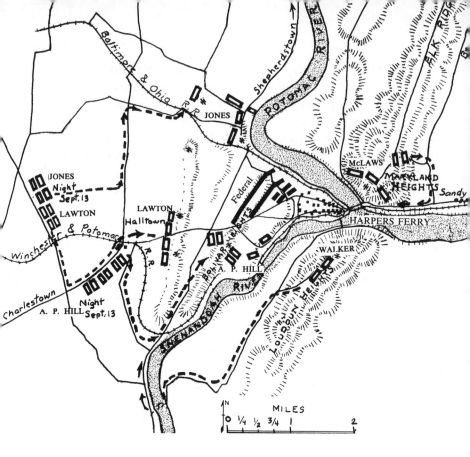

MAP 30. CAPTURE OF HARPERS FERRY

Showing the positions of Jackson's divisions on the night of September 13, and their routes forward. The positions of all divisions for the attack on Harpers Ferry are shown, McLaws being in the Federal works on Maryland Heights which he captured on the 14th. The artillery symbols indicate the various Confederate batteries and battalions. The solid lines are the Federal works on Bolivar Heights. The routes of Walker and McLaws to Harpers Ferry after the surrender are also shown.

to pieces if the Federals pressed their advantage in superior force. That in turn would mean the reoccupation of Maryland Heights by the advancing Bluecoats, the relief of Harpers Ferry, Lee's army cut in two, and possible destruction of the divided wings.

Fortunately for McLaws and the Confederate army as a whole, Union General Franklin, whose corps it was that took Crampton's Gap, proved to be somewhat less than enterprising. Hence McLaws was able, during the night of September 14, to recall all of the troops who had captured Maryland Heights except one of Barksdale's regiments and two guns. By morning he had five brigades less one regiment disposed in two lines across Pleasant Valley below Crampton's Gap, and it was this force which led Franklin to inform McClellan that he was outnumbered two to one. McLaw's bold front at a critical moment was thus sufficient to bluff a timid Franklin to gain the time necessary for Jackson to force the surrender of Harpers Ferry and for Lee to change his mind about calling the show off by withdrawing his army to Virginia.

Stuart's Effective Cavalry

Seen in retrospect, the effectiveness of Stuart and his cavalrymen in reporting vital information to Lee's headquarters was nothing short of amazing. Stuart himself was indefatigable in covering ground, but his score was not perfect, and he occasionally failed to pinpoint the strength and dispositions of Federal troops. Nevertheless the Confederate cavalry in 1862 was so superior to the Union cavalry in the matter of gathering enemy intelligence and executing counterintelligence missions that Lee's reliance on "the eyes of his army" had become almost a byword. Whenever and wherever a crisis occurred, it always seemed to be Jeb Stuart who stepped into the breach, made a whirlwind reconnaissance to ascertain the true facts, and gave Lee the answers that he needed to plan his next move.

It was Stuart's cavalry which screened Lee's army on the invasion of Maryland and prevented the Federal cavalry, as it moved west in the advance of McClellan's army from Washington, from penetrating the Confederate screen. It was Stuart's cavalry that secured the South Mountain gaps in rear of the army as it marched across the mountain ranges ahead of the approaching Federal forces. And later, when Lee found it necessary to hold the passes for an extended period because of the timetable upset in capturing Harpers Ferry, it was the cavalry that was called on to meet the emergency.

Stuart possessed an extraordinary grasp of the value of terrain for tactical purposes, and a keen eye for detail. He it was who took occasion to warn McLaws of the importance of watching the road that led from Harpers Ferry around the base of Maryland Heights to Sharpsburg, to make sure that none of the Federal garrison should escape by that route. Interestingly enough, Stuart's cautionary advice was overlooked or disregarded, for it was that very road that the Federal cavalry used without interference to escape from Harpers Ferry, when McLaws' attention was riveted on the dangerous situation that had developed in Pleasant Valley, on the opposite side of the mountain.

Jackson Slow to Act

There were times in Stonewall Jackson's military career when his customary sense of urgency was lacking. Most of the time he was a driver who gave his men no rest, nor spared himself in marches or battles until victory was achieved or his immediate mission accomplished. Occasionally, however, his actions seemed uninspired, a fact which in his case attracts attention for the simple reason that his standards of performance were so high that any deviation, however slight, became notable because it was so unusual. The investment of Harpers Ferry was one of those times.

Lee's directive of September 9 contemplated the capture of the Federal garrison at Harpers Ferry by Friday night, September 12. He believed that McLaws' force could bring it off with Walker's assistance from Loudoun Heights, while Jackson's corps was cutting the Baltimore and Ohio Railroad and closing the Federal escape route to the west. The schedule may have been a bit ambitious in point of time, because the three columns did not reach their assigned areas on the perimeter around Harpers Ferry until Saturday the thirteenth, on which day Jackson, by virtue of seniority, assumed the direction of affairs. Lee had not specifically stated in his order that Jackson should take command, probably because of his familiarity with Harpers Ferry and its environs and his realization of the difficulty of achieving unity of action in a tactical situation of that character.

The only means of communication between the Confederates on Bolivar, Maryland, and Loudoun Heights was by flag wigwag or messenger. Since the Federals controlled the town of Harpers Ferry and the bridge over the Potomac, Jackson's couriers would have to cross by distant fords, which would consume more time than could be spared. Flag signals were therefore utilized, but that also took time, assuming that the signal personnel on all three peaks were on the alert and functioning perfectly, which was not fully the case on this occasion. So far as Jackson could see by personal observation from his position west of Harpers Ferry, when he arrived late on the morning of September 13, there was no visible evidence of the occupation of either Maryland or Loudoun Heights, on the opposite side of the Potomac and Shenandoah Rivers. Jackson then tried flag signals, but they evoked no response from McLaws or Walker. Toward the end of the afternoon the sound of firing on the crest of Elk Ridge was heard, but Jackson could only guess what it meant. Failing to rouse McLaws and Walker by signal flags, he reverted to messengers, who returned after dark to report that both commanders had reached their objectives. Obviously nothing further could be undertaken till morning.

On the morning of September 14, which ushered in the battle for South Mountain at the two Gaps, Turner's and Crampton's, Jackson resumed his efforts to establish two-way communication with Walker and McLaws. Walker responded, advising that he had six guns in position on Loudoun Heights, but Jackson directed him to wait until fire could be opened from both sides of the river at once. Still unable to contact McLaws, a message was finally received through Walker to the effect that McLaws was occupied with the enemy in his rear, implying that his Harpers Ferry mission would have to be sidetracked for the time being.

So it came about that another whole day, Sunday, September 14, passed while Jackson fussed with inadequate communications. At the same time McClellan's army was pressing inexorably toward a full-scale battle with Lee's army, still widely scattered two days after Lee had hoped to have it reconcentrated, with Harpers Ferry safely in the bag. Jackson had not sent in a report to Lee since they had separated on the morning of September 10, nor had Lee dispatched any additional instructions to Jackson. Consequently both were in the dark as to the fortunes of the other.

Sunday evening, when the fighting had ended on South Mountain, and word reached Lee that McClellan's main body had crossed the valley to a position from which to effectively support the troops on the mountain, the Confederate leader dispatched a message to McLaws telling him to abandon his position on Maryland Heights and in Pleasant Valley, and with his two divisions to recross the Potomac. McLaws was further informed that the commanding general had resolved to withdraw the rest of the army that was still in Maryland by way of Sharpsburg to Virginia, crossing the Potomac at Shepherdstown.

Lee's disappointment at the failure of his optimistic invasion plans was not allowed to show, but it must have been intense. Gone was the bright hope that by this time his reunited army would be on its way to Harrisburg and the Susquehanna. Instead he must now salvage what he could in order to escape disaster in the process of reconcentrating on Virginia soil. On the other side of South Mountain was the entire Army of the Potomac. He could not hope to oppose that massive force with but three divisons, two of Long-street's and what was left of D. H. Hill's. Worse still, the rout of the Confederates at Crampton's Gap meant that the Federals now threatened him from two directions, even though the prompt withdrawal of McLaws should succeed in bringing his two divisions to safety. There seemed to be no alternative. Lee and Longstreet must also retire, and a night movement was thereupon ordered. Longstreet and Hill were informed of the decision, but were not told of Lee's intention to withdraw across the Potomac. That bad news was probably withheld for psychological reasons, or Lee may still have held the remote hope that some unforeseen circumstance might arise to improve his fortunes.

Federal Cavalry Runs the Gauntlet

As the clouds of apparent doom lowered on the Federal garrison at Harpers Ferry, Colonel B. F. "Grimes" Davis, commanding the 8th New York cavalry, conceived the idea of breaking through the Confederate cordon to join Mc-Clellan's approaching army. It was obvious that cavalry was of no use to the garrison in the present circumstances, and it made sense to try to save the horses and horse equipment, which would be of great value to the Confederates if they should fall into their hands.

The project was discussed with General White, Colonel Miles, and the commanding officers of the three cavalry regiments, the 8th New York, 12th Illinois, and 1st Rhode Island, on the evening of September 13. The possibility that the entire garrison might make the effort to escape the trap was considered, but Miles would not consent on two counts, that it would be in violation of his orders, and his belief that the infantry and artillery could not march fast enough to get away with it.

Miles hesitated, but after a heated exchange with Colonel Davis, who was determined to save the cavalry, he gave his approval of the attempt, which was to be made the following night. Preparations were carefully made; every officer and man was thoroughly briefed so that there would be no slip. Some hours after dark on the evening of September 14 the three regiments moved out with "Grimes" Davis at the head of the column, crossed the pontoon bridge over the Potomac and turned left on the road leading around the nose of the mountain to Sharpsburg. Taking up a fast trot, the cavalry found their route unopposed, chiefly because McLaws' force, which would certainly have been covering the east bank of the Potomac at the foot of Maryland Heights had they not been so busily engaged in Pleasant Valley, couldn't be two places at once.

It was a daring undertaking for so small a force to make a dash through country that would in all probability be swarming with Confederates. And as so often happens when a determined officer leads men of spirit in a bold gamble, the escape of the cavalry was completely successful, without the loss of a single horse or man. Even better, the Federal horsemen had the good fortune to come across a Confederate train (Longstreet's ammunition train) of 97 wagons, under escort of a detachment of 600 men on the Hagerstown Road, all of which they captured and led triumphantly into the lines of the advancing Army of the Potomac.

The Surrender of Harpers Ferry

Confederate accounts of the final phases of the investment leading to the surrender of Harpers Ferry on the morning of September 15 vary somewhat. General Walker, in command on Loudoun Heights, contended that Jackson informed him the garrison would be given twenty-four hours to remove civilians or surrender before the artillery bombardment commenced. In Walker's account, he stated that a further delay of that length would be fatal to Lee's plans; consequently, on the afternoon of September 14 he took advantage of the latitude afforded in Jackson's instructions by inviting Federal gunfire on two regiments that he exposed as a decoy. When the Federals responded, Walker had the excuse that he sought.

He ordered his guns to open fire; whereupon the other batteries of Jackson's artillery promptly followed suit.

Colonel Henry Kyd Douglas, of Jackson's staff, was emphatic in denying that Jackson intended to grant a 24-hour delay. Brigadier General Bradley Johnson, who was also present, definitely refuted Walker by quoting chapter and verse from the official file of Jackson's messages. The dispute over that particular matter is only of academic interest except for the impact of the additional delay on the smaller half of Lee's army confronting McClellan. If Harpers Ferry had not fallen on September 15, it is quite possible that McClellan could have destroyed Longstreet and D. H. Hill at Sharpsburg before McLaws, Anderson, and A. P. Hill reached the battlefield.

Soon after daylight on the fifteenth, fifty guns commenced a converging bombardment on the town of Harpers Ferry from Loudoun and Bolivar Heights. Many of the batteries enfiladed the Federal lines from the Charlestown Road to the Potomac. Others fired directly to the front, while those on the crest of Loudoun Heights took the Union line in reverse. The artillery fire continued until 8:30 a.m. with almost no reply from the overwhelmed Federal guns. About that hour Colonel Miles, the garrison commander, called a council of war of the brigade commanders, in the course of which he expressed the opinion that their case was hopeless, that further sacrifice of life would be fruitless. With evident reluctance on the part of some of the officers, the council voted unanimously in favor of surrender if honorable terms could be arranged. Miles appointed General White to negotiate with the Confederates, the officers separated, and almost immediately thereafter Miles was struck by a Confederate shell and mortally wounded.

Kyd Douglas has painted a vivid word-picture of the surrender scene:*

I found General Jackson at the church in the wood on the Bolivar and Halltown turnpike, and just as I

_____

*Battles and Leaders of the Civil War.

joined him a white flag was raised on Bolivar and all the firing ceased. Under instructions from General Jackson I rode up the pike and into the enemy's lines to ascertain the purpose of the white flag. Near the top of the hill I met General White and staff and told him my mission. He replied that Colonel Miles had been mortally wounded, that he was in command and desired to have an interview with General Jackson. Just then General Hill (A. P. Hill) came up from the direction of his line, and at his request I conducted them to General Jackson, whom I found sitting on his horse where I had left him. He was not, as the Comte de Paris says, leaning against a tree asleep, but exceedingly wide-awake. The contrast in appearance there presented was striking. General White, riding a handsome black horse, was carefully dressed and had on untarnished gloves, boots, and sword. His staff were equally comely in costume. On the other hand, General Jackson was the dingiest, worst-dressed, and worst-mounted general that a warrior who cared for good looks and style would wish to surrender to. The surrender was unconditional, and then General Jackson turned the matter over to General A. P. Hill, who allowed General White the same liberal terms that Grant afterward gave Lee at Appomattox.

The fruits of the surrender were 12,520 prisoners, 13,000 arms, 73 pieces of artillery, and several hundred wagons.

General Jackson, after sending a brief dispatch to General Lee announcing the capitulation, rode up to Bolivar and down into Harpers Ferry. The curiosity in the Union army to see him was so great that the soldiers lined the sides of the road. Many of them uncovered as he passed, and he invariably returned the salute. One man had an echo of response all about him when he said aloud: "Boys, he's not much for looks, but if we'd had him we wouldn't have been caught in this trap!"

To Stay or Not to Stay!

The night of September 14 was a difficult one for General Lee. Crampton's Gap had been lost to Franklin's Federal corps and it was clearly no longer possible to hold back McClellan's army at Turner's Gap. A message had gone to McLaws directing him to withdraw from Pleasant Valley as best he could and return to Virginia. Longstreet and D. H. Hill were told that South Mountain was to be abandoned, that their division would march to Sharpsburg. The ultimate destination was not mentioned.

Shortly after these decisions were taken, a courier from Jackson reached Lee with a note that started a new and more hopeful train of thought in the commanding general's mind. Jackson's report intimated, but did not make the positive statement, that Harpers Ferry would be captured the following morning (September 15). If that should happen, it might still be possible to salvage something from the wreckage of Lee's ambitious invasion plans. It was not in character for him to give up without a fight, so long as even a tiny chance to retrieve a situation remained to him. The message from Jackson was the first rift in the dark clouds of misfortune which had befallen the smaller wing of Lee's army in the past few hours.

Instead of withdrawing across the Potomac Lee revised his plan. He would concentrate at Sharpsburg, a small town west of Antietam Creek where a number of roads converge. Only three miles from the Potomac, Sharpsburg was seven miles southwest of Boonsboro and twelve miles from Harpers Ferry. With luck, and *if* Jackson's implied promise should be fulfilled, it might still be possible for the Army of Northern Virginia to be fully reassembled behind Antietam Creek by nightfall September 15, or the following day.

McLaws would face greater hazards than Longstreet and Hill, who would be unlikely to encounter Federal opposition in their direct march down the road from Boonsboro. Lee had not received any word from McLaws, who may or may not have gotten the earlier message directing him to retire to Virginia. The Federal corps that had taken Crampton's Gap was considered a serious threat to McLaws' rear, for Lee could hardly expect Franklin to be so unenterprising as actually proved to be the case.

With his new plan in mind, Lee sent modified orders to

McLaws to cross the mountain (Elk Ridge) or follow the river road, his destination to be Sharpsburg; he would cross the Potomac only if forced by circumstances to do so. The cavalry was directed to cover McLaws' rear from the vicinity of Rohrersville. Longstreet and Hill would accompany Lee to a new position at Keedysville,* three miles northeast of Sharpsburg. The original orders to Jackson and Walker, to rejoin the main body after the fall of Harpers Ferry, were modified only to the extent of substituting Sharpsburg for Hagerstown or Boonsboro. The dead and seriously wounded would unfortunately have to be left behind on South Mountain.

Longstreet and Hill withdrew that night from South Mountain under cover of darkness without the Federals becoming aware of their departure. As the column took the road to Sharpsburg, preceded by the wagon trains (which incidentally put a portion of Longstreet's trains in an unprotected position to be captured by Colonel Davis' Federal cavalry following their escape from Harpers Ferry), Lee sent still another message to McLaws, instructing him to go directly to Harpers Ferry if its surrender had been effected by the time the message was received. En route Lee decided not to stop at Keedysville, but to move on to Sharpsburg, which offered a better tactical position for disposing the army.

During the morning of September 15 the so-called "main body" of Lee's army completed its night march, crossed Antietam Creek, and moved into positions assigned by General Lee on either side of the Boonsboro road north of Sharpsburg. Hood's, D. R. Jones', and D. H. Hill's divisions, Evans' brigade, Stuart's cavalry, and the reserve artillery were all that Lee had on hand, some 18,000 men, a pitifully small force to meet McClellan's Army of the Potomac if Little Mac were to press his advantage. That, however, he had never been known to do, nor would he make the most of this opportunity, the last he would ever have as a soldier.

-----

*A village midway between Boonsboro and Sharpsburg, designated in Lee's orders as Centerville.

Toward noon a message arrived from Jackson announcing the surrender of Harpers Ferry. He reported that A. P. Hill's division would be left to complete the details, while the rest of Jackson's force would be ready to march after they had received their evening rations. Jackson inquired to what place they should move.

Although not unexpected, the good news was promptly passed on to the troops. It had arrived at an opportune moment; something had happened to the supply wagons and the soldiers were hungry. The fall of Harpers Ferry would not fill empty stomachs, but it did serve to boost morale with its assurance that the rest of the army would soon be on hand to join the three divisions already at Sharpsburg in fighting off the pursuing Federals.

The Lost Opportunity

This was McClellan's great opportunity, to strike with overwhelming force to crush the smaller half of the Confederate army at Sharpsburg before the Harpers Ferry troops could reinforce Longstreet and D. H. Hill. McClellan had for several days known all about Lee's troop dispositions and plans, but even with that knowledge he was so dilatory in his movements that the most he was able to accomplish by the night of September 14 was to capture one pass only through South Mountain. And so far as that success was concerned, it might just as well not have been achieved, because Franklin failed to exploit the breakthrough, and, so far as the record shows, McClellan did absolutely nothing to capitalize on his possession of Crampton's Gap.

The machinery of the Army of the Potomac was not too well synchronized. It was strongly built and could take a lot of punishment, but it moved slowly and somewhat ponderously. In comparing the skillful maneuvers and rapid marches of Lee and Jackson with the manner in which McClellan and Pope shifted their chessmen, the image of the lion and the elephant comes to mind. The conclusion is inescapable that McClellan, a topnotch organizer and administrator, was ineffective as a field general. His good fortune in having a copy of Lee's orders fall into his hands was dissipated because of the interminable time lag in putting the knowledge to good use. Reverse the roles and it is a good guess that Lee in McClellan's position would have given the Confederate army the worst licking of the war.

Where was McClellan's imagination? He had said that his plan was to cut Lee's army in two and defeat him in detail. Why did he fail to use his cavalry under Pleasonton, either to harass Jackson's force at Harpers Ferry, or to circle around South Mountain at its lower end and attack McLaws in Pleasant Valley? Why did he allow an entire corps, Franklin's, to sit idly by for several days doing nothing after the capture of Crampton's Gap? Even more to the point, how was it that, with virtually his entire army in hand at the foot of South Mountain, and only a part of D. H. Hill's division of 5,000 men holding Turner's Gap, McClellan was so deficient in the spirit of the offensive that he made little effort to brush Hill aside by weight of numbers or outflanking maneuver. Again, at daylight on September 15, when he learned that Lee had withdrawn from Turner's Gap during the night, why did he not immediately send at least Sumner's fresh corps pouring through the gap in pursuit?

Lee and Longstreet: A Contrast

The contrasting temperaments and strategic judgments of Lee and Longstreet are interestingly revealed in the Maryland campaign as on many other occasions. With Lee, offensive measures were paramount; Longstreet invariably preferred the defensive. While the objectives of each were identical, to win battlefield victories and if possible to destroy the effectiveness of their opponents, the approach was different. Lee relied on his usually accurate evaluation of the opposing army commander's capabilities and probable lines of action, always striving to keep him puzzled and off balance. Frequently that involved the taking of risks that could prove fatal if his opponent should outguess him. Longstreet on the other hand was a firm believer in minimizing risks. He inclined to the policy of taking a strong position, giving the enemy an opportunity to attack, and then, watching carefully for the opportune moment that arrives in every battle, to counterattack like a bolt from Heaven.

Longstreet had offered determined opposition when Lee ordered him back from Hagerstown to help D. H. Hill hold the pass at Turner's Gap. He preferred to yield the Gap without a fight, believing that the army should move at once to Sharpsburg, or better still, back to Virginia, on the premise that the Maryland campaign had already proved a failure and there was little point in compounding it by further combat with the odds so heavily in McClellan's favor. Longstreet, it will be remembered, had disagreed with Lee as to the wisdom of dividing the army for the Harpers Ferry diversion. He was therefore consistent in his views. The point which he seemed to miss was that by further delaying McClellan at South Mountain, Lee would be buying time for Jackson to finish his job at Harpers Ferry. To that extent Lee's judgment was correct, but only because McClellan's slow and, at times, seemingly singletrack mind, was incapable of turning over with sufficient rapidity to generate the power that the situation required.

DOUBLEDAY CROSSING THE ANTIETAM ON THE 16TH

CHAPTER 18

THE ARMIES PREPARE FOR ACTION

THE Army of the Potomac resumed the march on the morning of September 15 and commenced crossing South Mountain. Soon the Blue column was flowing toward Sharpsburg in a seemingly endless stream along the Boonsboro Road that the troops of Longstreet and Hill had followed only a few hours earlier.

McClellan's troops were no more than a three hour march behind Lee, but that unruffled general didn't seem to feel at all hurried. McClellan had never been known to act impetuously and Lee had little reason to believe that the Union commander would adopt a different course in the present circumstances. The Confederates were still on the road and approaching Antietam Creek when the Union soldiers appeared on the horizon six miles to the northeast. Longstreet's account of the invasion of Maryland described the Federal advance:

On the forenoon of the 15th, the blue uniforms of the Federals appeared among the trees that crowned the heights on the eastern bank of the Antietam. The number increased, and larger and larger grew the field of blue until it seemed to stretch as far as the eye could see, and from the tops of the mountains down to the edges of the stream gathered the great army of McClellan. It was an awe-inspiring spectacle as this grand force settled down in sight of the Confederates, then shattered by battles and scattered by long and tiresome marches.

Antietam Creek, although not too formidable a military obstacle, since it could be forded at a number of places except during spring or summer freshets, was a sufficiently prominent terrain feature to afford an excellent reference point and a natural dividing line between the two armies that were now taking position for battle. Flowing almost due south, but following a winding course, it passes Sharpsburg about a mile to the east. Four stonearched bridges crossed the stream within a few miles of the town, but only one would achieve distinction in the battle, and be known thenceforward as Burnside's Bridge. No effort was made by the Confederates to destroy any of the bridges, a rather surprising circumstance in view of the military situation which led Lee to make his stand there. However, he may not have had sufficient time for his engineers to place demolition charges, although it is more likely that he purposely refrained from destroying the bridges. The Federals, making their first move to cross, were permitted to do so without serious opposition, almost as though Lee wanted them to come in close for their assault, where his infantry and guns could mow them down as they crossed the open fields on the upgrade approach to the higher ground near Sharpsburg. The creek, varying in width from 60 to 120 feet, runs through a small valley, with the west bank more steep and broken than that on the east, where the slope is more gradual. Hence the advantage of terrain rested with the troops occupying the west bank, particularly at the two center bridges, where rugged bluffs and hillocks afforded an even more marked advantage to the occupants.

Farther to the east rose a line of prominent hills that promised excellent artillery positions for the Union troops on that side of the stream.

The town of Sharpsburg, where five important roads converge, is situated near the center of what was to become the battle area, which varied from 2½ to 4 miles in width between the Potomac River and Antietam Creek. The town itself rests on the western side of high ground, in a saucer-like formation, and all around was farmland, mostly under cultivation, with an occasional patch of woods. These woods, identified in accounts of the battle as East, West, and North Woods, were destined to play an important role in the battle; as would the Dunker Church*, on the Hagerstown Road at the eastern edge of West Woods, about a mile north of Sharpsburg.

The position upon which Lee had chosen to resist any further advance by McClellan was tactically sound. Strategically, however, it was vulnerable in the extreme, for in the event of a serious reversal, which would not be surprising in view of the disparity in relative strength, Lee could be thrown back into the Potomac at his rear, with the lone ford at Shepherdstown his only immediate retreat route. The peninsula between the Potomac and Antietam Creek was so shallow, averaging not more than three miles, that it barely provided room for the development of his army, leaving but little additional space for maneuver.

McClellan had his army, close to 90,000 troops, well in hand on the morning of September 15, with the major portion advancing without opposition against Lee's 18,000, and with only seven miles to cover before reaching the Antietam. On the face of it, an objective observer would be disposed to write Lee off as a bad risk on that day.

––––––

*Spelling today is *Dunkard*, a corruption of "Dunker" or "Tunker," from the German word to immerse (dunk). The sect call themselves "Church of the Brethren," or German Baptist Brethren, who practiced total, triple immersion in baptismal ceremonies.

The Confederate Position (See Map 32.)

As the Confederates filed across Antietam Creek, Lee disposed them in position along the high ground that includes the town of Sharpsburg. Facing to the east the line generally paralleled the creek, but well back from it, no effort being made to secure any of the bridges except the one southeast of the town (Burnside's Bridge), where a detachment was assigned to guard that crossing. North and east of Sharpsburg, where the center and left of the line were posted, the troops were placed to the east of the Hagerstown Road, which during the battle served the useful purpose of an avenue of communication between the several parts of Lee's command. West of the Hagerstown Road the ground was broken and uneven, in contrast to that on the east, which was rolling and unobstructed, much of it marked off in cultivated fields which

SHARPSBURG IN 1862, LOOKING EAST TOWARD THE CEMETERY

afforded to the Confederates a highly effective field of fire for infantry and artillery.

The initial line of defense was about three miles in length, with most of Stuart's cavalry and horse artillery occupying the extreme left flank, anchored on a prominent hill about six hundred yards northwest of Dunker Church and only a short distance from the Potomac River. From Stuart's right the line curved in a gradual arc to the south—the arc held by the divisions of John B. Hood and D. H. Hill in that order; the brigades of both, except Rodes' brigade, facing generally northeast. Evans' brigade was next in line, then D. R. Jones' division, on the high ground of Sharpsburg and the ridge south of the town. On the extreme right flank stood Colonel Munford's brigade of cavalry. The Confederate artillery, consisting of 125 pieces, all that were present on the fifteenth of September, were emplaced along the line wherever a profitable firing position offered itself.

The advance of McClellan's massive force, clearly visible to the Confederates throughout the better part of the day, seemed not to worry General Lee in the slightest. So confident was he that McClellan would be slow to fight that he expressed the opinion there would be no attack on *either* the fifteenth or sixteenth, although he had known for several days that McClellan had a copy of his own detailed orders of September 9. Lee believed that by the morning of the sixteenth Jackson, McLaws, and Walker would all be on hand, and in the meantime his Federal opponent would insist on taking precautions to make certain that every man and gun was placed to his own satisfaction before engaging in battle. It seemed that Lee's remarkable ability to evaluate his opponent's intentions would once more be proven, because his estimate of the situation was to be confirmed in all respects almost exactly in accordance with his forecast.

The Federal Advance

On the night of September 14 McClellan's strength had been augmented by the arrival of half of Porter's corps,

Sykes' Regular division, from Washington. Porter's other division, under Morell, was scheduled to join the rest of the army on the 15th. Humphrey's division of new troops had also reached Frederick, but did not depart for Sharpsburg until 3:30 p.m. on the 17th. McClellan now had at his disposal six corps in addition to Pleasonton's cavalry, giving him odds of substantially more than two to one, if he should delay until Lee's entire army was concentrated. Were he to act at once, as he should have, his superiority would be at least four to one. Of course McClellan didn't see it that way. According to his custom, he had estimated Lee's strength in Maryland at 120,000 men, an almost inconceivably gross exaggeration. Whether he believed his own estimates may be questioned, but exaggeration served his purpose, and on that score he was consistent throughout his military career. If on the other hand he really believed, as he stated on so many occasions, that Lee had two or three times the actual Confederate strength, always outnumbering his own, only then do McClellan's actions and orders make any military sense. On that assumption alone, however, McClellan is disqualified as a general charged with the responsibility of leading an army.

McClellan's orders for the pursuit directed Pleasonton's cavalry to lead off through Boonsboro, followed by the corps commanded by Sumner, Hooker, and Mansfield. Burnside and Porter would follow the old Sharpsburg Road. Franklin's corps was directed to move off the mountain at Crampton's Gap, into Pleasant Valley, and endeavor to relieve Harpers Ferry. As previously related, Franklin allowed himself to be unnecessarily stymied by McLaws in the Valley, and even when the Confederate general pulled his brigades out and marched to Harpers Ferry on September 15, Franklin did nothing but sit and wait for further orders. Thereafter McClellan either forgot about him, or purposely allowed him to mark time, because his corps failed to move until he was sent for on the evening of September 16. Even then he did not reach the battlefield until late in the morning of the seventeenth.

The Army of the Potomac appears to have been habituated, by their commanding general, to slow, short marches. McClellan consistently underestimated the capacity of his troops. If ever an opportunity for rapid marching and speedy development for attack was offered, this was it. Instead of which, with but seven miles to march, McClellan himself stated in his report that September 15 was too far spent when he reached the Antietam for him to consider an attack until the following day. No excuse was possible for such snail-like action, the only extenuation being that Burnside was even worse, for he dallied on the mountain until past noon, and it was not until McClellan personally pried him loose that Burnside's corps finally got under way. It will be well to remember this incident when the affair at Burnside's Bridge on the afternoon of the battle is reviewed.

In *McClellan's Own Story,** Little Mac describes his personal movement to the front on September 15:

> After seeing the ground where Reno fell, and passing over Hooker's battle-ground on the previous day, I went rapidly to the front by the main road, being received by the troops, as I passed them, with the wildest enthusiasm. Near Keedysville I met Sumner, who told me that the enemy were in position in strong force, and took me to a height in front of Keedysville whence a view of the position could be obtained. We were accompanied by a numerous staff and escort; but no sooner had we shown ourselves on the hill than the enemy opened up on us with rifled guns, and, as his firing was very good, the hill was soon cleared of all save Fitz John Porter and myself. I at once gave orders for the positions of the bivouacs, massing the army so that it could be handled as required. I ordered Burnside to the left. He grumbled that his troops were fatigued, but I started him off anyhow.

It is apparent from the above, which is typical of McClellan's writings, that a becoming modesty was not one of his attributes. The quoted extract also affords some ground for

-----
*Published in 1886 by Ellen M. McClellan.

speculation as to what effect Lee's initial greeting may have had on McClellan's time schedule. Certainly it was not accelerated by the accurate fire of the rifled guns from the other side of the creek, for McClellan permitted the night of September 15, and the following day and night, to pass before launching his attack.

The assignment of bivouac areas for the night appears to have satisfied McClellan that he was doing all that could reasonably be expected. No effort seems to have been made, by cavalry or otherwise, to reconnoiter the Confederate position, or gain some idea, by capturing prisoners, as to the strength and composition of the Confederates in front of him. We do not know, from anything McClellan has written, whether he had as yet a plan of action; if he did, it was only partly formulated, for no orders were issued that night, nor were any troop dispositions made that would place them in a position to attack.

That part of the Army of the Potomac, 70,000 strong, that had completed the march or would shortly arrive were massed in the vicinity of Keedysville, on either side of the Boonsboro Road, except for Burnside's corps, which went into bivouac opposite but some distance east of Burnside's Bridge, on the left of the army. The corps of Sumner, Hooker, and Porter were at Keedysville, with two divisions advanced in the direction of Antietam Creek, Richardson's and Sykes', one on either side of the turnpike. Mansfield was still marching on the road from Boonsboro, while Franklin, as already noted, was back in Pleasant Valley with 20,000 men. Artillery was sited along the hills looking down on the Antietam, and several long-range guns fired a few experimental shells into the Confederate lines. But the preparation of a comprehensive plan of operation for the army was deferred until the following morning.

McClellan and Burnside

On the morning of September 16, McClellan, accompanied by Artillery Commander Hunt and several other staff officers, rode the length of the Federal line on a reconnaissance to effect such realignment of positions as appeared necessary. He particularly liked the looks of the area in the vicinity of Burnside's Bridge, remarking that from the viewpoint of the Federals it was favorable for both offensive and defensive action, and that it covered as well the road from Harpers Ferry to Sharpsburg. But he noted also that Burnside was too far back from the bridge to be effective. He thereupon ordered him to move his corps forward to the bridge, occupy the heights immediately to the rear, and be prepared to interdict the Harpers Ferry Road.

In his postwar accounts, McClellan states that the preceding order was given to Burnside at noon, but that night had fallen before it was executed. This was the second occasion in two days upon which McClellan saw fit to criticize Burnside for being slow to respond to orders. The third occasion would be on the afternoon of September 17, when Burnside, according to McClellan, was many hours late in attacking the Confederate right, with results that would deprive the Union army of a decisive victory. If McClellan was seeking an alibi for his own shortcomings, Burnside was as convenient a candidate as any, more particularly in view of the fact that Lincoln had offered him the army command in preference to McClellan. That may have rankled somewhat in the mind of the latter, and been a contributory cause of his critical attitude toward his good friend and supporter, whose own subsequent failure as army commander was to become even more notorious than McClellan's.

Lee's Army Reconcentrates

General Lee's composure on the night of September 15, when with only 18,000 men he held a thin line at Sharpsburg against the overwhelming strength of the Army of the Potomac, assembled on the opposite side of the Antietam, reflects in great measure the quality and character of that superb leader of men. His attitude had completely changed overnight. The misgivings which had disturbed him the previous night on South Mountain, when the probability of a retreat to Virginia was uppermost in his mind, had vanished. His hope that the fall of Harpers Ferry would occur in time for his reunited army to oppose McClellan with at least a fighting chance for survival had blossomed into a conviction that the reliable Jackson would certainly be up on the morning of September 16. Lee was accustomed to odds of two to one in his opponent's favor, so that was no real handicap. McClellan had never been known as an aggressive campaigner, and in the past few days, even though he had shown unusual evidence of rapid (for him) movement, Lee felt sure that an attack, when it should finally come, would be preceded by the time-consuming measures that invariably characterized the Federal commander's prelude to action. Lee was equally confident, and with justification, that McClellan would telegraph his punch and thus allow the defense to counter from whatever direction the attack should be launched.

Nevertheless, Lee's decision to stand and fight on the Antietam was one of the boldest, all factors considered, that he had made up to this time. To risk disaster with the broad Potomac at his back was a gamble that few generals would have the courage to take. Longstreet considered it a foolish and unnecessary risk. It is doubtful that Lee would have so decided had Grant been in McClellan's place, or if he had foreseen the heavy losses to be sustained by the Confederates, with no compensating advantage. But Lee was first of all a fighter, with a keen understanding of human nature. The stakes inherent in bringing to a successful conclusion his invasion of Northern soil were huge; he did not wish his army to suffer the loss of morale that would inevitably follow a withdrawal from Maryland without a general battle; and he badly needed the supplies and material captured at Harpers Ferry, which might otherwise be recovered by the Federals. Moreover, he still believed that the Army of the Potomac was disorganized after Second Manassas and could not as yet meet his own army with a real chance of success. In his eyes, therefore, the risks that he was willing to take did not appear nearly so great as events would actually prove them to be.

From the position on the southwestern edge of Sharpsburg where Lee had pitched his headquarters tents in a grove of trees near Shepherdstown Road, the commanding general kept an anxious eye on that road to the south. Momentarily expecting the arrival of Jackson's corps on the morning of September 16, Lee chafed at the delay, for Jackson had advised him of his intention to start his troops on the fifteen-mile march from Harpers Ferry after they had finished their supper on the evening of the fifteenth. Stuart had visited Jackson at the Ferry after the surrender of the Federal garrison and then ridden to Sharpsburg to recount to Lee all the gratifying details. Lee had every reason to anticipate a night march by the normally fast-moving Jackson, who on this occasion must have weighed the need for haste, indicated in a message from Lee, against the condition of his troops. His ragged veterans had been marching or fighting continuously ever since they had left the Rappahannock prior to the Second Battle of Manassas, only a few weeks previously, and had been standing under arms most of the night of September 14, preparatory to attacking the Federal garrison at the Ferry at daylight, September 15. It was also a fact that straggling, after the fight at Manassas, had grown to immense proportions, and although Lee's army had been partly reequipped from captured Federal stores, it was still sadly in need of properly fitting shoes and other items of clothing. Even Jackson could not demand and continuously receive superhuman efforts from his vaunted "foot cavalry."

At midday September 16 Lee's period of watchful waiting came to an end as Jackson and Walker rode up to report their troops coming up behind them. McLaws, Anderson, and A. P. Hill were still absent, but Lee expressed confidence that the three divisions would arrive before the day was over, and, with the added strength of Jackson and Walker, that the situation could be kept under control. Jackson was directed to bivouac his troops on the army left, in rear of the line occupied by Hood's division, while Walker was told to place his division on the army right by daylight on the seventeenth.

During the morning the Confederate batteries expended considerable ammunition taking potshots at groups of Federal officers busy on reconnaissance across the Antietam. General McClellan, with members of his staff, was one of the targets upon whom the Confederate guns tried unsuccessfully to register. McClellan subsequently stated that he had been personally successful in getting the enemy to expose the position of battery after battery as he rode along the Federal line on the morning of September 16. However, the ineffective gunfire from the Sharpsburg heights led Lee, as he went along the line, to caution the gunners not to waste their shells, but to save them for the Federal infantry; a wise bit of advice on another count, for the Confederate guns could not hope to match Henry J. Hunt's better trained and equipped Union artillery, at Sharpsburg or elsewhere. Lee was too perceptive a general not to realize that his smaller number of guns would clearly get the worst of it in an artillery duel with the Federals, such as the one that his gunners had initiated and in which the Union gunners cheerfully joined. A great admirer of the effectiveness of the Union artillery, Confederate General D. H. Hill is credited with the remark that "the Confederate guns could not cope with the Yankee pieces—the contest was one of the most melancholy farces in the war."

McClellan's Battle Plan

For his battle headquarters McClellan had his wall tents pitched near the Pry House, situated on top of a hill on the north side of the Boonsboro Road, midway between Keedysville and Porterstown. The farmhouse overlooked Antietam Creek and commanded an excellent view of the terrain to the west of the stream, including those portions of the Confederate position that were not obscured by woods and the north-south ridge that prevented a view of most of the town of Sharpsburg, on the reverse slope of the heights.

Having completed his morning reconnaissance and issued

orders for certain troop realignments, McClellan was ready to give some thought to the business of readying his plans for the impending battle. Shortly after noon he had reached a decision on the general character of the attack. As stated in his preliminary post-battle report to Halleck:

> The design was to make the main attack upon the enemy's left—at least to create a diversion in favor of the main attack, with the hope of something more, by assailing the enemy's right—and, as soon as one or both of the flank movements were fully successful, to attack their center with any reserve I might then have in hand.

When McClellan's army had marched out from Washington in search of Lee's army, it was divided into two wings and a center column. Burnside had been given command of Hooker's First Corps and Reno's Ninth; Sumner his own Second and Mansfield's Twelfth Corps; and Franklin his own Sixth and

THE PRY HOUSE, SITE OF McCLELLAN'S HEADQUARTERS

Couch's division of the Fourth Corps (the rest of this corps having been left on the Peninsula). When Porter's Fifth Corps joined the army at South Mountain, McClellan kept it under his own command as a reserve.

So far as official orders went, there had subsequently been no modification in the chain of command, other than the elevation of Brigadier General Jacob D. Cox to temporary command of Burnside's Ninth Corps following the death of General Reno at Fox's Gap. Nevertheless, when the army reached the Antietam, Burnside found himself unceremoniously shunted off to the army left flank with only his own Ninth Corps, while Hooker's First Corps was held on the right under McClellan's direct supervision. Something had occurred to cool the intimate relationship which had long existed between McClellan and Burnside, ever since their West Point days together. Burnside suspected that Joe Hooker, who was not above conniving whenever it might suit his ambition for independent command, may have been the cause of McClellan's changed attitude, but on the other hand there is indisputable evidence that Burnside was strangely lethargic in all his movements and actions from South Mountain to the end of the campaign. It is also possible that McClellan intended the grouping of corps into wings to be solely for purposes of control on the march, and believed that greater flexibility would be achieved, when battle should be joined, by dispensing with the cumbersome wing formation and issuing his orders direct to the corps commanders. If so, it would have been a simple matter, and the part of wisdom, to make his decision official and so inform the three general officers most concerned.

At 2 o'clock on the afternoon of September 16, in accordance with orders from McClellan, Hooker's First Corps moved out from its position at Keedysville, crossed Antietam Creek at the upper bridge and two nearby fords, and, about 4:00 p. m., advanced to the Hagerstown Turnpike, where the column turned south. Marching along and on both sides of the road, with Meade's division in the lead, the advance elements about sunset ran into Confederate pickets, who were quickly driven in.

Lee, Jackson, and Longstreet were engaged in a discussion of tactical plans for the next day and studying the maps in the commanding general's headquarters in Sharpsburg when the Federal artillery in the late afternoon opened fire from the hills across the Antietam. Shortly thereafter a report came in that the Federals were crossing the creek at Pry's Mill. Longstreet was immediately directed to send Hood's division to meet the threat and Jackson was told to move into line on Hood's left.

What McClellan may have had in mind beyond putting Hooker's corps, unsupported, in an attack position for the following morning can only be conjectured. The disadvantage from the Federal viewpoint was that McClellan informed Lee by this action exactly where his attack would be aimed and thus gave timely warning of his intentions. Hooker's isolated position was an uncomfortable and dangerous one for a few hours, for it was not until almost midnight that Mansfield's Twelfth Corps followed Hooker across the Antietam, going into bivouac for the night about a mile or so northeast of Hooker's bivouac.

When the clash between the outposts of the opposing forces failed to develop into more serious fighting because of the darkness, the troops settled down for the night. McClellan sent word to Franklin in Pleasant Valley to bring his corps to the battlefield, while Lee, becoming more and more concerned over the non-arrival of McLaws and A. P. Hill, dispatched couriers with urgent messages to them at Harpers Ferry to rejoin with all possible speed.

THE CHARGE OF IRWIN'S BRIGADE, SMITH'S DIVISION, AT DUNKER CHURCH

CHAPTER 19

"THE BLOODIEST SINGLE DAY—"

FOR some inscrutable reason, the commanding generals of the Union armies during the first two years of the Civil War, almost without exception, habitually fed their corps and divisions into battle in a piecemeal and consequently wasteful, inefficient manner. Whether this was because they didn't know any better, or had so little confidence in their corps commanders that they were unwilling to allow them discretionary authority for effective troop leading, the failure of Northern leaders to gain victories against smaller and less adequately equipped Confederate forces may be attributed as much to that rigid concept of generalship as to any other single factor. One might have expected the Union leaders to learn something from Lee's repeated successes in the battles of 1862. But McClellan, Pope, Burnside, and Hooker, one after another, employed the piecemeal method of attack as though it were official doctrine. Unfortunately it was the men in the ranks who paid with their blood for such inept field generalship.

McClellan's initial tactical dispositions in the Antietam battle afforded a foretaste of the manner in which he would fight his troops. Instead of a coordinated, mutually supported troop movement, he sent Hooker's First Corps of three divisions across the Antietam all by itself, beyond supporting distance; it was not until nine or ten hours later that he ordered Mansfield's Twelfth Corps of two divisions to follow. Each corps commander was on his own; teamplay under such conditions was unlikely; McClellan at his headquarters was too far back to exercise timely and effective control. Although Lee had no intention of initiating an attack in the late afternoon of September 16, there was no reason why Hooker and Mansfield should not have advanced on a time and space schedule that would have permitted mutual support, under specific orders from the army commander in the form of a coordinated mission. No such orders were issued. So far as the record shows, Hooker and Mansfield were left to open the Battle of Antietam as semi-independent commanders, with Hooker in the lead and Mansfield in distant support.

In his final, lengthy official report on the battle, written months after the event, McClellan expanded on his preliminary report by stating specifically that his plan was to attack Lee's left with Hooker's First and Mansfield's Twelfth Corps, supported by Sumner's Second Corps, and if necessary by Franklin's Sixth Corps (which at the time was still on South Mountain); and, "as soon as matters looked favorable there" he would have Burnside's Ninth Corps attack the enemy right to carry the Sharpsburg heights. There was also an intimation that the final blow would be struck by the troops of McClellan's center, presumably Porter's Fifth Corps, after the attacks on Lee's left and right had gained the proper double-enveloping momentum. It all read very well indeed, *after* the battle, but it would have been more helpful had he told his corps commanders what he had in mind before they were committed, so that they might have executed their respective assignments intelligently as elements of the army team.

The Preliminary Skirmish

The opening skirmish in the Battle of Antietam occurred in the late afternoon of September 16, between a detachment of Stuart's cavalry on the Smoketown Road and Confederate General John B. Hood's two brigades, hastily shifted to the open wood later known as East Wood, and Union General George G. Meade's division of Pennsylvania Reserves (the vanguard of Hooker's corps). This fight, which took place near the D. Miller house, was a short, sharp, feeling-out process on both sides, with the artillery playing a supporting role. Hooker, who did not desire to make an all-out assault until morning, was merely getting set by jockeying for a strong position. He contemplated a movement aimed at Lee's extreme left flank, similar to his action as a division commander in the Battle of Second Manassas, when Pope's divisions on the Union right hammered successively at Jackson's left near Groveton.

Lee's left was in fact his more vulnerable flank, even though it rested on the Potomac River, which completed its final looping turn in the Sharpsburg area only a few hundred yards from the Confederate left, where General Stuart had posted his horse artillery batteries on a low ridge immediately north of Nicodemus Run. The Hagerstown Turnpike was less than a mile to the east of the Potomac at that point, allowing only limited space for maneuver, with the result that the position could be defended with less men than normally required per yard of front. By the same token, however, a successful penetration by the Federals there could conceivably pay off, for the reason that the river ran in a southwesterly direction for several miles at Stuart's rear, to open up maneuver space in which an aggressive Federal commander might operate to roll up Lee's line or attack him from the rear.

Hooker's First Corps bivouacked the night of the sixteenth on the northern slope of the ridge which dominates the area, the divisions of Doubleday and Ricketts in line, with Meade's division covering the front of both. Hooker himself passed the night at the farmhouse of J. Poffenberger, east of the Hagerstown Turnpike, in rear of Meade's division. But he was up before daybreak Wednesday, September 17, for an early look at the terrain over which he would shortly launch his divisions. The day dawned gray and misty, through which could dimly be seen gently rolling country, the most striking feature of which was the Dunker Church with its white brick walls, standing out like a gleaming pearl against the dark green background of the West Wood, not more than a mile from his point of observation. The church, on the west side of the Hagerstown Turnpike, rested as it were `at the apex of a large V, the left side of which (looking north) was the Hagerstown Road, the right the Smoketown Road, which merged with the Turnpike about where the church stood. The Smoketown Road passed through the western fringe of the East Wood; the West Wood paralleled the western edge of the turnpike. Between the two roads as they approached a junction, the apex of the V, Hooker could see a large field of high corn, which would become as famous as the Dunker Church or the sunken farm road (soon to be called Bloody Lane) that angled off in an easterly direction from the turnpike 600 yards or so south of the church. The upper portion of the V was covered in part by the North Wood, which reached out from the Hagerstown Road toward the East Wood to practically close the north side of the triangle of terrain above described.

The North Wood and the woods 400 yards to the east had been occupied by Hooker's corps in the course of its approach march. The Dunker Church, together with the East Wood and West Wood, were within the Confederate lines. From the standpoint of tactical maneuverability and troop concealment, the terrain at the point of contact of the opposing forces offered infinite possibilities for alert, observant troop leaders.

In round numbers, Lee's army on the field of Sharpsburg numbered at the most 28,000 men, supported by 200 guns, at daylight on September 17. McClellan's strength, disposed along

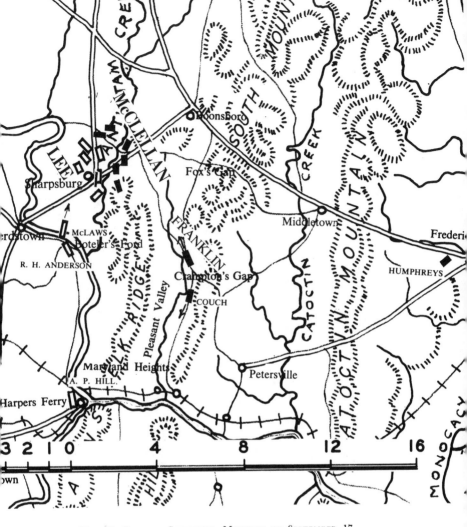

MAP 31. GENERAL SITUATION, MORNING OF SEPTEMBER 17

Showing the positions of the Union and Confederate major units at 5:30 a.m., September 17, 1862. Humphreys' division near Frederick does not march for 12 hours, reaching the battlefield only after the battle is over. Franklin's corps is starting from the western foot of Crampton's Gap, not reaching the field until 10 a.m. Couch's division ordered to Maryland Heights, gets a change of orders when it reaches the lower end of Pleasant Valley, and reaches the battlefield sometime that night or early on the 19th.

For the Confederates, McLaws and R. H. Anderson, shown crossing the Potomac at Boteler's Ford, reach the field at about 7 a.m. A. P. Hill's division begins to arrive near Sharpsburg at about 3:45 p.m.

the ridge across the· Antietam and in contact with the Confederates north of the town exceeded 70,000, with Franklin's corps the only one that had not yet come up. Lee's still absent divisions, those of McLaws, Anderson, and A. P. Hill, together with Hampton's cavalry brigade, would give him 15,000 additional men for a total of approximately 43,000, if they should arrive before it was too late. McClellan's exaggerated estimate that more than 100,000 Confederates confronted his slightly smaller army may have made him feel quite heroic, if he actually believed his own inflated figures, but the false image could not help but distort his tactical judgment and adversely influence his battle actions. By September 17 his knowledge that Harpers Ferry had succumbed was forty-eight hours old, long enough· for most of Lee's army to have been reunited at Sharpsburg and to neutralize the once-in-a-lifetime opportunity that the slow-moving McClellan had been too lethargic to exploit.

Hooker vs. Jackson

General Hooker was at this stage enjoying his role as a semi-independent commander of the Union army's attack echelon, a responsibility that McClellan had reposed in him with assurance of support from Mansfield's, Sumner's and even Franklin's corps if the army commander's plan to make the principal effort against Lee's left flank showed promise of fruitful results. It was "Fighting Joe's" big opportunity to prove that the sobriquet was something more than a typographer's error made in a newspaper correspondent's dispatch from the Peninsula which had correctly read: "still fighting— Joe Hooker"; but the euphonism had stuck and it was up to Hooker to make it good.

Hooker's three divisions had slept on their arms the night of September 16, astride the Hagerstown Road. As soon as it was light enough to see where they were going, the attack was launched, Seymour's brigade of Meade's Pennsylvania Reserves on the left and in the lead. The objective, the whitewashed brick Dunker Church, was a reference point that could not be missed by the most unobservant soldier, even though some may have wondered about the vagaries of human existence which required church attendance under such unusual circumstances.

Practically simultaneous musketry fire from keyed-up skirmishers in both the Federal and Confederate lines was followed immediately by the artillery from Hooker's batteries, several of which from well-sited positions poured their shells over the heads of the advancing blue-coats into the Confederate position. Across the Antietam Henry Hunt's rifled Parrotts, anxious to aid Hooker's attack, poured a devastating fire on that part of Jackson's line against which the Federal infantry advance was pointed. Hood's Texans, who the evening before had resisted Meade's probing attack, had been pulled out of the front line to cook a long-delayed hot meal, with the result that the Confederate defensive line was somewhat further to the south when the battle opened at daylight on September 17.

During the night the reduced divisions of McLaws and Anderson, which had been marching, climbing mountains, and fighting on various fronts including Maryland Heights and Pleasant Valley ever since September 10, had responded to Lee's urgent message to join the main body at Sharpsburg as quickly as possible. Shortly after dawn the straggling, wearied column reached the town at the end of a toiling march from Harpers Ferry, fifteen miles distant. The arrival of these reinforcing brigades meant that the Army of Northern Virginia, now fully reassembled except for A. P. Hill's Light Division, which was still paroling prisoners at Harpers Ferry, had a fighting chance to block the Union army, despite McClellan's superiority of more than two to one, counting Franklin's advancing corps as present.

Hooker advanced with his three divisions abreast, in the order, right to left—Doubleday, Meade, and Ricketts, with Meade's division somewhat advanced,—each division disposed by brigades in depth, the flanks (theoretically at least) overlapping the Confederate line so far as could be seen. The corps formation was such that, assuming the attacking line could

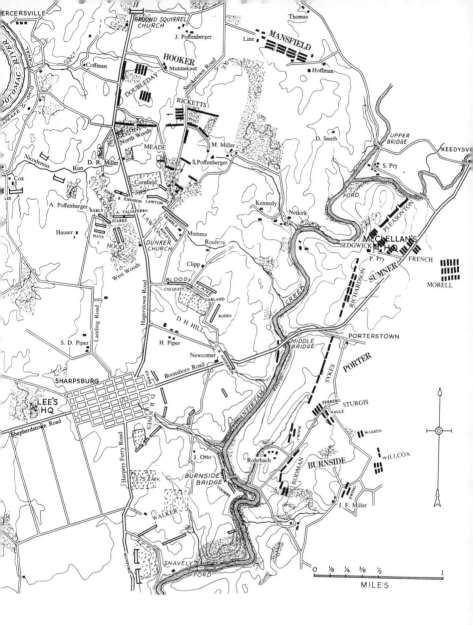

MAP 32. OPENING OF THE BATTLE OF ANTIETAM

The situation on the battlefield at daybreak, September 17. Hooker's First Corps, led by Meade's division, is beginning to attack south, with its right on the Hagerstown Road. Soon it will be partly astride this road. It is interesting to note that McClellan's headquarters is adequately protected.

On the original Board map the contour interval is 10 feet, but for simplicity all but the 50-foot contours have been omitted here.

proceed without breaking, it would sweep to the south through the West Wood, the East Wood, and Miller's thirty-acre cornfield which lay between the woods. Mansfield's Twelfth Corps, which had bivouacked a mile or so northeast of the First Corps, heard the noise of the opening engagement, sprang to arms, and moved promptly in support with the divisions of Williams and Greene.

In the early stages of Hooker's aggressive attack the Confederates were driven back in confusion. Brigade after brigade, including those of Stonewall Jackson's own division under Starke, was broken up or swept aside as the determined Federals pushed grimly ahead into the cornfield and the woods on either flank. Then it was that Jackson, rising to the occasion as he usually did when the going was tough, sent for Hood's division, busily engaged in cooking the first hot meal the men had anticipated for several days. Annoyed at the interruption, the fiery Texans came charging out of the West Wood to catch in flank Gibbon's Federal brigade, which had outrun the other First Corps troops through the tall corn. The fight had by this time become a general engagement, as the battle lines surged forward and back, with local successes and failures occurring in such rapid succession that it was impossible for the fighting units to know whether they were winning or losing. Losses on both sides were enormous, shells crashed indiscriminately into Federals and Confederates alike, blue and gray regiments melted into scattered fragments, as the early morning hours passed and the casualties steadily mounted.

Ricketts' division, on the left of Hooker's attacking force, together with Meade's division in the center, made slow but steady progress and gradually drove the Confederates into the West Wood, on whose edge the fighting became even more terrible. All of Jackson's two divisions, excepting only Early's brigade, were thrown into the battle. "The two lines almost tore each other to pieces," wrote Palfrey.* "Ricketts lost a third of his division, having 153 killed and 898 wounded.

---

*The Antietam and Fredericksburg, by Francis W. Palfrey. New York, 1882.

FEDERAL CHARGE THROUGH D. R. MILLER'S CORNFIELD

Phelps's brigade lost about forty-four per cent. Gibbon's brigade lost 380 men. On the Confederate side the carnage was even more awful. General Starke, commanding the Stonewall division, and Colonel Douglas, commanding Lawton's brigade, were killed. General Lawton, commanding Ewell's division, and Colonel Walker, commanding a brigade, were severely wounded. More than half of the brigades of Lawton and Hays were either killed or wounded, and more than a third of Trimble's, and all the regimental commanders in these brigades, except two, were killed or wounded."

The Confederate defense line was necessarily thin, because Lee didn't have enough strength to man a continuous cordon throughout the position he had selected, with each flank resting on the Potomac River. To the Federals, however, the Confederate left appeared to be solidly held, an illusion created by the guns under Stuart, who was in command on that flank. Manned by such able artillerymen as Pelham, Poague, and Pegram, the gunners kept shifting positions between bursts of fire in a successful endeavor to convince the enemy that there were no open holes through which to attempt a major penetration.

Much can happen in a thirty-acre cornfield whose stalks rise above the average man's head, particularly when hundreds of men using lethal weapons and with blood in their eyes are waiting in its invisible depths for the unwary to venture into the trap. Hooker seems to have realized that his attack was not progressing according to plan and that something had to be done quickly about that cornfield.

"From the sun's rays falling on their bayonets projecting above the corn I could see that the field was filled with the enemy, with arms in their hands, standing apparently at 'support arms,' " wrote Hooker in his official report. He thereupon ordered every available battery, five or six as he said, to open at once with canister. "In the time I am writing every stalk of corn in the northern and greater part of the field was cut as closely as could have been done with a knife, and the slain lay in rows precisely as they had stood in their ranks a few moments before."

Disaster loomed for Lee's army by 7 o'clock. Hooker's divisions had breached Jackson's line and the spearhead was being followed up from McClellan's seemingly inexhaustible reservoir of manpower. Hood's impetuous counterattack had temporarily halted the Federal advance, but Lee knew that it could be for a short time only, unless troops were shifted from other positions. Without hesitation he pulled G. B. Anderson's brigade of D. H. Hill's division out of the line east of Sharpsburg, and soon thereafter ordered Walker's division over from the right flank to Jackson's support. Lee's instinct would prove sound, however risky the decision to employ more than half of his available infantry, in addition to most of Stuart's cavalry, in defending only one-quarter of his four-mile line. Hood's Texans were the finger in the dyke, but there was no telling how soon the Federal flood waters would cause other cracks that could so weaken the defense structure as to cause it to crash in ruins. Jackson's situation was extremely critical, even though Hooker's attack had crested and then receded in the face of Hood's counterattack.

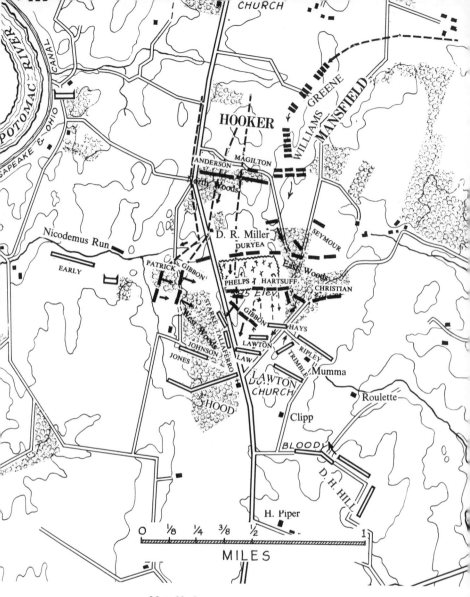

MAP 33. SLAUGHTER IN THE CORNFIELD

The situation about 7 a.m., when Hooker's attack had reached its height. The fighting is swirling around West Woods and in D. R. Miller's cornfield. Mansfield's Twelfth Corps (formerly Banks' First Corps) is coming in to join Hooker. About this time Mansfield is fatally wounded, being succeeded by Brig. Gen. Alpheus S. Williams, senior division commander in the corps. Hooker also receives a wound, albeit slight, and is succeeded by Meade.

This map shows Hood's regiments committed, but Lee has not yet moved up G. B. Anderson's brigade from farther south. Positions of units not shown hereon have not changed materially from those shown on Map 31.

Mansfield's Attack

Mansfield's Twelfth Corps had moved forward promptly from its bivouac at the opening of the battle, guiding on the Smoketown Road. His two divisions deployed to form a single line, Williams on the right, Greene on the left, and then paused to await an opening to join Hooker's battle. Before the corps entered actively into the fight and while still in the act of deploying Mansfield fell, mortally wounded.

Major General Joseph K. F. Mansfield, Class of 1822 at the Military Academy, was a Christian gentleman of high character. It was he who planned the Battle of Buena Vista in the War with Mexico, during which he rendered conspicuous service and was rewarded by being made Inspector General of the Army. He was 59 years of age in 1862, and his towering form and flowing white locks made him a conspicuous figure on the battlefield. Many of his troops were raw recruits, which may have been one of the reasons why he rashly exposed himself in leading them forward into their first battle.

As the Twelfth Corps was approaching the East Wood, Hooker rode up, shouted a few words to Mansfield, in order to be heard above the sound of the gunfire, and then galloped off. The sense of Hooker's message was that the Confederates were breaking through and pushing Hooker's divisions back, and that Mansfield must hold the East Wood to check them. The reason for the First Corps commander's haste was no doubt the impelling necessity to do something to halt the wild panic that had infected some of his men as an aftermath to the slashing counterattack spearheaded by the fiery Hood.

Mansfield was startled by the news, having been led to believe that Hooker's attack was succeeding handsomely and that the mission of his supporting corps would be to exploit the initial success by knocking the Confederates even more off balance. Instead of this it was now his task to restore the Union line and salvage all that he could of the advantage which appeared to be slipping from the Federal grasp.

His leading regiments had reached a rail fence bounding the

last field to be crossed before reaching the East Wood, which Mansfield thought was still in the hands of Hooker's corps. The men had deployed along the fence and opened fire on dimly seen figures moving through the woods. Mansfield spurred his horse forward and lifted him over the fence, shouting to the men to cease firing at their own comrades. When he

MAJOR GENERAL JOSEPH K. F. MANSFIELD, KILLED AT ANTIETAM

had managed to halt the fire he started forward toward the woods to find out which Union division held it, but was stopped short by a captain and sergeant of the 10th Maine Regiment, who insisted that the general was heading for the Confederate lines. About that time the graycoats opened fire, one bullet striking Mansfield in the stomach, another wounding his horse. Dismounting, he attempted to lead his horse to safety, but his wound was so serious that four men made a stretcher of their muskets to carry him off the field.

With Mansfield gone, the senior division commander, Brigadier General Alpheus S. Williams, assumed command of the Twelfth Corps, but before launching his attack consulted

General Hooker to ascertain the lay of the land, Hooker had just time enough to give Williams a few general directions when he received a slight wound in the foot and retired from the field, to be succeeded by General Meade. Hooker's First Corps had been badly shattered, losing almost 2,500 men in killed and wounded, so that for all practical purposes the corps was out of action. When Williams' two divisions pushed ahead to renew the attack, Meade withdrew the remnants of the First Corps to the ridge north of the Poffenberger house, where they had bivouacked the night before, to reorganize.

There were as usual conflicting reports on the condition of the First Corps after its attack and repulse. One account had it that Hooker's outfit had been completely shattered and that thousands of the men ran away from the battle. When Sumner came on the field he said that he was unable to locate any one from the First Corps except General Ricketts, who informed him that "he could not raise three hundred men of the corps." On the other hand, General Meade, who succeeded Hooker as corps commander, reported something less than 7,000 men that evening, which number still represented a rather tidy body of men. There was certainly confusion and plenty of straggling when the corps was pulled out of the line, but it was still an organized body and far from being "completely dispersed."

In occupying the West Wood and East Wood, the defensive positions of the Confederates, in addition to the cover afforded by the foliage, were greatly strengthened by the outcroppings of limestone whereby nature provided the same protection as breastworks. Furthermore, the Southern generals, experienced in utilizing terrain to advantage, had so disposed their brigades on Jackson's front that the Federal attacks were channeled directly into a funnel from whose sides the Confederates were able to fire from cover into the flanks of the attacking brigades. The same sort of reverse salient which Lee had set up for Pope at Second Manassas was again used to invite first Hooker's corps, then Mansfield's, to put their heads in the lion's mouth. Here at Sharpsburg, however, although McClellan repeated Pope's error of feeding his troops into battle in piecemeal fashion, the receptive lion lost his own teeth so fast in the chewing process that he escaped complete destruction by a hairsbreadth.

The massive Federal attacks against Lee's left were taking a heavy toll of lives on both sides in the early hours of the morning. Hooker's corps had failed to push its attack to a conclusion and was forced to withdraw, but Jackson's smaller defending force, although badly mangled, still fought on. D. H. Hill's division on Jackson's right was battling tenaciously, and now reinforcements from the center and right of Lee's line were thrown in to stem the attack by the Federal Twelfth Corps.

The confusion incident to the change of corps commanders resulting from the loss of General Mansfield was temporary, but undoubtedly took some of the strength out of the second Union attack. Williams was a good general, who led the fight as well as any could have done. Nevertheless, his attack, like Hooker's, failed to break the Confederates. The angle of attack of his two divisions, his own on the right, Greene's on the left, was in a southwesterly direction and more diverging than converging. Williams headed for the West Wood as Greene followed the ridge leading to the East Wood. The former took heavy losses from Confederates on his left and front, but Greene, meeting less opposition, was able to drive the defenders completely out of the East Wood. Greene even gained a precarious foothold near the Dunker Church, Hooker's original objective, a position which he was able to hold until early afternoon, when a Confederate counterattack drove him back.

By 9:00 a.m. the violent struggle north of the Dunker Church, and in and between the woods on either side of the cornfield, had been waged continuously and bloodily for four hours. Then came a lull in the battle, during which the manipulators of the human chessmen studied the board as they planned their next moves. Four thousand officers and men of

Hooker's and Mansfield's corps had fallen; the Confederate losses, while not so heavy, were equally great in proportion to the numbers engaged. The Federal tide had carried Greene's division through the East Wood and across the cornfield to effect a lodgment in the West Wood north of the Dunker Church, and Sumner's fresh Federal corps was advancing to take part in the battle.

But the Confederate line had not given way. Lee's left, badly shattered, had been bent but not broken. The resiliency of the Southern brigades was amazing. Jackson had even strengthened his defensive posture as a result of the forced retirement of Hood's division and a part of D. H. Hill's. Every available man had been thrown into the battle, yet the redoubtable Stonewall, far from admitting failure as the result of being driven back and having suffered a temporary break in his line, was watching the struggle from the West Wood and planning an aggressive counterattack with the help of troops that Lee had withdrawn from other parts of the line and placed at his disposal.

One wonders at the lack of imagination and ingenuity displayed by General McClellan, as he watched the battle through binoculars from the garden of the Pry House on the far side of Antietam Creek. The superior, long-range Federal artillery, massed on the ridges paralleling the creek, had been pouring metal into the Confederate line since daylight, but not a single Union infantryman of three unused corps totaling tens of thousands massed behind the guns, had been sent across the stream for any purpose. There was no reconnaissance, no probing attack, no flanking maneuver, no anything. Lee's center and right were allowed to rest peacefully in place, hour after hour, without even a threatening gesture from McClellan to prevent the Confederate brigades from being moved about at Lee's pleasure.

There can be but one plausible explanation of McClellan's reluctance to take advantage of the most favorable opportunity in two years of war for a Union army to wipe out Lee's army

THE FIGHTING ALONG THE HAGERSTOWN PIKE

and bring the war to a close. It was that the commander of the Army of the Potomac lacked a fighting heart, a defect from which it naturally followed that he would magnify the Confederate strength and play it so safe that tactical advantages would be frittered away. When the history of Lee's first invasion of Maryland is analyzed, it is difficult to credit the great Southern leader's postwar comment that McClellan was the Union army commander for whom he had the greatest respect. It may be questioned whether the remark was not quoted out of context, or possibly even with tongue in cheek.

Sumner's Corps Joins the Fray

The bloody fighting in which the First and Twelfth Federal Corps had engaged since daylight failed to accomplish its purpose of turning the Confederate left. The Federal line had made some progress, to be sure, but at a terrific cost in casualties, including many general officers. Greene's division of the Twelfth Corps had succeeded in seizing a portion of the West Wood and holding it, but without sufficient strength to do more than grimly hang on and hope for support.

Jackson's troops had been so badly chopped up during the early hours of the morning that the Federals could without question have overrun the line and rolled it up if only Mc-

Clellan had staged a coordinated, simultaneous attack along the entire front. He had the men to accomplish it; his powerful artillery had been in position along the high ground east of Antietam Creek for almost two days; and Lee was still short three of his divisions when the battle opened. Instead, McClellan sent in one corps at a time, over the same route, against the identical target, at lengthy time intervals that precluded mutual support and served only to give Lee the time he needed to shift forces from right to left to parry the blows.

It had been 7 a.m. before the Federal Second Corps, commanded by Major General Edwin V. Sumner, received orders to cross the creek in support of the two corps already engaged. There were three divisions in this corps, Sedgwick's, French's, and Richardson's, but only the two first named moved out together, Sedgwick at 7 and French at 7:30. Richardson didn't receive his orders until 9:30. Staff work at Union army and corps levels seems to have been somewhat less than efficient in this campaign.

Sumner's approach march to the battlefield followed pretty much the same pattern as had Hooker's corps—across the upper bridge and fords in a northwesterly direction, Sedgwick's division leading. Each division marched in three brigade columns, directly across country after crossing the creek, with intervals of approximately 70 yards between columns. These two divisions accounted for about 10,000 men, and their advance was made in so orderly a manner, with colors flying as though on parade, that the Confederates, awaiting the shock of their attack, watched the martial display with unconcealed admiration.

When the center of the corps reached a point opposite the Dunker Church, the columns at a given signal changed direction by the left flank and were at once in attack formation with divisions abreast, Sedgwick on the right, French on the left, each division in columns of brigades at 70 yards' distance between each brigade line. It was a picturesque maneuver, but its effectiveness may be open to question since the Confed-

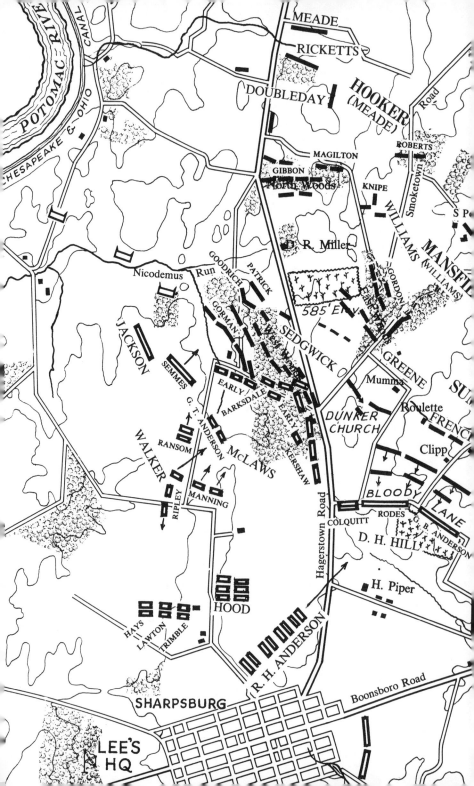

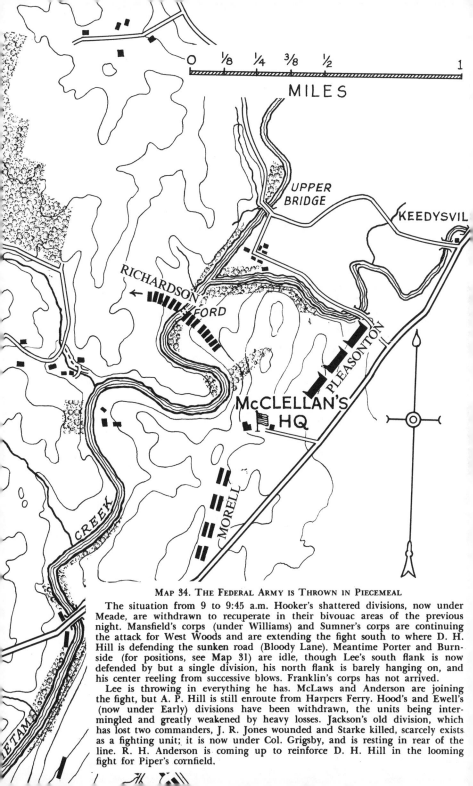

MILES

UPPER
BRIDGE

KEEDYSVIL

RICHARDSON

FORD

PLEASONTON

McCLELLAN'S
HQ

MORELL

CREEK

ETAM

MAP 34. THE FEDERAL ARMY IS THROWN IN PIECEMEAL

The situation from 9 to 9:45 a.m. Hooker's shattered divisions, now under
Meade, are withdrawn to recuperate in their bivouac areas of the previous
night. Mansfield's corps (under Williams) and Sumner's corps are continuing
the attack for West Woods and are extending the fight south to where D. H.
Hill is defending the sunken road (Bloody Lane). Meantime Porter and Burnside (for positions, see Map 31) are idle, though Lee's south flank is now
defended by but a single division, his north flank is barely hanging on, and
his center reeling from successive blows. Franklin's corps has not arrived.

Lee is throwing in everything he has. McLaws and Anderson are joining
the fight, but A. P. Hill is still enroute from Harpers Ferry. Hood's and Ewell's
(now under Early) divisions have been withdrawn, the units being intermingled and greatly weakened by heavy losses. Jackson's old division, which
has lost two commanders, J. R. Jones wounded and Starke killed, scarcely exists
as a fighting unit; it is now under Col. Grigsby, and is resting in rear of the
line. R. H. Anderson is coming up to reinforce D. H. Hill in the looming
fight for Piper's cornfield.

rates could see the whole show and prepare their reception in advance. As it happened, however, Jackson had formed a new line on a position somewhat farther to the south and there were no Confederates to prevent French from forming up on the left of Greene's division, still holding near Dunker Church, or to keep Sedgwick from moving his division into line on Greene's right.

Ewell's division, now commanded by Jubal Early, who succeeded Brigadier General A. R. Lawton after the latter was wounded, was just about all the infantry Jackson had left at the moment to meet this fresh assault, and Early was busily engaged, farther on the left of the Confederate line, opposing Williams' division of the Twelfth Corps. Greene advanced on the Dunker Church. Early struck him in the flank and Greene recoiled. But now Sedgwick's division was driving ahead, unopposed, and unless stopped would in a few moments be in position to take Lee's main line in flank.

Early's division, down to not more than 600 men, could not hope to deter Sedgwick's 6,000, but help was coming from General Lee. McLaws and Walker came swinging up from Sharpsburg in the nick of time and Jackson, watchfully awaiting the appropriate time, saw that this was the moment for which he had planned.

Lack of coordinated direction of the three Federal corps engaged had much to do with the repeated failure to achieve any conclusive results against Lee's left. There was no guidance or direction from McClellan. One corps commander, Mansfield, had been killed; another, Hooker, was wounded; and the third, Sumner, came on the field absolutely cold, unbriefed, depending entirely on his own eyes and guesswork. As a result, the divisions of the Twelfth and Second Corps became sandwiched together, so that it is unlikely that the right hand knew what the left was doing, or vice versa.

Jackson Counterattacks

The climax of the first phase of the Battle of Sharpsburg was reached about 10:30 o'clock with the arrival of McLaws and

DEAD NEAR DUNKER CHURCH

Walker. Hood's badly battered but still defiant division was withdrawn in favor of the reinforcing divisions, which deployed for attack as they moved swiftly into action. This was the psychological moment for Jackson's counterattack. Orders that had been drafted in anticipation of just such an opportunity were carried by galloping staff officers to McLaws and Walker to clear the West Wood, drive the Federals back and turn their right. Passing through the woods north of the Dunker Church, the Rebel yell signaled the advance as McLaws' brigades rushed impetuously ahead to hit Sedgwick's division in a driving flank attack that took that steady general by surprise and gave his strong division no opportunity to change direction. The effect on Sedgwick was disastrous, 2,200 men being shot down like sheep, and the remainder thrown into confusion. In a very few moments Sedgwick himself received his third wound, whereupon his leaderless troops faded rapidly to the rear. There they were halted, to re-form under the protection of a solid phalanx of artillery batteries judiciously placed in the forward edge of the North Wood and the ridge to the east.

"God has been very kind to us this day," remarked Stonewall Jackson as he rode along with Lafayette McLaws, observing the gratifying effect of his timely counterstroke. Part of Walker's division had in passing become engaged, in company with D. H. Hill's division, reinforced by that of R. H. Anderson, somewhat farther to the southeast. French's division of Sumner's corps, diverging from the direction of Sedgwick's advance, had encountered the left center of Lee's line rather than Jackson's. Consequently it was for the most part McLaws' division which followed Sedgwick's retreating brigades across the corpse-strewn cornfield, in a vigorous attempt to turn the retreat into a rout.

As it turned out, however, Jackson's gratitude was premature. The Federal artillery was not to be shaken. As they poured destruction into McLaws' hot pursuit, the Confederate ranks wavered, became more and more demoralized, and finally, having suffered casualties that totaled almost forty percent of the strength with which McLaws had entered the action, they were forced to give up and withdraw to the cover of the West Wood.

Nicely timed and bravely undertaken as Jackson's counterattack had been by McLaws' hard-fighting division, the scales were weighted against it by the fortuitous appearance of still another Federal division, which put in an appearance just in time to aid the artillery in depriving McLaws of a resounding victory on that part of the field. McClellan's plan had been to hold Franklin's Sixth Corps, when it should arrive, in a position of readiness on the east bank of the Antietam, to be put in where needed. Three Union corps in succession had been thrown piecemeal into the battle, at intervals throughout the morning, but neither singly nor together were they able to break Jackson's ever-dwindling but desperately fighting troops. The remnants of J. R. Jones' and Lawton's Confederate divisions, after a bitter fight, had finally succeeded, about 12 o'clock, in driving the obstinate Federal General Greene from

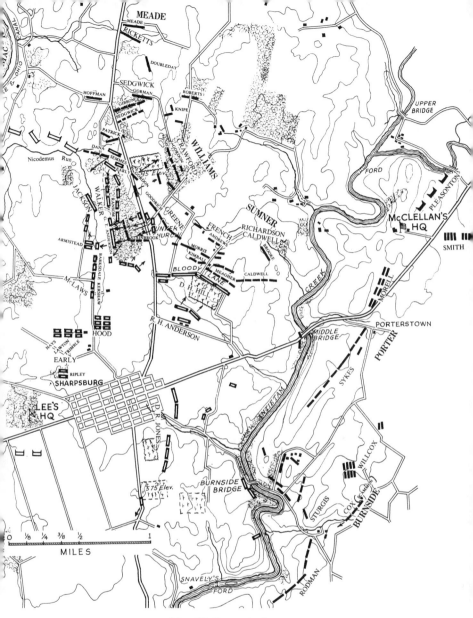

MAP 35. SUMNER'S ATTACK

The situation about 10:30 a.m. The Federals are being driven out of West Woods. Sumner is attacking toward Bloody Lane. Smith's division, the head of Franklin's corps, has arrived near McClellan's headquarters and will soon be committed, in part.

This map shows clearly the weakness of Lee's south flank, and the opportunity for a complete victory that was offered McClellan at this time if he had forced Burnside, Porter, and possibly Franklin to attack on the south.

Dunker Church, to which his division had so bravely clung while the tide of battle shifted on either side of him.

Coupled with McLaws' success, there is every reason to believe that Jackson could have put the Union forces to flight, in spite of the dogged defense by their artillery, if he had been able to call up a few additional brigades to push the pursuit. The fact that every unwounded man was already engaged, and McClellan had summoned Franklin's two-division corps to aid the Union effort against Lee's left, was too much for the badly shot-up, weakened Confederates of Jackson's wing. They had done their level best, had in fact achieved almost miraculous results against what should have been overwhelming odds, but they were not supermen. Jackson therefore pulled what remained of them back to the West Wood, where he placed the shattered remnants along its eastern border for rest and reorganization, as the battle shifted southward in its second phase.

Longstreet's description of the morning battle pictured the Confederate line as "swaying forward and back like a rope exposed to rushing currents. A force too heavy to be withstood would strike and drive in a weak point until we could collect a few fragments, and in turn force back the advance 'til our lost ground was recovered. Thus the battle ebbed and flowed with terrific slaughter on both sides. Federals fought with wonderful bravery and the Confederates clung to their ground with heroic courage as hour after hour they were mown down like grass. The fresh troops of McClellan literally tore into shreds the already ragged army of Lee, but the Confederates never gave back."

Franklin's Sixth Corps, composed of two divisions under reliable, experienced commanders, Major General William F. Smith and Major General Henry W. Slocum, had been marking time in Pleasant Valley after their success at Crampton's Gap, supposedly keeping Confederate General McLaws' division out of circulation. While they relaxed in that pleasant area two days, September 15 and 16, McLaws had withdrawn to rejoin Jackson at Harpers Ferry and later to follow him to Sharpsburg. We have just seen how busy McLaws had been since his arrival at the latter place after he had joined the battle. Franklin had at long last been summoned by McClellan, his two divisions reaching the Antietam during the morning of the seventeenth. For some strange reason McClellan's order to Franklin directed him to send Couch's division, which was attached to the Sixth Corps, to Maryland Heights. Presumably the purpose was to guard against a surprise attack on the army rear, an extremely remote possibility but a typical McClellan decision in the light of his habitual exaggeration of his opponent's strength and capabilities. Not that it made any real difference, since Couch would simply have increased the army commander's unemployed reserve at the Antietam. Couch reached the lower end of Pleasant Valley before being recalled, too late to participate in the battle on the 17th.

When Franklin found that he was needed to assist the three stymied corps who had preceded him across the Antietam, he moved promptly. Smith's division was the first to reach the field, and although only one of his brigades became engaged it was enough to restore the balance and bring the exhausted Confederates to a halt. Franklin joined Sumner to talk things over and find out what had happened. What he learned led him to believe that the situation was made to order for a strong counterattack, in the belief that the Confederates on that flank were played out and his fresh corps, despite its forced march, could bring it off successfully. Sumner disagreed, influenced unduly by the lack of success of his own three divisions following those of Hooker and Mansfield. Franklin had more than 10,000 fresh troops, and they were good divisions, in position and ready for immediate use. They could almost certainly have put the finishing touches to Jackson's decimated divisions and it was nothing short of a military crime that the attempt was not authorized. Here again McClellan remained in character, supported Sumner's view, and refused Franklin's request that he be permitted to attack. The disappointing result was that

Smith and Slocum sat the battle out in relative peace and quiet just as they had been doing for two days in Pleasant Valley.

"The Bloody Lane"

The Battle of Antietam is accurately recorded in Civil War history as the bloodiest single day's engagement on any front. In achieving that doubtful honor, it may be equally accepted that THE famous "sunken road" about 600 yards southeast of Dunker Church (sunken lanes were characteristic of farmlands in the vicinity of Sharpsburg) led even the famous cornfield in the competition to attain high score in number of casualties per square yard.

The bitter struggle on Jackson's part of Lee's line, which continued with practically no pause from dawn to nearly midday, came to a halt mainly because of mutual exhaustion. The Confederate bulldog had managed to chew up without actually destroying the major part of three Union corps, the First, Twelfth, and Second, a feat that could not possibly have been accomplished if those three corps had been utilized in a coordinated attack under a competent, aggressive army commander actually present on the field. On the other hand, almost half of Lee's infantry had been rendered temporarily hors de combat in the course of denying McClellan the privilege of throwing the Army of Northern Virginia into the Potomac.

The stage for the second phase of the battle centered on the sunken farm road which, leading out from the Hagerstown turnpike at a point about a third of a mile south of the Dunker Church, ran east for half a mile to the farm of H. Piper, and then continued around Newcomer's cornfield. This was the Confederate sector entrusted to D. H. Hill's division, on whose right extended two of Longstreet's divisions under "Shank" Evans and D. R. Jones, manning the original defense line that Lee had prescribed upon the army's arrival at Sharpsburg.

Sumner's Federal Second Corps, as previously noted, included the divisions of Sedgewick, French, and Richardson.

Sedgwick and French came on the field together, but Sumner's information was incomplete and faulty, with the result that the direction of his attack was at right angles to the route Hooker's and Mansfield's corps had taken in their.successive assaults on Jackson's position. The quick fate that overtook Sedgwick has been described, but what of French and Richardson?

It seems that while Sedgwick was advancing unopposed through the East Wood, across Miller's cornfield, and into the West Wood, French led his division too far to the south and found himself, rather than attacking the left of Lee's line, in conflict with D. H. Hill's division, which occupied the left center of the Confederate position between Jackson and Longstreet. French's spirited attack on Hill was making progress when R. H. Anderson, who had just completed with McLaws his forced march from Harpers Ferry, and was on the way to join Jackson by Lee's order, was informed that

FRENCH'S DIVISION FIGHTING AT ROULETTE'S FARM

D. H. Hill was in trouble and needed help. Anderson, together with one of McLaw's brigades, turned aside to support Hill and the desperate encounter around Bloody Lane was in full swing.

McClellan had planned simultaneous attacks against Lee's left and right. When those attacks should be progressing according to plan and, presumably, Lee's flanks were in process of being rolled up toward the center, McClellan expected to launch a third assault at the center and that would be it. But McClellan wasn't doing much of anything to effectuate his plan. About all that can be said of his actions and orders on the morning of September 17 is that he directed his corps commanders, one after another, to cross the creek and attack Lee's left flank. By 10:30 o'clock the fight on Lee's left had scored a staggering total of almost 13,000 casualties, 7,000 of which were Federal, the rest Confederate losses. Even before the flames on that flank had died down, however, the battle center of gravity had spontaneously shifted farther south. It was not planned that way, but battles are seldom tidy affairs that work out as intended by the guiding hand of army headquarters. In this instance French's aim was inaccurate and his blow landed on D. H. Hill.

From ten until one o'clock the fighting raged in the new area with mounting intensity as one side or the other received reinforcements. For the Confederates, several brigades of Walker's division had joined the fight, and Richardson's division of Sumner's corps came up to add his strength to French's. Since Longstreet now had a number of his divisions engaged, he took command of the battle as it swung back and forth, now swirling close to the Dunker Church, then around the Roulette house and barns, and in the sunken road (Bloody Lane) and Piper's cornfield just south of the sunken road, flanking it on the south.

The heavy Federal guns had for a long time been concentrating from the far side of the creek on the Confederate batteries and the Union gunners had done their work well.

So much of Lee's artillery was put out of action that at the height of the battle on this part of the line there remained but twelve guns to raise feeble outranged voices. French and Richardson between them forced the Confederates back until the sunken road became their main line of resistance, to which they clung with fanatic heroism. The depressed road proved to be almost as effective as a trench for defense, its natural strength reinforced by protective fence rails that were piled in place by the defenders.

The tenacity of the Confederates in their efforts to hold the sunken road was matched by the gallant persistence of the Union attackers. For more than an hour repeated efforts were made to take the desired objective, as the masses of

THE SUNKEN ROAD (BLOODY LANE) AFTER THE FIGHTING

the dead were stacked like cordwood in the narrow lane. The weight of the Union drive, with the arrival of Richardson's fresh division, eventually proved too much for the Confederates. Several of their regiments broke. The Federals rushed up to the lane and from the upper bank poured in such a devastating fire as no group of human beings could hope to sustain. The extent of the carnage was appalling. Then and there the name Bloody Lane was coined; no more apt description could be applied. French and Richardson cleared the field of Confederates and seized the ridge beyond the cornfield, but the two Federal divisions had paid a high price for their success. Division commander Richardson was mortally wounded, and the Union losses reached a figure in excess of 2,900. The Confederates suffered even greater losses and except for their artillery, organized defense in that area had ceased to exist.

McClellan Misses His Greatest Opportunity

Here was the opportunity of a lifetime for McClellan to drive a wedge through the center of Lee's position. But he not only wasn't there; it is doubtful if at his remote command post he had more than a hazy notion of the tactical situation, where the actual fighting occurred. The Pry house, McClellan's choice as his field headquarters, had the advantage of being on high ground east of the Antietam, overlooking the Sharpsburg area to the west and south. It was a perfectly safe spot, but it was much too distant from the battlefield for the Union commander to be able to react instantaneously and effectively, as Lee was wont to do, when it was minutes, not hours, that counted. At a distance of two miles as the crow flies, and somewhat further by road, to the key areas such as the Dunker Church and Burnside's Bridge, the position selected was at least consistent with McClellan's philosophy of never moving faster than a figurative slow walk.

Franklin was on the field, however, with the divisions of Slocum and Smith, and although he saw the opportunity to cut through at the hinge where Jackson's position connected with Longstreet's, he was unable to sell the idea to McClellan. Why the army commander sent Franklin's 10,000 troops to the front and then refused to let them get in the fight must remain one of the unsolved mysteries of the Battle of Antietam. At the very least it struck a new low in army generalship.

The Confederate loss of the sunken lane brought to an end the second phase of the battle, with Lee's battered divisions, bloody but still defiantly unbowed, holding grimly to their somewhat retracted original line. They were "badly whipped," in Longstreet's own words, but they wouldn't admit the fact, and since McClellan hadn't the least idea that Lee was in such desperate straits, and seemed incapable of making the kind of effort necessary to disclose the facts, the Southern commander was far from being licked at this stage of the battle.

BURNSIDE'S BRIDGE, FROM THE CONFEDERATE SIDE

CHAPTER 20

THIRD AND FINAL PHASE

O F THE three stone bridges that crossed Antietam Creek within the battle area, the only one to become a bone of contention was the bridge farthest south, three-quarters of a mile southeast of Sharpsburg, where the Rohrersville-Sharpsburg road crosses the creek. The ridges bordering both sides of the stream at that point were wooded and quite steep, creating a canyon-like area that was ideal for defense but decidedly unpromising for an attacking force.

The right of Lee's line, manned by D. R. Jones' division of Longstreet's corps, rested on the wooded bluffs above the bridge, with three batteries judiciously placed where they could effectively rake the bridge to discourage any Federal attempt to run the gauntlet of direct, plunging fire. Mc-

Clellan's engineers after a reconnaissance had reported that the only ford in the vicinity of this crossing, which would go down in history as Burnside's Bridge, was located half a mile below, in a deep bend of the stream. The Union force to whom was assigned the task of attacking Lee's right consequently faced the unhappy prospect, if it was to use the bridge, of approaching along a narrow roadway in column formation under the concentrated fire of Confederate artillery and musketry, with no chance of fighting back until the bridge was crossed and the troops that managed to escape destruction fanned out in battle order on the far side.

Careless Reconnaissance on Burnside's Flank

The Union failure to reconnoiter the Antietam thoroughly for available crossings was sheer criminal negligence, for there were any number of places where infantry could cross, even if they should have to hold their rifles above their heads. Crook's men found a ford 250 yards upstream from Burnside's Bridge, and Scammon's brigade crossed a quarter of a mile downstream and about half-way from the bridge to Snavely's Ford, where Rodman's division was ordered to cross. There were other crossings as well, so it would appear that McClellan's engineers must have made merely a superficial reconnaissance. That however does not exonerate Burnside, Cox, or any of their division commanders for accepting at face value what must have been obvious to any one who took the trouble to examine the creek for a few hundred yards in either direction.

Burnside's Ninth Corps was selected by McClellan to execute the attack on the south flank, but the orders were not issued until September 17. The only instructions given Burnside on the fifteenth, when the Army of the Potomac reached the Antietam, directed him to go into bivouac on the army left. Burnside's choice of a camp area, in rear of the hills along the creek and about a mile below the bridge, did not suit McClellan, who considered it too far removed from the battle area. Burnside was told to move his divisions closer to the bridge, which was accomplished in due course, although the corps commander was criticized for taking too long to effect the change of position.

Federal Command Confusion

The command situation in McClellan's army had become somewhat anomalous in the course of the campaign. Burnside was originally designated as commander of the Right Wing, composed of Hooker's First Corps and Burnside's Ninth, the latter temporarily under Cox, who normally commanded the Kanawha division. The order prescribing the wing organization had never been rescinded, but McClellan chose to ignore that fact when Hooker was directly ordered to attack Lee's left while Burnside, with only his own corps, was sent to the other end of the Union line. Burnside chafed under what he regarded as an affront, but placed the blame on Hooker's well-known ambition for independent command, on the assumption that "Fighting Joe" had wangled the post of honor from McClellan, more or less at Burnside's expense.

From Washington to South Mountain, Jesse Reno led the Ninth Corps until he was killed at Fox's Gap. Since then, the senior of the four division commanders in the corps, Brigadier General Jacob D. Cox, had been acting corps commander. Cox suggested to Burnside that the latter resume command of the corps, whose staff had accompanied Reno's body to Washington for burial, but Burnside, reluctant to vacate the higher wing commandership, declined to act on the suggestion. This made for ineffective control on the south flank, with Burnside and his wing staff breathing down the neck of a nominal corps commander whose own division staff was inadequate for its dual mission.

During the day, September 16, McClellan had visited the Ninth Corps, ordered Burnside to move his divisions closer to Antietam Creek, and later wrote that he had advised Burnside "he would probably be required to attack the enemy's right on the following morning." But Burnside received from

McClellan's remarks the impression that the Ninth Corps would be expected merely to create a diversion of sufficient strength to hold the Confederates on Lee's right in place, in order to prevent them from being shifted elsewhere to bolster the line.

McClellan seems to have lost some of his usual confidence in his close friend Burnside as a result of the latter's unexplained delay in moving his troops off South Mountain in the direction of Sharpsburg on the morning of September 15. The impression was sharpened when McClellan found the Ninth Corps in too withdrawn a position east of Antietam Creek on the sixteenth. It may have been that combination of events that prompted the army commander to virtually ignore Burnside on the latter occasion by having the army staff directly assign the divisions of the corps to the positions which McClellan thought they should occupy. At any rate, before settling down for the night, the corps had been redisposed as follows: Rodman's division at Snavely's Ford a half-mile below Burnside's Bridge; Sturgis' division covering the bridge, on either side of the road leading to it. Cox's division was split, one brigade attached to Rodman, the other to Sturgis. Willcox's division was placed in reserve a short distance to Sturgis' left rear.

Toomb's brigade of D. R. Jones' division, somewhat isolated from the rest of the division, held the hill mass closest to the bridge on the Confederate side of the stream, which effectively covered the crossing. Supported by several batteries, sited to enfilade the bridge and its eastern approach, Toombs' small force of 600 infantrymen would be endangered chiefly by being outflanked in the event a Federal division should cross by the lower ford and come in on Toombs' rear. Lee was aware of the danger, but had no troops to spare until Walker's division arrived from Harpers Ferry on the afternoon of September 16. At daylight on the morning of the battle, September 17, Walker was ordered down to guard Snavely's Ford, until the situation on Jackson's front became so tense that Lee pulled Walker out, about 9 o'clock in the morning, to lend his strength to the left and left center where Mc-Clellan was making his main effort.

Burnside chose for his field headquarters a high knoll northeast of Burnside's Bridge, which boasted a haystack that afforded a prominent landmark for messengers to spot. The location proved to be a front row seat for watching the battle to the north, for from that position the observer could see as far as the Dunker Church and up to that point at least could follow the movements of the troops of both armies as the fighting surged back and forth.

Burnside's Corps Alerted

During the early morning hours of the 17th McClellan sent Burnside a message to form his troops and hold them in readiness to assault the bridge, but not to initiate the attack until McClellan should give the word. Evidently the army commander wanted to wait until the attack on the army right had registered a success before committing the Ninth Corps. General Cox was with Burnside at his hilltop headquarters when an officer of McClellan's staff rode up with the order to attack:

> Headquarters, Army of the Potomac,
> September 17, 1862—9:10 a. m.
>
> MAJOR-GENERAL BURNSIDE:
> GENERAL,—General Franklin's command is within one mile and a half of here. General McClellan desires you to open your attack. As soon as you shall have uncovered the upper stone bridge you will be supported, and, if necessary, on your own line of attack. So far all is going well.
>
> Respectfully,
> GEO D. RUGGLES, Colonel.

The distance from the Pry house, McClellan's headquarters, to Burnside's command post was about two miles, which would indicate that the above order was received by Burnside sometime between 9:30 and 10:00 o'clock, depending on the speed of the courier's horse and the rider's sense of urgency. In view of the subsequent controversy over the delay on Burnside's part in responding to McClellan's "repeated orders to attack," as the latter described it, the timing of the order is significant. Acting corps commander Cox has written that the actual attack order dated 9.10 a.m. was the first that Burnside received, McClellan's allegations as to an 8 o'clock order to the contrary notwithstanding.

Two things are clear. In the first place, McClellan missed a great opportunity by not ordering the Ninth Corps to attack simultaneously with Hooker's First Corps at daylight, against Lee's respective flanks. There was nothing to lose and everything to gain, including a ten to one chance to inflict a decisive defeat on the Confederates before midday. In the second place, Burnside was unconscionably slow in initiating and carrying out his part of the army mission. Whether the attack of the Ninth Corps was to be a diversionary or full-fledged effort makes little difference, for it is quite obvious that Burnside on September 17 was operating in what was either a mental vacuum or a state of suspended animation.

As a matter of fact, not one of McClellan's three wing commanders had much to recommend him for what would today be referred to as army command. Each of the three had been placed by McClellan at the head of two army corps, each corps comprised of either two or three infantry divisions. Neither Major General William B. Franklin nor Major General Edwin V. Sumner had demonstrated in their earlier assignments that he possessed unusual talents for high command or more than average military competence to mark him for advancement. Length of service and their respective positions on the army officer list offer the logical explanation for their assignments. McClellan's popularity with the men in the ranks of his army cannot have failed to cause him to analyze the reasons therefor, and it is just possible that a desire to win friends may have caused him to be less critical of the performance of his generals than the welfare of the army required.

Franklin and Sumner, the latter over sixty years of age, were "present or accounted for" during the Maryland campaign, but that was about all. Neither seems to have influenced the action to any extent in a constructive way. On the negative side we have seen how uninspired was Franklin's leadership at Crampton's Gap and subsequently. Nevertheless both generals managed to retain their positions as corps commanders through the rest of the year 1862 and until after the Battle of Fredericksburg, following which heads rolled in great profusion. Although Sumner, a fine, loyal, fire-eating, old-school type of Regular Army officer escaped the axe which caught Franklin and Burnside in the aftermath of that great December disaster to Union arms, Sumner died in the early part of the year 1863, and there is some reason to believe that his death was hastened by more than physical causes stemming from the Maryland and Fredericksburg Campaigns.

McClellan and Burnside

Major General Ambrose E. Burnside's case was of a far different character. His career was intertwined with and to a certain extent paralleled that of McClellan. They attended West Point at the same time, were intimate friends then and later, and were associated as corporation officers in a western railroad after both had resigned from the Army. Each commanded the Army of the Potomac at different times, but neither was successful in that capacity. Both possessed inventive ability of a sort, McClellan having developed the McClellan saddle and Burnside having created an early model of the breech-loading rifle. The blood of the politician ran through the veins of both; McClellan aimed high to seek the Presidency and failed; Burnside set his sights lower and after the war won the governorship of Rhode Island for three successive terms, and then moved on to the United States Senate.

Burnside's chief asset was a winning personality. He possessed an unusual charm of manner and knew how to turn it on to his advantage. It may not be fair to attribute his rise to prominence in the Union Army entirely to his personal magnetism, but there is little doubt that he would have been just another Civil War general without 'it. Even more than that, perhaps, for in the absence of such a powerful aid to recognition, Burnside's weakness of character would almost inevitably have been discovered before, rather than after, the historic military blunders associated with his name. The most penetrating analysis of Burnside's character came from General Palfrey, an army officer who knew him well, and who wrote that "nobody could encounter his smile and receive the grasp of his hand without being for some time under a potent influence . . . and yet his presence was an element of weakness where he was a subordinate, and was disastrous when he held a great command." What more apt comment on Antietam and Fredericksburg could be offered!

Ineffectual Union Tactics

Noting that McClellan was feeding his troops against Lee's left in corps driblets, Burnside adopted a similar plan on a small scale against the Confederate right—if indeed his feeble initial effort, when finally undertaken after an interminable and inexcusable delay, can be dignified by the use of the word plan.

The morning hours of September 17 were the critical ones; critical in the sense that McClellan's hope of victory rested on a coordinated attack, the only kind that offered a real chance for success against Lee and his capable lieutenants, all of whom were highly skilled in taking advantage of every opening and in extracting the maximum gain from any demonstrated weakness or false move on the part of their opponents. The inconclusive effect of the successive attacks by Hooker's First Corps, Mansfield's Twelfth, and finally Sumner's Second, can fairly be charged to McClellan's inadequate planning and direction of the battle, once started. Nevertheless, the three attacks had taken a heavy, almost insupportable toll from Lee's army, less than half the size of McClellan's and therefore unable to sustain equal numerical losses with the Federals.

The Union fortunes would have been best served by the battle plan which McClellan stated in his official report he intended to carry out, namely a double envelopment of the Confederate line. The army commander's failure lay more in the execution than the conception, for the battle as actually fought by the Union army was a disjointed series of corps attacks, uncoordinated by army headquarters and generally unrelated to one another. The men and officers of the various divisions fought as bravely and well as the Army of the Potomac ever had—the fault certainly does not belong on their doorstep.

The manner in which Pleasanton's cavalry division of five brigades was employed after the arrival of the Union army at the Antietam was a piece out of the same cloth. McClellan knew what had happened at Harpers Ferry and must be credited with the intelligence to realize that Lee's missing divisions would be coming up to Sharpsburg by one or the other of the only two available roads, both of which could and should have been covered by Pleasonton's horsemen, between Sharpsburg and the Potomac to the south. It was the only logical assignment that could be given to the cavalry under the prevailing tactical conditions, and it would have served a four-fold purpose, to secure the army left flank and open Snavely's Ford for an easy crossing of the Antietam by the troops of the Ninth Corps; to harass Lee's line of communication to the Potomac; to keep McClellan informed of Confederate movements in that direction; and to delay the arrival of Lee's reinforcements. Any one of the four missions would have served a constructive purpose; combined they could mean the difference between victory and defeat. Instead, except for a brief skirmish across the middle bridge, the Union cavalry was relegated to bleacher seats opposite the center of the battle area where they watched the game in a dismounted status, together with Porter's reserve corps and Franklin's two immobilized divisions, while the rest of the Army of the Potomac fought and bled and died in fragmentary fashion until the sun went down, with the Confederates still holding approximately the same positions to which which Lee had assigned them on the morning of September 15.

In spite of the inability of three Union corps, half of Mc-Clellan's army, to achieve the objective of cracking Lee's left or breaking the hinge between Jackson and Longstreet on the left center of the Confederate line, the punishment dealt out by those Union divisions was so severe, and the margin of Confederate disaster so thin, that a determined Union effort at either end of the line, or at the center, or at all three points, must have accomplished Lee's downfall long before A. P. Hill's absent Light Division could reach the field. McClellan had at his disposal three practically unused corps, Franklin's, Fitz John Porter's, and Burnside's, a total of eight divisions. With the exception of one brigade of Smith's division, not one of them had been thrown into the battle during the fierce fighting of the early morning, or at any subsequent period during the entire battle, which can only mean that McClellan had no conception of the extent to which the contest on the north flank had weakened Lee's much small army. When affairs came to a pass that found D. H. Hill fighting in the ranks with a rifle, and General Longstreet personally helping to serve a Confederate gun, both of which phenomena actually occurred during Sumner's attack against Hill's sector, one is likely to wonder at the lack of competent Northern leadership that could so utterly fail to exploit such an opportunity.

Contrast the moral courage and aggressive fighting spirit of General Lee at the very moment when his center had been swept so clean of defenders that a Union army corps could have driven through the huge hole with but few losses. D. H. Hill had set the example by staging a "lost cause" counter-attack with a few hundred men, which of course got nowhere as attacks go, but which did apparently have an important psychological effect on Sumner's divisions, who had just driven the Confederates back from Bloody Lane. For Sumner, conscious of his own heavy losses and ignoring what his men had done to their opponents, chose that moment to dissuade Franklin from pushing his own two divisions into the vacuum which neither Sumner nor McClellan, who had ridden over for a few minutes for a close-up view of what had happened during the morning hours, had the vision to recognize.

It was then that the alert, quick-thinking Lee decided that the moment was opportune for an attempt by Jackson and Stuart to turn the Federal right and, in Jackson's words, "drive McClellan into the Potomac." What Lee was going to use for men and guns was apparently unimportant—surely his lieutenants could scrape together a few regiments and a couple of guns for the purpose. Jackson was all for it, and managed to locate a regiment and two batteries of Walker's division who were given the mission of working around Mc-Clellan's right when Stuart's guns opened as a starting signal. Simultaneously with the flank movement, several thousand other Confederates would support the advance on the left. When, however, after a careful reconnaissance Stuart's cavalrymen discovered that the Federal right was solidly anchored on the Potomac, the projected attack was abandoned. It wouldn't have had the chance of a snowball in the nether regions, but the point was that Lee and his key generals, the flaming spirit of the offensive still burning brightly, never seemed to know when they were licked. This explains in part why they seldom failed to outgeneral and outfight their slower-witted, heavier opponents.

Burnside's Dubious Performance

Without exonerating McClellan from full responsibility for failure to achieve a clean-cut, ringing victory over Lee's army in the Battle of Antietam, which by all the rules of warfare should have been the outcome, the corps commander who had it in his power to turn the trick in spite of the army commander's hesitant tactics and ineffective battle leadership was Ambrose E. Burnside, the wingless wing commander who permitted his personal feelings to control what little military judgment he may have had.

If Burnside, smarting over the apparent affront which McClellan had administered by detaching Hooker from Burnside's wing and giving Hooker the mission of leading the attack on the Confederate left, made a conscious decision to emulate McClellan's slow pace in committing his troops to action, he certainly succeeded. The four divisions in the Ninth Corps were just as good as those of the other divisions of the army, and deserved better leadership than Burnside could furnish. Several of them had demonstrated their fighting qualities only a few days earlier on South Mountain. Except for a couple of hours in the early morning of September 17 their only Confederate opposition across the Antietam above Burnside's Bridge was the small brigade of Brigadier General Robert Toombs, who was more of a Southern politician and orator than a general, at least by Confederate standards. It was true that Toombs' thinly held line occupied a tactically favorable defensive position, but that applied only to an attempt to storm it by a frontal charge over the small bridge, an unimaginative maneuver that any experienced platoon commander would have avoided in favor of an enterprising flank attack by using the available, nearby fords.

Burnside had been alerted by McClellan in person on September 16 to the probability that he would be ordered to attack Lee's right the following morning. Early on the morning of the battle Burnside received a message from army headquarters to form his divisions and be prepared to launch his attack when McClellan should give the word. At 9:10 the attack order was signed and on its way to Burnside.

The sequence of the series of orders leaves no doubt that Burnside was fully aware of McClellan's intentions and should have had his divisions on their marks, like sprinters, awaiting only the starter's pistol to send them speeding down the track. All the alibis in the world cannot excuse Burnside for delaying his attack a minute beyond 10 o'clock, which was the very hour that marked the critical phase of the battle north of Sharpsburg. Had the Ninth Corps jumped into the fight at that time, the psychological effect alone might very well have served as the last straw for the embattled, wearied, decimated Confederate divisions, who with the exception of Stuart's cavalry and artillery on Lee's extreme left flank had all fought their hearts out in the magnificent struggle against McClellan's vastly greater numbers and clearly superior artillery. As of that hour, and for the five hours that followed. Lee had no reserves that he could call upon, in contrast to McClellan's nine fresh divisions, which up to that time had not participated in the fighting.

Burnside's Bridge

The stone-arch bridge over the Antietam in front of Burnside's corps was the major obstacle to getting the Union attack under way mainly because Burnside lacked imagination and ingenuity in planning how to put his divisions across the stream. He knew of the existence of Snavely's Ford a half-mile down stream, but made no effort to reconnoiter above or below the bridge for possible additional fords, an inexcusable oversight because several such crossings did in fact exist, as the troops were later to discover for themselves. The corps commander appeared to be hypnotized by the bridge, the approach to which was under the direct fire of Toombs' Confederates from the opposite hill. The more Burnside tried to figure out what to do, the more bemused and confused he became. He couldn't seem to make up his mind to attack directly across the narrow bridge, so he temporized and tried out a few probing advances with small detachments, with no success. Each time the Federals moved out toward the bridge Toombs' Georgia regiments opened with everything they had and drove them back. It was supremely important to the Confederates that they discourage the bluecoats from becoming too zealous, for they knew full well that once they were over the bridge it would be impossible to hold them back with the small force under Toombs' command.

Rodman's division was given the mission of crossing by Snavely's Ford, to come in on the Confederate flank and rear. For several hours, until about nine o'clock, Walker's Confederate division guarded that point, but it had then been recalled by Lee to strengthen the defenses above Sharpsburg. Consequently from nine o'clock on the way was open for Rodman to advance unopposed, but it took his division a long time to march down to the ford, so long in fact that several regiments of Sturgis' division were finally able to force a crossing at the bridge itself before Rodman had completed his relatively short march.

While Burnside watched from his hilltop headquarters, General Cox as corps commander directed the Union efforts to carry the bridge. Crook's brigade of the Kanawha division made the first attack, moving out a short distance above the bridge, covered by a firing line from Sturgis' division. Coming under heavy Confederate fire as soon as the troops showed themselves, Crook was stopped in his tracks and had to withdraw. The second attack was made by a brigade of Sturgis' division, supported by artillery, with no better success.

600 Confederates Pin Down 13,000 Federals

Precious hours were passing while a comparative handful of Confederates on Lee's right flank held up an entire army corps of four Union divisions, 13,000 strong, thereby buying the priceless time that Lee desperately needed for A. P. Hill to come up from Harpers Ferry. The fighting at the northern end of the line had practically ceased, with the exhausted troops of both sides lying on their arms and glaring at each other like two badly wounded animals without energy to renew the fight, before the final and successful attempt was made to cross Burnside's Bridge.

Meanwhile, as Burnside in his indecision continued to put off the hour of the concerted attack that McClellan had directed, messenger after messenger galloped over from army headquarters with urgently repeated orders for Burnside to get on with his assault. That general was either in a blue funk, or had made up his mind to ignore McClellan, for all he did was to brush off the messengers as though they didn't exist. Finally it was borne in on the impatient army commander that something was wrong with his friend Burnside. What he should have done was to ride over to see for himself why his lieutenant was acting so strangely, and to exercise his own authority on the spot. Instead of which he continued his policy of fighting the battle by remote control, contenting himself this time with sending his inspector general, Colonel D. B. Sacket. Sacket was told to order Burnside "to take that bridge, at bayonet point if necessary" and to stay right with the reluctant general until the order was executed.

That did it, but it was almost one o'clock when Sacket delivered his message, three long hours after Burnside had first received the order to launch his assault. Still disgruntled, Burnside evidently realized that he could stall no longer if he wished to hold his job. Sending for General Cox, Burnside told him to carry the bridge at all hazards, a decision that could just as well have been reached three hours earlier, with results that might have changed the course of the war.

Two Union Regiments Cross the Bridge

Cox directed Sturgis to select two regiments from Ferrero's brigade, which had not yet seen action in the battle, form them in a double column so that after crossing the bridge they could fan out to right and left while on the run without losing their regimental integrity, and charge the bridge. Sturgis chose the Fifty-first New York under Colonel Robert B. Potter, and the Fifty-first Pennsylvania under Colonel John F. Hartranft, and to lend weight to the charge, a light howitzer was set up to deliver point-blank fire on the far edge of the bridge. When everything was set, Federal skirmishers all along the line laid down a heavy musketry barrage, the howitzer blasted the further side of the bridge, and the two regiments dashed across. The casualties, as expected, were fairly heavy, bunched as the men were on a narrow front, but

THE ATTACK ACROSS BURNSIDE'S BRIDGE

there was no hesitation, and Toombs' Confederates fled to the safety of their division line.

The precipitous heights on the Confederate side of the stream, formidable as they appeared, were heavily wooded and therefore useful for sharpshooters only at the edge nearest the bridge. Nevertheless, volley fire directly on the road paralleling the creek, by which the Federals were forced to approach the bridge, and on the bridge itself, achieved a shotgun effect that was plenty lethal in spite of the interfering trees and foliage.

At the base of the hills, which were almost vertical for the last few feet, was an area of defiladed space, free from the Confederate musketry fire but still enfiladed by artillery fire, where the attacking Federals paused momentarily to deploy after rushing the bridge and before starting to climb the hills.

The Union spearhead having penetrated the Confederate defense, it was easier sailing for the rest of the Ninth Corps for awhile. Rodman's division crossed at Snavely's Ford,

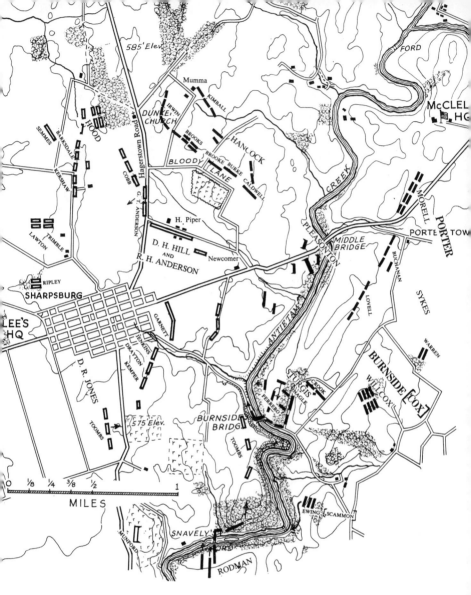

MAP 36. THE ATTACK AT BURNSIDE'S BRIDGE

Situation on south flank at 1 p.m. At this time R. H. Anderson's and D. H. Hill's divisions have lost all organization, regiments and brigades being broken up and intermingled, and in positions along the stone fences of the Hagerstown Road and behind the ridge running from the road to and beyond Piper's barn. Only G. T. Anderson's brigade has preserved its cohesion.

Burnside's famous assault across the stone bridge which now bears his name is shown in its initial stages, with Ferrero's brigade leading the way up the steep slope against heavy fire. Rodman is crossing farther downstream, at Snavely's Ford, this crossing being just as successful if not as spectacular.

Sturgis and Crook and Willcox by the bridge and the two additional fords that had by that time been discovered 250 yards north of the bridge, and 400 yards south of it. Under Cox's direction the heights above the Antietam were occupied by the Union forces, as they prepared to advance on Sharpsburg along the ridge to the north. However, all these movements had taken time, because of the narrow defile of the bridge, and it was three o'clock in the afternoon before the corps dispositions were completed, the light artillery in position, ammunition resupplied, and the troops properly placed for an extension of the advance.

The Maryland Campaign was a historic one in several ways, one of its more unique aspects being the fact that two future Presidents of the United States were combat participants. Even more unusual is the fact that both were members of the same regiment, the 23rd Ohio Volunteers. The regimental commander, Lieutenant Colonel Rutherford B. Hayes was wounded when his regiment, a part of the Kanawha Division of the Ninth corps, made its successful attack at Fox's Gap. Sergeant William McKinley, age 19, in charge of the commissary department, distinguished himself during the Battle of Antietam in a less flashy, but nonetheless heroic manner, when on the erstwhile Confederate heights above Burnside's Bridge he personally and without orders carried hot coffee and food across the bridge and up the hill, under fire in both directions, until every man in his regiment had been served. One has only to have had a similar experience to appreciate the stimulating effect on the morale of that particular Ohio regiment.

Lee's battered divisions on the left and center of his position had with almost unbelievable tenacity held their sagging line against the superior weight of men and metal thrown against them during the long hours of the morning. Few battles in history have recorded such bloody carnage as that of the Antietam. More than 10,000 men had been killed or wounded in the early attacks by Hooker and Mansfield, and additional thousands of casualties were added in the struggle between Sumner and D. H. Hill in and around the sunken road. Confederate reserves were nonexistent, but still McClellan held out two army corps, Porter's and Franklin's, as well as Pleasonton's cavalry division, while he waited impatiently for the slow-thinking and even slower moving Burnside to swing into action with his Ninth Corps on the southern flank.

McClellan himself had been fumbling the ball ever since the fortunate circumstance which had given him Lee's blueprint for action back at Frederick on September 13, four days earlier. General Grant was later to describe McClellan as "one of the mysteries of the war," a characterization that only partly explains why he missed *all* of the opportunities gratuitously offered him by General Lee, master of the calculated risk. McClellan's explanation as to why he did not commit Franklin and Porter with their four divisions, at the moment when Lee was figuratively staggering on the ropes, was that he felt it necessary to hold out a strong reserve in case Lee should mount a counterattack, which, obviously, was the last thing that the Confederates could have managed.

Nevertheless, and in spite of McClellan's martial timidity and Burnside's lethargy, it looked, at 3:30 in the afternoon, as though the boom was about to be lowered on the Army of Northern Virginia. The Confederates still holding the line north and east of Sharpsburg were about fought out, McClellan was holding five unused divisions in that same area that could be thrown into the final phase on short notice. while Burnside's four divisions under Cox, across the creek and deployed in battle formation, were moving steadily up the southern slopes of Sharpsburg, squarely on Lee's right flank.

The Ninth Corps Enters Sharpsburg

With Willcox's division on the right, Rodman's on the left, each supported by a brigade of the Kanawha division, Cox advanced to meet D. R. Jones' Confederate division, which, having shifted position, was disposed diagonally across the Federal front and guarding the approaches to the town of Sharpsburg from the south. Sturgis' division was held in reserve on the high ground recently vacated by the Confederates. On the other side, Jones' six brigades were strongly posted behind the stone fences and crests of the crossridges, supported by all the artillery Lee was able to transfer from the now quiet other sectors.

As soon as Willcox's men came into view on the open ground between Antietam Creek and Sharpsburg, the battle opened with a fury that matched the earlier struggle to the north. Over fields and through farmyards the fiercely fighting Federals slowly but steadily pushed Jones' hard-pressed, outnumbered brigades until Cox had effected a lodgment in the lower end of Sharpsburg and occupied the high ground southeast of the town. About that same time, Pleasonton's dismounted cavalry crossed the creek at the middle bridge, drove back the Confederate skirmishers at that point, and cleared the way for four horse batteries to move across and engage the Confederate artillery in the vicinity of Cemetery Ridge, on the eastern edge of Sharpsburg. Still later in the afternoon, while the Ninth Corps continued its forward progress on the south flank, several battalions from Sykes' division crossed to lend support to the horse batteries that were still in action (Pleasonton's cavalry had been withdrawn). The pressure from two sides was more than the few Confederate guns on the crest could resist; Cemetery Hill was abandoned to the Federals.

In the heat of the battle, as Willcox inclined to the right in his advance, Rodman moved somewhat to the left to face the Confederates occupying the ridges to his left front, and thus diverged from Willcox's line of advance. It was now 4:30 o'clock. The ammunition wagons had been unable to keep pace with the Federal advance, due partly to traffic delays over the Burnside Bridge, so that it became necessary to call a temporary halt to Willcox's thus far successful assault while the ammunition was hurried forward to replenish empty cartridge boxes.

A. P. Hill to the Rescue

The dramatic climax to the Battle of Antietam had within itself all the ingredients for a best selling historical novel, although the leading characters were too engrossed in the problems of the moment to give any thought to histrionics. George B. McClellan, Thomas J. Jackson, Ambrose E. Burnside, and Ambrose Powell Hill had all been cadets together at West Point, McClellan and Jackson in the Class of 1846, Burnside and Hill in the Class of 1847. McClellan and Powell Hill were room mates, but Hill lost a year on account of illness and graduated a class behind McClellan. "Tom" Jackson as a cadet displayed many of the characteristics which, then as later, kept other men at arms length, but McClellan and Hill were warm friends, while Burnside and Hill, also close friends, led their class in undergraduate escapades if not in scholarship.

Nellie Marcy, attractive daughter of Colonel Randolph B. Marcy, later Chief of Staff to General McClellan, was one of the most popular of the "army brats" and quite naturally caught the eye of the young army officers in Washington, among them George McClellan and Powell Hill. The former room mates and intimate friends both fell in love with Nellie. Ambrose Burnside, admirer and loyal supporter of McClellan, did all he could to assist him in the competition for Nellie's hand, while father Marcy, learning that McClellan was about to resign from the Army and enter the railroading business, allowed as how that afforded more promise for the future. So that was one battle that McClellan won and Hill lost. Nellie became Mrs. McClellan and Powell Hill, concealing his disappointment, attended the wedding.

The scene now shifts to a small town in Maryland, some years later. Lee's Army of Northern Virginia, locked in a deadly struggle with McClellan's Army of the Potomac, has been bled white and is hovering on the brink of disaster.

Outnumbered more than two to one, it is standing on the defensive and with no reserves at hand to meet a possible final thrust from McClellan's powerful and as yet uncommitted reserve of five divisions. Lee's first invasion of the North, at 4:30 o'clock on the afternoon of September 17, stands a good chance of coming to an inglorious end. Jackson's veterans had succeeded in chewing up two Federal corps and assisted Longstreet in fending off a third. The fourth, Burnside's Ninth Corps, after a long delay was now pushing close to Sharpsburg and threatening the safety of Lee's entire defense line. Had McClellan only known it, Lee's army was ripe for the coup de grace.

There remained the remote possibility that the Confederate army could be saved by a miracle, but the time was getting awfully short within which even a miracle would prove effective. Lee's one last hope was A. P. Hill's Light Division of 3,000 effectives, whom Jackson had left behind at Harpers Ferry to wind up the task of paroling the thousands of Federals who had surrendered in time to free most of Jackson's corps for the more important task of fighting McClellan at Sharpsburg.

An urgent message from Lee to Hill, which the latter received at 6:30 in the morning, aroused him to the danger facing the army on the Antietam. Leaving Thomas' brigade to wrap up the remaining details of the Harpers Ferry job, Hill promptly put his five other brigades on the road to Sharpsburg. Dressed largely in Federal uniforms, which were a vast improvement over their erstwhile conglomerate wearing apparel, the hard-bitten veterans of many a tough march and battle moved at a rapid gait along the dusty road to Shepherdstown, with hardly a pause for breath.

Why Hill took the long seventeen-mile route via the Shepherdstown Road rather than the much shorter route across the Potomac at Harpers Ferry is not known. He may have figured that the Federals would make him fight to reach Lee if he chose the latter, whereas it was pretty certain that he could cross the Potomac without opposition at Boteler's (Blackford's) Ford, and an additional march of five miles would be preferable to not getting there at all. Thanks to his old friend Burnside, the extra two hours of marching were not wasted, although by a very slim margin.

Major General Ambrose P. Hill, age 36, a native Virginian with a fiery temper, loved a fight, preferably against the Yankees. Between battles, however, he apparently had no scruples against taking on his superiors in the Confederate army, to keep his hand in as it were. There was the time after the Peninsular Campaign, for example, when Hill tangled with General Longstreet and challenged him to a duel in the fashion of a true Cavalier, but that affair was smoothed over. It was Stonewall Jackson, however, who most frequently rubbed Hill the wrong way. A feud between the two generals, which started at Orange Court House during the march that preceded the battle at Cedar Mountain, was only concluded at Chancellorsville, nine months later, when Jackson's career was brought to a close through an accidental volley from his own men.

Jackson was a stern disciplinarian who would brook not the slightest deviation from the letter of his orders, whether by a private in the ranks or a major general commanding a division. He could be uncompromisingly unpleasant in exerting his authority, and there were occasions when he carried matters to extremes by jumping to unfair conclusions without permitting the object of his wrath to explain what might only appear to the general to be a violation of his orders. There were times when Jackson criticized Hill for marching too slowly, and others when he objected that the Light Division traveled too fast for units in rear to keep up.

The crisis between the two occurred on September 4, 1862, after the Battle of Second Manassas, when Jackson's corps was crossing the Potomac at Leesburg, on the way to Maryland. Jackson's standing orders were that division commanders must see to it that their units moved out at the hour Jackson ordered, no later, and that the division commander himself would ride the column to prevent straggling, which plagued the Confederate army so badly after Manassas. On the day in question, Jackson found that his orders were not being followed in Hill's division; there was straggling in the rear and the division commander in Jackson's opinion was doing nothing to prevent it. So Jackson rode forward and halted Hill's leading brigade without notifying the division commander. Hill rode back to see what was wrong, inquiring angrily as to who had ordered the halt. The brigade commander pointed to Jackson, sitting his horse and watching the tableau. The enraged Hill rode up to Jackson and, informing him that if he proposed to issue orders directly to brigade commanders he had no need of a division commander, offered Jackson his sword. "Keep your sword," responded Jackson curtly, "and consider yourself under arrest." Jackson then rode off.

From that time on, and until Jackson's corps approached Harpers Ferry on September 14, A.P. Hill rode at the rear of his division without exercising command. It was only when action was imminent that Jackson lifted the arrest status temporarily to restore Hill to command of his division for the purpose of battle.

A. P. Hill, the impetuous man of action, was little given to putting his thoughts on paper, unlike the many generals who at the drop of a hat recorded their views before, during, and after battle. For that reason he has until recently been the forgotten general of the Confederacy, despite his magnificent record as commander of the Light Division, which he molded and led throughout the war until his promotion to corps command after Chancellorsville. Lee considered Hill his best division commander, and it was his name that hovered on the lips of both Stonewall Jackson and Robert E. Lee in the last moments of their lives.

It may have been due to quirks of fate, or the possibility that A. P. Hill was simply a man of destiny, figuratively waiting in the wings for the climactic moment of the drama. When the time came, it always seemed to be A. P. Hill, at the head of the Light Division, who led his hard-hitting veterans onto the stage to turn imminent defeat into victory, or the next best thing to it. He had turned the trick at Cedar Mountain and was about to repeat the performance at Sharpsburg, but with far greater dramatic effect. The fact was that Powell Hill was a fighting leader with a driving urge that would spare neither himself nor the men of his command, no matter how many swords he might have to break over the backs of laggard lieutenants, by way of transmitting his own fire into those under him. He had a natural flair for the dramatic, and his red shirt, symbol of combat, was invariably exposed to the eyes of his troops whenever battle was imminent.

There is no record of Hill's words or thoughts as he drove his men relentlessly forward over the long, dusty miles that brought them closer to Sharpsburg and the anxious army that awaited the relief of his coming. He might well be recalling his youthful friendship and rivalry with McClellan for the hand of Nellie Marcy. It is doubtful if he was aware of the fact that Ambrose Burnside was the Union general whose troops would be the first he would encounter, but thoughts of McClellan must have passed through his mind, and quite possibly hastened the tempo of his march. The image of Stonewall Jackson, his bete noir, certainly flashed over the screen of his consciousness, for Hill kept exhorting his straining foot soldiers with "close up, close up," the very words that Jackson invariably used to exact even greater exertions from his already fast-marching foot soldiers.

The Climax

The battle on the south flank, along the Sharpsburg ridge and in the lower part of the town, was being conducted ably and with dogged persistence by Burnside's divisions under Jacob Cox, once the bridge had been crossed and maneuver space made available. There was no glamour in this particular fight, just hard, killing work, up hill from Antietam Creek, in the face of heavy gun fire from the artillery Lee was able to

BURNSIDE'S ADVANCE TOWARD SHARPSBURG

assemble from all parts of the field. The Confederates had been given plenty of advance notice of Burnside's obvious intentions, so there could be no surprise. The Federals of Willcox's, Rodman's, Sturgis', and Cox's own Kanawha division had to endure a hurricane of fire from Longstreet's Confederates, who were just as determined to stop this new outfit as Lee's divisions on the north and east sectors had been against Mc-Clellan's first and second attempts on their left and center.

Field commander Cox, directing the Union effort from the center of the corps position, quickly became aware of the gap caused by the diverging attacks of Willcox and Rodman. The configuration of the ground and the Confederate movements were such that the Federals were given little choice; but a gap could be dangerous, so Cox ordered Sturgis forward from reserve to fill it. The leading Federal brigades at this stage had advanced more than a mile beyond the bridge; their forward progress had been slow but steady, and although their casualties were heavy the divisions were understandably elated that they had broken the Confederate defense on its right and appeared on the verge of achieving a victory over the vaunted Southerners of Lee's famous army that had so far never met defeat.

Cox's attack on his right had succeeded in occupying the high ground southeast of Sharpsburg and a part of the town itself. The effort on the left was also making progress and had reached a point about 1,200 yards from the Sharpsburg-Shepherdstown Road, Lee's return route to the Potomac if a retreat should become necessary. Should that road be cut before Hill's division arrived, even the slow-to-fight McClellan would then, at long last, commit his powerful reserve—against which there could be but feeble resistance, and it would then be all over.

It was 2:30 o'clock when A. P. Hill galloped ahead of his troops to meet Lee and inform him that five of his six brigades were making a forced march and should be up in one and one-half hours. They had been on the way since 7:30 that morning and the road they were following required a seventeen-mile march, if everything went well. There was more than the usual straggling because of the heat and dust, to say nothing of the killing pace at which their red-shirted general had been driving them. Hill was going to get his troops there if only half of them should make it by the time the grueling foot race was over.

The word of his arrival quickly spread through the ranks, with electrifying effect. This meant that there was still hope, though why only one more half-size division could be expected to balance the scales against the overwhelming strength of the Union army would seem to defy all logic. The answer lay in the fighting spirit of Lee's army, together with the unsurpassed leadership of its commanding general and his principal lieutenants, when disaster threatened even more than in times of victory.

No help could be looked for from Jackson or D. H. Hill, while Longstreet's divisions had been whittled down at the center to the point where they would be lucky to merely stay alive. With the exception of D. R. Jones' brigades, and the artillery, now using antipersonnel canister to slow Cox's assault on the Confederate right, Lee hadn't a single unit to help the hard-pressed Jones, who was fighting desperately to prevent his line from giving way at the seams.

An anxious Lee kept looking to the south, as the inexorable minutes passed, wondering whether Hill's men would come up in time. Everywhere he looked there were only Union troops and they were pushing the weary Confederates all along the line, almost—but not quite—to the point of no return, that psychological moment when the bravest spirits falter, a few men panic, and the game is up.

Toombs' Confederate brigade, the same that had immobilized Burnside's four divisions on the heights east of the Antietam, opposite Burnside's Bridge, all morning and well into the afternoon, had fallen back when the stream was crossed and was now fighting on the right of Jones' division. To Toombs' rear, in the open fields between the two important roads leading south from Sharpsburg to Harper's Ferry and Shepherdstown respectively, fields of tall Indian corn along the right provided partial screen from observation by those north of Sharpsburg and to the east.

As General Lee watched, suddenly a column of troops appeared out of nowhere, moving at a fast gait across the fields and along the road from Boteler's Ford. Calling to his side a lieutenant who happened to be carrying a telescope, Lee told him to take a good look to see if he could identify the troops. If they were Federals, it could mean the end, because this new mass of fighting men were in the rear of Jones' line—and they wore blue uniforms. The lieutenant took a long look, turned to the General, and informed him that the units were carrying Confederate flags. A. P. Hill's division at last! The men couldn't be from any other organization; the battle was not yet lost!

As Hill's division reached the combat area, two of the five brigades, Field's and Pender's, were detached to cover the

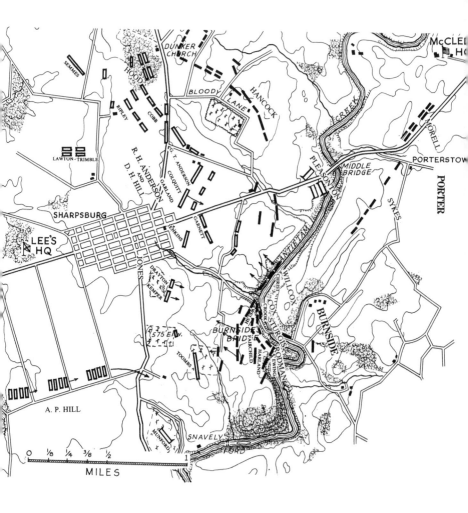

MAP 37. A. P. HILL TO THE RESCUE

The situation at about 3:45 p. m., when Burnside is advancing from his bridgehead, while A. P. Hill's Light Division is approaching the battlefield from Boteler's Ford. The situation on the north flank is as shown on the following map.

approaches by Snavely's Ford and the lower reaches of the Antietam. The other three, under Branch, Gregg and Archer, moved into line at the double and charged. In the mad scramble, Branch was killed, Gregg wounded, and 374 casualties sustained by the three attacking brigades, but a loss of 20 percent of Hill's effectives, far less than many of the other Confederate divisions which had stood on the defensive, was a low price to pay for what the short, fierce, flank attack achieved. A. P. Hill again at the psychological moment saved the day for Lee's army, tottering on the brink of complete disaster as it had been just a few moments before the Light Division came up.

Scammon's Federal brigade of the Kanawha division, in reserve behind Rodman's division on the left of Cox's line, saw the Confederate reinforcements about the same time, changed front to the left and drove the leading skirmishers back on their main body. One of Rodman's brigades included a regiment that was receiving its baptism of fire. Becoming confused in the cornfield this regiment lost its cohesion and was struck at the same time, at an angle, by the rush of A. P. Hill's men, who charged to the tune of the wild Rebel yell. Division Commander Rodman, in an effort to restore the line, was mortally wounded. Cox managed to realign his divisions to repair the break, but the sudden, unexpected counterattack by Hill's 1,800 yelling demons unnerved the Federals and forced them back. The retirement was made in good order, but it was a decisive check, and on that note the Battle of Antietam ended. Burnside's divisions remained on the west side of the Antietam, holding the high ground they had won at a cost of more than 2,300 casualties, while the Confederates, wisely deciding not to push their good fortune too far, busied themselves in intrenching the line of the road to Shepherdstown with a view to securing that vital withdrawal route, Lee's lifeline to Virginia.

Lee Defies McClellan

As the merciful darkness settled over the blood-soaked fields north, east, and south of the little town of Sharpsburg, lantern

MAP 38. THE CLOSE OF A BLOODY DAY

Situation from about 5:30 to 6 p.m. Hill's division is attacking on the south flank to stop Burnside's advance. The fighting on the north flank and center has already virtually ceased except for a long, fruitless charge made by the 7th Maine Regiment of Smith's division.

Note how the Confederate cavalry is disposed to extend the flanks of Lee's army to the river. Pleasonton's Federal cavalry seems to be in safe position, well protected by infantry; it does not appear that Pleasonton's men will be asked to take unnecessary risks.

carrying litterbearers threaded their way among the dead and wounded, sorting out the latter for removal to the barns, churches, and other buildings designated as temporary hospitals. There the overworked surgeons of the two armies administered first aid, amputated arms and legs, or gave what relief they could to those who were beyond saving. It was of course impossible to immediately gather up all the wounded, of the many thousands who lay where they had fallen, calling piteously for water, for the loved ones at home, or, stoically silent, waiting and hoping for help or even death to end their suffering.

The famous Dunker Church, at the very heart of the heavy fighting in the morning, was one of the houses of worship to serve as a hospital. Wounded soldiers of both sides sought and found sanctuary there, in spite of the Federal shells which found a mark in its white brick walls. The church was badly damaged, but the thrifty parishioners of German decent rebuilt it in 1864, only to have it blown down by a heavy windstorm in the year 1921, so that today's visitors to the Antietam battlefield can see only its foundation stones.

Lee's headquarters tent was in the same grove at the southwestern edge of town where he had first set it up upon the arrival of his army from South Mountain. One after another his generals rode in from their several posts to report the status of their corps and divisions and to confer on plans for the next day. Their feelings can only be imagined. All knew how close to disaster the army had been, nor were they under any illusions as to the fate that still hung over their heads. They could be and were justly proud of the way their troops had thrown back the massive Federal attacks, but they were all realists enough to know that a well-planned and skillfully executed Union assault on September eighteen could, and probably would, drive them into the Potomac or cut to pieces what remained of their army.

Almost 11,000 of their men and officers had become casualties in a single day at Sharpsburg, in addition to nearly 3,000 at South Mountain, Boonsboro, and Harpers Ferry. Other thousands had fallen out during the hard marches since the Battle of Manassas and were still among the missing. The army would be fortunate if it could now muster 30,000 men able to wield a musket or yank a lanyard, while McClellan's army, after its cumulative losses of somewhat more than 13,000, still had over 62,000 able bodied soldiers, half of whom had not been engaged at Antietam.

Jackson, the two Hills, Hood, Stuart, Early, and D. R. Jones, among other generals, were all there. It was not a council of war—Lee was in the habit of consulting his lieutenants and then announcing his decision—but it was obvious from the character of the reports that all the generals, Jackson included, believed that a retreat across the Potomac was not only logical but inevitable, if the army expected to remain intact to fight another day. Lee talked with each in turn, calmly gathering information and seemingly unmindful of the distressing situation which the successive reports managed to portray. Concerned over the safety of Longstreet, who had not arrived, Lee inquired if any had seen him. About that time Old Pete put in an appearance, to Lee's evident relief, for he put his arm on Longstreet's shoulder with the remark: "Here is my old war horse at last."

After sifting the reports, and much to the amazement of the assembled generals, Lee announced calmly that the army, clearly incapable of offensive action, would not retreat, but remain in its present defensive position; if McClellan chose to attack, they would meet it. The men were to remain in the lines and cooked meals would be carried to them. Stragglers between Sharpsburg and the Potomac were to be gathered up and returned to their units. The Maryland campaign was not yet over. On that note the generals were dismissed to return to their organizations.

Psychological warfare? In a sense it was, but it was more than that. Lee was supremely confident that his army, defeated as it was, could still outfight McClellan if the latter should at this late date overcome his timidity and dare to risk all in a second day's battle. Perhaps Lee still hoped that an opportunity might offer for that outflanking maneuver which he had wanted to try with Stuart and Jackson on the afternoon of the first day. Clearly he hated the thought of retreat, an admission that the Maryland invasion was a failure, even though his hard-fighting army had deprived McClellan of a victory. For Sharpsburg was certainly a stalemate—a new experience for the Army of Northern Virginia and one which was not relished by its commanding general.

McClellan Still Hesitates

The wounded Confederate tiger, at bay and still dangerous, stood fast on the night of September 17 and throughout the following day, daring the still hesitant McClellan to attack if he had the courage and the will.

During the morning of the eighteenth, two reinforcing Union divisions, Couch's and Humphreys', arrived on the field with over 12,000 men, but according to McClellan the boys were tired from marching and "needed rest and refreshment" before he would think of asking them to fight! The contrast with A. P. Hill's Confederates needs no comment.

History records that McClellan lacked both courage and character. His official report of the battle reveals his indecision and the reasons why he allowed the second day to pass without lifting a finger to exploit what he alone considered a victory. In his own words, wherein he kept alive the fiction that Lee's strength was 100,000 or more men (2½ times the actual Confederate manpower), McClellan reveals his inadequacy as a fighting army commander:

> Night closed the long and desperately contested battle of the 17th. Nearly 200,000 men and five hundred pieces of artillery were for fourteen hours engaged in this memorable battle. We had attacked the enemy in a position selected by the experienced engineer then in person directing their operations. We had driven them from their line on one flank and secured a footing within it on the other. The Army of the Potomac, notwithstanding the

moral effect incident to previous reverses, had achieved a victory over an adversary invested with the prestige of recent success. Our soldiers slept that night conquerors on a field won by their valor and covered with the dead and wounded of the enemy (no mention of the even greater Federal losses).

After a night of anxious deliberation, and a full and careful survey of the situation and condition of our army, the strength and position of the enemy, I concluded that the success of an attack on the 18th was not certain. I am aware of the fact that under ordinary circumstances a general is expected to risk a battle if he has a reasonable prospect of success; but at this critical juncture I should have had a narrow view of the condition of the country had I been willing to hazard another battle with less than an absolute assurance of success.

There was much more of the same, a rationalization ad nauseam to bolster McClellan's case for deferring a resumption of the battle, but the quoted section is sufficient in itself to contrast the character of the opposing commanders, Lee and McClellan, and to justify the former's willingness to take the calculated risk that he did.

Lee Withdraws

Although Lee had indicated to McClellan his willingness to continue the battle, he had probably learned of the arrival of Union reinforcements, and had another day to think over what his generals had advised on the evening of the seventeenth. It would be prudent, however disappointing, to retire to Virginia and seek a more favorable opportunity to accomplish the purpose which the now fruitless invasion of Maryland had failed to achieve.

The word was passed to his lieutenants. After midnight, September 18-19, the retrograde movement was initiated, with Longstreet in the lead and Fitz Lee's cavalry brigade to cover the withdrawal. All night long and well into the morning the Confederate columns plodded south and splashed through the waters of the Potomac at the ford a mile and a half below

Shepherdstown. There was no interference from the Union army, not even an attempt by the cavalry to harass the retreat, which suggests rather strongly that McClellan had permanently surrendered the initiative to his "defeated" opponent.

Safely across the Potomac with all his troops, wagons, and wounded, Lee moved the army a short distance back from the river and went into bivouac, leaving the reserve artillery with 44 guns and a couple of small infantry brigades to discourage a possible Federal attempt to effect a crossing by the ford the army had just used.

Shortly after midnight of the 19th, General Pendleton, whom Lee had charged with the responsibility of guarding the ford, woke the Commanding General with an alarming report that McClellan had sent Porter's corps across the Potomac at an upper ford while the Federal artillery pounded the rear guard with a heavy bombardment. The excited minister-turned-gen-

BOTELER'S FORD, FROM THE MARYLAND SIDE
Scene of the disaster to the 118th Pennsylvania Regiment.

eral told Lee that the infantry had retreated and all the Confederate guns had been captured.

Lee, although disturbed by the news, was reluctant to undertake a counterattack in the darkness, but Jackson, when summoned, took a more serious view of the matter. With Lee's permission, he sent A. P. Hill's division back to the river at once. Having turned back Burnside's corps on the afternoon of the seventeenth, Hill's men were keen to add a few more laurels to those already earned by the Light Division. Hill found that Pendleton had been badly misinformed, in that a Union brigade had crossed at Boteler's Ford and had captured only four rather than forty-four guns, all the others having been safely brought off by the retreating Confederate rear guard. On seeing the approach of Hill's whole division, the Federal brigade commander at once started to pull back across the river. Unfortunately one of his regiments, the 118th Pennsylvania, failed to get the order, and remained to receive the full impact of A. P. Hill's customary fiery assault. The Federal soldiers, who had been in the service only three days prior to Antietam, stood their ground bravely for a short time, but presently broke and poured back over the steep embankment, almost a cliff. Some were impeded by fallen timber, others floundered in the river. The Confederates rushed to the top of the bank and poured destructive fire into the fugitives, hitting many in the act of trying to clear the timber and others in the water. A number who took refuge in a mill building were killed by their own artillery, which was firing with defective fuzes. The regiment lost 71 killed, and several hundred wounded and captured.

After this sad affair, McClellan made no further effort to pursue the Confederate forces. For all practical purposes the campaign was over.

The North, at first, accepted McClellan's victory claim at face value. Later, when all the facts emerged, there was a less enthusiastic reaction. But for President Lincoln, patiently waiting and hoping for even a quasi-victory to afford an excuse

LINCOLN VISITS MCCLELLAN AFTER THE BATTLE
In addition to McClellan and the President we can identify, to the right of
Lincoln, Henry J. Hunt, Chief of Artillery; Fitz John Porter; two unknowns;
Gen. Slocum; and the volatile cavalryman Judson Kilpatrick. Who else can the
reader spot? Allan Pinkerton ought to be lurking somewhere. Who is the
bearded ruffian at the far left?

to issue his Emancipation Proclamation, the fact that Lee's invasion had been turned back and the Confederate army had been the first to leave the field was believed sufficient to establish a foundation for the historic pronouncement. The bloodiest single day's battle of the Civil War was therefore not fought in vain. For it was made the vehicle whereby the War Between the States was transformed from a family dispute into a crusade for human freedom. Truly it can be written, of that famous battle on the banks of the Antietam, that God works in a mysterious way His wonders to perform.

Lee Congratulates his Army

Shortly after the return to Virginia, Lee issued to his troops General Orders No. 116, in language somewhat less restrained than was customary with him. Perhaps he felt that the exertions and sacrifices of the summer campaigns deserved more attention than usual; it may also have been in his mind that he had demanded, and received, military efforts that stretched the limits of human endurance. An uninhibited recognition of his army's superior achievements, without boasting, might have a salutary psychological effect, even to the extent of a healthy future reduction in the straggling that had characterized the recent operations in Maryland. The congratulations of the commanding general were conveyed to his army in these words:

> Since your great victories around Richmond, you have defeated the enemy at Cedar Mountain, expelled him from the Rappahannock, and, after a conflict of three days, utterly repulsed him on the plains of Manassas and forced him to take shelter within the fortifications around his capital. Without halting for repose, you crossed the Potomac, stormed the heights of Harper's Ferry, made prisoners of more than 11,000 men and captured upwards of 75 pieces of artillery, all their small arms and other munitions of war. While one corps of the army was thus engaged, the other insured its success by arresting at Boonesborough the combined armies of the enemy, advancing under their favorite general to the relief of their beleagured comrades. On the field of Sharpsburg with less than one-third of his numbers, you resisted from daylight until dark the whole army of the enemy and repulsed every attack along his entire front of more than 4 miles in extent. The whole of the following day you stood prepared to resume the conflict on the same ground and retired the next morning without molestation across the Potomac . . . History records few examples of greater fortitude and endurance than this army has exhibited . . .

APPENDIX

Text

A great deal of background reading as well as much detailed research is a prerequisite to the writing of a relatively short and general treatise on a campaign as complex as that of Second Manassas-Antietam—the same as for any complete account of a smaller segment of the Civil War or a definitive biography. To cite such sources, paragraph by paragraph, would unduly increase the size and cost of the book while contributing little to the enjoyment of the average reader. Many even protest that they are distracted and annoyed by voluminous footnotes. For those who wish to pursue their investigations into bibliographical crannies, the accompanying reading list will be helpful and the citations in some of the books will point the way to additional research. At the same time, the determined searcher for obscure details will not have his fun spoiled by a too-plain blazing of the trail.

The basic materials for a study of the Civil War are now fairly well known, especially the primary sources. In general the only documents remaining unexplored are collections of private papers and correspondence which have not yet been published or deposited in institutions open to the general public. A possible exception, in the case of the Antietam campaign, is a manuscript history by General Ezra A. Carman, in the Manuscript Division of the Library of Congress, described more in detail in the sections following. The researcher who is interested in new discoveries would do well to examine this lengthy and valuable document, as well as the Carman manuscripts on other Civil War campaigns.

Reading List

Battles and Leaders of the Civil War, Vol. III. Contributions by Union and Confederate Officers. New York: The Century Company, 1884.

Blackford, Lt. Col. W. W., C. S. A. *War Years With Jeb Stuart.*

Carman, Gen. Ezra A. *The Antietam Campaign* (manuscript); a very bulky and detailed study, deposited in the Library of Congress, Manuscript Division. Gen. Carman's maps are in the Map Division.

Carter, Capt. R. G., U. S. A. *Four Brothers in Blue, From Bull Run to Appomattox.* Washington: 1913.

Cox, Maj. Gen. Jacob D. *Military Reminiscences of the Civil War,* 2 volumes. Charles Scribner's Sons, 1900.

Cullum, Bvt. Maj. Gen. George W. *Register of the Officers and Graduates of the U. S. Military Academy,* 3 volumes. Houghton-Mifflin and Company, 1891.

Foote, Shelby. *The Civil War, Ft. Sumter to Perryville.* New York: Random House, 1958.

Freeman, Douglas Southall. *R. E. Lee,* and *Lee's Lieutenants.* New York: Charles Scribner's Sons, 1935 and 1944.

Hamlin, Percy Gardner. *Old Bald Head (General A. S. Ewell).* Strasburg, Va.: Shenandoah Publishing House, Inc., 1940.

Hassler, Warren W., Jr. *General George B. McClellan—Shield of the Union.* Baton Rouge: Louisiana State University Press 1957.

Henderson, Colonel G. F. R. *Stonewall Jackson and the American Civil War,* Vol. II. New York: Longmans, Green and Co., 1927.

Livermore, Thomas L. *Numbers and Losses in the Civil War.* Bloomington: Indiana University Press, 1957.

McClellan, George B. *McClellan's Own Story.* New York: Charles L. Webster and Co., 1887.

McClellan, H. B., C. S. A. *The Campaigns of Stuart's Cavalry.* Boston: Houghton, Mifflin & Co., 1885.

Palfrey, Francis W. *The Antietam and Fredericksburg,* Vol V of *Campaigns of the Civil War.* New York: Charles Scribner's Sons, 1882.

Ropes, John Codman. *The Army Under Pope.* New York: Chas. Scribner's Sons, 1882.

The Story of the Civil War; Part II, The Campaigns of 1862. New York: G. P. Putman's Sons, 1898.

Schenck, Martin. *Up Came Hill, the Story of the Light Division and Its Leaders.* Harrisburg: The Stackpole Company, 1958.

Sorrel, Moxley G. *Recollections of a Confederate Staff Officer.* New York: Neale Publishing Co., 1905.

Steele, Matthew Forney. *American Campaigns,* 2 volumes. Washington: War Department Document No. 324.

Thomason, Maj. John. *Jeb Stuart.* New York: 1934.

Vandiver, Frank. *Mighty Stonewall.* New York: McGraw-Hill Book Co., 1957.

Virginia Campaign of General Pope in 1862, The. Papers read before the Military Historical Society of Massachusetts in 1876, 1877, and 1880. Vol. II. Boston: Ticknor and Co., 1886.

War of the Rebellion: *Official Records of the Union and Confederate Armies.* Government Printing Office: 1882-1900.

Williams, T. Harry. *Lincoln and His Generals.* New York: Alfred A. Knopf, 1952.

Maps

Good maps are essential to a full understanding of any military operation, and are greatly appreciated by most readers of books dealing with the Civil War. The Atlas to the *Official Records of the Rebellion,* and the original maps produced by the Confederate cartographers Jed Hotchkiss and W. W. Blackford, the Federal mapmaker Micheler, and others, are to be found in the Map Division, Library of Congress and the National Archives. These maps, excellent in draftsmanship and showing the terrain in fine detail, are useful. Unfortunately they are for the most part quite inaccurate as to horizontal control, often show roads which did not exist, and plot the courses of streams apparently from a superficial inspection of the terrain. The errors are not uniform and cannot be corrected for except by a complete resurvey and a redrawing. Vertical control is sketchy, consisting mostly of hachures which only portray the general location and existence of hills and mountains, but not their relative elevations or exact shapes. A notable exception is the large-scale map of the Antietam battlefield which was surveyed accurately by engineers, after the war, under the direction of a board comprising both Federal and Confederate officers. On this map General E. A. Carman, a member of the board, has plotted the troop dispositions in a series of 14 situations during the one day of the battle. The completed series of·maps were published by the Government Printing Office as an official document, and photo copies may be obtained from the Library of Congress. Carman, who commanded a regiment at Antietam, was assisted by Jed Hotchkiss, Harry Heth, and others, in his postwar studies.

In order to obtain comparable accuracy for the Manassas campaign, modern contoured maps obtained from the U. S. Geological Survey have been used for the basic topography. On these maps, redrawn and simplified somewhat by omitting some of the contours and other details which might clutter the reproduced versions, have been plotted the roads, fords, bridges, towns, woods, and other topographic features as they existed in 1862. This information has been obtained from the Civil War maps referred to above, plus the Board Map used in the Fitz John Porter hearing in 1878. In the case of the Manassas battlefield, the stream lines and the road system on the old maps were especially inaccurate. Fortunately the Park Historian, Mr. Naisawald, kindly supplied corrected data obtained as a result of much terrestrial and air reconnaissance. For example, though the "unfinished railroad" is easily distinguishable on the ground, the Haymarket-Sudley Road is not, and many of the roads shown on the early maps were merely cowpaths or tracks made by the heavy troop columns marching across the pastures and fields.

The Chantilly battlefield provided a special problem, since even many of the participants did not locate it within several miles of where the fight occurred. With Mr. Naisawald's assistance, this battlefield, only three miles west of Fairfax, has been identified beyond a shadow of a doubt. It is to be hoped that some day it will be adequately marked. Again, the Cedar Mountain battlefield required extensive reconnaissance, and the preparation of new maps.

The general maps are mostly from a set of 1:125,000 maps originally surveyed by the U. S. Geological Survey about 1880. They are contoured, and show the roads and towns much as they were in 1862. Being no longer reproduced in quantity, they are little known, but photo copies may be obtained.

The endpaper maps are photos of a plastic relief map made by the U. S. Army Engineers, which shows the towns and highway system as they exist today. The purpose is to show readers how they may follow the general routes of the maneuvering forces, and aid them in visiting the battlefields in their own cars. At the same time these maps give a good impression of the terrain.

The plotting of troop positions and movements for the

Battle of Second Manassas, August 28-30, is from official maps at the headquarters of the Manassas Battlefield National Park. The Park Superintendent, Mr. Francis Wilshin, maintains a set of 12 detailed situation maps on which the troop positions were plotted in 1957 by himself, Park Historian L. VanL. Naisawald, and Dr. Warren Hassler, Jr., of the History Department, Pennsylvania State University. Dr. Hassler provided full documentation.

The troop locations on the Antietam battle maps are from the 14 official maps produced by the Board of Officers previously mentioned, and originally sold as an album by the Government Printing Office.

The dispositions for the Battle of Cedar Mountain are from the Official Records and the Atlas thereto. The dispositions during the Battle of Chantilly are from the Official Records and a map accompanying a paper presented before the Military Historical Society of Massachusetts by Bvt. Brig. Gen. Chas. F. Walcott, USV. Further data furnished by Mr. L. VanL. Naisawald.

The symbols representing troop units are similar to those in use during and after the Civil War. Federals are solid black, Confederate units are open rectangles. For the battle maps, as differentiated from the maneuver maps, plotting is down to regiments, this enabling us to show the organization, frontage, and depth of the several brigades and divisions. It also permits a more accurate plotting where component parts of divisions and corps are scattered. Cavalry units generally occupied more frontage but less depth than the symbols indicate. With a few exceptions, artillery batteries are omitted, it being impracticable to plot them on such small maps, and considering the scope of the book.

ORGANIZATION, STRENGTHS, AND LOSSES

The Campaign of Second Manassas (Bull Run)

The data presented herein are derived from reports and returns of units, to be found in *The Official Records of the Rebellion*, Series I, Vol XII, Parts II and III; Vol XIX, Parts I and II; *Battles and Leaders of the Civil War* (Century Co.), Vol II; "Strength and Forces under Pope and Lee," by Lt. Col. William Allan, C. S. A., in "The Virginia Campaign of 1862," *Military Historical Society of Massachusetts*, Vol II (1886); and Thomas L. Livermore, *Numbers and Losses in the Civil War*.

During the campaigns of August-September, 1862 neither side rendered satisfactory strength returns. Many reports, especially for the Confederate forces, are missing entirely from the *Official Records*. In compiling data for the Federals, one must rely mainly on Pope's return for July 31, supplemented by a number of divisional and brigade returns and a few corps returns for August 9, 10, 16, and 21. These returns are incomplete, inconsistent, and subject to differing interpretations. The Confederate situation is much worse, only Ewell's division having rendered a complete return for the period in question. Furthermore it is suspected that the Confederate data as to "Captured or Missing" are, in some cases, very incomplete; for example Jackson reported only 4 men missing after the Battle of Cedar Mountain. Data for the units other than Ewell's has been derived by consulting secondary sources. Allan's and Ropes' figures have been freely used here, especially for comparison, though it may be suspected that Allan underestimated Lee's strength. A hint of this is seen in the fact that on July 27 Lee in a telegram to Jackson referred to A. P. Hill as having over 18,000 men, whereas most authorities never credit Hill with more than 12,000. Again, Ewell reports his strength as being 7,500 or 8,800, depending on which column of his report is used; yet he is usually stated to have not to exceed 5,000.

Nevertheless, the figures cited in the following tables conform to the commonly used smaller totals for Confederates.

TABLE I—THE BATTLE OF CEDAR MOUNTAIN, AUG. 9, 1862

The Federal Forces, a Part of Pope's Army of Virginia

Unit	Commander	Strength	Killed	Wounded	Losses Captured or Missing	Total
II Army Corps	Maj. Gen. Nathaniel P. Banks					
1st Div	Brig. Gen. Alpheus S. Williams	3,700	171	588	453	1,212
2d Div	Brig. Gen. Christopher C. Augur	3,150	120	699	127	946
Arty		800	7	27	6	40
Cavalry brig	Brig. Gen. George D. Bayard	1,150	10	45	6	61
	Totals for the corps	8,800	313	1,364	598	2,275

The Confederate Forces, a Part of the Army of Northern Virginia

Unit	Commander	Strength	Killed	Wounded	Losses Captured or Missing	Total
Provisional corps or "wing"	Maj. Gen. Thomas J. Jackson					
1st Div	Brig. Gen. Charles S. Winder					
	Brig. Gen. William B. Taliaferro	4,000	158	574	0	732
Light Div	Maj. Gen. Ambrose P. Hill	12,000	56	368	2	426
3d Div	Maj. Gen. Richard S. Ewell	7,200	17	178	2	197
Cavalry brig	Brig. Gen. Beverly H. Robertson	1,200	(casualties included in 1st Div)			
	Totals for corps	24,400	231	1,120	4	1,355

Summary	Strength on field	Losses
Banks	8,800	2,275
Jackson	24,400	1,355

TABLE II—THE CAMPAIGN OF SECOND MANASSAS, AUG. 27–SEPT. 1, 1862

*The Federal Forces, Major General John Pope's Army of Virginia,
With Reinforcements from The Army of the Potomac*

Unit	Commander	Strength	Killed	Wounded	Captured or Missing	Total
Army of Virginia						
I Army Corps	Maj. Gen. Franz Sigel	3,800	97	368	139	604
1st Div	Brig. Gen. Robert Schenck	2,500	47	294	60	401
2d Div	Brig. Gen. Adolph von Steinwehr	2,800	74	374	86	534
3d Div	Brig. Gen. Carl Schurz	2,000	70	296	81	437
Indep brig	Brig. Gen. Robert H. Milroy	200	4	22	0	26
Corps arty						
Totals for corps		11,000	292	1,345	367	2,004
II Army Corps	Maj. Gen. Nathaniel P. Banks	3,000	0	0	15	15
1st Div	Brig. Gen. A. S. Williams	4,000	4	36	68	108
2d Div	Brig. Gen. Geo. S. Greene					
Total for corps		7,000	4	36	83	123
III Army Corps	Maj. Gen. Irvin McDowell	9,000	324	1,560	844	2,728
1st Div	Brig. Gen. Rufus King	9,000	192	845	875	1,912
2d Div	Brig. Gen. James E. Ricketts					
Arty & Cav		500	(casualties incl. in div totals)			
Totals for corps		18,500	516	2,405	1,719	4,640
Attached units						
Reynold's div	Maj. Gen. John F. Reynolds	4,700	66	399	211	676
(from Porter's corps)						
Piatt's brig	Brig. Gen. A. Sanders Piatt	800	16	94	112	222
(from Sturgis' Res. Corps)						
Scammon's brig	Col. E. Parker Scammon	1,800	14	50	42	106
(from Cox's div)						
Beardsley's cav brig	Col. John Beardsley	1,500	3	15	65	83
(atchd I Corps)						

| | | | *Losses* | | | |
Unit	Commander	Strength	Killed	Wounded	Captured or Missing	Total
Buford's cav brig (atchd II Corps)	Brig. Gen. John Buford	1,500	15	35	150	200
Bayard's cav brig (atchd III Corps)	Brig. Gen. Geo. Bayard	1,500	13	44	70	127
Totals for cav. brigs.		4,500	31	94	285	410
1st Brig 1st Div (VI Corps)	Brig. Gen. Geo. W. Taylor	600	9	126	204	339
VI Corps						
Army of the Potomac Troops						
III Army Corps	Maj. Gen. Samuel P. Heintzelman					
1st Div	Maj. Gen. Philip Kearny	4,500	110	741	178	1,029
2d Div	Maj. Gen. Joseph Hooker	5,500	154	793	280	1,227
Totals for corps		10,000	264	1,543	458	2,256
V Army Corps	Maj. Gen. Fitz John Porter					
1st Div	Maj. Gen. Geo. W. Morell	5,600	178	772	277	1,227
2d Div	Brig. Gen. Geo. Sykes	3,400	152	583	180	915
Corps arty		1,100	1	7	1	9
Totals for corps		10,100	331	1,362	458	2,151
IX Army Corps	Maj. Gen. Jesse L. Reno					
1st Div	Maj. Gen. Issac I. Stevens	4,000	94	585	67	746
2d Div	Maj. Gen. Reno	4,000	109	415	252	776
Totals for corps		8,000	203	1,000	319	1,522
Aggregate for Pope's army		77,000	1,746	8,445	4,258	14,449
The Confederate Forces, General Robert E. Lee's Army of Northern Virginia						
Jackson's command	Maj. Gen. Thomas J. Jackson					
Jackson's div	Brig Gen. William B. Taliaferro	5,000	223	877	6	1,106
Light Div	Maj. Gen. A. P. Hill	12,000	259	1,583	3	1,845
Ewell's div	Maj. Gen. R. S. Ewell	7,200	370	1,169	28	1,567
Totals for Jackson's command		24,200	852	3,629	37	4,518
Longstreet's command	Maj. Gen. James Longstreet					
Anderson's div	Maj. Gen. Richard H. Anderson	7,000	72	264	8	344
Jones' div	Brig. Gen. David R. Jones	5,200	156	1,108	6	1,270
Wilcox's div	Brig. Gen. Cadmus M. Wilcox	4,000	50	279	4	333
Hood's div	Brig. Gen. John B. Hood	3,800	50	827	13	972
Kemper's div	Brig. Gen. Jas. L. Kemper	4,000	113	857	7	977
Evans' Indep Brig	Brig. Gen. Nathan G. Evans	2,200	133	593	8	734
Arty		2,500	9	29		38
Totals, Longstreet's command		27,800	665	3,957	46	4,668

	Strength				
Cavalry division ....Maj. Gen. J. E. B. Stuart (Brigs. of Fitz Lee & Robertson)	3,000	37	161	36	234
Aggregate for Army of Northern Virginia	55,000	1,554	7,747	119	9,420

Note: In the above, an assumption was made that the casualties for F. Lee's cavalry brigade were the same as those for Robertson. The latter and Pelham's battery, only, rendered returns.

Summary:

	Strength on field	Losses
Pope	77,000	14,449
Lee	55,000	9,420

Comment: Two other authorities have derived the following over-all statistics:

	Strength	
	Pope	Lee
U. S. National Park Service (Manassas)	78,000	55,000
John Codman Ropes	70,000	54,300

The lack of accurate data as to the artillery and cavalry, and the various assumptions made, account for many of the differences as to strengths cited by various sources.

TABLE III—BATTLE OF SOUTH MOUNTAIN (FOX'S AND TURNER'S GAPS)
(From *Battles and Leaders*)

	Forces engaged	Losses	
Federals	24,000	1,800	approximate
Confederates	15,000	1,600	approximate

TABLE IV—BATTLE OF CRAMPTON'S GAP
(From *Battles and Leaders*)

	Forces engaged	Losses	
Federals	6,500	533	
Confederates	2,200	749	(partial report)

TABLE V—BATTLE OF ANTIETAM

As for the Manassas campaign, the strength and casualty returns from both armies are incomplete and inadequate in all respects. After considering several sources, it has been decided to use the statistics derived by Bvt. Brig. Gen. Ezra A. Carman, USV, to be found in Chapter 23 of his manuscript *History of the Antietam Campaign* (Manuscript Division, Library of Congress). Not only was Gen. Carman a regimental commander in the battle, but he was a member of a Board which convened for a number of years after the war to study the battle and survey the battlefield. On this board were Gen. Harry Heth, CSA, Maj. Jed Hotchkiss, CSA, and others, with whom Carman consulted. He also corresponded and visited with most surviving unit commanders and adjutants on both sides, in an effort to piece out the official reports. He likewise consulted unit histories and other documents as well as the *Official Records*. In view of this, it is believed that his conclusions are probably as reliable as can be obtained. Carman points out that Confederate figures are based on "numbers engaged" and that therefore a like frame of reference must be used for the Federal data if a fair comparison is to be obtained. Such strength figures are, of course, far less than the number of men available on the Federal side, as has been pointed out in the text. For the Confederates, however, the numbers "engaged" were probably close to the number then available. There had been heavy losses in Lee's army owing to illness, hunger, hot weather, lack of water and shoes, and other causes such as the rapid and prolonged marches which whittled down the strength of Confederate units as a result of inordinate straggling. Many of these men rejoined their units after the battle. On the Union side the gross difference between number "available" and number "engaged" was caused to a large extent by McClellan's poor generalship. But in fairness to the lower unit commanders, it must be stated that all units were also below their roster strength owing to detachments, details, sickness, furlough, and so on. Most researchers feel that such subtractions exceeded 20 percent.

The figures given below are extracted from the Carman manuscript. For the Federals, there is also a column showing the "roster strength" of the several corps, as reported by McClellan.

ARMY OF THE POTOMAC
Major General George B. McClellan

| Unit | Commander | Roster Strength | Strength "engaged" | Losses | | | |
				Killed	Wounded	Captured or Missing	Total
I Corps	Maj. Gen. Joseph Hooker; Brig. Gen. John P. Hatch; Brig. Gen. Abner Doubleday				1		1
1st Div			3,425	140	638	34	812
2d Div	Brig. Gen. Jas. B. Ricketts		3,158	172	946	86	1,204
3d Div	Brig. Gen. Geo. G. Meade; Brig. Gen. Truman Seymour		2,855	105	466	2	573
I Corps totals		14,856	9,438	417	2,051	122	2,590
II Corps	Maj. Gen. Edwin V. Sumner				2		2
1st Div	Maj. Gen. Israel B. Richardson; Brig. Gen. John C. Caldwell; Brig. Gen. Winfield S. Hancock		4,029	210	941	16	1,167
2d Div	Maj. Gen. John Sedgwick		5,437	373	1,593	244	2,210
3d Div	Brig. Gen. William French		5,740	300	1,324	136	1,760
II Corps totals		18,813	15,206	883	3,860	396	5,139
IV Corps							
1st Div only	Maj. Gen. Darius N. Couch				9	(Sept. 18)	9
V Corps	Maj. Gen. Fitz John Porter						
1st Div	Maj. Gen. Geo. W. Morell			not engaged			
2d Div	Brig. Gen. George Sykes (5 bns only)		2,274	12	85	1	98
3d Div	Brig. Gen. Andrew A. Humphreys			not engaged			
Res Arty			950	5	5	1	11
V Corps totals		12,930	3,224	17	90	2	109
VI Corps	Maj. Gen. William B. Franklin						
1st Div	Maj. Gen. Henry W. Slocum			not engaged			
2d Div	Maj. Gen. William F. Smith (Irwin's Brigade only)		2,585	71	335	33	439
VI Corps totals		12,300	2,585	71	335	33	439
IX Corps	Maj. Gen. Ambrose E. Burnside; Brig. Gen. Jacob D. Cox						
1st Div	Brig. Gen. Orlando B. Willcox		3,248	46	285	7	338
2d Div	Brig. Gen. Samuel D. Sturgis		3,254	136	532	11	679
3d Div	Brig. Gen. Isaac P. Rodman		2,914	220	787	70	1,077
Kanawha Div	Brig. Gen. Jacob D. Cox		3,154	36	192	27	255
IX Corps totals		13,819	12,693	438	1,796	115	2,349

| | | | Losses | | | |
Unit	Commander	Strength Engaged	Killed	Wounded	Captured or Missing	Total
XII Corps	Maj. Gen. Joseph K. F. Mansfield; Brig. Gen. Alpheus S. Williams	10,126				
1st Div	Brig. Gen. Williams; Brig. Gen. S. W. Crawford; Brig. Gen. Geo. H. Gordon	4,735	160	864	54	1,078
2d Div	Brig. Gen. Geo. S. Greene	2,504	115	522	31	668
Corps Arty		392				
XII Corps totals		7,631	275	1,386	85	1,756
		55,956				
Cavalry Div	Brig. Gen. Alfred Pleasonton	4,320	7	23		30
Aggregate, Army of Potomac		87,164	2,108	9,549	753	12,410

ARMY OF NORTHERN VIRGINIA
General Robert E. Lee

| | | | Losses | | | |
Unit	Commander	Strength Engaged	Killed	Wounded	Captured or Missing	Total
Longstreet's command	Maj. Gen. James Longstreet			2		2
McLaws' div	Maj. Gen. Lafayette McLaws	2,961	160	933	26	1,119
Anderson's div	Maj. Gen. Richard H. Anderson	4,000	172	954	152	1,278
Jones' div	Brig. Gen. David R. Jones	3,392	103	605	50	758
Walker's div	Brig. Gen. John G. Walker	3,994	184	839	97	1,120
Hood's div	Brig. Gen. John Hood	2,304	123	815	87	1,025
Evans' Indep. Brig.	Brig. Gen. Nathan G. Evans	399	13	60	11	84
Corps Arty		596	14	103	2	119
Totals, Longstreet's command		17,646	796	4,311	425	5,505
Jackson's command	Maj. Gen. Thos. J. Jackson					
Ewell's div	Brig. Gen. A. R. Lawton; Brig. Gen. Jubal A. Early	4,127	196	1,102	40	1,338
Light div	Maj. Gen. A. P. Hill	2,568	70	341	6	417
Jackson's div	Brig. Gen. John R. Jones; Brig. Gen. William E. Starke, Col. A. G. Grigsby	2,094	145	486	17	648
Hill's div	Maj. Gen. Daniel H. Hill	5,795	352	1,439	519	2,310
Totals, Jackson's command		14,584	763	3,368	582	4,713
Reserve Arty		621	4	47		51
Cavalry	Maj. Gen. J. E. B. Stuart	4,500	10	28	11	49
Aggregate, Army of Northern Virginia		37,351	1,546	7,754	1,018	10,318

COMMENTARY
by D. Scott Hartwig

As a young boy growing up at the time of the Civil War Centennial, I once selected *From Cedar Mountain to Antietam* from the shelf of Civil War books at the local public library. Why I picked this particular book, I cannot recall precisely, but I believe it was because I had heard something about Antietam that aroused my curiosity. It was one of the first books on the American Civil War I ever read. Apparently, it made a lasting impression upon me, for I have had a passion for the Civil War and a lifelong fascination with the Battle of Antietam and Maryland Campaign of 1862 ever since.

The passion I, and thousands of others, have for our Civil War did not diminish with the passing of the Civil War Centennial in 1965. It grew stronger, and our study of this conflict, whose repercussions were still being felt in that final year of the Centennial, probed ever deeper. In our insatiable quest to learn more, dozens of undiscovered collections of wartime papers, manuscripts, diaries, and journals of men and women who had experienced the war were uncovered. These expanded our knowledge of the war and the people who fought it and often challenged previously accepted interpretations of events. It has been more than three decades since General Stackpole published *From Cedar Mountain to Antietam*. New scholarship has revised or challenged interpretations that were embraced by General Stackpole and other historians in 1959.

Stonewall Brigade at Cedar Mountain

One relatively minor incident illustrates this point. It concerns the alleged disgraceful behavior of the famous Stonewall Brigade at the Battle of Cedar Mountain. General Stackpole writes (p. 66–67) that this brigade "broke" and streamed to the rear in panic. He does, however, note that this was according to General Branch, whose brigade came to the support of the Stonewall Brigade. Space limitations may have precluded General Stackpole from elaborating upon this incident. Robert K. Krick, in his masterful tactical study *Stonewall Jackson at Cedar Mountain*, gave the incident careful attention, in both the text and a separate appendix. His conclusion, which was ably supported by rare sources that he had unearthed, was that General Branch's claim that the Stonewall Brigade was routed at Cedar Mountain was utterly false: It was merely Branch's unsavory effort to shed more glory upon himself and his command at the expense of another unit. Of the five regiments that composed the Stonewall Brigade, only the 27th Virginia fled the field. The remaining four regiments held their position and fought stoutly. In vindicating the performance of this brigade Krick noted, "At Cedar Mountain the Confederate army captured three Northern flags. Each and every one of the three was captured by the Stonewall Brigade. That accomplishment does not begin to mesh with Branch's self-serving picture of a 'celebrated' but 'beaten and broken,' 'routed and fleeing' brigade."[1]

George B. McClellan and Command of the Army of the Potomac

Another controversial point, considerably more important than the conduct of the Stonewall Brigade, concerns the question of command of the Army of the Potomac during the Maryland Campaign. Maj. Gen. George B. McClellan's memoirs, which were published in 1887 following his death, contain the remarkable claim that when he led the Army of the Potomac out of Washington, in September 1862, he did so on his own authority, without orders from President Lincoln. According to McClellan, the question of who would command the army in the field was still undecided when the army sortied forth. "I determined to solve the question for myself," wrote McClellan, "and when I moved out from Washington with my staff and personal escort I left my card with P.P.C. written upon it, at the White House, War Office, and Secretary Seward's house, and went on my way." McClellan went on to thrill his readers with the claim that "I fought the battles of

South Mountain and Antietam with a halter around my neck, for if the Army of the Potomac had been defeated and I had survived I would, no doubt, have been tried for assuming authority without orders, and, in the state of feeling which so unjustly condemned the innocent and most meritorious General F. J. Porter, I would probably have been condemned to death."[2]

The two men who might have disputed McClellan's version of things, Lincoln and Halleck, were both dead by 1887. Consequently, numerous authors and historians, including General Stackpole, accepted McClellan's account. After all, there were no written orders from Lincoln, Halleck, or Secretary of War Stanton placing McClellan in command of the field army in the voluminous correspondence published in the *Official Records of the War of the Rebellion*. The only order on record was one dated September 2, 1862, from the War Department that placed McClellan in command of Washington's fortifications. This lent further credence to McClellan's claim. If there were no written orders, perhaps McClellan's account was accurate. The administration and the War Department were in a state of confusion following the defeat of Pope at 2nd Manassas, and it seemed plausible that a general of McClellan's ego might have assumed command on his own authority. To General Stackpole, the evidence available supported this view. He concludes that "the President's decision was to put McClellan in command only of the troops in the defenses of Washington. He had no intention of allowing the general to lead the army into the field or to fight a battle, and said so, without any reservations, to a number of intimates" (p. 293). But this accounting of affairs has recently been taken to task as inaccurate.

At the root of the confusion over McClellan's command status in Maryland is the absence of written orders restoring McClellan to command of the army in the field. The issue is further obscured by the notion that following the withdrawal of the Army of the Potomac from the Peninsula, McClellan was relieved of command and the army was turned over to Pope. McClellan was never relieved of command. During the 2nd Manassas Campaign his army was largely removed from his control and placed under Pope's orders. McClellan was still in command of the Army of the

Potomac, although by August 30 the only troops of that army still under his direct command were his headquarters personnel. Then came the defeat at 2nd Manassas and the scare in Washington that resulted in Lincoln's placing McClellan in command of all troops as they came within the fortifications. In this instance it was necessary to issue a written order defining McClellan's authority to avoid confusion with Pope, who was already questioning his own status.

On September 5 Pope was relieved of command. On that same day Lincoln and Halleck, after an unsuccessful effort to convince Ambrose E. Burnside to accept command, visited McClellan at his house in Washington. Halleck, in testimony to the Congressional Committee on the Conduct of the War, stated that in the meeting Lincoln point-blank said to McClellan, "General, you will take command of the forces in the field." Although Lincoln later denied that he had placed McClellan in field command (p. 293), noted Civil War historian and biographer of McClellan, Stephen W. Sears, doubted Lincoln was speaking honestly. Sears wrote, "Lincoln's denials were most probably efforts to distance himself from the matter so as to avoid political repercussions."[3]

McClellan's orders then were verbal. There was no need for written orders. Since McClellan had never been officially relieved of command of the Army of the Potomac, there was no need to reappoint him. Lincoln's verbal instructions were all that was necessary to clear up any uncertainty McClellan may have had concerning his status of command. Perhaps by the time McClellan penned his memoirs he had simply forgotten his meeting with Lincoln and Halleck on September 5, or perhaps, as Stephen Sears wrote, McClellan's account "was another of the fictions he spun so effortlessly."[4]

The Army of the Potomac in the Maryland Campaign

The vast disparity in troop strength between the Army of the Potomac and Army of Northern Virginia has been highlighted by virtually every study of the Maryland Campaign. General Stackpole writes that McClellan "had seventeen veteran divisions at his disposal, some 90,000 men altogether," which gave him "almost a

two-to-one superiority over Lee . . ." (p. 308). By simply comparing numbers it would seem that McClellan possessed an immense
advantage over Lee. But then, sheer numbers do not guarantee
battlefield victory. There are countless other factors, such as leadership, morale, equipment, training, and experience, that contribute to success. In many of these critical areas the Army of the
Potomac fell short of its adversary.

To begin with, it was the Army of the Potomac in name only.
This was not the superbly organized and equipped army McClellan had commanded on the Peninsula. Only the 2nd and 6th
Corps, Sykes Division of the 5th Corps, and Couch's Division of
the 4th Corps had participated in the Peninsula Campaign. The
1st and 12th Corps had both belonged to Pope's Army of Virginia.
Ambrose E. Burnside's 9th Corps had been conducting independent operations along the Carolina and Virginia coasts, and the
Kanawha Division of Brig. Gen. Jacob Cox had been drawn from
its area of operations in the Kanawha Valley in western Virginia.
Essentially, the "Army of the Potomac" in Maryland was three
separate armies: the Peninsula army, Pope's army, and Burnside's
independent 9th Corps. McClellan had to draw these forces together in eleven days, from September 3 to September 14, when
he met Lee at the Battle of South Mountain.

The army that McClellan took from Washington numbered not
90,000, but slightly over 74,000 men and 290 guns. Lee entered
Maryland with an army of close to 50,000 men, nearly all of
whom were disciplined veterans. Of McClellan's 74,000 men,
only about 54,000 were veteran troops. Nearly 20,000 men were
raw recruits with only the sketchiest of training, if they had any at
all. Of the 20,000, between 15,000 and 16,000 belonged to new
regiments, raised in answer to Lincoln's July call for 300,000
volunteers. Furthermore, 3,000 to 4,000 recruits were raised by
various states, principally New York, Massachusetts, and Pennsylvania, and sent to veteran regiments in the field. The large,
new regiments were reinforcements of dubious value. Although
the men were brave, because of their general lack of training and
discipline they were unpredictable under fire and clumsy to ma-

neuver. G. F. R. Henderson, a British observer of the Civil War, commented on the problems inherent with untrained troops:

> An ill-disciplined army lacks mobility. Marching, strange as it may appear to those who have never served with troops in the field or in protracted peace exercises, makes the greatest demands on the subordination of the men and exertions of the officers. It is no light task to bring a battalion of a thousand bayonets intact on to the field of battle at the proper time. Something more than enthusiasm is required to enable a mass of men to overcome the difficulties of bad weather and bad roads, or the sufferings of fatigue and hunger.[5]

Many of the men in the new regiments were utterly ignorant of the use and care of their weapons. In one extreme example, as the 9th New Hampshire prepared to enter the Battle of South Mountain, the men had to be shown how to load their muskets. In another instance, Charles Mills, a lieutenant in the veteran 2nd Massachusetts, remarked in a letter to his mother that Col. Ezra Carman, commanding the newly arrived 13th New Jersey, "told Colonel Andrews yesterday that they had never been drilled in loading and firing, and have done nothing but march since they left home, I do not imagine that they will prove very valuable auxilieries [sic] on the field."[6]

The knowledge that 20 percent of your army's infantry had little or no training would give any professional soldier pause before he took on the veteran Army of Northern Virginia in battle. This was not McClellan's only problem. The withdrawal from the Peninsula and defeat at 2nd Manassas had left the army's logistics in a state of chaos, which initially limited its ability to maneuver. Its artillery was in a state of disorganization. Brig. Gen. Henry Hunt, who McClellan appointed as his chief of artillery on September 5, reported, "When the army left Washington, I was compelled to obtain on the roads the names and condition of the batteries and the troops to which they were attached. Not only were the batteries of the Army of the Potomac dispersed as stated, and serving with other divisions than their own, but I had no knowledge of the artillery of the other corps that had joined from the other armies other than what I could pick up on the road." The Army of the Potomac in September 1862 was a heterogeneous collection of forces hastily thrown together to meet an emergency. It exceeded the Army of Northern Virginia — despite that army's own problems — only in numbers of men and quality of equipment. In leadership, organization, troop quality, and morale the Army of Northern Virginia was the superior force. This does not excuse McClellan's failures as a general in the campaign, but it helps us understand the limitations of the army that he commanded.[7]

The Lost Order

Bruce Catton called the loss and discovery of the Army of Northern Virginia's Special Orders no. 191 "the greatest security leak in American military history — the only one that ever finally affected the outcome of a great war."[8] Its impact upon the Maryland Campaign, specifically, its unfortunate consequences for Lee's army and the opportunity it offered McClellan that was subsequently squandered, has made it the source of intense scrutiny and debate. A key point of debate is when Lee learned that the order had fallen into enemy hands. General Stackpole states (p. 321) that a Frederick citizen friendly to the Confederacy who was present at McClellan's headquarters "picked up the startling news of the disclosure of Lee's plans" and sped off to warn the Southern high command.

General Stackpole's opinion was no doubt influenced heavily by Douglas S. Freeman's magnificent work, *Lee's Lieutenants*. In Volume 2 of that work Freeman offered the same opinion that Stackpole repeats sixteen years later: Lee knew that McClellan had discovered a copy of S.O. 191 by the 14th of September. In his 1935 biography *R. E. Lee*, Freeman opined that Lee did not know McClellan had a copy of the order. Following the publication of that work, the son of Col. William Allen, a former ordnance officer in the Army of Northern Virginia and later professor at Washington College while Lee was its president, provided Free-

COMMENTARY 467

man with two memoranda that had been among his father's personal papers. The memoranda had been recorded, one by Allen, the other by E. C. Gordon (then a clerk at the college) following separate conversations with Lee on February 15, 1868, about the Maryland Campaign. In both conversations, Lee discussed the "lost order." In his discussion with Gordon, Lee's comments about when he learned McClellan had found S.O. 191 are ambiguous. To Allen, however, he was more specific. Allen wrote in his memorandum, "Stuart informed him [Lee] of report of a Md. gentleman, who said he was at McClellan's H.Qrs. when Lost Dispatch was found and that he (McC.) openly expressed his delight." The effect of these documents was to revise Freeman's opinion, which he reflected in *Lee's Lieutenants*.[9]

This accounting of when Lee learned that S.O. 191 had fallen into McClellan's hands was directly challenged by Stephen W. Sears in *Landscape Turned Red*, published in 1983. Concerning Lee's statement to Allen, Sears wrote, "There is substantial evidence that in this instance Lee's memory failed him." Significantly, neither Stuart or D. H. Hill mentioned the "lost order" in their wartime reports. Lee did, but his report was not prepared until the summer of 1863. This was after the publication of McClellan's Maryland Campaign report, in which the Union commander reported for the first time publicly that he had come into possession of a copy of Lee's orders. Sears also produced a letter to D. H. Hill from Charles Marshall, Lee's wartime aide, written in 1867. Marshall wrote, "I remember perfectly that until we saw that report [by McClellan] Gen. Lee frequently expressed his inability to understand the sudden change in McClellan's tactics which took place after we left Frederick." Sears wrote, "Thus the conclusion seems inescapable that Lee learned from the Maryland civilian only that the Federal army had suddenly become active" and nothing more. Moreover, it is extremely improbable that McClellan or any member of his staff would have revealed anything to an unknown civilian in a state known to harbor Southern sympathizers. At most, the civilian learned only that McClellan had received a piece of intelligence that had generated great excitement at army headquarters and had prompted increased activity of that army. Finally, Lee's actions from the night of September 13 to September 16 are not those of a general who possesses the knowledge that his opponent holds the orders precisely detailing the extreme vulnerability of his army. Sears wrote, "It defies belief that Lee would not have met such an obvious crisis by ordering Longstreet to the rescue with a night march, by ordering D. H. Hill to Turner's Gap that night with every man at his command, by ordering McLaws to take positive and immediate measures to avoid being trapped, or even by taking Longstreet's advice and pulling back out of immediate danger to Sharpsburg. But he issued no such explicit orders; instead he took the precautions of a general puzzled by the suddenly inexplicable moves of his opponent."[10]

McClellan and the Battle of Antietam

There is little debate that McClellan fought a clumsy, ill-coordinated battle at Antietam. Opportunities aplenty were squandered. McClellan, as the army commander, must bear the ultimate burden of his army's failure to realize the victory that was possible. But the blame for the failure of the Union army to achieve a decisive victory should not rest solely upon his shoulders. Other random events and the demoralization of a key general at a critical point of the battle contributed substantially to the disappointing performance of the Union army.

General Stackpole writes (p. 394) that "lack of coordinated direction of the three Federal corps engaged (1st, 2nd, 12th) had much to do with the repeated failures to achieve any conclusive results against Lee's left." McClellan, however, made an effort, albeit a clumsy one, to achieve a coordinated attack upon this point by three corps. McClellan's problem in organizing his offensive was one of leadership. Who would direct the effort of these forces? He disliked 12th Corps commander Joseph Mansfield, a general with limited combat experience. He had little confidence in Edwin Sumner, the senior corps commander of the army. After the Battle of Williamsburg on May 5th, McClellan wrote his wife that "Sumner had proved that he was even a greater fool than I had supposed & had come within an ace of having us defeated."

Gen. Philip Kearny wrote of Sumner during the Peninsula Campaign, "He has neither capacity, nor sane judgement. He is a proverbial blunderer." Sumner, clearly, was not to be trusted with directing McClellan's principal offensive effort.[11]

McClellan wanted Joseph Hooker. The 1st Corps commander was a fighting general and a soldier in whom McClellan had confidence. At the outset of the Maryland Campaign he had placed Hooker in command of the 1st Corps, which McClellan believed to be suffering from a lapse of discipline and morale, because he believed the New Englander could "make them fight if anyone can." The problem was that Hooker was junior in rank to both Mansfield and Sumner. If either or both of those corps went into a coordinated attack with the 1st Corps, by seniority, Hooker would fall under Mansfield's or Sumner's orders. McClellan attempted to circumvent this arrangement by committing Hooker to battle first, then reinforcing him with Mansfield, followed by Sumner. As Mansfield's and then Sumner's corps reached the fighting they would then be subject to the directions of Hooker, who was the general at the scene. It might have worked — although the entire arrangement says something about the quality of the senior leadership available to McClellan — but McClellan was late in moving both Mansfield and Sumner into the battle, and Hooker, who had fought with courage and ability, was wounded and carried from the field. "The Rebel marksman who wounded Hooker," wrote Stephen Sears in *Landscape Turned Red*, "put Bull Sumner precisely where McClellan did not want him — in the field in an independent command."[12]

Sumner arrived on the field at a critical moment in the battle. Lee's left had been severely shaken and may not have been able to withstand a coordinated attack by even two divisions of the big 2nd Corps. Sumner arrived at the East Woods at the head of Sedgwick's Division at about 9 A.M. What followed is explained by General Stackpole in a single paragraph (p. 395) that describes how McLaw's and Walker's divisions struck John Sedgwick's flank with devastating consequences. Sumner's role in this disaster is not discussed. Yet Sumner, more than any other single officer, was responsible for Sedgwick's heavy defeat — a defeat that had a wide-ranging impact on the rest of the battle at Antietam.

After arriving with Sedgwick's division at the East Woods, Sumner made a brief effort to learn the situation that lay before him. He spoke with Hooker, who was wounded and being carried from the field, but the 1st Corps commander was only semi-conscious and could offer little information. Sumner also encountered Brig. Gen. Alpheus Williams, commanding the 12th Corps after Mansfield's mortal wounding, who attempted to brief him on the situation. But Sumner paid little attention. His conclusion, formed from the barest of information, was that Hooker's corps was defeated and dispersed. Of the 12th Corps dispositions he evidenced little interest and made no effort to coordinate the attack of his corps with Williams's troops. Neither did he make an effort to coordinate the efforts of his own corps. Without waiting for French's division to arrive, or even to leave any instructions or staff officers to provide French with directions, Sumner marched off toward the West Wood at the head of Sedgwick's division—a corps commander leading a divisional assault. The division was deployed in a formation favored by Sumner: three brigades in successive lines, with barely forty paces between each line. Because of this formation, wrote Alpheus Williams, who observed the attack, "We lost a good deal of our fire without any corresponding benefit or advantage." Sumner, who had made little effort to learn the enemy's strength and position, then guaranteed the slaughter of Sedgwick's division by moving them into action nearly perpendicular to the front of the Confederate army, leaving the division's flank exposed to an attack upon its flank. When this attack struck, Sedgwick's closely formed brigades were unable to deploy to defend their flank. "The colonel of a regiment in the second line told me he lost sixty men and came off without firing a gun," wrote Alpheus Williams. The result was a massacre of fine, veteran soldiers and a turning point of the battle.[13]

Although personally a very brave man, Sumner was severely shaken by the slaughter of Sedgwick's veteran command. Francis Walker, a staff officer in the 2nd Corps and later the corps historian, wrote that after Sedgwick's defeat Sumner lost courage—"the courage which, in the crash and clamor of action, amid disaster and repulse, enables the commander coolly to calculate the chances of success or failure." William B. Franklin found Sumner to be "much depressed" in the early afternoon. The disaster in the West Wood had completely sapped the offensive spirit of the normally aggressive Sumner, and he imagined the Union right to be in grave peril of defeat unless it was bolstered by reinforcements. He signaled to McClellan soon after Sedgwick's defeat, "Re-enforcements badly wanted. Our troops are giving way." McClellan responded by dispatching Franklin's 6th Corps. When Franklin arrived, he made preparations to assault the West Wood. Moments before his attack was to step off, however, Sumner rode up and ordered it suspended. His reason, Franklin recalled, was "that if I was defeated the right would be entirely routed, mine being the only troops left on the right that had any life left in them." Sumner exaggerated. There were plenty of troops in the 1st and 12th Corps that were still intact and capable of further combat. But the statement offers a view of Sumner's state of mind.[14]

Franklin appealed Sumner's decision to McClellan by dispatching a nearby staff officer to army headquarters. Orders returned for Sumner "to get up his men and hold his position at all hazards." Sumner directed the staff officer who carried the orders to return to headquarters "and ask General McClellan if I shall make a simultaneous advance with my whole line at the risk of not being able to rally a man on this side of the creek if I am driven back." This prompted another round of communications between McClellan and Sumner that only further established that Sumner was a demoralized general. Finally McClellan rode to the front after 2 P.M. A personal meeting with Sumner dispelled any notion McClellan might have had about renewing the offensive on his right. "He was afraid to risk the day by an attack there on the right at that time," recalled Franklin.[15]

The wounding of Hooker and demoralization of Sumner were critical to the outcome of the Battle of Antietam, largely because of their effect on the mind of George B. McClellan. McClellan imagined the Confederate army to be far more powerful than they actually were. To conduct an offensive on September 17th was out of character for him. Nevertheless, he did attempt it. But when

Hooker was wounded and Sumner began communicating gloom and doom after Sedgwick's disaster, McClellan gave up the offensive and began thinking defensively. Stephen Sears wrote, "To this point, however cautiously he was committing his forces McClellan had the initiative in the fighting. With the rout of Sedgwick's division, however, he surrendered control of events and never regained it."[16] Had the command arrangement worked out as McClellan had originally planned it, the battle's outcome, and history's treatment of McClellan, may have been dramatically altered.

"It all happened a long time ago," Bruce Catton wrote of Antietam, "and that part of the reality which is represented by smoke and flame and bloodshed casts a thin shadow now, its original darkness bleached out by the years. Yet something endures. . . ."[17] Indeed. Years after Catton wrote those words, and after General Stackpole published *From Cedar Mountain to Antietam*, our fascination with the great American tragedy remains very much alive. The vast array of literature on the conflict that is being published today rivals in quantity what was published during the late nineteenth century. Among the titles returning to the shelves after a long absence is this one. It is my hope that its readers will find the spark of interest in these pages that I once did as a young boy, to go beyond this volume and seek more knowledge of the massive conflict that shaped the nation we live in today.

NOTES

1. Robert K. Krick, *Stonewall Jackson at Cedar Mountain* (Chapel Hill and London: University of North Carolina Press, 1990), 384–88.

2. George B. McClellan, *McClellan's Own Story* (New York: Charles L. Webster & Co., 1887), 551.

3. *Report of the Joint Committee on the Conduct of the War* (Washington, D.C.: Government Printing Office, 1863), 451, 453, 438–39; Stephen W. Sears, *George B. McClellan: The Young Napoleon* (New Haven and New York: Ticknor & Fields, 1988), 264.

4. Stephen W. Sears, *Landscape Turned Red: The Battle of Antietam* (New Haven and New York: Ticknor & Fields, 1983), 77.

5. Jay Luvaas, ed., *The Civil War: A Soldier's View* (Chicago: University of Chicago Press, 1958), 145.

6. Edward O. Lord, *History of the 9th New Hampshire Volunteers* (Concord, 1895), 21; Gregory A. Coco, ed., *Through Blood and Fire: The Civil War Letters of Major Charles J. Mills* (Privately printed, 1982), 27. McClellan received one division of the 5th Corps and an infantry brigade as reinforcements before September 17th. This raised his total strength to something over 80,000. Lee, due to heavy straggling, was reduced to slightly less than 40,000 men at Antietam.

7. U.S. War Department, *The War of the Rebellion: Official Records of the Union and Confederate Armies* (Washington, D.C.: Government Printing Office, 1880–1901), XIX, Part 1, 205.

8. Bruce Catton, *Mr. Lincoln's Army* (New York: Doubleday & Co., 1951), 224.

9. Douglas S. Freeman, *Lee's Lieutenants, Vol. 2* (New York: Scribner's, 1942–44), 715–23.

10. Sears, *Landscape Turned Red*, 350–52.

11. Stephen W. Sears, *The Civil War Papers of George B. McClellan* (New Haven and New York: Ticknor & Fields, 1989), 257; William P. Styple, ed., *Letters from the Peninsula: The Civil War Letters of General Philip Kearny* (Kearny, N.J.: Belle Grove Publishing, 1988), 146.

12. Sears, *Landscape Turned Red*, 220; Sears, *Civil War Papers of George B. McClellan*, 450.

13. Milo Quaife, ed., *From the Cannon's Mouth: The Civil War Papers of General Alpheus Williams* (Detroit: Wayne State University Press, 1959), 128.

14. Francis A. Walker, *History of the Second Army Corps* (New York: Scribner's, 1886), 117; Robert U. Johnson and Clarence C. Buel, eds., *Battles and Leaders of the Civil War, Vol. 2* (New York: Century, 1887–88), 597; *War of the Rebellion, OR*, XIX, Part 1, 134.

15. James H. Wilson, *Under the Old Flag, Vol. 1* (New York: D. Appleton, 1912), 113–14; Johnson and Buel, *Battles and Leaders, Vol. 2*, 597.

16. Sears, *Civil War Papers of George B. McClellan*, 310.

17. Catton, *Mr. Lincoln's Army*, 331.

Bibliography

Catton, Bruce. *Mr. Lincoln's Army*. New York: Doubleday & Co., 1951.

Coco, Gregory A., ed. *Through Blood and Fire: The Civil War Letters of Major Charles J. Mills*. Privately Printed, 1982.

Freeman, Douglas S. *Lee's Lieutenants: A Study in Command*. 3 vols. New York: Scribner's, 1942–44.

Johnson, Robert U. and Clarence C. Buel, eds. *Battles and Leaders of the Civil War*. 4 vols. New York: Century, 1887–88.

Krick, Robert K. *Stonewall Jackson at Cedar Mountain*. Chapel Hill and London: University of North Carolina Press, 1990.

Lord, Edward O. *History of the Ninth New Hampshire Volunteers*. Concord, 1895.

Luvaas, Jay, ed. *The Civil War: A Soldier's View*. Chicago: University of Chicago Press, 1958.

McClellan, George B. *McClellan's Own Story*. New York: Charles L. Webster & Co., 1887.

Quaife, Milo, ed. *From the Cannon's Mouth: The Civil War Letters of General Alpheus S. Williams*. Detroit: Wayne State University Press, 1959.

Report of the Joint Committee on the Conduct of the War. 3 vols. Washington, D.C.: Government Printing Office, 1863.

Sears, Stephen W. *The Civil War Papers of George B. McClellan*. New Haven and New York: Ticknor & Fields, 1989.

Sears, Stephen W. *George B. McClellan: The Young Napoleon*. New Haven and New York: Ticknor & Fields, 1988.

Sears, Stephen W. *Landscape Turned Red: The Battle of Antietam*. New Haven and New York: Ticknor & Fields, 1983.

Styple, William P., ed. *Letters from the Peninsula: The Civil War Letters of General Philip Kearny*. Kearny, N.J.: Belle Grove Publishing, 1988.

U.S. War Department, *The War of the Rebellion: Official Records of the Union and Confederate Armies*. Washington D.C.: Government Printing Office, 1880–1901.

Walker, Francis A. *History of the Second Army Corps*. New York: Scribner's, 1986.

Wilson, James H. *Under the Old Flag*. 2 vols. New York: D. Appleton, 1912.